H. V. MORTON'S L

30

7/6

H. V. MORTON'S LONDON

being *The Heart of London*
The Spell of London and
The Nights of London
in one volume

WITH TWELVE ILLUSTRATIONS

SEVENTH EDITION

METHUEN & CO. LTD. LONDON
36 Essex Street Strand W.C.2

First published in this form . October 31st, 1940
Second Edition . . . December 1940
Third Edition . . . January 1941
Fourth Edition . . . April 1941
Fifth Edition . . . August 1941
Sixth Edition . . . December 1941
Seventh Edition . . . 1942

'The Heart of London' was first published on
June 11th, 1925. Twentieth edition 1941

'The Spell of London' was first published on
February 11th, 1926. Fourteenth edition 1937

'The Nights of London' was first published on
November 11th, 1926. Eleventh edition 1941

INTRODUCTION

AN acquisitive young reporter, with an immense appetite for London, was once allowed to wander out at will into the highways and the byways, as long as he returned in the evening with something to write about. So far as my recollection goes, he never came back empty-handed, and it is on record that he kept up the story of his explorations day by day for many a month. He was upheld in his quest by the conviction that, in such a wonderful and mysterious place as London, it was impossible for him to stand anywhere for half an hour and see nothing of interest. And, in this, I think he was right.

I now regard these snapshots of London and London life, gathered here for the first time into one book, with some respect, not for anything that is said in them, but because of the amount of vitality and enthusiasm that went to their making. Nothing was too much trouble, and no appointment to be neglected, no matter how seemingly ridiculous, if it appeared to promise yet another glimpse into the life of the capital.

Now in this year, 1940, and in a changed London, I have put together these sketches with the knowledge that they describe a London upon whose vivid scene a curtain has fallen. London since the Armistice, the London which I explored with so much tireless pleasure, is now seen to have been a definite period in history. In times of peace periods run on and on, often overlapping, and it is necessary for men to examine them, and to say precisely where one began and another ended. But war does this instantly. It ends a period, just as the peace that follows begins another. August, 1914, ended what was left of nineteenth-century London. September, 1940, concluded a period which perhaps future historians may call the Long Armistice or the Twenty-one Years Truce. But ended for ever it is and the present London, at war as never before in its history, the London of A.R.P.; A.F.S.; and H.G.; the London of Black-out, Evacuations, and Sandbags is an interim London from whose streets elegance, leisure, and freedom from care have departed for the time being. No one can say what London will be like after the war. That it will be a new London is obvious: a London as different from that of 1918–40 as the London since the Armistice differed from the capital of Edwardian Britain.

So it seems to me worth while to put out these little snap-shots which, in their own way, illustrate the London of the past twenty-two years. It was, to me at any rate, a happy time, and I shall always look back upon it with undimmed affection.

The human background of London will, of course, remain unchanged as long as the population is counted by the million; and I expect someone, like the earnest young reporter who wrote these essays, will always be able to go about the crowded streets and speculate upon the motives which sway their inhabitants. But the crowds of London move against a back-ground which is hardly the same from year to year: a back-ground always changing and, one may be permitted to think, not always for the better. Londoners, indeed, are like players who rehearse a play while the scene shifters are at work. Looking up from their lines, they see that a splendid palace has been succeeded by a monstrous cube of concrete; but they were too busily engaged at the time to notice the transformation.

I am reminded in these essays that, in the 'twenties, old Devonshire House was removed from Piccadilly; that an obscure building, lying between the Strand and the Thames, housed a novel organization known as 2 L O; that Croydon Aerodrome and its Paris liners was something of a novelty; that in the City men still hoped one day to be able to speak to New York; that a voyager upon the Thames could once see barges laden with German 'reparation goods'; and that when the City of London was rebuilt after the Four Years' War, Roman pottery was to be found below the basements of Victorian and Georgian London, the last remaining relics of Roman London we shall ever discover, for the roots of modern buildings go down to the London Clay.

It is interesting to hark back to the days when the Cenotaph enshrined a sorrow that was still new and raw, when the Unknown Warrior's Grave in the Abbey seemed to an over-confident generation to be the grave of the last soldier. I am also pleased to be reminded that, in the 'twenties, the London omnibus was open to the weather, and had not developed into the huge red glass-houses of the 'forties.

On the whole, however, the pages that follow deal less with the changes of London than with the unalterable emotions of London folk. Whatever the new London is like, I think the Londoner will remain much the same as I have seen him, rightly or wrongly, in these pages.

Of his attitude to London, I am not so sure. The ignorance of, and the indifference to, London, which are characteristic traits of the Londoner, as he goes up to earn his daily bread and fights his way home again on an evening train, are bound to be altered by the war. During the past year, I do not know how many thousands of Londoners have been in intimate attendance on the giant, trained to save it from possible destruction. Men who in former years hardly knew where their town hall was to be found, now sleep there regularly, and have become familiar with many a municipal mystery. Men and women, to whom a fire hydrant was once a technical term which cropped up occasionally in the newspapers, can now draw you an accurate map of the water-supply of their district. Countless diligent wardens know by heart streets which, until recently, were an untracked wilderness to them, although they lived just round the corner.

London, once so aloof and so vast a mystery, has, in the anxiety of these times, become comprehensible in her danger; and Londoners by the thousand have ceased to be merely lodgers in London, and have found a new importance as helpers of London. It must have astonished many a man that London could require his aid. So it is that the capital has ceased to be an amorphous monster, and has most surprisingly become a series of borough boundaries.

This cannot fail to have a profound effect upon the attitude of the Londoner towards the new London. I like to think that it will bring about a better London; and it is indeed difficult to believe that a city like London can pass through the ordeal which now faces it without gaining in spiritual grace. So, with faith in the future of London, let me offer you these snapshots, taken in the highways and byways of the world's greatest city during the sometimes gay and often happy period of the Short Peace.

H. V. M.

August, 1940

CONTENTS

THE HEART OF LONDON

ix

THE SPELL OF LONDON

THE NIGHTS OF LONDON

ILLUSTRATIONS

When a man is tired of London he is tired of life; for there is in London all that life can afford.

DR. JOHNSON

THE HEART OF LONDON

An ever-muttering prisoned storm,
The heart of London beating warm.
JOHN DAVIDSON, 'Ballads and Songs'

WHEN eight million men and women decide to live together on the same spot things are bound to happen.

London, in lineal descent from Thebes and Rome, is one of those queer massings together of humanity which Civilization dumps on a small plot of earth before handing the lease of Destiny, not knowing whether to laugh or cry about it. Great cities are strange inevitable phenomena. It is wrong to compare them with hives, for in a hive the wish of the individual has been unquestioningly sacrificed to the good of the community. Had we ascended from the bee perhaps the greatest happiness we could achieve would be an unspectacular death in the service of the London County Council. But in London, as in all modern cities, it is the individual who counts. Our eight millions split themselves up into ones and twos: little men and little women dreaming their private dreams, pursuing their own ambitions, crying over their own failures, and rejoicing at their own successes.

Fear built the first cities. Men and women herded behind a wall so that they might be safe. Then came trade; and cities grew into lucky bags in which men dipped for profit. Essentially they remain lucky bags to this day. London's millions pour into London and carry off their loot every Friday; but that, thank heaven, is not the whole story. A city develops Tradition and Pride. London has greater tradition and pride than any other city in the world.

So when I ask myself why I love London I realize that I appreciate that ancient memory which is London—a thing very like family tradition for which we in our turn are responsible to posterity—and I realize that I am thrilled, puzzled, charmed, and amused every day of my life by that flood-tide of common humanity flowing through London, as it has surged through every city in the history of civilization. Here is every human emotion. Here, in this splendid theatre, the comedy and the tragedy of the human heart are acted day and night. Love and treachery, beauty and ugliness, laughter and tears chase one another through the streets of London every minute of the day, often meeting and mixing in the strangest fashion, because London is just a great mass of human feeling, and Man, never clearly labelled 'Hero' or 'Villain' as in melodrama,

3

is capable of so much moral complexity that you might almost say that good and bad exist in him at the same moment.

Had I been born a few thousand years ago I feel sure that I could have written much the same book about Thebes or Babylon, because the only things that change in life are fashions and inventions. The human heart was patented long ago and the Creator has not seen fit to bring out a later model.

One night after dinner a woman fixed large eyes on me and confided that in a previous incarnation she had been Cleopatra. She was my tenth Cleopatra. She told me that there was no romance in modern life, and, looking a little withdrawn as if remembering some Alexandrian indiscretion, she said: 'No surprise, no—you know what I mean?—no real poetry.'

I always think it best not to argue with queens; but I believe that the surprise, the romance, and the poetry of a modern city are fiercer than they were in the past. The drama of the ancient autocracies was played with so small a cast. The rest was suffering. People with large eyes were never in their past lives anything less than queens or princes, and thus their naturally vivid memories of a small and brilliant circle dim a recollection of the dumb majority beneath their wills. In spite of the supply of desirable lamps in Bagdad the census of owner-drivers must have been negligible, so that the average inhabitant must have lived through the romance of those days sitting in the same patch of sun, bitten by insects and trodden on by negroes.

In London, and in the free cities of this modern world, the drama of life widens, the characters increase and the unchanging human heart, no happier perhaps in the long run, beats less timorously than it did, yet leaping in sympathy to the same old loves and fears and hates.

Every day our feelings vibrate to some stray unimportance. Life is full of portentous triviality. Is it not strange that our minds often refuse to recognize some sensation—a word like a worn-out boot—while they react immediately to something so small as to be almost foolish? You may be bored stiff by the front page of the evening paper, but you go home remembering some common thing seen or heard; some little humanity: the sight of a man and a girl choosing a child's cot, two people saying good-bye at a street corner, the quiet hatred in a man's eyes—or the love. . . .

Let us now go out into London.

Where the Eagles Sleep

ONE o'clock in the City of London. Crowds overflow the pavement into the narrow, twisting road. Young men in striped trousers, ruled like ledgers, black coats sober as a bill of lading, rush or saunter, according to their natures, towards a quick lunch-bar, where a girl with golden hair will give them beer and mutton. Girls, arm-in-arm, discuss those eternal verities—dress, love, and another woman—as they go primly or coyly, according to their nature, towards two poached eggs and a cup of tea. Here and there a large man in a silk hat, who may be a millionaire or a bankrupt, chases the inevitable chop. And the traffic roars, throbs, and thunders.

But behind a hoarding that shouts dogmatically of soap and shirts and pills things are quiet. Out of the chaos yet another bank will rise. Workmen sit around in picturesque groups eating. On their knees are spotted handkerchiefs in which lie gigantic sandwiches cut by wives in the early dawn. They carve them with clasp-knives and carry them to their mouths, the clasp-knives upright in their hands, grazing their cheeks. They drink from tin cans, and wonder, in rich monosyllables, 'wot' will win the three-thirty.

I stand on the edge of a vast pit in which, down through successive strata—brick, tiles, black earth, powdered cement —lies the clay on which London rests. It is a deep, dark hole. It is as if some surgeon, operating on the body of the city, has bared it to the spine. I look down with awe at the accumulation of nearly two thousand years of known history piled, layer on layer, twenty-four feet above the primal clay.

How amazing to gaze down into that pit where the record of London lies clear as layers of cream in a cake: Victorian, Georgian, Stuart, Plantagenet, Norman, Anglo-Saxon, and Roman. There it stops, for there it began. Below, nothing but clay and ooze, hundreds of thousands of years of un-recorded Time, century after century written in clay, forest after forest, springing up, dying, the great trees crashing into lonely death; and who knows what awful drama of creatures struggling in green undergrowth and river slime long before the first man climbed a tree on Ludgate Hill and looked round fearfully on that which was not yet London?

5

A workman clambers into the pit, prods around with a stick, and shouts up to his mate:

'Hi, Bill, here's a bit more!'

And pat-pat-pat on the parapet fall hard, encrusted fragments that look like flat cakes of sealing wax. I pick them up, knock off the caked earth, and find a beautiful little fragment of deep red pottery, one the rim of a delicate vase, another the rounded base of a little cup, and in the bottom something is written: 'Fl. Germanus. F.' Just that.

What does it mean? It means that I have seen the roots of London pulled up, the roots that go back to Rome. 'Fl. Germanus. F.' is the trade mark of Flavius Germanus, a potter who lived in the time of the Caesars, and 'F' stands for 'Fecit,' meaning 'Flavius Germanus made it.' What a message to receive in modern London behind a hoarding which advertises pills.

* * * * *

A sackful of Rome is dug up in the City of London every week when a new bank is built. For we stand on the shoulders of Rome. Men from the London and the Guildhall Museums watch the excavations like lynxes, collect the little bits of red pottery, the coins, the bits of green and mauve glass, this wreckage of that first London; that far-flung limb of Rome crowning its single hill.

* * * * *

As I stand there, so modern, such a parvenu, an omnibus ticket still in the strap of my wrist-watch, I hold the cup of Flavius. What do I see? I see the first London and its colonists pegging out their camp. Then Boudicca, blood, fire, a ruin. The second London rises from the smoke, a London old enough to have a story to tell the young men; and round this London they are building a wall.

Gradually, as a vision in a crystal clears and forms out of mist, I see a smaller, colder Rome standing with its marble feet in Thames water. I see rows of wood and red-tile houses running within the walls in straight lines like tents within a castrum; I see the marble capitals under our grey skies, the majestic circular sweep of the theatre, the white gleam of the

Forum, the gates with their statues, the baths at the gates, the long straight streets crowded, noisy, varied. I see the shaggy Britons and the Gauls move to a side as the Roman troops come clattering over the stones, their helmets shining, swords at hips; the marvellous short sword that carved out an Empire as a girl might cut a cake.

And the heart of this little English Rome, how did it beat? I imagine that it knew the enterprising business man opening up new markets, the enthusiastic soldier always dreaming of sending the Eagles north, the inevitable Phoenician with his galley at the docks and his shop somewhere in the city, the bad boy sent to colonial London to expiate, and women making the best of it, always three months behind Rome in fashion: wives and sweethearts who had followed their men into barbary. O, the homesickness and heroism of colonization! How many old men must have wept to see their careful vines wilt in the London clay; and I wonder if Londinium Augusta numbered among its inhabitants the optimistic gardener who bored his friends with a vision of olives in a neat Italian row.

There would come a time in this first London when a small boy would say to his mother: 'Tell me about Rome!'

And she would sit facing the broad Thames, talking of Italy as a homesick woman in Winnipeg might talk of England:

'Do you see those galleys coming up under the bridge like water beetles? They come from Ostia—from Rome. They bring soldiers and—sometimes people go home in them! Yes, dear, perhaps when you grow up you too will go. The sun always shines there, and it is seldom cold as it is here. When your father was a little boy like you . . .'

So the tale would go on.

Then I see the market-place, the marvellous mixture of race which Rome drew to her cities: the dark Iberian soldier pressed into service for duty on the Wall, the Gaul, the German, the negro, the merchants with their wares, the amber from the Baltic, the pearls, the perfumes from the East, the brown fingers holding out gold chains as the Roman ladies go by. . . .

What chatter of a six months old scandal as the women walk to the baths; what discussion of Rome's latest *coiffure*, her newest pin, her smartest sandal! At the docks the creak of timber and the straining of a released rope, the 'one, two, three' as the oarsmen dip their great blades in the Thames; and a galley goes home with letters to Caesar from the Governor of London.

Londinium Augusta! There is nothing between her and Verulamium but a straight road through the forest, then another road, more forests, and proud Camulodunum on its hill. Three fortified islands in a green sea. So England takes shapes out of the mists of Time; so London begins.

And I like to think, to round off the picture, that, on a cold night of winter, when brittle green stars glitter in the sky, some grey old wolf creeps to the edge of the Hampstead woods and licks his jaws as he looks towards the first lights of London. Then he yawns and blinks his eyes as a dog blinks and looks away from something he does not understand. So he pads noiselessly among the trees with the unhappy feeling that things are different; that—something has happened to the Hill!

A YOUNG girl with eyes like the fish-pools of Heshbon sits on an upturned crate outside a butcher's shop. Her fingers glitter with rings, and when she laughs she throws her fuzzy head back, exposing a plump, olive-coloured throat, as Moons of Delight have been doing throughout the history of the Orient.

She is beautiful after her kind. In five more years, however, she will look like a side-show. Her lithe grace, her round face, her firm, white neck will be submerged in regrettable tissue. The eye passing over her façade will find it impossible to excavate her recent beauty. She will be like a thin girl who has become somehow merged with a fat woman. She will be 'herself with yesterday's ten thousand years,'—and yesterday winning all along the line. That is the burden of the Jewess.

At the moment, however, she is ripe as a peach is ripe before it falls into the hand. Were I a Sultan, swaying above the street in a litter, I would roll a lazy eye in her direction, make a minute movement of a jewelled finger, and, later at the palace, would address her:

'Moon of Great Beauty and Considerable Possibility,' I would say, 'whither comest thou, O Radiance, and who is thy father?'

Whereupon she would spit at me with her eyes and reply:

'Cancher see I'm respectable . . . cancher? You're a nice chep, you are, sitting up there dressed like a dorg's dinner and talkin' like thet . . . lemme go . . .'

For though her eyes are the eyes of Ruth among the alien corn, her larynx is that of Bill Sykes. The street in which she sits, shedding this varied atmosphere, is lined on either side by a row of rough booths. It is a mere track between two bright hedges of merchandise. Here the fruit-sellers expose their pyramids of red-gold oranges, their African plums, their pineapples; there the sellers of shoes wait patiently beneath their pendulous racks. The sellers of cloth walk up and down with bright, stabbing colours, daringly mixed, slung across their shoulders, and the drink merchants, with their cooling brews—never absent from an Oriental market—stand beside their ample golden globes.

Through this lane of bright colour the crowd moves—the women young, straight, and mostly beautiful in a dark, passionate way; the old women fat and round; the men sallow, bearded, and incredibly wrinkled. Among them pass the abject creatures so well known in the East, who clutch a handful of vegetables or three inferior lemons, with which they try to undersell the regular merchants.

Where is it? It might be Cairo, Bagdad, Jerusalem, Aleppo, Tunis, or Tangier, but, as a matter of fact, it is Petticoat Lane in Whitechapel—a penny ride from Ludgate Hill.

As I walked through Petticoat Lane, I thought that, if we had a sunny climate, this part of Whitechapel would become one of the famous showplaces of the world. Here you have the East without its lepers, without small-pox, without the flies, without the impertinent stinks. This is the scene of rich and amusing variety which, were it only a few thousand expensive miles from London, under a blue sky, would attract the attention of artist and traveller.

The attitude towards commerce is as old as barter. I saw a neatly bearded woman, whose brown coat looked as though it was draped over a barrel, go up to a fishmonger, standing beside two gigantic codfish and a number of smaller fish.

'How much?' asked the woman, indicating a group of still life.

'Six shillings,' replied the fishmonger, with a keen glance from small, black eyes.

'One and ten,' remarked the woman, reflectively turning a plaice upside down and prodding it with a fat finger.

Whereupon a singular change took place in the fishmonger's aloof attitude. He was insulted, outraged. Suddenly, picking up a plaice by the tail, he said with a threatening gesture:

'I'll wipe it acrost yeh face!'

The customer was not outraged as a woman would have been in Oxford Street; she just shrugged her fat shoulders, as she would have done in Damascus, and moved away, knowing full well that before she had retreated very far she would be recalled—as indeed she was. After a brisk argument she bought the fish for two and fourpence and they parted the best of friends.

I have seen the same drama played on a carpet in Alexandria.

*   *   *   *   *

What strange foreign eatables you see here: vile-looking messy dishes, anaemic cucumbers, queer salted meats, varied sausages of East European origin, the inevitable onion, and, of course, olives. Smoked salmon has customers at ten shillings a pound.

But the people are more interesting than their surroundings or their food. Such gnarled, lined faces, such live eyes, such a patriarchal air. That is the old orthodox generation. The new? Such smartish young semi-Englishmen prospering in trade on an education for which the old generation has starved itself. They can pronounce their w's and their th's. They have an eye on Hampstead or even on the Golden West. The daughters of Israel, powdered and rouged, flit with their dark, and often alluring, eyes from dressmaker's shop to dressmaker's shop, pert and self-assured, well dressed even in their working clothes.

This rift between the old and the new generations is the first thing that strikes you. There seem several hundred years between them. What tragedies does it conceal, what human stories? Many an old man nodding over his crowded counter has sent a son to the 'varsity. This is not fiction, and those will not believe it who do not understand that Israel has always given over its heart to its children. If the elements of domestic tragedy are not here, where are they?—for Israel, scattered in its wanderings and oppressed, never lost the Tables of the Law, never forgot the old things, never became quite deaf to the sounds of tents in a wind; but now the old men can say to their children: 'My thoughts are not your thoughts, neither are your ways my ways.'

*   *   *   *   *

In a narrow street full of jewellers' shops I saw a bent old patriarch gazing into a window at a nine-branched candlestick; on the opposite side of the road came a young girl in her sand-coloured silk stockings and her tight black coat, swinging a silver bag—very far from the flocks and herds was she! Again I saw a limousine stop at a tiny shop. An old woman ran out, a young man leapt from the car to meet her, and when he kissed her there was joy shining in her eyes. Joseph? The Prodigal Son?

*   *   *   *   *

I caught a penny omnibus back to England with the feeling that I might have spent two hundred pounds and seen less of the East, less of romance, and much less of life.

IN the greyness of the dawn liners from the Seven Seas slip
into the docks of London; and men and women gather there
to meet friends. Some even meet their sweethearts. They
are the lucky ones.

It was not yet light. Dawn was a good hour away, and it
was cold. I was travelling away from London towards
Woolwich in a jangling, dirty workman's train. On the platform at Fenchurch Street I had noticed several other people
obviously on their way to meet friends, but they had been
assimilated in the gloom of the long train; and I was glad, for
I was enjoying myself in a carriage full of dock workers: a
carriage that reeked of smoke and manly conversation. The
train ploughed wearily on through the darkness, stopping at
stations.... Stepney East.... Burdett Road.... Bromley.
... Canning Town.... Bleak, unfriendly places under their
pale lights. More early Londoners stormed the carriage at
each station and split pleasantries rather like roadmen hitting
a spike:

'Goo' mornin', Bill. . . .'

'It ain't a goo' mornin'. It's a blinkin' cold mornin'!'

The laughter could not have been louder if the retort had
been made by a judge or a king!

The conversation was both technical and sporting. The
technical discussion centred round the life and shortcomings
of a certain foreman, who, I gathered, although he knew less
about a ship than a —— —— school-teacher, was, if not a
man of iron, at least a man of blood. So they said. Football
and racing! They knew the parentage, habits, and hobbies
of every League player, also the result of contests going right
back to ancient times. They all had 'a bit' on the three-thirty.

*   *   *   *   *

North Woolwich! In the still air of dawn I could feel the
nearness of shipping. I could not see much, but I knew that
I was surrounded by ships. The docks were not awake. The
steam winches were not screaming, the hammers were stilled;
yet over the dark docks lay the presence of great ships home
from sea. . . .

I walked on past the shrouded cranes, standing in their straight lines near the water's side. I came upon a tall ship looming up like a cliff. I could make out a man leaning over her deck far above. I asked him if this was the ship I wanted. He opened his mouth, and there descended curious, unwilling sounds, like something trying hard to escape from his throat and then changing its mind and trying to get back again. I think he was talking Japanese.

So I walked along to the stern of the ship to read the name, and there I met a man gazing upward, too. It turned out that we were both looking for the same ship, so we walked on together.

'What an experience it is,' he said. 'I wonder how many people in London have ever done this. I'm generally asleep at this time of the morning. How early London wakes up. Think of those workmen's trains. . . .'

'Are you meeting a friend in the ——,' I asked.

He coughed slightly and said, 'Yes,' and the way he said it told me that it was going to be a romantic occasion.

Then dawn. If there is anything more wonderful in London than dawn coming up over the tangled shipping of the docks I would like to know of it. First a silvery light in the air, a chilly greyness, then a flush in the east, and, with startling suddenness, every mast, every funnel, every leaning crane is silhouetted jet-black against the pearl-coloured sky. . . . Unreal . . . still . . . silent.

Gradually the docks awaken. Men walk along the wharfside, doors are opened. In the depths of little ships men rise and become busy with ropes; there is, from some, a smell of frying bacon; on tall ships mast lights grow pale in the dawn light, men in swinging cradles yawn and start painting a ship's hull, and from far off comes the ring of the first hammer of a new day.

As the light grows, one's sense of smell improves. This is strange. The air is now full of a pungent smell of hemp and tow and tar, and even distant docks, stored with their merchandise, seem to contribute their part as the dawn wind blows.

There is a flush of pink cloud high up in the sky, such a delicate flamingo pink that changes, spreads, and fades even as you look. It becomes gold, and you know that at any

THE DOCKS AT DAWN

moment the sun may rise up like a tocsin and call the world to work.

*   *   *   *   *

We found the ship.   A mountain she was, towering up above us with tiny holes in her side like the entrances to caves. She smelt of fried fish, bacon and eggs and coffee. . . .

Soon after I was aboard I had to look the other way, for I had seen my friend holding a girl in his arms and I had heard him say:

'And how are you, darling?'

'Splendid!' she cried. 'Let me look at you! Come into the light.'

So you see wonderful things happen to some people when ships find their way to London Town.

SOME things, such as umbrellas, suit-cases, trousers, boots, bedsteads, and hats, both male and female, can become so old that it would be a decency could they disintegrate and vanish into thin air. Nothing can be quite so old and dissipated as an umbrella. But, no; the effortless Nirvana which these things have earned is denied them; they are spread out on the cobbles of the Caledonian Market (North London) every Friday, in the hope that their pitiful pilgrimage may continue.

When I walked into this remarkable once-a-week junk-fair I was deeply touched to think that any living person could need many of the things displayed for sale. For all round me, lying on sacking, were the driftwood and wreckage of a thousand lives: door knobs, perambulators in *extremis*, bicycle wheels, bell wire, bed knobs, old clothes, awful pictures, broken mirrors, unromantic china goods, gaping false teeth, screws, nuts, bolts, and vague pieces of rusty iron, whose mission in life, or whose part and portion of a whole, Time had obliterated.

It seemed that all the queer things in all the little shops in London's by-streets had been poured out in a last desperate effort of salesmanship, while on every hand, above the Oriental clamour of stall-holders and the negative remarks of the public, rose the all-prevailing cry:

'Come on, ma, take it for sixpence . . . fourpence? . . . twopence? All right, then I'll *give* it you. . . .'

I must say, however, that I never saw this threat carried out.

As I walked between the aisles of junk, I remembered the story of a friend who went to this market out of curiosity, and came away unexpectedly in a taxicab with a priestess. He had bought a mummy for ten shillings. And well can I believe it. I longed for something like this to happen to me, for that is how life should go. When you look forward to a thing, or search for it and find it, you are invariably disappointed because your mind has had time to experience it and possess it and tire of it long before it comes. But the joy of sudden, unexpected things seldom fails. I have always envied J., not his priestess, because, he told me, she smelt like a French third-class carriage and had to be buried at night,

but his meeting with her. That must have been wonderful.
He was walking along thinking about door knobs or bell wire
when he saw her: 'My God, a mummy! Man or woman?
Woman! How romantic! Probably she was beautiful and
young! She used to shake a sistrum at Karnak beside the Nile
and wear a lovely pleated skirt and nothing underneath. . . .'

For a second, perhaps two—anyhow just long enough to
hand over a ten-shilling note—I think he loved her as much
as you can love a mummy, and although his affection waned
in Bloomsbury, when he had to help her out of the taxi, it
must have been worth it just for the sharp delirium of that
meeting—he ardent, romantic; she a bit distant, but still
eternally feminine.

I walked on trying not to expect that anything so wonderful
would come my way. Near the entrance a man offered me
someone's skeleton for seven-and-sixpence, and when I said
'No' he put down the box in which it is kept and remarked to
his wife: 'Now, don't put your foot through the skull, Emma.'
At the next stall a young mother was buying a cradle festooned
in black lace that had once been white.

I watched a man buy three dentist's door plates for three
and sixpence, and the dealer generously threw in a bowler
hat that looked like the hero of a hundred brawls.

Then, here and there among the dense, fingering crowds of
women in search of cheap saucepans, and those odd lengths
of cloth which women of all classes accumulate, I saw the
dealers from the more fashionable districts looking for something for five shillings to sell later in the West End for five
pounds. There were also countless treasure-seekers, men and
women—smart, well dressed—collectors of antiques, nosing
round like setters for Chippendale chairs, Japanese prints,
Chinese jade, and Queen Anne silver.

Half the collectors in London make it a point to visit this
place every Friday in search of loot; and they walk round like
pirate kings ready to pounce on the instant.

Most curious and sad to look upon were the old shoes, poor
down-at-heel, crinkly-toed things, standing dressed by the
right on their last parade, some with a remote Jermyn Street
look about them, others all that remains of someone's ancient
corn-ridden aunt. Among a pile of boots which looked as
though they had walked every yard of the road to ruin, I
saw, tall and upright, a pair of women's riding boots, proud

still in their decline. I also saw a pair of gold dance-slippers, somehow naked and ashamed.

A large woman was turning this way and that a slim little bride's dress with the faded orange blossom still sewn on it. A white veil went with it, gashed and torn. The fat woman moved on, lured by a decayed washstand, and, onward still, to flirt a moment with an old brass bedstead. I saw other hands—big coarse hands—pulling this forgotten little bride's dress about, pawing it. What a pity it could not melt away and save itself from this supreme insult.

* * * * *

In a corner lying on a sack I saw an Egyptian antiquity. I pounced!

'How much?'

A young man answered me with a cultured accent.

'Fifteen shillings, sir.'

I wondered what on earth this superior person was doing there standing back behind a sack spread with antiques. Was it his hobby, or was it a bet?

'I think,' went on the cultured voice, 'you will agree with me that the hieroglyphs were added at a later period. Perhaps the Ptolemaic age, though I think the figure is much older, possibly Eighteenth Dynasty.'

I was surprised to hear this in the Caledonian Market.

'No, indeed, sir, I do not do this for fun: I do it for bread and butter. Since the war, you know! Yes; I make enough to live. I have a *flair* for antiques. I buy cheaply and sell reasonably, and collectors always come to me.'

Strange spot, the Caledonian Market!

As I went out, I was offered another skeleton for ten shillings.

Cenotaph 〇 〇 〇 〇 〇 〇 〇

TEN-THIRTY A.M. in Whitehall on a cold, grey February morning.

There is expectancy at the Horse Guards, where two living statues draped in scarlet cloaks sit their patient chargers. A group of sightseers waits at the gate for the high note of a silver cavalry trumpet, for the click of hoofs on the cobbles and a shining cavalcade beneath an arch: the pageantry that precedes that silent ceremony of changing a guard that 'turns out' for no man but the King.

Laden omnibuses go down to Westminster or up to Charing Cross, and, as they pass, every passenger looks at the two Life Guards in their scarlet glory, for they are one of the sights of London that never grows stale. Taxicabs and limousines spin smoothly left and right, men and women enter and leave Government offices: a Whitehall morning is moving easily, leisurely, elegantly, if you like, towards noon.

And I walk on to Westminster, and, in the centre of the road, cream-coloured, dominant, stands the Cenotaph.

* * * * *

More than six years ago the last shot was fired. Six years. It is long enough for a heart to become convalescent. Sharp agonies which at the time of their happening seem incapable of healing have a merciful habit of mending in six years. A broken love-affair that turned the world into a pointless waste of Time has ended in a happy marriage of six years. A death that left so much unspoken, so much regret, so much to atone for, falls in six years into its pathetic perspective a little nearer Ninevah and Tyre.

I look up at the Cenotaph. A parcels delivery boy riding a tricycle van takes off his worn cap. An omnibus goes by. The men lift their hats. Men passing with papers and documents under their arms, attaché and despatch cases in their hands—all the business of life—bare their heads as they hurry by.

Six years have made no difference here. The Cenotaph—that mass of national emotion frozen in stone—is holy to this generation. Although I have seen it so many times on that day once a year when it comes alive to an accompaniment of pomp as simple and as beautiful as church ritual, I think that I like it best just standing here in a grey morning, with its feet in flowers and ordinary folk going by, remembering.

     *   *   *   *   *

I look up to Charing Cross and down to Westminster. On one side Whitehall narrows to a slit, against which rises the thin, black pencil of the Nelson column; on the other Westminster Abbey, grey and devoid of detail, seems etched in smoke against the sky, rising up like a mirage from the silhouette of bare trees.

The wind comes down Whitehall and pulls the flags, exposing a little more of their red, white, and blue, as if invisible fingers were playing with them. The plinth is vacant. The constant changing trickle of a crowd that later in the day will stand here for a few moments has not arrived. There is no one here.

No one? I look, but not with my eyes, and I see that the Empire is here: England, Canada, Australia, New Zealand, South Africa, India . . . here—springing in glory from our London soil.

     *   *   *   *   *

In a dream I see those old mad days ten years ago. How the wind fingers the flags. . . .

I remember how, only a few weeks ago, as a train thundered through France, a woman sitting opposite to me in the dining car said, 'The English!' I looked through the window over the green fields, and saw row on row, sharply white against the green, rising with the hill and dropping again into the hollows—keeping a firm line as they had been taught to do— a battalion on its last parade.

The Cenotaph and no one there? That can never be.

     *   *   *   *   *

Look! Near the mottled white and black of the War Office far up Whitehall a platoon of Guardsmen come marching. They swing their arms and stride out, carrying their rifles at a perfect 'slope.' They are young, the 'eighteen-year-olds' we used to call them in 1918 when they were called up to form the 'young soldiers' battalions.' I remember how frightened some of them were at this thing that had happened to them, and how often, when one was orderly officer padding round at night, a boy soldier would be crying like a child in the darkness at some harshness, or in a wave of homesickness.

The old recipe has worked with the Guards! On they come, a platoon of tough Irish soldiers, their solemn faces grim and set under their peaked caps, their belts snow white with pipeclay.

They approach the Cenotaph:

'Platoon!' roars the sergeant. 'Eyes—right!'

He slaps his rifle butt, and the heads swing round.

'Eyes—front!'

*   *   *   *   *

The Cenotaph stands there with a wind pulling . . . pulling like fingers touching the Flag.

WHEN normal London folk have gone home to bed the coffee-stalls come trundling out of the mysterious dark to stay until dawn at street corners and bridge-heads. Ask your friends if they have ever sought refreshment at a coffee-stall. I wager that perhaps only the Bad Boy of the Family or Dance Club Jane have experienced the happiness of sausages at 3 a.m. in this temple of romance.

The coffee-stall at the street corner is the only thing left in our modern world that approximates to the medieval inn or guest-house. Hotels are graded and standardized, and you know exactly the kind of people you will find in them. Good hotels are so much alike that patrons often have to ask the hall porter whether they are in London or Rome.

But the little coffee-stall, set netwise at street corners to catch queer fish, is dramatic. If ever I write a play the first act will take place round a coffee-stall; but I am told that this has been done; and no wonder. Here it is that you, like some traveller in the old days before the last dragon died, will meet varlets and squires, knights on some bright errantry, damsels in distress, and many a wandering fool: all the old characters of Romance like moths round a flame, dropping in out of the night to snatch a sausage and then off, mysterious, elusive, into the night.

There was a mist round the coffee-stall when I found it: one of those strange, fugitive fogs that drift like ghosts at night in the hollows. In the mist the stall was a glow-worm, yellow and furry, warm and desirable, a home to wanderers and fly-by-nights, comforting with its smell of hot coffee and its pungent, inviting sizzle.

Six or seven people, black against the yellowness and the banked Woodbines and the tiers of depressing cakes, gazed round suspiciously as I came in out of the incalculable dark, for after a certain time of morning every plain man may have the mark of the devil on him. Round this stall were the following people:

A young man with a silk hat on the back of his head and a white evening scarf hanging over a white shirt front.

A young girl with yellow, shingled hair and a pair of silver dance-shoes peeping from a moleskin cloak.

An arch young woman, who was making hopeless eyes at the young man in the silk hat out of sheer enthusiasm, as she ground cigarette stump after cigarette stump into her saucer.

Three or four workmen from neighbouring road repairs.

Two men holding little black bags, who may have been telephone officials, burglars, printers, disguised peers, or returning prodigal sons.

From the young man in the silk hat, I eavesdropped that everything was 'topping' and that Millie was 'awfully struck' on Arthur, and from his pretty partner I gathered that coffee and buns at 3 a.m. were awfully good fun, and that she had sprung a ladder in her stocking.

'But why,' she asked, 'are coffee-stalls licensed to sell stamps?'

The arch young woman looked up swiftly, and said all in one breath:

'So that men can write home and tell their wives why they were kept late at the office. Who's going to stand me a coffee?'

No one laughed; then, surprisingly, one of the solemn bagmen put down the money, and, as solemnly, went on talking to his companion about horses. The arch lady turned her back on them, drank her coffee, borrowed a broken mirror, rouged her lips, said, 'Well, cheerio, all!' and vanished, archly.

A taxicab driver arrived with a clatter, excavated three-pence from that deep remoteness where all taxicab drivers keep their money, and departed with the young man and the young woman. The bagmen went off with a non-committal air, which made me wonder whether they were off to break into a house or to sleep beneath a scriptural text.

'All sorts, sir, I gets here,' said the coffee-stall man, as he sloshed about among the dirty plates. 'You remember that cat burglar, him what broke into Grosvenor Gardens the other night? I've had him 'ere. 'Safact! Talkin' to a reel lord, he was, too! Yes; I get a lord now and again, but they ain't no different from ordinary people. They eats their sausages like everybody else, and leaves the gristle like everybody else, and only puts tuppence under the saucer. Why, you might be a lord for all I know——'

He paused, then, in case I might get proud and haughty, he added:

'Or a cat burglar. . . . Well, as I was sayin', up comes this 'ere cat burglar, smart as you like, puts a little black bag where your leanin' now—full of jools it was, but I didn't know—and he asks for a cup of corfee and a barth bun. He chips into the conversation and talks to 'is lordship, quite the gentleman. "Nice chap that," says 'is nibs after he'd gone. "What is he?" "I dunno," I tell him; and at that moment up run a couple of coppers, all hot and bothered. "'Ave you seen a dark young man wearin' a blue double-breasted suit, height five foot ten and a narf and of a pale complexion?" "Thousands," I says, going on wiping up; I could see something was up and I wasn't splitting. Then they told me about 'im, and I told them about 'im, and off they ran like a couple of ferrets. Catch him? Not likely. . . . Good morning, sir!'

Suddenly into the circle of light stepped a man carrying a cat that had been born white. A thin, melancholy cat and a thin, melancholy man, middle-aged, rain-coated, and grim. He placed the thin cat on the oilcloth counter, and the man behind at once poured out a saucer of milk.

The cat slunk to it guiltily. The man watched it as if he had never seen a cat before, and stroked its back. Then he buttoned it inside his raincoat and went away.

'Collects cats, he does,' said the coffee-stall man, as he banged about among his unwashed china. 'Says they follow him. Most nights he comes along with a stray cat, buys it milk, takes it home and looks after it. Regular walkin' cats' home, he is. . . . Balmy, of course. . . . Good morning, sir. . . .'

Round the bend of the road swung the first gold tramcar. It was officially 'to-morrow.'

Ghosts of the Fog

FOG in London.

Men are like flat figures cut in black paper. All things become two-dimensional. Carts, motor-cars, omnibuses are shadows that nose their way painfully like blind beasts. The fog has a flavour. Many flavours. At Marble Arch I meet a delicate after-taste like melon; at Ludgate Hill I taste coke.

Everywhere the fog grips the throat and sets the eyes watering. It puts out clammy fingers that touch the ears and give the hands a ghostly grip.

Children alone love it. They press small faces to window-panes and watch lights like little unripe oranges going by in the murk. A taxicab becomes something ogreish; a steam-lorry is a dragon spitting flame and grunting on its evil way. Men who sell things in the streets become more than ever deliciously horrible. They never arrive normally; they loom; they appear, freezing the blood, howling their wares like the lonely wolf in a picture book.

I go out into the fog and enter an incredible underworld. The fog has turned London into a place of ghosts. At one moment a man with a red nose and a moustache like a small scrubbing-brush appears with the suddenness of an apparition. There must be millions of such men with exactly similar moustaches, but this one is segregated from the herd. He seems unique in his isolation. I am prepared to believe he is the only one of that type in the world. I want to examine him as a learned man examines an insect on a pin. He seems a rare and interesting specimen. I want to cry 'Stop! Let me appreciate you!' But no; in a flash he goes, fades— disappears!

There comes a girl, pale and beautiful—much more beautiful than she would be on a fine day, because the eyes are focussed on her alone. She has the allurement of a dream, or a girl in a poem.

What is this in Oxford Street? Two motor-cars locked together. Fifty grim, muffled ghosts stand round watching and blowing their noses. On any day but a foggy day it would be a mere nothing: an excuse for a policeman to lick his pencil and write in a book. To-day it is a struggle of prehistoric

25

monsters in a death-grip. So must two clumsy, effete beasts of the Ice Age have fought locked in each other's scaly arms.

'Hi, there, put a bit of beef behind it. . . . Come on, mate —heave!'

Deep, angry voices come from the grey nothingness. A girl ghost says:

'Oh, isn't it awful? My eyes smart like anything."

Two big yellow eyes bear down on the scene. Men ghosts jump about in the road. They shout, they wave a red light, the monster with the two blazing eyes swerves, there is a vision of a red-faced man in a peaked cap and his gloved hands on a steering wheel:

'Keep your rear lights on, can't you! You ought to be in the cemetery. . . . that's where you ought to be and that's where you'll blinkin' well end!'

He passes on with his message.

*   *   *   *   *

In Finsbury Square a crowd of ghosts watch ten devils. Men are putting down asphalt. To-day they are not men: they are fiends pushing flaming cauldrons. The roadway is a mass of tiny, licking, orange-coloured flames. The devils take long rakes, and the little flames leap and flicker and fall over and between the prongs like fluid. Red-hot wheeled trolleys, with a blasting flame beneath them are dragged backwards and forwards over the roadway, heating it, licking at it, and roaring like furnaces.

The wind blows the flames this way and that way, lighting up the faces of the men, glittering on their belt buckles and making their bare arms fire colour.

The ghosts stand with white faces watching. More ghosts come. One little ghost has a peaked cap and an urgent message in a patent leather pouch. He stays a long time.

*   *   *   *   *

Near the Bank I come face to face with the greatest optimist of this or any other age. Here is a man entirely obscured by fog standing on the kerb making a tin monkey run up and down a piece of twine. Think of it! If you are sad or broke or things are going wrong, think of this man selling tin monkeys in a thick fog.

'How many have you sold?' I ask him.

'Fower,' he says.

Four tin monkeys sold in a thick fog.

Marvellous!   Incredible!

Battle ⚭ ⚭ ⚭ ⚭ ⚭ ⚭ ⚭

THEY lie in long, bright wards, which are full of a clean but brightening hospital smell of warmth, flowers, and drugs. A neat-waisted nurse moves between the beds, smiling, bending, whispering, easing a pillow, passing from weary smile to weary smile, so young by contrast with these sufferers, so healthy, so calm, so reliable.

The women are mostly middle-aged, but their plaited hair, lying in two little coils over their shoulders, gives them a youthful look, so that you realize what they were like when they were eighteen. Some are pale, their poor, thin arms the colour of unbleached wax; many look so well that you marvel that they should be there. It is the same in the men's wards. Cancer! That malignant, hissing word that lurks like a spectre at the back of so many minds has brought these men and women to one of the most noble hospitals in the world—the Free Cancer Hospital in the Fulham Road.

I admit that when I entered my first ward I shrank, in the shameful cowardice of my health, as I once did when a leper in the East rose on his stumps out of the dust and touched my arm. To see the unimaginable horrors which you may be called on to suffer, to see lying before your eyes the unthinkable depths to which your fine, strong body could sink is a fearful ordeal.

Yet what did I see? I saw greater than this black thing whose vileness no words can mitigate, the forces of Heroism and Hope: Heroism in the long, quiet wards, Hope in the operating theatres, in the laboratories. Here in the middle of London, with streams of omnibuses thundering beyond the railings, is a day and night battle with agony. Tragedy and triumph follow each other through these white halls, and over all is that spirit of enthusiasm, as of an army banded to fight for a cause.

*   *   *   *   *

Instead of shuddering at the flesh, I reverenced the spirit that rises up and fights this unknown terror, fights it with the knife and with the test tube and with the X-ray, and goes on fighting, goes on hoping. Have you ever in a storm at sea thrilled to the driving, thrusting strength and balance of a ship riding the tempest? If so, you will know how I felt in this hospital that steers its course through an ocean of suffering.

'This is the laboratory!'

A man in white overalls was bending over a microscope. Another man in white was examining the changing colour in a test tube. The rigid set of their shoulders denoted utter concentration. Hundreds of glass globes and bottles lay round about, ghastly exhibits from which I swiftly turned away.

Day in and day out, year after year, the research department of this hospital searches into the mysteries of cancer. Doctors try to cure or alleviate the disease in one part of the building; in another scientists work with their minds on that day when it may be possible to prevent it. Is there a more splendid room in London?

* * * * *

The chronic ward! Through glass doors I saw, in one, men, in another, women. They were away from the other patients in whom the disease has been caught in time. I tried not to look at the seared faces; I turned from the broken lives with a soreness at my heart. Some of them have been there for years, some are there for life. Over many of them was a strange, still peace which made me see, but I may be wrong, a nurse hurrying down those calm corridors with a merciful hypodermic syringe in her hand.

* * * * *

Visiting day! Can you imagine the quiet heroism of it? The wife who comes to see the husband who has been taken away from her, the husband who creeps in towards a bed in which, so small and girlish and white, she lies waiting for him? The flowers, the little cheerfulness, and, behind it all, the doubt, the wondering, the ache, the sense of injustice and the merciful deceit.

'Well, you'll soon be well and home again, dear.'

'Yes! And how's Johnny? How I'd love to see that dog again!'

Then anxiously, swiftly in reply:

'But you *will*, you old silly, you *will*!'

'Yes, of course, perhaps I will.'

'Good-bye!'

'Oh, come back, my dear. Just once more! How lovely your hair smells. . . .'

Can you imagine how often the most cheerful visitor crumples up when the weary eyes from the bed cannot see beyond the closed door?

*　　　*　　　*　　　*　　　*

Who is Dr. William Marsden?

How many Londoners know? He was the man who seventy-one years ago founded this hospital, and behind it lies a story as tragic as any in its wards. When going home late one night Dr. Marsden, who was then a young medical student, found a girl in a dying condition on a doorstep near Holborn. He took her to a hospital, where she was refused admission because she bore no letter of introduction from a subscriber. The next day she died. The young medical student resolved that, if he succeeded in life, he would found a free hospital for which there would be no qualification for admission but poverty and suffering.

He became famous, he loved, he married. Then his own wife was stricken with cancer, and nothing could be done to check the disease. Out of her death, and the death of the unknown girl, sprang this splendid work that shines like a good deed over London.

FAT babies, white dogs running, nursemaids with the wind pulling at their snuff-coloured veils, and at least six sharp intervals of sun strong enough to paint three shadows on the grass. That was how Kensington Gardens looked the other day, that delicious annexe to a thousand nurseries, that lovely land of young things insulated from our common world by a row of spiked railings.

I went up the Broad Walk revelling in this untroubled side of life, joyfully appreciating other people's babies, patting other people's dogs, admiring a smart turnout that lacked only a crest on the dove-grey perambulator, noting with pleasure the tall, neat young Kensington mothers with their lamp-post figures in well-cut tweed. When the sun came through it was like a game of musical chairs. The nursemaids stopped perambulating. Wind-blown walkers came to a standstill. They sat down on green seats.

So did I.

Next to me was a maiden of about three, a little unopened rose-bud of a girl, whose crisp gold hair escaped from a woollen cap with a yellow woollen tuft on top like a tangerine. Her short legs, in grey woollen trousers, stuck out in space so that she, sitting on a grown-up's seat, was in exactly the same position she would have assumed had she been sitting on a floor. Her brother was perhaps five. He wore a peaked cap of corduroy, leggings, and a fawn coat with an absurd belt at the back.

These two were holding hands, a difficult feat, I imagine, when hands are so small and woollen gloves so bulky and fluffy. They were discussing railway travel. He said that the carriage wheels say 'lickety-lick, lickety-lick,' which I thought was true, but she, womanlike, contradicted him, saying that they go 'tell-at-a-train, tell-at-a-train,' which I thought was also true. Then suddenly he said loudly three times, because his nurse was reading a novel:

'Nannie,' he said, 'I'm going to marry Madge!'

She looked shocked, put down the novel, and said:

'No, Master John, little boys don't marry their sisters, ever.'

'I know,' said Master John. 'Not now, of course, but when I grow up and get big. Some day when I'm——'

Here he opened his arms to denote size and maturity.

'Yes; but then you'll marry some other boy's sister,' said the nurse.

'I won't—not never!' cried John furiously. 'I'll marry Madge! Other boy's sisters are silly asses. They play with dolls!'

The sun went in and they went away, nurse telling him that 'nice boys' don't say 'silly asses'—ever!

Ten minutes in the Broad Walk make you think a lot about small children. How much character they show at an age when they seem hardly to exist as reasonable beings! See how some lag behind, how others are unhappy unless they are in front, exploring, climbing, meeting great dogs on which, at the last moment, they turn their backs in fear. Watch how some just endure a walk placidly, while others shine with the adventure of it, seeing every detail, wondering, questioning. Look how some collect things busily: sticks by the armful, stones by the pocketful. Restless, acquisitive little creatures. All instinct with motives planted in them before birth.

How amusing it is to watch it all. Such tiny, instinctive people.

*   *   *   *   *

The Round Pond flecked by wind. White gulls. Ducks with green velvet heads. Not one ship slanting across this ocean; not one. Only a boy prodding the water with a stick:

'Too cold to sail a ship!' I said.

'It isn't,' he replied scowling. 'But mother thinks it is.'

'And she's right!' I said, wishing to rebuke him.

'She isn't!' (Slap, slap on the water.)

'She is!'

'She isn't!'

I felt that this conversation had all the elements of eternity, so, after delivering a last word in defence of the mothers of Kensington who release the navies of the Round Pond at exactly the right temperature, I left this scowling die-hard admiral to his melancholy.

*   *   *   *   *

Then, on a path under bare trees, I saw a fat, round fairy in salmon pink. Just standing, she was. I sat down to look at her. She advanced slowly. Among the bare trees someone called, 'Joan, Joan!' She reminded me of a faun I saw once on the Rock of the Loreli on the Rhine. It advanced in just this same doubtful, solemn manner; one movement on my part would have sent it with beating heart into the thicket. So she advanced. I smiled; she smiled. Then she touched my coat with one finger, laughed, and—ran unsteadily away over the path under bare trees. Flirt!

I left Wonderland, and caught an omnibus to Piccadilly in a good temper.

Faces in the Strand ⌀   ⌀   ⌀   ⌀   ⌀

WHEN you ride up the Strand on top of an omnibus—and probably in rain—please remember that someone is envying you with all his heart, that someone would give six months' pay to sit in your damp seat[1] and see the lines of traffic converge on Charing Cross.

To the west in Canada, to the south in Africa, to the east in India, and far over the sea in Australia and New Zealand, are the lonely men. Where the red border line of Empire ends on the map in an alien colour are the little outposts in which these men work and dream. At the end of day they ram down the tobacco in their pipes and think of home with the characteristic sentimentality of the exile, for solitude makes a man very like a child. 'Lord, to be in London now!' How many times in the twenty-four hours does this cry go up all over the earth? We who take our London carelessly as a matter of course can have no conception of its meaning to these wanderers who, feeling the ache of home-sickness, are too old to cry.

*   *   *   *   *

The Strand!

That means London in shack, bungalow, and camp. It means more: it symbolizes—home! Not Piccadilly, not Pall Mall, not fashionable Mayfair or Belgravia, but the curious old Victorian Strand.

What a street it is. It does not belong to London. Piccadilly, Regent Street, and Oxford Street stole its birthright long ago. It belongs to the Empire. Look at its shops. They are full of pith helmets and spine pads, veld shirts and tropical drill, ammunition belts and puttees. Your smart subaltern going out to join the Indian cavalry may buy his clothes in Savile Row, but your old colonial, who has been

[1] In 1925, when this was written, London omnibuses had open roofs, and the seats were protected by black tarpaulin covers which travellers could adjust in wet weather. Nowadays the London omnibus is an enclosed juggernaut and wet seats are things of the primitive past. Also, the Strand has changed since 1925. It has been widened in parts, and it is no longer an exclusively masculine street. Silk stockings are probably now more in evidence there than pith helmets and spine pads.

34

pegging down the flag somewhere for the best part of his life, comes back to shop in the Strand, to walk in the Strand, to exult in the Strand. . . .

*   *   *   *   *

Take the faces. In days when colonials come home you will find nothing more interesting in London. The exile makes straight for the Strand; if he does not know it he makes its acquaintance at once, joyfully, reverently; for he has heard men speak of it as men speak of their mothers. As he walks along he begins to believe that he has really come home.

You will see him shouldering his way gingerly through the crowds with the gentleness of a big man not used to pavements, and he looks up at the landmarks, a shop where he bought a gun once, a restaurant where once Mary . . . well, never mind, that was over long ago. Or he may be that strange thing, a tenderfoot in London, a tenderfoot from the prairies or the veld or the Afghan frontier. He is fulfilling his destiny: He is walking down the Strand! When he gets back men will say to him: 'Well, and how did you find London?'

And he will start a story consciously and proudly with:

'I was walking down the Strand one morning——'

Ah, he has struck a chord at once. Surely you visualize the smile that will go round the circle of men deep in their cane chairs. 'I was walking down the Strand!' Can you begin a story in the tropics in a more arresting way? You set a whole flock of memories a-flying. . . .

What sentimental journeys the Strand has seen.

You must have been stopped at some time near the Adelphi by a burnt-up, middle-aged man who asks the way to a bar or a restaurant unknown to you. When you say you don't know it, a disappointed look creeps into his eyes, and he apologizes and goes off, very straight and lonely, in the crowd.

Conrad in quest of his youth? Perhaps. Possibly for years, while he waited for leave, he was promising himself a visit to this place. No doubt the stars saw him sitting out alone at night thinking of it, hearing the thunder of the Strand, seeing its lights, and himself slipping into his old seat at a corner table where he used to sit with old X, who was killed in 'British East.' . . .

All the time the Strand was altering, denying such exiles their beloved landmarks.

*   *   *   *   *

So they drift a little sadly and disconsolately along the Strand, feeling as you feel when, after a long absence, you visit a place known to you when you were a child. Nothing is so big as you thought, nothing so impressive as once it was. That tiny paddock was once a prairie—that small house a castle.

The Strand to them is somehow different—cheaper, smaller, vaguely disappointing. Those pale-faced men hurrying along. How strange. What an altered atmosphere! And where are those lovely little faces that used to look from beneath Merry Widow hats?

*   *   *   *   *

Then, six months after, in a solitude of stars and palms, with a hot wind blowing over the plains:

'O Lord, to see the dear old Strand now!'

The big stars shine, the moon swings up above the distant hills, and the old love comes back into the heart of the lonely man. . . .

Women and Tea   *ᴑ*   *ᴑ*   *ᴑ*   *ᴑ*   *ᴑ*

A TEA-SHOP is the milestone that marks the end of a day's work.

In the provinces, and particularly in the north and in Scotland, where men take tea with passionate sincerity, the tea-shop occupies an appropriately massive position in daily life. London's tea-shops are, however, talk-shops, refuges from a day's shopping, trysting-places after a terrible eight hours' separation.

O, the eyes that meet over a muffin every afternoon in London; the hands that thrill to a casual touch beneath the crumpet plate. . . .

London's tea-shops are of many kinds, from the standardized shop to the good pull-up for millionaires constructed on the Paris plan, where slim Gruyère sandwiches hide in paper coats, and cakes taste of Benedictine, and bills have a queer habit of working out at fifteen shillings.

Then, of course, there is the cosy type of tea-shop run on amateur lines where genteel young women, who do not seem to have forgotten William Morris, bend wistfully over the meringues in brown or sage green *crêpe de Chine* gowns and an air of shattered romance. Such places have fanciful names designed to attract those with a passion for peace. They are always opening or going smash, and there is a widespread belief in the suburbs among enterprising young women that this is the way to an enormous bank account.

'Thanks awfully!'

That's what they say when you pay the bill, and such a sad, sweet smile goes with it. Andromeda chained to a cheese cake.

     *   *   *   *   *

I entered a large musical tea-shop in the heart of Shopland yesterday. The atmosphere was as feminine as that of a perfume store. It was No Man's Land. I steered my conspicuous way to a table through a jungle of musquash, moleskin, and beaver. The only other men there were in the toils of women, politely tapping their *éclairs*, and wearing photographic faces, behaving as men never behave away from this uplifting and ennobling atmosphere.

37

I heard a girl describe a bridesmaid's dress; another girl was talking about a baby; a third had discovered John Galsworthy. Two young married women were discussing their husbands, how really sweet they were, how they hated cold mutton, how amusingly irritable they were, and how upset they were when their wives shingled their hair. . . .

A slight stir was caused by the entrance of husbands to claim their wives. One, a handsome young man, was charmingly introduced with shy pride; another, an elderly, bluff, old-established husband, was received quite calmly like an overdue muffin. Then the human event that electrified the entire tea-shop happened, that marvellous touch of nature that unites Kennington with even the best parts of Kensington.

A small, smug child, distinguished only by a red balloon on the end of a string, set up a wild and awful howl. It was dramatic in its suddenness. Everybody looked round in the belief that the infant had sat on a pin. Instead they saw the red balloon drifting with a gay and careless determination towards the roof. Reaching its destination, it bumped gracefully twice and remained there, nestling against an overblown cupid.

Immediately the entire tea-shop, hitherto split into self-centred groups, became one in its endeavour to rescue the red balloon. Young men, anxious to distinguish themselves, stood on chairs and made grabs for the string with umbrellas; dogs, which until then had been asleep and unsuspected, awakened and barked.

In the centre of the stage stood the smug, small child, breathless with anxiety, pointing to the roof, grief-stricken that his balloon had played him false, yet encouraged by the stir his tragedy was causing in so many grown-up lives.

A grim old man, melted by the event, obtained a long pole employed in pulling down shop blinds. He succeeded in driving the balloon from its fastness and sending it fatuously bumping into another. Meanwhile the entire shop held its breath, expecting these good intentions to end in a loud plop and a worse tragedy. There was a gasp of relief as this ancient hero gave way to a man in an apron with a step-ladder.

He did the deed.

The tea-shop settled down. The smug child that had united

an afternoon's assembly left unnoticed. Over the tea-tables rose again the talk of bridesmaids and husbands and shingles and Maud's hennaed hair. The orchestra played some more Puccini, and a small boy, who had profited by the commotion to seize his fourth *éclair*, gave an enormous sigh of joy.

SHORTLY after midnight a decently dressed young man glanced furtively round Trafalgar Square, hesitated a moment, and then swiftly ran up the black steps of St. Martin's Church. I came up behind him as he tapped the door.

There was the sound of a drawn bolt, and the door swung back. The young man stammered. He was blue with cold, and—there was something else:

'I'm—I'm broke,' he said. 'I've never done this before. I've always had a bit of money; but—well, I've nowhere to sleep to-night, and—please can I come in?'

The door opened wider, and a pleasant, middle-aged policewoman said:

'Come along!' I followed.

*   *   *   *   *

Down in the crypt of St. Martin's Church, the church whose doors never close, I saw a remarkable sight. Broad, white arches spanned a dim gloom. Certain benches were set facing the east, as in the church above, and others were placed round the crypt. Lying, sitting upright, and huddled in every position of which the human body is capable, were men and women, homeless wanderers over the hard face of the earth.

There was no sound in the white crypt but variously keyed snores and the small scratch of a policewoman's pen as she kept a record of Christ's guests, for such they are; and as I looked at them these words sang in my heart: 'Come unto Me, all ye that labour and are heavy laden, and I will give you rest.'

Sanctuary. That was it. They had the hunted air of having run hard to find this place, and, having found it, had abandoned themselves to safety. There was something else. They reminded me of a picture that used to thrill me when I was a child: troops, rolled in their cloaks beside dead fires, sleeping before a battle. Their battle was To-morrow.

*   *   *   *   *

There was a young girl who could not sleep. She was wrapped tightly in a blue mackintosh. She sat with her eyes wide open, gazing before her. There was a grey-haired woman sleeping upright in a pew, a poor, rakish hat on a pile of prayer-books beside her. Three or four other women slept near together, leaning against each other, as if for warmth.

Most of the men slept. Some had no overcoats, and lay huddled with their tousled heads on hassocks. Others had placed their coats over their heads. One or two wore spats, and appeared from their clothes to be prosperous. Then you looked at their boots, and read a story of tramp, tramp, tramp. One elderly man, awakened suddenly, shot out an arm to look at his wrist-watch. But there was no watch there, and he drew his hand swiftly under his coat again as though it hurt.

*   *   *   *   *

'Some extraordinary dramas have been acted on the steps outside in the small hours,' said a young man officially connected with the church. 'Once a girl was saved from white-slavers; once I brought in a boy so blue with cold that I had to open the furnace doors and thaw him. Most of the "down-and-outs" know this church. We manage to set up many of them again, some sink back or just disappear. Yet we never lose faith in human nature. A homeless person is allowed to shelter only for three nights in succession. After that we try to find some other abode for them, so you see our visitors are always changing.'

He opened a door, and I found myself in a cellar full of old clothes. Boxes of collars lay on the floor. A knowing-looking silk hat crowned a pile of old hats. Women's skirts and men's trousers hung from pegs. Boots and shoes stood neatly dressed by the right.

'This is our wardrobe,' he said. 'Our first principle is to give a homeless person food and then whatever clothes we can. You can't expect to hear the truth on an empty stomach.'

'Are you often deceived by people who drift in here out of the night?'

'Now and then. It's nothing compared with the friends we make, the delightful characters we discover when the ache and pain of hardship have worn off. We divide men into three groups: Those who have been to prison and have a grudge against the world; those who went to the war as boys and came

back men with boys' minds; and those who simply will not
work and can't run straight. We have heard every fairy tale
in the world, and we know a scrounger at sight!'

*   *   *   *   *

I tip-toed back through the white crypt. The pale girl was
still awake. The grey-haired woman still slept—old, worn-
out, uncared-for, and life gone by. Men slept and stirred
uneasily as if afraid of the dawn that was stealing on to draw
them again into the battle. How many would rise gloriously;
how many fall? We talk of human nature in the rough, heart-
beats, life. Here it is in the middle of London every night,
each sleeper a real drama of struggle, each man and woman
midway in that Valley of the Shadow through which all lives,
spiritually or materially, must pass.

'We don't care what they are,' said the young man. 'If they
are in trouble, that is enough.'

I hardly heard him, for I was thinking that in this white
place is the Spirit of Christ.

A Bit of Bagdad

THE only place where you could sell an elephant, a werewolf, or your second best aunt without attracting the slightest curiosity is Club Row, a Sunday market famous throughout the eastern regions of London. Turn out of Shoreditch along the Bethnal Green Road and presently you see a large cloth-capped crowd. You approach.

A dramatic, sinister man, who lost his razor early last year, detaches himself and sidles up to you with his right hand suspiciously hidden in the breast of his coat. Is he an anarchist? Just as you expect him to bring out a bomb and cry 'Down with Civilization,' he quickly produces a six-ounce pom and whispers in a voice like a rusty door hinge: 'Come on, half a dollar!' Other dog men approach. They offer handfuls of pups, or they submit dogs of larger growth, which sit round in a circle looking up at you questioningly, hopefully. You want to buy the lot. Then an Airedale bites a collie and you find yourself the centre of a splendid battle, from which you escape into the heart of the mob.

Here life is magnificent. Thousands of things are happening at once in Oriental variety. This is what Bagdad was like in the days of the Caliph. This is what the Mouski in Cairo is like to-day. As you stand wedged between people who hold sacks that writhe and cluck, a man waves a couple of buff orpingtons in your face and pushes past to stand himself a glass of jellied eels. An elderly parrot-like old lady is marooned helplessly, with a green aloof-looking parrot, exactly like herself, perched on her hand. Pigeons coo, hens cackle, cockerels crow, dogs bark, canaries sing, and you gain the impression that anything—anything—is yours for 'half a dollar.'

I was interested in the little groups round contortionists, catch-penny men, and herb doctors. We have driven these medieval characters from more polite places, and it is almost with a thrill that east of Aldgate Pump you find yourself in the hearty atmosphere of a fair as old as England. One man, who said that his face was as well known as the dome of St. Paul's, walked rapidly up and down with a mysterious paper packet over which he held a pair of dental forceps. Every one wanted to see what marvellous thing he would pick out

43

of the packet at the psychological moment. All the time, as he walked backwards and forwards, he talked of indigestion and flatulence with Elizabethan frankness. He discussed food as if it were a revolver.

'If the steak repeats, if the onions repeat, if the pudding repeats, if cheese repeats. . . .'

Then, working up to his climax, he dived the forceps into the packet and produced a beautiful heliotrope-coloured pill! Did he sell any? He did!

Under a railway arch a young man with a faint Scottish accent had been handcuffed and chained. Round his neck he wore a steel collar; on his head a steel cap which, he said, was 'an exact replica of the cap used for capital punishment throughout the United States of America.' (Thrill in the audience!)

'And now,' he remarked (with a touch of his Scottish accent), 'before I release myself, my partner will take the liberty of passing the hat round!'

The fringes of the crowd melted away. After a prolonged struggle, interrupted by a donkey and cart bursting violently into the arena, the young man unshackled himself, dived for the hat, looked at the pennies, and remarked, 'Well, now; if any sportsman would care. . . .'

But the crowd had stampeded.

How delightfully childish it all is. In order to sell chocolate, one man had taken off his coat and had put on his head an irresponsible looking opera hat.

In side streets I came on a bicycle market. I wondered how many were doped like racehorses. A stray bicycle found carelessly outside a house becomes something quite different with the aid of a paint brush! How many old crocks had been dressed up with new lamps and saddles, I would not care to say! Here trade was booming. I saw a man who had bought a dog, a birdcage, and a pair of pink braces, treat himself to a pair of handle-bars. It must be wonderful to wander through Bagdad like this, meeting things on the way, living an hour full of infinite possibilities, not knowing whether you will arrive home with a bullfinch or a bicycle! After watching this market closely I realized this: people do not go there to buy things, but to have things sold to them!

*   *   *   *   *

On the way out I saw something worth while. A melancholy bull pup, sitting in the road with all the world's troubles in his eyes, was picked up by a little girl.

'I want him because he looks so unhappy.'

A chauffeur in a green coat paid out five shillings.

'Darling . . . darling,' said the girl, holding the squat little body.

They took him to a motor-car that had been left round the corner. So he left a street corner in Bagdad to be a prince among pups.

Kismet!

'PRISONERS Only.'

A door in Bow Street Police Station opens on a small tiled room in which each morning all the prisoners on their way to the celebrated dock gather to await the call.

It is an exclusive apartment. Visitors are not allowed. Unless you break a shop window, punch a policeman in the stomach, or become publicly full of spirit you will never see it. It was due only to the courtesy of Bow Street that I was allowed in for a moment yesterday like an ordinary prisoner. Here I found a strange assortment of human beings gathered together by Fate—or should I say alcohol?—for most of Monday morning's crime originates in a bottle.

The room is tiled, and looks like an ordinary waiting-room until a policeman opens the door that leads out to a courtyard and then you see a second door composed of stout iron bars. About twenty or thirty men were sitting round the room talking to the policemen who had arrested them. Most of them were weary, some of those who had been let out on bail looked smart, a few still retained traces of their fateful debauch, and all had lost the divine afflatus which had flung them into a pair of blue arms. The atmosphere was rather like that of a headmaster's study in which is gathered a group of bad boys waiting for the cane.

A stoical old man dozed peacefully in a corner. So might dear old Falstaff have bared his grey hairs in a moment of humiliation. A navvy with the head of a Roman emperor sat huddled in his clay-soiled clothes, silent, grim. He reminded me of Trajan's bust in the British Museum. He should have been dressed in a toga instead of sitting in Bow Street with a fine of five shillings hanging over him. A young man with a mild face sat near him, the kind of young man who keeps rabbits in a back yard. I wondered what odd circumstance had brought him in conflict with law and order. Among a group of seedy and tattered people I noticed a smart man wearing spats and holding a neat umbrella.

It was the strangest roomful you can imagine.

*　　　*　　　*　　　*　　　*

It was unaccountably British. I do not imagine that the

46

police and prisoners of any other nation meet together as captor and captive in the same cheery, social atmosphere.

In Berlin, I imagine, it must be exceedingly unpleasant to be a prisoner, and in Paris, also, it cannot be exactly jolly. In Cologne I once saw a German policeman draw his sword and charge a little boy who had left a banana skin on a patch of neat, cultured turf; and in Paris once I saw a gendarme do unnecessarily unfriendly things to his captive. But our Roberts are not like this, and when they are face to face with their prey in the station they seem almost apologetic about it: 'You broke the law and I did my duty, and that's that. Let's forget it!'

That is the atmosphere in the 'Prisoners Only' room. Thumbs in belts, the policemen talked with their prisoners about racing, the weather, and, as far as I could gather, anything but drink and brawls. What instinctive good breeding! Here and there a prisoner who took his captivity lightly laughed and joked with the man who brought him there.

'What'll I get?' one prisoner asked.

'Oh, about twenty years without option!' replied the constable. Then a man with a notebook became busy with the day's evil-doers, a name was called, and, as the first prisoner pulled himself together and strode out dockwards, a flutter of interest went round the waiting-room; and the old man awakened with a start and asked where he was.

*　　*　　*　　*　　*

Under the Royal Arms sat Sir Chartres Biron, white-haired and exceedingly wise to human nature. He was dealing with a pathetic collection of women prisoners who had been waiting in a 'Prisoners Only' room of their own. Constable after constable described scenes of revelry in which it was alleged that certain inadequate Bacchantes in black bonnets had been urged to deeds of violence.

Some women pleaded guilty and got it all over quickly. Others clasped and unclasped their hands—appealing, thin, worn hands grimed with work—and tried to impress Sir Chartres that 'two glasses of port' had been the cause of all their trouble. They were fined and went their way, some with an assumption of belated dignity, others jauntily. One old lady was so pleased with her sentence that she danced down the corridor between two lines of policemen promising never to look upon the wine again.

* * * * *

Then one by one my friends of the waiting-room came up for justice: drunk and disorderly, drunk in charge of a motor-car, creating a disturbance, using insulting language. They all looked sorry for themselves and exceedingly foolish. Five deaf and dumb youths had, it appeared, pushed a policeman off the pavement. The mother of one of them interpreted the case, talked to them in baby language, asked them if they had really 'banged' the policeman. They nodded their heads and tried to speak, but only vague, tortured sounds, heart-rending to hear, came from their mouths. They filed out, bound over.

Then Caesar strode into the dock, said he had been drunk, accepted his fine without a trace of emotion, and walked from the dock with an invisible cohort before him and—a visible bottle sticking out of his coat-tails!

* * * * *

When he has done his day's work does Sir Chartres Biron feel more like laughing or crying, I wonder?

Boys on the Bridge ～ ～ ～ ～ ～

BOYS are always leaning over London Bridge, as right-minded boys have been leaning these five hundred years and more. Beneath them the Thames, that loved river of ours, swirls and eddies round the piers, sucking at the weathered stone as it runs seawards, out and away.

When I joined them the other day, I noticed, with an authentic thrill, that against the grim wharves men were doing interesting things in ships. No matter how trivial the act—the hauling of a rope, the turning of a winch, the painting of a hull—it becomes somehow vital and significant to anyone on dry land. To a London office boy who has been told not to linger by the wayside—ah! how exquisite, how irresistible!

Sometimes little, important jets of steam rose from a cargo boat, marvellously suggesting departure and the imminence of great adventure; enviable free men whose boots had never trod an office stair popped their heads out of hatchways and lumbered up on deck; a string of linked barges, dingy, low in the water, went by behind an impertinent tug, which nosed the tide sideways, pulling and puffing. On the hindmost barge a man was frying bacon in a jet-black pan. O, exquisite! O, irresistible! Was this not life? Was this not romance?

To me a fat white woman was singularly significant. She appeared from the bowels of a barge and, moving slowly to starboard with a nautical roll, hung an intimate item of her laundry right in the eye of London Bridge. Then she looked round her with that composed placidity which sustains the suburbs (just as if she were in Brixton and not on the high seas), and after giving one of her sleeves a roll to keep it above her fat elbow, she went below with the important air of the busy female who believes that her industry is the hinge on which life turns smoothly. No cut-throats on that barge, no swashbuckling, no silly ideas about the Spanish Main there, but everything nice and tidy, and wipe your boots on the mat and mind you don't stay out too long after closing time! Wonderful how a woman—any woman—softens a masculine scene and awakens the boy in man to a swift respect—as if the matron had appeared suddenly on the scene of a scrum on a dormitory landing! The wild places of the earth do not care much about a man. He can't do much. When the woman appears the aspens shiver and the tamarisks tremble and even the oak is fearful, for a lone man is transitory and woman is permanent: she means a home and a whole lot more men; she is the beginning of civilization.

So the fat woman made her barge interesting to me: she brought it into society, she humanized the wild old Thames. All this was high above the office boys who pressed their stomachs to the stone, and clambered for a foothold in the balustrading, so that they might take a better view of all this glamour. . . .

Thames, you muddy strip of magic, how many London heads have you turned; how many sirens come in from sea on every tide to sing those wicked songs against which we poor chained creatures sometimes wax our ears in vain?

　　　*　　　　*　　　　*　　　　*　　　　*

I looked at the faces of the spellbound office boys. They gazed like gargoyles from the parapet. Most of them were dull and stolid; but you never can tell. Their cheeks bulged with sweets and their eyes regarded the river with the same intent vacancy that they would have given to a spectacular road repair.

One face only seemed to me to hold the hunger that burns. It belonged to a thin, pale lad who possessed no physical strength, the type that would rather have been Hercules than Homer; the frail type that dreams of swords and ambuscades and blood. He looked over the water towards Tower Bridge with eyes that were wide—whether with imagination or indigestion I cannot say! I can only tell you this: he was the kind of pale, useless mass of parental despair that through history has met the turning point of existence in an idle hour, when imagination, blazing suddenly like fired straw, illuminates a dream on which to build a life.

What was he thinking, I wondered. Had I asked him he would have said sullenly, 'Nothing,' and would have slouched away, ashamed.

I wondered if he were seeing in Thames water those things that thousands of London boys have seen—argosies and ventures and foreign places, the drive of water past a vessel's bows, leaning sails, and small white towns whose palm trees stand with their feet in calm lagoons.

LONDON BRIDGE

Who knows? This is the dream of London Bridge. This is the challenge that the Thames flings down to London every day and every night, crying it aloud to the huddled streets and to the crowded places, calling it softly in the market-place. This is the old magic. It has given to London merchants, adventurers, sailors, poets, and millions of poor, discontented men who must need take their burning hearts to Balham and shut their ears.

*   *   *   *   *

Slowly conscience dawned in the minds of the boys. One by one they went away, their places immediately filled by others.

Away they went into the traffic, to become lost in the ant-hills of commerce, carrying who knows what high resolve from that stolen moment beside the river.

*   *   *   *   *

More barges came slowly downstream. High and shrill sounded the hoarse protest of a siren, imperative and wild, and I seemed to feel, right in the heart of London, where all things are so ordered and inevitable, the ancient call to the open places that comes with the smell of tar and the sight of masts rising to the sky.

IT is three o'clock in the morning. Piccadilly Circus is empty of life and movement—save for a prowling policeman trying shop doors, and a group of men directing water from a giant hose over the gleaming, empty road.

A taxicab is an event, and a stray person walking quietly into the Circus holds dramatic possibilities. The mind fastens on him. Who is he? He may be a great criminal, or a great lover walking home after a dance with his head full of glorious dreams, or he may be a burglar, or a young man who has just inherited a million, or a young man without a place to rest his head. The emptiness of Piccadilly at three a.m. is awful, unnatural, death-like. . . .

Yet London is not asleep. Hundreds of people in London never seem to sleep. Come into one of the all-night cafés which have sprung up within the last year or so. It is full. It hums with talk and laughter. Waiters move about between the crowded tables. There is a constant clatter of cups and saucers, and the air is blue with smoke. In contrast to the desolation of the empty streets outside, it is an astonishing place. At first you think there is nothing to distinguish the café from the same place at normal hours. You look again and realize the difference. The people are different. The woman with three or four brown paper parcels—the shopping woman—is absent. There are no children. There are few elderly people.

Those present are mostly young people distinguished either by an air of lassitude or an unnatural gaiety.

At the next table a girl is eating lobster salad. Lobster at three a.m.!

*   *   *   *

Who are these people? You begin to wonder about them. Some are obvious—extremely obvious—some are mysteries.

In a corner a man in evening dress has dropped in for a cup of coffee with the nice girl with whom he has been dancing. She keeps her velvet evening cloak tightly round her, and looks about at the other people, trying to place them. It is, to her, an adventure. Her partner's glance at her over the broad rim of his cup suggests that he is desperately trying to prolong the 'night out.' He is a clean, blond young man, and he pretends to take no notice of the elderly satyr at another table who is openly admiring the girl in the cloak. But she sees and gives the satyr a cold Kensington eye, hard as an eviction order.

Quite a number of other dancers seem glued to rolls and coffee, unable to go home. They laugh and discuss the dance. Someone says: 'I must be in the office at nine!' They laugh and order more coffee.

A group of men with music cases under the chairs talk in a corner. They are a jazz band which has just finished work. There are a number of solemn, self-centred men smoking quietly, alone. They may be night-workers, post office officials, or what not, waiting for the next tramcar.

There are inevitable Japanese students. They sit together talking, occasionally taking an expressionless survey of the company. What are they doing? Studying night life? Winding up an innocent party?

Most interesting are the unplaceable people: the number of foreign-looking young men who argue together: the type of man who at the precise crack of Doom with graves opening and the world closing, would try to sell you a cheap pearl tiepin. A number of night birds are evidently in the habit of drinking coffee at three a.m. There is movement from table to table, group to group. Dotted about the room are girls who would describe themselves as dance instructresses or cinema actresses.

Four or five men who look as though they have been celebrating a friend's last night of bachelorhood enter with exaggerated politeness, apologizing for occasional conflicts with chairs and tables. They order black coffee. Another man comes up to their table. They all leap up and shake hands.

'The last time I saw you was in Bagdad!' he says. 'What's happened to old "Whisky Willie" of the Gunners? You remember that night. . . .'

This sort of talk still goes on in London where young men are linked together by common memories of the War.

*　　　*　　　*　　　*　　　*

As we go from the brilliantly lit room, the emptiness and the chill of sleeping London meets us at the door. Long lines of lights shining on desolate pavements, a shuffling figure under a lamp, a slow taxicab cruising near the kerb, and then, surprisingly, like a ghost of old London, a hansom cab standing in Piccadilly, the ancient horse, head down as if remembering past things.

In the cold air is the vague promise of a new day, a faint rumble of market carts as if London is stirring in her impressive slumber.

HE was sitting in the acrid unpleasantness of a London fog holding a steering-wheel and—the lives of men and women. It was Sunday.

Inside the well-lit, and almost pleasant, omnibus a young man, wearing his Sunday hat, and a young girl, completely Sundayfied, sat holding hands as they pretended to read a newspaper. They saw no more than each other's eyes, and what more could they possibly have seen? Portentous women with unnaturally clean children entered or made a fussy exit from time to time, bent, no doubt, on that awfulness of a London Sunday—a visit to relatives. On some faces you could read a kind of comfortable condescension that somehow suggested a glittering descent on poor relatives; on others a dutiful resignation—the composure of an ordained martyr preparing to meet the lions—and you pictured a stiff and patronizing tea in a distant but exalted suburb, with criticism underlying an afternoon of smooth insincerity.

All the time the Man at the Wheel exhibited a broad and stocky back to the human comedy he was carrying; sometimes his face, tense and questioning, was turned towards the lit interior as he tried to gauge the right moment to accelerate after the descent of an agile passenger. Mostly, however, he just sat there peering into the white cotton-wool world of fog that was hung with saffron lights, his big hands in gloves, expertly and suddenly taking his vehicle from an unexpected near rush of light as a tramcar clanged past. And the passengers did not notice him. They had paid twopence to be taken in safety through the fog.

*   *   *   *   *

I sat there admiring him.

I have never heard of any poet writing an ode to a London omnibus driver, but he always seems to me a subject worthy of heroic metre. He may not possess the social charm of the old horse-omnibus driver, who, according to legend, wore a top hat, and used his whip-butt on London as a lecturer uses a wand. He is a more solemn character. Machines always leave their mark on men. The big petrol engine has created a grim, silent, crouching character who, fortunately for London and Londoners' wives and families, has no time for social pleasantries as he urges his great, red, double-decked steed through the thousand perils of a crowded street.

He has, I think, developed a sixth sense. His whole being seems conscious of inches. Watch the way a press of omnibuses in High Holborn or Tottenham Court Road, or any other famous hold-up, will edge and nudge a way with a mere inch between their mudguards, all so skilfully and calmly done as though the scarlet sides of the vehicles had nerves—invisible feelers—that carried warning of danger to the rough, deft hands at the wheel.

As we crawled through the fog, I watched his taut concentration, admired his judgment as he executed a circling movement round a candidate for suicide, as he jammed on the brakes within a yard of a halted motor-car, as he put on speed over a thin patch of fog, and as he shot ahead past a less speedy driver.

Now and then he had to crawl through a whiteness as dense as that terrible billowing mist that rolls down a Scottish mountain. Here and there pin-points of fire shone out, changed swiftly on approach into objects like long hair aflame in the wind, and, nearer still, stood revealed as tall fog flares shooting in fire from metal standards.

At the terminus I watched the drivers dismount, stiff and cold, pull off their big gloves, and hit their cold hands across their chests. Wet particles of fog shone on their moustaches.

Pretty bad at Camden Town, and Baker Street was like a tunnel! Couldn't see a yard at Brixton. Fine and clear at the Crystal Palace. . . . So these adventurers of the London fog compared notes before, groping in remote recesses, they found money to buy coffee from a stall. Then a whistle, the roar of a chilled engine, and off again on their perilous pilgrimages across London.

Surely every man who has driven through fog with eyes that ache, and imagined phantoms at each cross-road, will be glad to raise his hat to the bulky figure behind the wheel of a London omnibus as he steers his living cargo to safety with no thought of praise because—it's all in the day's work?

I WAS cheered to find that St. Paul's looked quite firm and permanent when I walked up Ludgate Hill the other morning. How deceptive are the works of man! Who would have guessed that this mountain was feeling its age a bit, moving ever so slightly under the weight of its Dome?[1]

The pigeons wheeled in flight. A girl stood covered in them, while less bold birds walked, nodding quickly, round her feet pecking crumbs. Up the fine, bold sweep of the steps walked many people. I think that they were perhaps Londoners paying their first visit, hoping that they would get it over before the cathedral collapsed, for they looked up warily as they advanced as though alarmed by accounts of splitting piers, and then, finding nothing unusual, they went on their way, maybe surprised to find no cant to the Dome or any visible fissure.

As I walked over the black and white diamonds of the nave I realized that, although I have attended services normal and national in St. Paul's, I had never climbed to the Whispering Gallery. When Americans had talked to me about it I had lied and had pretended that I knew it. So I determined to wipe out my shame.

I walked down the south aisle, admiring the gold shafts of light striking through the dusk of the church, noting the number of young women who go there to sit quietly and read sacred and profane literature, and remarking how one appreciative beam of light had caught a splendid head of Burne-Jones's hair, making it blaze in the comparative darkness like fire in a lonely thorn bush. I met all kinds of people wandering on tip-toe with that vague, lost air people assume in churches; and then I came to a little office near the south transept in which I paid sixpence for a ticket—the best sixpennyworth, as I afterwards found, in all London.

'I thought,' I said to the verger, 'that I'd better go up there before it comes down here.'

'That won't be for a long time, sir,' he said, with a reassuring smile, a sentiment I passed on at step two hundred and forty-one to a charming old lady, who asked if I thought it was 'quite wise' to go right to the top.

[1] There were at this time some grave fears for the safety of Wren's masterpiece; and these led to extensive reconstructions.

What a climb it is! If ever I go foolishly walking or climbing in Switzerland again, I will get into training on this spiral staircase. Once up and once down every day, and no mountaineer's muscles would be firmer, no walker's wind less treacherous. It is a fine, free, and uncrowded gymnasium.

Half-way up is a museum and a library, where I, puffing slightly, prodded about among old stones, the ruins of Old St. Paul's. Then up, up, up and round and round again until I came to a little door where a quiet, churchy man was sitting who said it was the Whispering Gallery.

In the Whispering Gallery I was not so impressed by the man in occupation as I was by the astonishing bird's-eye view of tiny people walking far below on a little chess-board of a pavement. Then suddenly I heard a whisper. I looked across to the other side of the gallery. The guide was whispering against the wall. His message came to me like a spirit voice from the Beyond, rather terrifying and sepulchral: 'The diameter of the dome is a hundred and eight feet,' said the Voice, and then it plunged into an account of Sir Christopher Wren. I walked away, congratulated the Voice, which seemed gratified, and said, 'How dissatisfied and hard of hearing some people are!'

High up below the dome of St. Paul's you have thrills. As you walk out on a large stone platform, London lies below in a huddle of buildings and smoking chimneys. You pick out landmarks. How narrow even the widest streets look. To the east, over the big black bulk of Cannon Street, is the faint outline of Tower Bridge in the mist. Only the broad Thames has size. Men are midgets, an omnibus is blotted out from time to time by the flight of three pigeons; your eye rakes offices, exploring all floors at a glance, floors packed with typists. You feel like a bee-master looking into a hive; and all the time a rumble reaches you, the restless voice of the city.

*   *   *   *   *

Almost as wonderful as the smoky map of London spread below, is the feeling that you, so leisurely examining St. Paul's while the rest of London is rushing about trying to pay the rent, are having a holiday in a foreign city.

You feel a superiority over all those poor harassed people. You perceive a new angle to London life. You join the idle

ST. PAUL'S

drifting population of sightseers; and you feel rather sorry you did not bring your camera with you, just to help out the illusion that you are in a Florentine mood.

Vergers, too, observe towards you the courtesy extended to strangers within the gate. There is a subtle difference in their manner. In their 'Yes, sirs,' and 'No, sirs,' and in their pointing and smiling you can feel the affection which churches have always, and quite rightly, extended to pilgrims. One man obviously considered me a distinguished visitor from foreign parts. He went out of his way to instruct me in history that I know quite well, and I wondered whether the only straight and honourable thing to do was to make a clean breast of it and stop him with:

'Look here, I live in Knightsbridge and work in Fleet Street, and I'm frightfully sorry about it, and all that. I know it's most unusual and you won't believe me, but there it is.'

I had not the courage. I gazed insincerely into his enthusiastic eyes and said 'Really!' and 'By Jove!' and 'How interesting,' at appropriate pauses, so that, when eventually I left him, I went surrounded, for him, with all the beauty of a bird of passage.

IN the old comic papers you will find a stock character whose nose is red, whose coat collar is Astrakhan, whose hand is always drawn in the act of conveying drink to a clean-shaven, mobile mouth—a mouth always uttering the words: 'When I played Hamlet, laddie, in '84 . . .'

He is, or rather was, the out-of-work actor. No actor has of course ever been out of work: he 'rests' sometimes for so long a period that idleness becomes a habit. Lack of employment seems to cover the actor with disgrace. In most other professions men make no secret of being out of a job, but the actor acts both on and off the stage.

The out-of-work actor to-day (you find him in Leicester Square and the Charing Cross Road) has changed since the comic papers pictured a tragedian whose ambitious argosies had evidently foundered in, as Homer would put it, a wine-dark sea. To-day you find him in a bar, merely because he will meet there other actors and agents and pick up news of his heartless and overrated profession; but in his hand is a glass of ginger beer. His clothes are well-cut and he wears a public school tie. His spats draw attention to his worn boots, always the sign of a man's condition, and as he drawls lazily in his Oxford voice, real or assumed, he tries hard to give the impression that, resting, as he is, on the enormous profits of his genius, he must keep an important appointment in Mayfair at one-thirty or the duchess will be absolutely furious.

Poor brave people! No matter how overdue the rent may be they never lose their *panache*. To-day the fight to walk on in a musical comedy and say heartily: 'Girls, let's go to Paris!' and the feminine fight to answer coyly in good Kensingtonian: 'Oh, what a quate topping ideah!' is fiercer than ever. Added to the usual legitimate 'resters' are thousands of film actors, both male and female, thrown on the streets because the British film trade is in the doldrums.

If you could only know the bitterness of the fight for the job that does not exist, the daily march round the agents' offices, the young man who puts his head round a door, smiles, says 'Nothing doing'—the humiliation of not having a shilling.

What keeps them going? What encourages girls to wash their one pair of real silk stockings overnight, brush their furs carefully, and turn out each day, apparently prosperous, to try another joust with fate? It is belief in themselves, the inability to do anything else, and, above all, it is a vision of fame and a name flung high against the stars over Piccadilly —the dream that *might* come true. Many a man and many a maid, who feel they possess a descending lift instead of a stomach, see that name of theirs every night twinkling, glistening, beckoning, making it all seem worth while. That keeps them going.

* * * * *

I sat for an hour in a film agent's office which deserves the title of Heartbreak House. Six months ago the crowds of heroes, villains, heroines, and villainesses who clamoured for heroism or villainy became so great that they had to sit four deep down the stairs. Since that time the word has gone forth that there is no work to be had and no point in seeking it; but still every day they come, hopeful, bright-eyed, the girls all airs and graces, the men eager, self-reliant.

In the waiting-room were six or seven exceedingly pretty fair-haired girls of assorted ages. Some friend had once committed one of the cardinal sins and told them how like Mary Pickford they were. They were now reaping the harvest of this dangerous suggestion. There was an old man with the face of a judge, a young man cut out to be a hero, and a number of vague people who looked in restlessly, and as restlessly went away.

An enormously fat woman occupied the doorway, talking rapidly:

'No fat parts going? Oh, well, I suppose something'll turn up some day. Nothing like hope, is there? And it's not easy for me to keep my weight up with everything so dear these days. Suppose I got thin? What would I do then? Oh, what a life, what a life!'

* * * * *

The agent entered the room. All the pretty girls pursed their lips and assumed a photographic smile, putting up what they hoped would be a barrage of beauty to demolish all obstacles.

'Sorry, I can do nothing for you. There's no work!'

Slowly the smile faded, and each girl looked five years older than girls of that age have any right to look. They fussed a moment with their handbags, brushed imaginary crumbs from their knees, lingered as if hoping against hope that some producer would dash into the office and cry, 'Girls, I want you!' and then, with a sigh, departed; fawn coats, moleskin, and black coats.

'Pretty awful, isn't it?' said the agent to me. 'You wouldn't think they were out of work. That's part of the game: they must look smart!'

* * * * *

A big negro put his head round the door, took off a battered bowler, exposed his gums, and said:

'Mornin', boss. Does any guy wanter a good ord'nary nigger?'

As he went out he came into collision with a tall, pale young man who wore spats but no overcoat. He, too, was sent away.

'We get lots like that,' said the agent, 'well-bred young fellows wearing college ties, who manage to keep their spats white though their shoes probably need soleing. In fact, we get all sorts. But all the men and women who come up here looking as though a thousand a year would be an insult would be grateful for two pounds a week. They all look smart.'

* * * * *

That is part of their tragedy.

They may be 'resting,' but they cannot afford to stop acting. The only consolation is that, as everybody knows, luck turns, the darkest hour precedes the dawn, and so on, and so on!

Hope has kept more people alive than Harley Street.

HOW often in a London street do you try to pierce the mystery of another's life, to visualize the loves, the hates, the joys, the sorrows that have painted lines on some unknown, passing face?

I saw them in High Holborn. They stood out from the tense, jostling crowd because they seemed to have no object in life, nowhere to go, nothing to do; they were aimless, lost. They stood out also because they were so poor. Poverty is a relative thing; but no man is really poor until life becomes a desert island that gives him neither food nor shelter nor hope. They were such obvious failures at this game of getting and keeping called success. If they had suddenly shouted in pain above the thunder of the passing wheels they could hardly have been more spectacular in their misery, this man, this woman, this child.

He slouched along a few yards in advance of the woman. He looked as though Life had been knocking him down for a long time, then waiting for him to get up so that it might knock him down again. His bent body was clothed in greenish rags and his naked feet were exposed in gashed boots. He was not entirely pathetic. He was the kind of man to whom you would gladly give half a crown to salve your conscience; but you would never allow him out of sight with your suit-case.

She carried her baby against her breast in a ragged old brown cloth knotted round her shoulders. Perhaps she was twenty-five, but she looked fifty because no one had ever taken care of her, or had given her that pride in herself which is necessary to a woman's existence. She had not even the happiness of being wanted or necessary—a condition in which the altruistic soul of woman thrives. This man of hers would obviously be better off without her. She had once been pretty.

The shame of it. To parade her woman's body draped in rags through streets full of other women in their neat clothes, to meet the pitying eyes of other wives and mothers, and to drag on, tied like a slave, behind this shambling, shifty man. Is there a crucifixion for a woman worse than this?

*   *   *   *   *

He walked ahead, so that she had plenty of time to wonder why she married him. Now and then he would turn and jerk

63

his head, trying to make her quicken her pace. She took no notice, just plodded on in who knows what merciful dullness?

Then the sleeping child in her old brown shawl awakened and moved with the curious boneless writhing of a young baby. The mother's arms tightened on it and held its body closer to hers. She stopped, went over to a shop window, and leant her knee on a ledge of stone. She placed one finger gently into the fold of cloth and looked down into it. . . .

I tell you that for one second you ceased to pity and you reverenced. Over that tired face of chiselled alabaster, smoothed and softened in a smile, came the only spiritual thing left in those two lives: the beatitude of a Madonna. This same unchanging smile has melted men's hearts for countless generations. The first time a man sees a woman look at his child in that way something trembles inside him. Men have seen it from piled pillows in rooms smelling faintly of perfume, in night nurseries, in many a comfortable nest which they have fought to build to shield their own. No different! The same smile in all its rich, swift beauty was here in the mud and the bleakness of a London street.

They went on into the crowd and were forgotten. I went on with the knowledge that out of rags and misery had come, full and splendid, the spirit that, for good or ill, holds the world to its course.

Two beggars in a London crowd, but at the breast of one— the Future. Poor, beautiful Madonna of the Pavement. . . .

GIRLS were running after omnibuses, lawyers were running after briefs, and reporters were running after things called 'stories' as I turned from Fleet Street to enter that little Round Church in the Temple which is one of the most splendid things in London.

Utter peace. A dim, tinted light filtered through the east windows, and at my feet lay the stone figure of Geoffrey de Mandeville, Earl of Essex, bandit and excommunicate. He lies in full chain armour, his shield across his body, his spurs at his heels, and his long sword beside him, just as he might have lain eight hundred and eighty-four years ago, when they found him in the fen country and sent an arrow through his head. What trouble his death must have caused the Templars. They could not bury him in holy ground till the Pope had granted him absolution, so they sealed him in a lead coffin and hung him on a tree near Holborn. When Rome wiped out his sins, they plucked him from the tree and brought him to this Round Church that was born of the first Crusade.

As I stood over Geoffrey de Mandeville, my thoughts raced across Europe, across the Mediterranean, over that sandy yellow waste known as the Desert of Sinai, and on to that city standing high on terraced rock—Jerusalem. Of what else can one think here in the Round Church? Its roots go back to Robert, Duke of Normandy, Tancred and Bohemund, Godfrey de Bouillon, and that fiery triumvirate, Frederick, Emperor of Germany, Richard Cœur de Lion of England, and Philip Augustus of France.

This quiet little church remembers Saladin; its stones have rung to the chain mail of men who saw the lances of the infidel like a forest against the sky, of men who knew how Frederick Barbarossa came like a storm out of the west to hurl his hosts on the gates of Jerusalem.

Jerusalem. . . . Standing there so near to the roar of London, yet centuries away from it, I recalled white nights on the Mount of Olives, the Holy City spread below over its hills, a dome rising up from violet shadow into the moonlight, a group of cypress trees pointing dark fingers to the stars, and, from the faint ribbon of road, the trit-trot of a donkey's hoofs going on to Bethany.

The link with Jerusalem is true and straight. It was after they returned from the First Crusade that the Templars built this church to remind them of the round church that guarded the grave of Christ. There are only three others like it in the country, at Cambridge, Northampton, and Little Maplestead, Essex. This church was conceived in Palestine. As I looked at it I recalled the waxen face of a monk whose thin beard was like black silk. I met him in the Church of the Holy Sepulchre in Jerusalem. I had been torn here and there by the confused crowds of pilgrims. I had been mixed up in various sacred processions, I had seen the hungry fervour in which those anxious for salvation had kissed the end of a stick after it had been poked through a hole in an arch so that it might touch a fragment of the Column of the Scourging. And I went on towards the Chapel of the Holy Sepulchre, six foot by six foot, in whose tiny space hang forty-three lamps. Here I saw a poor Greek woman creep in and fall into a torrent of tears on that marble slab which hides the tombstone of Christ. The monk met me outside, such a smooth wax fellow, and led me to a little chapel in which he produced a pair of old spurs and a sword with a hilt shaped like a cross. Godfrey de Bouillon's. So he said.

I whispered the name in the Round Church. It all links up.

*   *   *   *   *

It is so quiet to-day in the safe keeping of the law. You would never dream that those lawns sloping to the Thames were, eight hundred years ago, the beginning of that long, hard road to Palestine, the nest of the Templars, those priest warriors who began their history so splendidly poor that two men rode one horse, and ended, so richly and dangerously, that two kings and the Pope of Rome broke them as three millionaires might smash a trust.

Nothing now remains of all that ancient fire but the Round Church and a few stone crusaders lying with their feet towards the east. Some names linger on, their meaning quite changed. The serjeant-at-law owes his title to the 'Fratres Servientes', the serving brothers of the Templars; and the judges' title of 'Knight' of the Common Pleas takes us back eight hundred years.

Between the crusaders, lying cap-à-pie with Paynim knights

TEMPLE CHURCH

beneath their spurred heels, are two brass tablets let into the floor. One is in memory of the members of the Inner Temple, and the other of members of the Middle Temple who laid down their lives in the war.

*   *   *   *   *

So these crusaders, with eight hundred years dividing them, are rightly commemorated together in this quiet, lovely place, whose atmosphere, once so charged with stress and strife, is now purged by time of all passion, either good or evil. But the ghosts live on, and it would not astonish me to hear that some quiet, harmless lawyer, going to his chambers at night down that sloping path past the church, had encountered an armed host ready for the march, from whose throats burst, like an organ note: 'Deus vult!'

That was the cry that built the Temple, and, spreading out over the land like a flame, fired men's hearts, leading them into the desert in defence of the holy places of Christendom.

DOWN Whitechapel way is a place famous for dealing out sleep by the fistful twice a week.

None of your six thousand pounds Albert Hall fox-trots here. This is Knockout Land. It is, I imagine, the nearest thing to a bull-fight you will see in England. Good, hard, slamming fifteen-round contests follow each other, with the ropes trembling and the fight fans howling like a pack of hungry wolves, and two half naked men with strawberry-coloured noses, hitting, gasping, reeling. . . .

A great high hall, blue with smoke, steel-girdered at the roof like a railway station. It is packed by a cloth-capped crowd, predominantly Oriental—a crowds of swift murmur and sudden silences and sharp, instantaneous uproars. Good tempered now, but—O my!—suppose somebody started a row! There is not one woman present. The elegant girls in evening gowns who sit out Albert Hall prize fights have no place here. It is a gathering of fight fans. In the centre, under bright, white lights, rises the ring. The men in it are like men on a raft floating on a sea of restless, white faces.

Suddenly five or six men near the ring leap to their feet and shout 'Five to one on Cohen!'

The hall becomes thick with wagers. Arms shoot out, men shout, no record is made (except that in a keen Hebrew mind), and everyone is quite happy about it. Even if the Jew were not so commercially reliable, who would dare to be crooked here!

Look! The seconds in their white sweaters are busy. Two fighters enter the ring. Their bodies glisten in the light. One is white, the other olive-coloured, Eastern. They square up, crouch, dance round each other, then pat, pat-pat, pat-pat-pat —crack! A howl goes up from the crowd! That was a hit! Smash! Another one! Right! to the ropes! Back he comes, a little wild, and his opponent is driven away under the speed of his assault. Blows rain on each body, pink patches appear on chests and chins, both men dodge this way and that, a bell rings. Time!

'Chocolates!' cries a man with a tray.

I want to laugh. A less chocolate-like crowd I have never

seen. Jellied eels, perhaps, beer undoubtedly, beefsteaks certainly; but milk chocolate—how astonishing!

Round fifteen! Both men are all in. They have pounded each other to pulp. I wonder if they can hear the yells and roars of the audience. Their legs drag. They are weak with hitting. You can see what they meant to do as a blow falls short, you can reach out and enter their exhausted minds, sympathize with them in their hazy world as they dog each other to plant the knockout for which everyone is waiting.

Smash! Right on the chin! The smashed one reels to the ropes, but comes back for more trouble, with his mouth sagging and something in his expression which suggests to me that he is not really here at all, but possibly wandering through some field rich with buttercups, with a little old public-house round the bend in the road. . . . Smash! He's taken another one! The scene in his dazed mind changes! He awakens from some stellar night, and comes alive again out of careering constellations to rush, with the desperation of last strength, on his opponent. Crack-crack—bang! Surely the knockout; surely he cannot stand any more? His head must be like iron, his jaws like steel.

He reels, his arms drop, his nightmare mind tries to grapple with the padded realities waiting for him, he makes an effort to hit. The other man is now ready to land him one that will lift him off his feet. He is the gladiator standing over him with lifted sword and—no appeal to the amphitheatre. It is only a question of a second now. Something brutal and masculine inside me desires to see him knocked out; something weak and feminine inside me wishes it was not necessary.

The victor draws back his head, the muscles ripple along his wet back, he shoots out an arm; and the other man crumples like a marionette at the end of a cut string. He lies in a corner of the ring, moves a leg once, and is still. I feel sure he is dead. In two minutes, with water trickling over his reddened face, he staggers to his feet, smiles a painful, swollen smile, shakes hands with the man who put him to sleep, and gropes out into the obscurity of the yelling crowd.

*   *   *   *   *

'And how much do they get for fighting here?'

'Oh, thirty-five bob,' replies an official. 'Sometimes as much as fifty.'

I wonder what our elegant bruisers would think about it as I make my way out into the darkness of the wet streets.

Ghosts ⌀ ⌀ ⌀ ⌀ ⌀ ⌀ ⌀

I SOMETIMES wonder how many Londoners have been inside No. 13 Lincoln's Inn Fields!

Here we have the most remarkable museum in this, and probably any other, country. Sir John Soane, the architect who designed the Bank of England, died eighty-eight years ago, and left an instruction in his will that his house, packed with treasures, should be thrown open to the public in the condition in which he left it. The furniture has hardly been moved, the pictures hang in the same positions, and, if old Sir John could come back, he would enter his library and go over to his desk, hardly knowing that over three-quarters of a century have intervened since he said good-bye to the things he loved with all his heart and soul.

If ever the presence of a dead man printed itself on a house, this is the house. I went there the other day and found the shutters drawn. It was after closing time; but the caretaker asked me inside and courteously took me round.

It was like entering a house when a family is away. I had to pull myself together and realize that this family was eighty-eight years away. There is a certain air about a house whose contents have been arranged by someone who loves it. No museum curator could imitate it. I could, in imagination, see Sir John pottering round with one of his latest treasures, wondering where to put it. He looks in bewilderment. The rooms are so crowded! He finds a place, not the best place, but his place; and there it has remained and will remain down the ages.

Another ghost. Lady Soane. Dear woman, she loved these things too, so the biographers say, but it must have given her feminine heart many a twinge to see Roman pillars, gigantic stone fragments from Greek temples, life-size statues, a cast of the Apollo Belvedere, and, at last, the biggest and finest stone coffin ever taken from an Egyptian tomb, enter her home one by one.

'Oh, John,' her ghost said, 'how full the house is. Where are we going to live?'

And John, beaming and running his hand over a smooth green bronze, replied, pointing to something new:

'Isn't that perfectly lovely. I think I'll have to knock down the dining-room wall!'

No woman in the history of housekeeping has ever endured a more overwhelming artistic invasion.

*   *   *   *   *

Sir John began life as the son of a bricklayer; which is some encouragement to all collectors of the antique. As he got on in life, he collected more precious things, spent two thousand pounds on an object the British Museum could not afford, and gradually surrounded himself with one of the choicest collections any private individual has possessed.

How many things enthusiasm can accomplish in one life-time. It is inspiring to walk through this old house and to realize that everything was collected by one man while he built up his career.

Pictures—notably Hogarth's 'The Rake's Progress'—antique gems, bronzes, manuscripts, books, ancient glass, bas-reliefs, the first three folio editions of Shakespeare, and thousands of other things, came to him as steel to a magnet. It is not a house: it is a curio shop.

He must have puzzled over space. You would never guess unless you were shown how he made one wall do the work of two or three. He devised walls which opened like the leaves of a book, each leaf, or side, being hung with pictures. Clever Sir John; and how Lady Soane must have praised him as the tide of treasure rose higher and higher round her tea-table.

*   *   *   *   *

Down in the basement he kept the splendid alabaster coffin of the Pharaoh Seti I, a marvellous thing cut from one solid lump of alabaster. This was the object that Belzoni saw gleaming in the dark tomb in those days when no man could read the weird hieroglyphs which cover it.

What a beautiful thing it is. As I looked at it, I remembered Belzoni's account of its discovery in that vain, amusing, yet always interesting, 'Narrative of the Operations and Recent Discoveries within the Pyramids, Temples, and Tombs and Excavations in Egypt and Nubia,' published in 1820. This man's adventures among the tombs of Egypt, at a time before Egyptology was a science, are sufficient to make any modern archaeologist lie down and howl with envy at his opportunities; and burn with rage at the opportunities he missed.

After describing the location of the tomb, and how the debris of three thousand years was cleared, Belzoni pictures his entry, his progress through columned halls, his discovery of a rope that fell to dust when touched. He wandered for days like a boy in a fairy tale through this tomb, the most splendid in the Theban Necropolis.

'But the description of what we found in the centre of the saloon and which I have reserved till this place,' wrote Belzoni, 'merits the most particular attention, not having its equal in the world, and being such as we had no idea could exist. It is a sarcophagus of the finest Oriental alabaster, nine feet five inches long, and three feet seven inches wide. Its thickness is only two inches; and it is transparent when a light is placed inside of it. It is minutely sculptured within and without with several hundred figures which do not exceed two inches in height, and represent, as I suppose, the whole of the funeral procession and funeral ceremonies relating to the deceased. . . . I cannot give an adequate idea of this beautiful and invaluable piece of antiquity, and can only say that nothing has been brought into Europe from Egypt that can be compared with it.'

Just as the reports of the late Lord Carvarvon's discovery sped through Thebes like wildfire, so did Belzoni's luck circulate, with the result that one day the Turkish authorities rode up, headed by Hamed Aga of Keneh. Then, as now, antiquities to the native meant simply gold. The Aga, after glancing vaguely round the tomb, ordered his soldiers to retire, then, turning to Belzoni he said:

'Pray where have you put the treasure?'

'What treasure?' asked poor Belzoni.

The Aga then told him a story—so like those in circulation at Luxor in 1923, when it was rumoured by natives that every woman visitor to the tomb of Tutankhamen came away with gold jewellery concealed in her skirts. Belzoni denied the rumours of fabulous wealth, and of a reported large golden cock crammed with diamonds and pearls. The Aga was crestfallen.

'He seated himself before the sarcophagus,' wrote Belzoni, 'and I was afraid he would take it into his head that this was the treasure and break it to pieces to see whether it contained any gold.'

Fortunately he did not.　He merely delivered himself of the remarkable observation that the tomb of Seti I 'would be a good place for a harem, as the women would have something to look at,' and then, happily for Egyptology and the Soane Museum, departed.

＊　　　　＊　　　　＊　　　　＊　　　　＊

'Is this place haunted?' I asked the caretaker, just to see what he would say.

'No, sir!' he replied scornfully.　'I've heard noises, but it's mice.　There isn't such a thing as ghosts, believe me.'

But he's wrong; for I saw old Sir John as plainly as anything in those high, leisurely rooms, arranging things, prying into them with a cut crystal, and touching them with fingers that caressed.

Aladdin's Cave ∽　∽　∽　∽　∽　∽

AS I passed through a steel door set in spiked steel railings, a hefty commissionaire secretly pressed a bell that gave the alarm downstairs, so that when I appeared two equally hefty commissionaires sprang out and asked for the password.

No; it was not the Bank of England, or the Tower of London, or Buckingham Palace: it was one of the deepest safe deposit vaults in London. Each person who rents a safe there chooses a password—any word he likes; 'Annie Laurie,' or 'Mrs. Jones's Baby,' or 'Good Queen Anne.' Till the commissionaires know him by sight, the depositor is held up every time he goes to his safe and is asked to stand and deliver. If he forgets the password, he is turned away unless he can prove his identity and his right to unlock his treasures.

Fabulous millions are locked away underground in the safe deposits of London. The companies themselves do not know how much treasure they guard day and night. Now and then the inquiry of an insurance company reveals that a fourteen-inch safe holds a million pounds' worth of treasure.

When the commissionaires had looked me over with an expression which inferred that I probably carried on me acetylene blowpipes, a few six-shooters, and a dozen Mills bombs, they called the secretary, who had promised to take me through Aladdin's Cave. The vaults resembled the interior of an Atlantic liner. In every direction stretched long lit corridors with doors every few feet along them. What doors! Some of them had handles like a giant's dumb-bells and locks like young cartwheels.

The door of one vault was half open. Inside it, a man was sitting at a table counting diamonds. A pile of white diamonds on a piece of brown paper! Stuck on the wall with the splash of a gum brush was—surprising sight—a coy Kirchner girl adjusting the suspender at the extremity of a shining silk leg.

On we went down the corridor, the secretary, pointing out the vault of the Duke of This and Lord That, making my head reel with a story of title deeds and heirlooms and treasures beyond price. Another door opened and the owner came out. At first I thought he was about to give us some of the gold plate with which the room was vulgarly full.

'Could you,' he said, 'lend me a pencil?'

We gave him one.

On another floor I found the ordinary safes, much less spectacular than the vaults, but, I think, more interesting. Here it is that men and women hide their smaller treasures. You can have quite a nice little safe, big enough to take a pair of shoes, for twenty-five shillings a year.

I entered an avenue of them, looked at their clumsy hinges and their astonishing locks, wondering what mysteries they contain. In how many of them lie letters that would break up homes? In how many are documents that would explain why So-and-So never married? In how many of them are the riches of people whose friends think them penniless? In how many are merely silly things?

'I think the strangest thing we guarded,' said the secretary, 'was a penny. For thirty years a man paid three pounds a year to guard that penny. No; he was not mad—only superstitious. He believed that if he lost that penny he would have terrible ill-luck. When he first deposited it, he was poor, but he died worth a hundred thousand pounds, and his executors then came and took away his mascot.'

Another strange treasure was the hoof of a Derby winner. The owner made a fortune from his victory, and when the horse died his wife had the hoof mounted, and they kept it for years in a special safe.

Hundreds of safes in every deposit vault are filled with the jewels of wealthy women. Now and then the owners come and look at them, and sometimes, before a ball or a reception, they take them away for a night or two. Hundreds also contain the treasures of women who do not seem wealthy. What they contain no one knows. Once when a safe that had not been claimed for twenty years was broken open—it belonged to an elderly spinster—bundles of faded letters were found tied with faded ribbon, all that was left of an old romance.

What other secrets lie hidden underground in these cold, tiled avenues—what strange human stories that will never be known?

In one of the waiting-rooms I saw an ancient man with a white beard. He was sitting over the contents of his safe, feebly fingering documents and poring over them, his nose almost touching the papers. The sight of him roused questions.

How easy to write a dozen speculations about him, his life, and his little tray full of musty deeds and letters. . . .

*   *   *   *   *

Outside over the wet pavements hurried the men and women of London, unconscious that beneath their feet lay millions and—mystery.

IN two thousand years' time will there be brambles growing
on Ludgate Hill, I wonder, and will a shepherd graze his sheep
in Piccadilly Circus? It happened to Thebes and Carthage. . . .

If the tamarisks should come back to town I desire to be
reincarnated at that time in order that I may join in archaeo-
logical speculation on the fragment of an extinct animal
('probably a lion') dug up on the site of Trafalgar Square!
It would also be jolly to reconstruct the plan of Bush House
on the strength of three window-sills, a lift bell, and a typewriter key. There are great days in store for those who will
shake up our dust and worry our ghosts, and even attempt
to discover our gods. I can see Macaulay's New Zealander
having the time of his life among the ruins of London; and
surely one of his most splendid adventures will take place at
the base of Cleopatra's Needle. Did you know that beneath
that famous stone is buried a kind of Victorian Tutankhamen's
treasure, placed there to give some man of the future an
idea of us and our times? Did you realize that the London
municipal authorities could do anything so touching?

In 1878 sealed jars were placed under the obelisk containing
a man's lounge suit, the complete dress and vanities of a
woman of fashion, illustrated papers, Bibles in many languages,
children's toys, a razor, cigars, photographs of the most
beautiful women of Victorian England, and a complete set of
coinage from a farthing to five pounds. So the most ancient
monument in London stands guard over this modernity, rather
like an experienced old hen, waiting for Time to hatch it.

Poor sad old stone. . . .

*   *   *   *   *

I went down to look at it yesterday when the Thames, in
full tide, dancing in the sunlight, was giving the Embankment
great slapping kisses. Tugs were chugging upstream with their
ugly duckling barges; and the jet-black finger of Ancient Egypt
pointed to the sky, so slim and beautifully proportioned, so
tall that, when I looked up, it seemed to be falling against
the wheeling clouds.

Two little boys were riding a sphinx. Men and women

CLEOPATRA'S NEEDLE

stopped, looked up at the monument, saw the pale sunlight
finding its way into those funny little carvings, a few moved
round to the rear of the platform and gazed with open mouths,
seeing an incomprehensible stone, wondering about it perhaps,
may be feeling that there was a story behind it somewhere,
somehow.

A story? Heavens! What a story. Shall I tell you what
I saw, as I stood there with the tramcars speeding past and
the criss-cross traffic busy on its way?

*   *   *   *   *

I saw a great tunnel of Time three thousand four hundred
years long. Imagine the time that separates us to-day from
the Spanish Armada and then *multiply it by ten*: that is almost
three thousand and four hundred years. London was unknown.
Greece was unborn, and there was no Rome on the Seven
Hills. But Egypt had thrashed its way through the mumps
and measles of civilization and was already ancient. In that
distant blaze of light moved epicures and artists, soldiers and
priests, and, in the great palace of Thebes, sat the most
powerful man in the world, the Pharaoh Thothmes III, Lord
of the Two Lands, giver of life and death.

And Pharaoh decided to perpetuate his greatness in the
eye of Time. In other words, he probably remarked after
dinner one night: 'I want obelisks for the temple at Heliopolis.
That pylon looked rather bare, I thought, the last time I was
there. You might see to it, will you?'

Whereupon chariots were harnessed and messengers sped
south to the red granite quarries of Assuan.

*   *   *   *   *

Now see the architect drawing the shape of Cleopatra's
Needle in the virgin rock. See hundreds of naked backs bent
over the stone, pounding, pounding, pounding month after
month in the savage heat with no tools but hard balls of
dolomite; and the whips crack over the sweating bodies and
flicker in the heat and hiss like the tongues of serpents.

In a year the whim of Pharaoh is bashed from the quarry
in blood and tears. His titles are set upon it, and it stands,
painted and glorious, fronting the Temple of the Sun in

Heliopolis. On its tip is a cap of electrum that catches the sun, so that travellers in the desert, looking towards the city of On, see a pillar with a fire blazing upon it. . . . Look!

A cloud of dust; and, in the heart of it, gilded chariots. The white horses are pulled up on their haunches; the nodding ostrich plumes on their head-collars rise and fall; the fan bearers come forward; the troops stand at ease, and, above the kneeling priests, is the Pharaoh, that ancient superman, inspecting his monument from a burnished car.

'Quite good. The god is pleased.'

*   *   *   *   *

Time passes. Moses, who was a priest in Heliopolis, sees the obelisk every day. The frogs of the Plagues hop and chirrup on its plinth. Over a hundred years pass, and Rameses the Great, who loved himself dearly, carves his name on the column, usurping it. A thousand years pass, and it is moved to Cleopatra's capital at Alexandria. Here it survives four great empires. Thrones rock and fall, dynasties fade like mists. The world changes. Two thousand years pass by, and a new race of men come to power. They pick Cleopatra's Needle out of the sand, enclose it in a huge steel cylinder, give it a deck, a keel, a rudder, put a crew aboard and tug it across the sea towards England. Prosperous winds favour the voyage for the first few weeks; then, in the dreaded Bay of Biscay, Cleopatra's Needle pitches with such violence that the tug's captain cuts her adrift with her crew aboard her. How different from her last voyage three thousand years previously, when the Egyptian slaves floated her on the sunlit Nile for the delight of Pharaoh. As she rolls and tosses, five sailors from the tug volunteer to go out to the abandoned obelisk ship. They are swept under and are drowned. Eventually the Cleopatra's crew are saved; and the tug watches her drift away over the stormy seas. Sixty days pass, and then news is received that Cleopatra's Needle was tugged into Vigo by a ship whose owners received two thousand pounds for their services. Eventually, tugged by an M.P.'s yacht, the Egyptian stone arrives in England.

Here, forty-seven years ago, they placed it beside a cold, grey river; and some unknown hand penned the following epitaph to it in the morning:

This monument as some supposes
Was looked on in old days by Moses;
It passed in time to Greeks and Turks,
And was stuck up here by the Board of Works.

*   *   *   *   *

It has remained beside the Thames ever since, with the last great adventure still in store. One night the wrath of Ra, the fury of Set, the god of evil, descended like thunderbolts from a dark sky.[1] Chips of the granite pediment flew away. The plinth was bruised as a city is bruised in war, and overhead, in the shaft of a searchlight, lay a silver fish in the sky—a fish that hummed like a hornet and laid most devilish eggs. What a strange night for ancient Egypt. . . .

*   *   *   *   *

Sad, cold stone—the saddest monument in all London. We are killing it. It was once red granite. Now it is coal black; and its glory is being eaten away year by year. Forty-seven years of London have done it greater hurt than the three thousand years that went before. It did not deserve this; for the splendour of the past is centred upon it, and beneath its feet is a message for the future.

[1] Several bombs fell near Cleopatra's Needle in September 1917.

6

VICTORIA STATION is the scene of a daily romance every morning—the departure of the Continental boat expresses. When the fog comes with rain and driving sleet, and every Londoner loathes London just a little, I can extract a certain pale kind of pleasure by buying a penny platform ticket and watching other people start off to the snow or the sun.

I can never decide whether the act of extracting enjoyment from other people's luck is the lowest, or the highest, form of fun. There is always a sting of envy about it.

*　　　*　　　*　　　*　　　*

When you love travel, and have lost count of the number of times the chocolate-coloured Pullmans have whirled you through Kent to the edge of the sea, and on to far places, that morning assembly of travellers shakes you to the heart. You know what is in store for them. You follow them down to Dover; you see them in the swift Channel boat; you hear the blue-bloused porters of Calais crying 'Soixante-dix, m'sieu. I meet you at ze douane!' You visualize the idiotic fight in the French Customs; you see the long Paris Rapide waiting with steam up, the wrinkled old Frenchwomen in white caps and knitted black shawls who sell fruit; and you hear the funny little penny whistle, like a child's trumpet, that sends the great train racketing and thundering through France, or Basle and Switzerland, or Marseilles, and then—oh, marvellous far places in Africa!

Which is more wonderful? To awaken at the Swiss frontier, with snow muffling a cotton-wool world of chasms and peaks, or to awaken in the sunlight of Southern France to a glimpse of the Mediterranean?

*　　'*　　　*　　　*　　　*

That wide, hedgeless plain with its silver-grey olive trees, its red-roofed houses, and its vignettes of rustic activity; little men in fields walking behind the plough, at stable doors bringing out a solemn, ragged mule, give me that. And give me, too, the ever-recurring joy of the uncomfortable swinging

French *wagon restaurant* full of various people; Englishmen, who look so comically English as soon as they cross the Channel, Frenchmen, whose black spade beards cascade over white table-napkins, which they tuck into their collars before they devour their food, and the good-looking Parisienne, with her carmine mouth and her finicky, much-manicured hands, breaking bread and salting meat while her eyes sweep over, and beyond, the bald heads of appraising British husbands.

'Liqueur, m'sieu?'

The man with the tray of little bright bottles staggers up and, notable sight, the elderly virgin of some distant vicarage sips an unusual brandy. Marvellous France!

So, knowing all this so well, I watched the boat train crowds with the keenest enjoyment the other morning. There were girls who would be tumbling about in the snow before many days were gone, or sitting in the paleish summer of the Riviera in white, pleated skirts. There went the hardened traveller with the well-worn rucksacks and the skis, the excited, flushed traveller making a first journey, and—lucky fellow—a man with a pith helmet over his arm.

Nothing is more awkward to pack than a pith helmet. Even socks and shaving tackle will not sit comfortably in it. When carried with an air, it advertises the fact that you are not a mere Swiss fan or a poor Riviera lizard, but an honest-to-goodness traveller, possibly even an explorer. In the Channel boat people will look at you, as you bear this symbol of the sun on your arm. You will stand out above all others. Perhaps in the bar some one will say:

'Going far?' and you can flick the ash of your cigarette carelessly and say:

'No; only to Timbuctoo!'

A great thing is a sun helmet!

Then there was the lady of quality off to Monte Carlo, with trunks full of dresses, and one trunk lightly packed to contain more dresses which she will accumulate in Paris. There was a pale woman who had obviously been ordered South. Her husband stood beside the Pullman door telling her to take great care of herself and get well, and, just before the train left, he shyly, like a boy, gave her a little packet in white tissue paper, which she opened, and the tears came into her eyes as she held the small jeweller's box in her hand. Yes; there are such husbands!

All the time the cosy lamplit tables of the Pullman cars gradually filled. At one a man turned to the weather report, where, under a weird map of barometric pressure, he would read about the Channel crossing; at another, a woman gazed thoughtfully through the menu, wondering if it would be wise to eat a grilled sole.

*   *   *   *   *

Sharp to the last second of the minute, the Continental boat express slipped out of Victoria with its load of people in search of health and pleasure. A flutter of handkerchiefs, a turn away, and the tail coach disappeared with those squat mail boxes on it which are deposited by a crane in the hold of the ship and lifted out in France, fixed on a railway wagon, and consigned to the G.P.O. in Paris.

As the boat express went off, the diminishing grind of its wheels seemed to sing to me of olive yards and orange groves and long white roads in sunlight, and, somewhere far down in the south, a ship. . . .

SUPPOSE you were walking down that delicious slope of Piccadilly, the Green Park rails on your left, and suddenly you saw Sir Claude, the wicked young squire, chucking a shepherdess under the chin while he slapped his riding boots with a hunting crop. Suppose . . .

This happens! Turn down Whitehorse Street, and in two seconds bald heads in club windows, pretty sandy-legged ladies, the flood stream of omnibuses, are forgotten. They have never existed. They are two hundred comfortable years off in the womb of Time. You stand in the eighteenth century, in a London of maypoles and gallantry and much sly sin, of coaches and cavalcades, inn parlours and buxom serving wenches. Even your spats feel elegant. You desire to snap an ivory snuffbox, to wave a fine cambric handkerchief, and to kiss a good-looking chambermaid. Odds truth, sir, you are under the influence of Shepherd Market! At any moment my Lord Maxbridge may turn the corner on the arm of Sir Timothy Strophe, poet and wit, and you will, of course, stand, leaning on your ebony cane, promising to look in at the Cocoa Tree to-night and to join my lord later (bow) at his box at Vauxhall. And did you hear what the Prince said last night of Lady T., and how young Charles H. took it? And did you know that Captain X. lost nine hundred guineas at cards on a single throw at White's, and that the Marquis de St. A. has sent his seconds to Lord M., and that Sir Richard T. has been black-balled at Brooks'? Gad, sir!

That, at least, is how it takes me!

Looked at with the eyes only, Shepherd Market reveals itself as a queer, haphazard warren of streets packed with little shops whose onions overflow on the pavement, whose cabbages sometimes collapse into the gutter, whose fish and meat are much in evidence. Here you have the atmosphere of the Pantiles and the formation of any square in any old county town you care to remember.

This is picturesque. Behind any grand modern street you seem to see a surveyor or an architect bending over a blue paper, drawing straight lines. These shops and squares have grown up naturally, as a clump of flowers grows—some here, some there; some big, some small. What splendid individuality.

Here, within a stone's throw of Piccadilly, shopkeepers display big galvanized dust-bins on the pavement. You might be in Salisbury market-place. A china shop sells pretty little teapots of the kind which spinster ladies drive into Ipswich to procure on market day. All manner of antique shops sleep in the shadows. In one window I saw really good china, in others Georgian silver and rushlight holders.

It is Georgian or Victorian, according to taste. You can people the uneven pavements with ghosts of your own choosing. No matter how many gallants and dames you discover, there are a few later characters whom you expect to meet at every turn. The colonel's wife! Where is she? You look round anxiously. She should be walking stiffly round with her cane, a couple of Sealyhams rolling affectionately at the hem of her tailor-made skirt. The bishop's lady, too, a tall, lined woman in a religious black hat; the dean's daughter, romantic and anaemic and addicted to green velvet; Lady Potts, from 'The Hall,' in a dog-cart, large, florid, and suspiciously golden; the three hefty unmarriageable daughters of the major-general (retired), with their bicycles; the pretty wife of a junior subaltern—all the stock characters of an English cathedral city or garrison town.

Instead, so strange is this rural atmosphere, go London folk, smart women from flats in Curzon Street, and men passing through on their way to their clubs.

*   *   *   *   *

How did this patch become insulated from the fierce current of London life? I will tell you. They used to hold a fair here every May as far back as Edward I. Then, in 1738, a Mr. Shepherd built a cattle market on the spot. The butchers' shops had theatres on the second storeys, so that the dwarfs and drolls and vagabonds might in fair-time amuse the crowds. In 1750 so many regrettable things happened here that the fair was suppressed as a public scandal. (It must have been very wicked!)

So this is the heritage of our Shepherd Market, this concentrated essence of old England set down within sound of the wheels of Mayfair. If you visit it, notice how the old butchers' shops linger on, relics of the Shepherd Market of 1738. I imagine that there is here more prime Welsh mutton to the square yard than in any other street of its size in London.

WHEN I was walking along the Embankment on a path of pale sun, I saw a young man and a young woman leaning over the grey stone watching the river. There were white gulls wheeling, and the river was high; and this man and this woman were still and intent. When I stood beside them, I found they were looking, not at the river, but at the Future.

Under cover of their leaning arms, they were holding hands. They were in the last stage of love, their eyes like fields full of moon-calves. His clothes were Sundayfied and his boots were new and brown—the colour of a retired Indian general.

Her hat had been made at home in a hurry. And they were standing lost in the illimitable wonder of each other. They were not in London. They were in that aerial country on the boundaries of paradise, from which such men and women descend to a small red box in the suburbs and the current price of eggs.

I could compose their imaginary dialogue easily. I could tell you that he whispered about the fifteen pounds in the bank, that they murmured daringly of banns, and an oak suite on the instalment system. But, no! They said nothing, because they had reached that condition when words cease to capture meaning.

And I thought how well worth writing of are the lovers of London, the ordinary little lovers, whose sitting-out places are the parks, whose adventures are omnibus rides to Kew, whose extravagances are tea and buns.

Every Sunday they walk London. Every week-day you can see them in the solemn City snatching a half-hour at luncheon, she with an index finger purpled by a new ribbon, he very clerkly and correct. And you must never think them mean when, having watched each other eat steak and kidney pie as if they were sitting at a mystery play, they call for separate bills.

He pays his one and threepence and she pays hers. How significant that is. Had he been philandering with her they would have had a far nicer luncheon in a much nicer restaurant, and he would have carelessly ordered an ice and ended up recklessly with coffee and perhaps even a sinister *crème de menthe*. And he would have paid the bill, giving her the impression it was a mere nothing. She would not be allowed to know that his hand, groping mysteriously in his pocket, was trying desperately to discover whether there was enough left for seats in a cinema, whether—dash it all!—that little coin in the dark of his slender pocket was a penny or a much-hoped-for half-crown.

Ah, a bad sign. The road to bankruptcy is paved with boasting and insincerity and such little showings off! Let him once discover the Girl, and then, with life imminent, they get down to truth, and she discovers that he is not the lordly thing he pretended to be, that he is not earning a splendid fiver a week but a solemn two pounds ten. Crisis? Oh, dear, no!

There then begins a wrestle with a skeleton disguised as a bank account. They both stand guard over it. An extra packet of cigarettes is a betrayal, a reckless splash at a movie is a crime against a new home that exists nowhere but in two hearts. So he pays his bill and she pays hers, and all the time the modest little pile grows, leading them to those helpful organizations which give two hundred pounds worth of property for ten per cent down and the rest over eternity.

* * * * *

They are happy, are these little lovers of London; as all honest, simple things are happy. No great winds of passion or ambition blow like storms in their hearts. They wish to escape from their surroundings into something which is their own. They dream of the little house, just like every other little house in the row, and they dream of locking the front door on life and opening their arms to each other.

In the great hive of London you can see them meeting, hungrily snatching a moment from their separate labours which are just a means to an end. In the City she comes, lighting his heart with her beauty, and she goes, leaving him feeling that the light has been turned off inside him. At Kew in lilac time you will find them in sweet green avenues; the red buses bear them and their Dream to country places; and one day you will meet them in a tube train bending self-consciously over a furniture catalogue. . . .

* * * * *

Dante and Beatrice came out of their dream beside the Thames and walked away. Dante's new boots squeaked. Arm-in-arm they went along the sun path, two ordinary little actors in the great play, with that stillness about them that suggests how full two hearts can be.

If one could only peep into their lives again in ten years' time. That, however, is tempting Fate.

In Uncle's Shop ✑ ✑ ✑ ✑ ✑ ✑

OUTSIDE on its rusty supports hung the sign of the proud Medici—three gold balls.

Inside the pawnbroker's shop nothing was proud, except perhaps a grandfather clock that stood in a corner like an old aristocrat who has buttoned his coat, cocked his hat, and decided to go down hill with an air. For the rest—just junk lingering in this sordid, waiting-room atmosphere to be reclaimed and taken home. I looked at it and saw it as junk; then I looked again, knew that some of it had been hard to part with, was, in fact, transmuted by affection so that its very frayed unloveliness brought tears to the eyes. Those cheap, badly-made china shepherdesses designed to simper across a mantelpiece at the girlish gallant whose flirtatious salute was ruined because the hand that once held his hat had vanished—how remarkable that anyone had made them, how remarkable that anyone had cared sufficiently to buy them! There they were in the pawnshop, and perhaps some poor woman scraping up fourpence interest to keep them hers, gazing at her bare mantelpiece, longing for their sugary smiles, the cheap, conventional romance of them. . . .

* * * * *

'Something'll happen soon,' said the pawnbroker to me. 'You just have to wait.'

So I waited for comedy or pathos in the dim crowded shop that smelt of undusted china and old boots. Beyond the stacked window—so full of clocks and fractious bronze horses, of watches and silly shaped silver vases—I saw a busy London district; people passing and repassing, tramcars at congested cross-roads, omnibuses, women shopping and stopping to talk, their baskets over their arms. I became aware of a man in a blue overcoat examining the window.

'He's an old hand at "popping" things,' said the pawnbroker.

'You know him then?'

'Never seen him before; but I can tell.'

'How?'

'Well, just watch the way he's going over my stock. I bet he's sized up every blessed thing in the window. It's the jewellery he's interested in. He's wondering if I'm over-stocked with gold bracelets. See, he's counting them. He's not sure. He's coming in. You listen!'

The man in the blue overcoat entered, and spoke in a firm, rather condescending, manner.

'Look here,' he said, 'would you care to give me anything on this? I shall be getting it out some day.'

He threw on the counter a gold bangle.

'Ten shillings,' said the pawnbroker.

'Dirty dog!' said the man, and walked out.

'Old X. round the corner'll give him a pound for it,' said the pawnbroker calmly. 'He's rather low in bangles.'

A well-dressed young man in a great hurry rushed in and detached a watch from his chain:

'I've never done this before!' he said. 'But I want some money quickly.'

It was a good watch, thin as a wafer. Gold.

'Two pounds?'

'Right!' Off he rushed.

All sorts came in, reflected the pawnbroker, you could never tell. Some needed money desperately and some just wanted it at the moment. Young men pawn watches to pay the landlady, to back a horse, to take a girl out to dinner, to stave off a creditor, to buy food. A decent coat disguises motives. Sometimes a 'real lady,' who had been playing too much bridge, 'popped' something really worth while, and always in a quiet shop like this; sometimes 'flashy' people came with diamonds, and then you had to keep your eyes open.

*　　*　　*　　*　　*

In came a little wisp of a woman. She put sixpence on the counter. I noticed her thin wrists and the criss-cross grimed lines on her fingers. She called the pawnbroker 'sir.' When she had gone he showed me the article on which she was paying interest. It was a small box with mother-of-pearl diamonds set in the lid, many of them missing. She had been paying interest for two years.

In every pawnshop there are thousands of things like this box: links with happier days perhaps, things which sentiment enthrones in the heart. One could build up a dozen stories round this box: the gift of a mother, a dead husband, a son?

A Pandora's box full of the winds of old happiness? I leave it to your imagination.

*   *   *   *   *

Then, at the tail of a number of people, some of whom were obviously pledging their overcoats for a long drink of beer, came a woman with dark rings round her eyes, and she said:

'My husband's ill . . . very ill . . . and I must, I simply must. . . .'

She wrestled unhappily with her left hand and placed on the counter a plain gold ring. . . .

'That was horrible,' I said.

'Look here,' replied the pawnbroker. He opened a drawer and ran his fingers through a pile of wedding rings. 'They keep them to the end,' he explained, 'but——'

'I understand. I've seen quite enough. I think I'll be moving on.'

HAVE you ever calculated how much respect you can buy with a sudden half-crown?

A railway porter will give you quite a lot, an hotel porter will unbend slightly, and under its influence even a taxicab driver, if the fare is about seven and sixpence, will appear fairly human. But if you want your money's worth, go briskly into Aldridge's or Tattersall's on the day of a horse sale, walk up to a man who wears a white jacket and holds a whip, give him half a crown and say at the same time: 'Selling any hunters to-day?' You know at once that you have made a hit. As an American would say, he reacts immediately. In one swift eye-sweep he has made a mental note of you; he knows the kind of horse he thinks you ride, the way you ride it, and so on. He looks knowing, a quality shared by all men even remotely connected with the sale of horseflesh, and, slightly closing one eye, he whispers:

'Come with me, sir!'

You are in a stable facing the posteriors of many horses. The hunters, the aristocrats of the sale, are boxed together in a corner, but there are big hefty carthorses and sturdy hacks of every kind. You look down the catalogue: 'Bay mare, has been ridden side-saddle and astride.' What lovely girl rode her side-saddle and astride, you wonder, called her 'Nelly,' and came to the stable every morning with a lump of sugar?

'Look out, sir!' says your admirer, as he taps Nelly's hocks lightly with his whip, causing her to swerve round and show you a dilated pupil and a suspiciously poised near-side hoof. 'Now, sir, that's your 'oss, that is!'

You don't deceive him. You don't explain that you are only doing this for fun, to while away a weary hour, to banish ennui. On he goes, a natural-born auctioneer. She's your weight, she is, and she has a lovely mouth, she has, and he wouldn't be surprised if she was a marvellous jumper, he wouldn't. . . .

For one half-crown and a minimum amount of attention you can spend hours with this man prodding flanks, feeling hocks, and running your hand over withers, but the best thing to do is to run down the horses, call them 'rough stuff,' and go off into the yard where they are having a sale.

Now horse fancying has created a unique type of man
familiar to you in the country, but never seen in London
except at these sales. When you regard them *en masse* the
effect is remarkable. You feel that if a coach-and-four suddenly drove in they could all take seats and drive out looking
like one of Cruikshank's illustrations in Dickens. People would
say: 'What are they advertising?'

They are horse-faced, thin, bow-legged, and some of them
actually suck straws—most difficult things to find in London
these days should you contract the habit. They wear little
fawn coats with pearl buttons and tight little gaiters well up
on the tops of their boots; and they walk with a roll.

You have seen a wicked man in a night club on the movies
look at the heroine. He screws up his eyes and looks straight
at her ankles, and then slowly insults her with his eyes as his
gaze ascends. These horsey men look at horses just like that:
their eyes glance contemptuously at hoofs, linger sneeringly
on fetlocks, wander disparagingly over other parts of the
anatomy, then they say: 'Wind sucker,' or 'Roarer,' or 'Eats
her bedding,' and light a cigar.

*   *   *   *

Into the ring is led a chestnut mare.

She is a lovely thing, and you can tell by the way she
trembles and tosses her head that she is not having a good
time. She does not understand. There are many things she
does understand. She understands the man into whose waistcoat it is so good to place her moist muzzle, she understands
the slightest move of him in the saddle, and she loves to obey
when, feeling the faintest pressure of his knees, she breaks
into a canter over soft grass, and falls again into a trot, to
find his hand patting her sleek neck.

Why isn't he here? He has never let others take control
of her before! In a moment, no doubt, he will come and drive
all these men off; and then they will go out together to their
own place as they have always done. She looks round.
Whinnies. But her man is not there.

Then the auctioneer, a little fellow in a silk hat, explains
that this splendid chestnut mare, sound in wind and limb and
eye, is being sold to save her summer keep. The horse fanciers
come a step nearer, they whisper, they begin to bid. . . .

Bang! The hammer descends. The little chestnut mare starts suddenly as if she knew that she had got a new master.

*　　　*　　　　*　　　*

They lead her out under the wide arch of the livery stable, and in the proud tossing of her head and her backward looks you seem to read: 'Where is that man of mine, and why—why doesn't he come?'

I HAVE realized one of my first ambitions. In the dark engine cab of an Underground train I have shot like a comet through light and darkness, the glittering tail of the train thundering behind packed with people on their way from Bow to Ealing.

A bell rang. The driver looked out over the track where three gleaming steel rails met in a point outside a tunnel. He pulled over a lever and the train started. It was the strangest sensation. I forgot the six packed coaches at the back of us. I forgot the cargo of calm newspaper-reading men and novel-reading girls which we were carrying across London. In the semi-darkness of the driver's cab an ordinary Underground journey had become strangely adventurous and exciting.

The driver accelerated. His pointer moved round a dial, and the train answered his small movements, gathering speed and noise. I was conscious only of being in the grip of a tremendous force that was hurling us over those three gleaming rails. We took the tunnel at a good thirty-five miles an hour, and the noise we made changed to a hollow roar! I could feel the train swerve and rock slightly as we rounded a curve; but I could see nothing save here and there a green light close to the ground. If you can imagine that you are tied to a projectile shot from a gun in the night, you have an idea of driving an electric train through a tunnel.

Stations show first as a faint yellow glow cut across by the jet-black semicircle of the tunnel. The next second you can see their curving rows of lights; they straighten out, and then the platform at which you will pull up lies level as a knife edge before you. Mark Lane . . . Mansion House . . . Blackfriars . . . Temple . . . Charing Cross.

Charing Cross is big. As you sweep in, the driver has time to collect a lightning series of snapshots! A bookstall, a cigarette booth, lit and yellow, a pretty girl coming down the steps carrying a bag, a fussy old lady asking a ticket inspector how to get to Baron's Court, and a sudden stir and interest of Ealing-bound people who detach themselves from the crowd of waiting passengers. Just a flash! All seen in the fraction of a second! Bells ring down the train. A loud one clangs in the engine cab. And off you go again through the blackness towards Victoria.

Few things are more uncanny in mechanical London than the system of automatic signalling which permits a chain of electric trains to move over the same line at minute intervals with no chance of a collision.

Little green lights beckon you on, telling you the way is clear. As you pass them red lights at your back change to green, beckoning on the train behind; and so it is all the way along. Now and then you meet a red light. You stop! The light changes to green. On you go! The marvellous thing is that if, in a moment of colour blindness, you tried to override a red light your train would correct you. It would refuse to go on!

At Kensington we shot out into the open air. Gaily, madly, we raced over the shining rails, marvellously, so it seemed to me, taking a sharp bend, smoothly continuing along the straight. It was like flying without the perpetual anxiety of flight. Once, with the awful insolence of the cocksure, I thought the driver had erred.

'Good Lord!' I said. 'That was a red light, and *you've gone on*!'

Instead of kicking me out on the metals, as he should have done, he smiled and remarked:

'Wrong signal! That red light governs the loop line!'

Safe! On we thundered triumphantly Ealingwards, with the green lights smiling a benediction on us, telling us that the next ahead was at least a minute ahead, telling the next behind that we, in our turn, were sixty seconds on the right side of safety.

'Do you ever get bored with driving the Ealing express?'

'No,' replied the driver, 'I like it! I wanted to do this ever since I became a conductor. Most conductors want to be drivers. The first time you take a train out alone is what you might call a bit of excitement, but it soon wears off.'

'You don't feel as though you were flying?'

'No, you soon lose that feeling.'

'You never get the wind up?'

'No, you can't go wrong if you keep your eyes open and your repair bag in good order!'

*   *   *   *   *

In a cabin where a signalman kept his eyes on an illuminated map over which little black snakes were crawling—trains coming and trains gone—I met an inspector who had been on London's electric railways for over thirty years!

'The changes I've seen?' he said. "Yet it's marvellous what we did in the old days. Do you know that we used to take eighty thousand people a day to exhibitions in the old steam trains? I'm not saying that we weren't a bit packed and a few children on the rack, but—we did it! Now, of course, everything is bigger, quicker, and better, and—you can have the good old days! I remember them and prefer these!

'Why, bless my soul, in the good old days we had to have a regular baby hunt nearly every night under the seats of the old trains. Anybody who didn't want a baby seemed to leave it in the Underground.'

*   *   *   *   *

I bought a ticket like any ordinary unenlightened passenger and went back to London in a 'smoker' with my thoughts straying to the man in the engine cab ahead, sitting there with his eyes glued to the little *crème de menthe* lights that tell him he can fly and thunder on through the darkness.

A STRIPED awning leads to the church. A narrow strip of
scarlet carpet runs from kerb to porch. Policemen hold back
the crowd.

Women—always women; and in such numbers, too, and in
such remarkable variety. The lily-livered misanthrope on a
passing omnibus growls: 'Another wretched wedding. . . .
What women see in them I cannot imagine.' Of course he
cannot. Women, with their relentless grip on essential realities,
see in them the work of the world, the justification of all
living—but, naturally, they do not reason it out like that.
They go to 'see the bride,' or, dare I say, to see themselves as
the bride, either as they once were or as they hope to be.

How remarkably they gather! At one moment the street
is normal save for that tell-tale scarlet strip; the next, as a
swarm gathers out of the blue sky, so gather the wedding
fans, ready, if need be, to prod a policeman in the ribs with an
umbrella in order to watch another woman walk through a
wedding-ring into a home. . . .

Shall we join the ladies?

*   *   *   *   *

'Steady on there. Don't push.'

That is the policeman. There is a surge and writhing of
this solid mass of womanhood.

'Officer, could you stand just a little . . . Thank you.'

''Ere, Robert, can't you move your fat self? I'm only a
little one.'

All kinds of women: Kensington and Balham and Clerken-
well; virgins, matrons, and grandmothers; some happy, some,
no doubt, unhappy. What does that matter? Another bride
is stepping out into life with the future in her eyes, and joy
and sorrow presiding over her marvellous destiny.

*   *   *   *   *

'Who is it?'

'Lady Agatha Penwhistle!'

Not you see, 'Who is *he*?' What does *he* matter? Half the

women have never heard of Lady Agatha. To them she is not Lady Agatha. She is something far more important: she is a bride; she is—Everywoman.

In the dark arch of the church porch a certain anticipatory liveliness is noted. Pink young men in morning clothes, white gardenias in their buttonholes, fuss helplessly, asking each other whispered questions, pointing, hesitating, muddling. Marriage is a bad day for young brothers. The boys at the porch have been tumbling over pews and mixing up the bride's guests with those who owe allegiance to the bridegroom. It has been a fearful sweat for them. The sight of Sis at the altar, too, was pretty awful. Of course, George is an awfully decent cove and all that; but still, you know . . . so small she was, and so pathetic in white, kneeling there. . . .

One of the young men runs down the steps and officiously opens the door of a limousine in whose silver brackets shine white carnations. The crowd watches every movement. He blushes under the scrutiny. Silly asses, they are! Then as he runs back the doors are flung wide. Suddenly the church vibrates like a great cat purring. The stones seem to rock, as, with a crash, the hysterical triumph of Mendelssohn bursts forth and goes galloping down the wind like a messenger. There are people crowding round the porch. She is coming. . . . She, the eternal, unchanging, marvellous She!

Look, there is a movement in the porch, and then . . . 'Oooh, isn't she lovely!'

The Girl in White!

Her veil flung back, her straight, slim form moving down the steps, the white satin gleaming as she moves, her bouquet against her breast, and her silver toes peeping in and out from beneath her gown. She smiles.

'Good luck, my dear!'

A swift turn of her head. Who said that to her? Her eyes brim, for it was very lovely. She gazes over the women's faces—those, at this time, generous women's faces.

So she passes.

*   *   *   *   *

As she goes the women put away their handkerchiefs, for they have all been crying a little, some with joy and some out of the depths of knowledge.

To all of them standing there She represented That Which Once Was, That Which Might Have Been, That Which May Be; and something more—oh, much more. For that brief second she was the Ideal. She was Happiness.

I think also that when the older women found themselves in tears they were seeing through a glass darkly, through the glass of this girl's life, and in their hearts they knew that, come weal, come woe, they had seen a sister at the pinnacle of her life.

*   *   *   *   *

'Good luck, my dear!'

NELL GWYNNE must have had some trying moments. When she fell into a red-haired woman's rage facing Charles II with clenched hands, Charles probably stood there looking at her just as he looks at the few people who from time to time gaze at him in the Westminster Abbey waxwork show.

Women hate to be looked at like that, whether the man who looks is a king or is merely someone else's husband. 'Now, Nelly!' he seems to be saying. 'Now, Nelly!' Cold, distant, on the apex of his pyramid of superiority, with his sallow, cynical face framed in its cascade of curls, how mad he must have made her—and all the others—for women who permit themselves hysterics do detest having them against a human granite quarry. That sad, superior Stuart eye, that heavy, drooping mouth, that thin, supercilious pencil line of a moustache etched straight over, but a little above, his upper lip. So contemptuous, so cutting, so sarcastic. You can positively hear the dead beauties saying, 'Charles, I never know what you are *really* thinking,' or 'Charles, do smile, just once,' or 'Charles, dearest, why do you look at me like that? Have you forgotten . . .' Heart-rending for them, but—also attractive, you know!

How many calculated storms must have beaten in vain tears against that stern rock of a face as he stood there, his Majesty the King, just waiting for the tempest to abate. It must have been one of the most useful expressions in history.

*　　　*　　　*　　　*　　　*

Waxworks? Pooh!

That is what most visitors say as they trail round Westminster Abbey, wrestling painfully with the past, trying to flog their imaginations with dates.

How many realize that these waxworks were made by men who saw these kings and queens in life? They are authentic portraits, less flattering perhaps than the works of greater artists, and for that very reason more interesting. In fact, I prefer this waxwork of Charles II to Lely's splendid portrait. I am sure it is more like Charles.

From the time of Henry V till about 1700 every dead monarch was modelled in wax. This effigy was then dressed in the king's finest suit, and was carried through the streets of London in his funeral train. Westminster Abbey was once full of these marvellous relics—'The Ragged Regiment' they used to be called, or 'The Play of Dead Folks.' To-day only eleven are shown, the broken limbs of the others, the gruesome heads and hands, are locked away from public sight. Poor Edward I and Eleanor, the third Edward and Philippa, glorious Hal and Katharine, Henry VII and Elizabeth of York, James the First and Anne of Denmark, lie all jumbled together; a sight that would have made Hamlet wince.

Was there ever a more pathetic puppet show?

Enough remained of Queen Elizabeth for a clever restorer to give us a new idea of her. There she stands covered in jewels, holding her sceptre, her rich, red, velvet gown falling to a pair of surprisingly adequate brocade shoes. But this is not the imperious queen we know, this is not Gloriana, who could put on a Tower of London expression and whip men with her tongue. This is a sad old woman. She has uncanny, unhappy eyes; such a lonely face.

William and Mary, who attract every Dutch visitor to London, are a heavy, homely couple. She wears purple velvet over a brocaded skirt, and he was so small that some thoughtful person mounted him on a footstool so that he might match his tall wife. Queen Anne is also on view, but she, too, is rather heavy and homely. Those are the royalties.

In a corner is Frances, Duchess of Richmond, who is said to have been the Britannia of the coinage. Just think of this! Frances Teresa Stewart in wax looking across at a waxen Charles II! What irony! She, you remember, was the lady Pepys thought so lovely; and he had a good eye. What scandal a wax figure can recall. 'La Belle Stewart' never cared for chatter, however, and you can imagine how Charles looked when he learned that the beautiful scandalous creature, who might have been Queen of England, had eloped one night from Whitehall with the Duke of Richmond. It must have been a bad day for everybody in St. James's Palace.

In the next case is Katherine, Duchess of Buckingham, who on her death-bed developed an enthusiasm for her funeral. She had previously arranged it in detail with the Garter King-of-Arms, and she lay there worrying if the trappings would be all right, and fearing to die before the undertakers sent the canopy for her approval.

'Why don't they send it,' she cried, 'even though all the tassels are not finished?'

Poor lady! Her pomp is ended, and her brocaded robes sadly in need of the dry-cleaner.

Nelson is there, modelled shortly after death, wearing his uniform, his neat, thin legs in white kerseymere breeches and silk stockings, and the Government 'hat tax' stamp still to be seen inside his hat.

Full of human interest they are, but Charles is the gem. Time has been unkind to the fine point lace at his neck and at his wrists. It is almost black. His jaunty hat, with its drooping ostrich plumes, would disgrace a brawl; yet I defy you to laugh at him. His Majesty looks at you from the dust of centuries, and you are inclined to hate the people who have written their names with diamonds on the plate glass, including the author of that famous quatrain which ends:

> He never said a foolish thing,
> Nor ever did a wise one.

Still he has an air with him, and when he entered a room, his melancholy eyes burning in that sallow, set face, just think how the ostrich plumes swept the dust, and how the lovely naughtiness of his day curtseyed in gold brocade. . . .

I WONDER how many people who live in London lodgings look in their mirror during their occasional shaves and think: 'There goes the rightful Duke of Brixton!'

O the wild dreams of London! The old man who starves himself that he may search year after year for a document which conceals a coronet is only less tenacious than the elderly virgin whose sole passion is the belief that somebody way back in history 'did her down' over a will. There are humble, ragged people who must be positively shocked when they cut a finger and discover that their blood is just ordinary red. There are others who believe themselves to be the ground-landlords of New York or Philadelphia, who go on living in the splendid hope that some day—some day—that missing document will turn up to smooth out the injustices of time.

The Record Office in Chancery Lane is the magnet which draws all these queer people year after year. Those unofficial dukes and earls go off each morning with their luncheon in paper bags to hunt up their ancestors. They are all so certain. So convincing. You can put your head quite close to theirs and never hear the bee.

Their fingernails may be in mourning for their lost departed, their collars may be greyish, and their cuffs frayed, but they have butlers and scarlet carpets in their hearts; and in their eyes a hunger most awful to see. There is a legend that one searcher, who insisted on being called 'my lord,' became tired of trying to justify his claim and, in a moment of enthusiasm, hired a peer's robes and actually succeeded in entering the House of Lords during a State ceremony. What a moment!

There he stood for a time among his peers. It must have been the greatest moment of his life. It was during the State opening of Parliament, and the House of Lords was waiting with lowered lights for the moment when the King and the Queen, with white-satined pages holding the royal trains, would enter. At the precise moment, the lights leap up and send a green and fiery glitter rippling along the throats of the peeresses in the gallery. In this scene stood the peer from Bloomsbury, or Brixton, or Balham, watching with who knows what delicious thrills the Gentlemen-at-Arms standing at the doors holding their halberds in white gauntleted hands while

the lights glanced off their golden helms. What a moment!
And what, I wonder, betrayed him? Why did they ask him
to go? Did he show too much confidence in his rightful surroundings, or did he say, 'Granted, I'm sure,' to the duke who
trod on his foot? I wonder. . . .

When I entered the Record Office yesterday, the curious
round room, like the smoking-room of an Atlantic liner that
has taken to book-collecting, was full of students and historians
poring over spidery Elizabethan script or muttering the English
of Chaucer's day beneath their breath. Now and again someone with the strawberry leaf complex wanders in here, puts
an old hat on the chair, and calls for documents with the air
of a rather weary Malvolio. Generally speaking, the legacy
and title hunters gather next door in the Legal Search Room.

Here I found an assortment of women and men. Some
were solicitors and barristers looking up records, some were
trying to claim funds in Chancery, and others the usual fortune
and title hunters.

This is merely a fraction of the interest this building holds
for us. It houses twenty-six miles of shelves packed with
historic documents and millions of unhistoric documents.
Here are the bones of English History. Come into the Museum,
known so well to those who have a *flair* for the right things,
the Americans. Here in two portly volumes is 'Domesday
Book,' writ in a fair monkish hand. Shelves are stacked with
letters from kings and queens, generals and admirals, cardinals
and peers: humour, pathos, tragedy, passion. In one of these
Wolsey, 'the King's poore, hevy and wrechyd prest,' asks
Henry VIII to forgive him and take him back into favour.
Queen Elizabeth's hand is set to a number of letters, and to
her are missives from many men, including two who loved
her. Robert Dudley, Earl of Leicester, says in one: 'I humbly
kiss your foot,' and the imprisoned Earl of Essex is represented
by a brief letter written for the eyes of Gloriana alone.

You can read letters which recall cannon shot on the high
seas, and letters which give a vision of deep political plotting
and such-like villainy. 'God has given us a good day in
forcing the enemy so far to leeward,' wrote Sir Francis Drake
aboard the 'Revenge.' 'I hope in God the Prince of Parma
and the Duke of Sedonya shall not shake handes this fewe
days.' Quite near you will find the last confession of Guy
Fawkes.

When you have enjoyed the flavour of these old days you may meet on the stairs an ordinary cat. At least so it seems. It is Felix, and he has been walking through history for centuries. It is the only cat officially on a Government staff —in spite of anything women secretaries in Whitehall may tell you! It receives a penny a day from Government funds! I believe that the terms of its appointment include a clause that it must keep itself clean, catch rats and mice, and bring up its children. If anybody killed the official cat in ancient times he had to forfeit a sufficient quantity of wheat to cover the body.

*   *   *   *   *

The officer in charge of the Legal Search Room sits with the official list of lost money before him—the funds in Chancery, which, by the way, are only sufficient to make one decent full-blown millionaire—as millionaires go nowadays.

'Yes,' he said, 'there are some strange searchers.

'In the summer many good, democratic Americans come over to trace their ancestry back to William the Conqueror!'

'And the lost heirs,' I said—'the would-be dukes?'

'Ah!' he replied. 'Ah!'

He sighed.

I noticed a shabby old man mournfully shuffling out. I felt certain that there was the ghost of ermine over him, and I hope that now and then, just to keep his poor heart up, his landlady drops a curtsey when she brings in the kippers, and says: 'Dinner is served—*your grace*.'

Fish ∽ ∽ ∽ ∽ ∽ ∽ ∽ ∽

AT the uncomfortable hour of five every morning a man in a peaked cap rings a big bell in Billingsgate Market and the lights go up. Then the haddocks and plaice, which you eat in due course, begin their commercial career.

Shouting? Yes; most decidedly! The ozone which exudes from prostrate cod seems to have a singular effect on the lungs of the fish trade. In the old days, I am told, they used to shout fishy slogans such as: 'Had-had-had-haddock!' or 'Wink-wink-wink-winkles!' But only now and then, when some enthusiast becomes filled with the spirit of the past, do you hear anything so interesting. It is mostly a swift, sharp, business-like affair, with a little violent auctioneering over in the corner. Lying in the Thames, at the Wharf which is on one side of the market, is a Danish trawler with North Sea salt caked on her funnel. Men run up and down the gangways carrying her cargo, while, from every corner of the compass, railway carts converge on that tangle of narrow streets which begins at the Monument. If you like statistics, you will be interested to know that, on an average, eight hundred tons of fish pour into Billingsgate every day, and most of it comes by train.

I wandered between lines of dead fish. Nothing on earth can look so dead as a fish. In a place of this kind it is difficult to believe that fish have ever lived, have ever sported gallantly in the sea, making romantic love and building homes, and generously seeing to it that we shall go on having fish after soup.

Incredibly dead codfish, and inconceivably defunct skate, lay strewn in rich profusion, herrings with red eyes and white-bellied plaice—all the fruit of the ocean mixed up with ice. Queer, fascinating things are apparently weeded out before they reach Billingsgate; there is none of the strange, snarling fish you see at Boulogne or Dieppe, none of the comic monstrosities with green whiskers which enchant you in Marseilles. Billingsgate is essentially an edible dump. Everything that comes into it is solemnly designed for the kitchen.

Between the flabby corpses walk men and women—fishmongers, hotel buyers, and the like—prodding, examining, comparing, now and then tasting a shrimp—at five a.m., too! —sometimes cracking an experimental mussel.

109

Officials of the Worshipful Company of Fishmongers patrol the place. They represent one of the few old guilds which are still actively interested in the trades they represent. These inspectors have the power to condemn anything unfit for sale.

*   *   *   *   *

And the smell!

How many cats sniff it at the Bank, I wonder! Smell is a marvellous thing. It can awaken tender memories of love and passion, of moments under a moon, blowing roses, blue nights. Were I a woman, I would never allow the man I loved to go far without a bottle of my favourite scent. A photograph is a dead thing; a smell is alive. How strange, I thought, that Billingsgate should appeal to the same sense that thrills to a laced handkerchief. Here you have the harmony and discord of smell. Billingsgate, in this musical metaphor, is like a cat walking across a piano—worse, it is a blare of smell, an assault on the senses. I wondered if, with study, a keen nose could, in time, learn to disentangle the various strains that go to swell the mass effect, as a musician is able to deafen himself to a symphony and to follow the steady hum of an individual 'cello.

Remembering a handkerchief I once had, so long ago that I can write of it as if it were a museum specimen, I asked myself this problem: Suppose a fishmonger fell in love in Billingsgate Market, would fish remind him or would it not? At first I was inclined to say no, but, on reflection, I thought yes. He would meet the girl every day for months among the lobsters. He would see her come to him down an avenue of oysters. He would whisper to her above the whiting, and they would kiss among the kippers. Gradually turbot would come to have a deeper meaning for this man. He would hesitate over the whitebait, and—remember. When the first Danish herrings came in during February he would have to pull himself together and be strong. Years after, if he wished to call up a memory of the loved one, what simpler than to unpack a box of bloaters? But the agony of living in such a hall of memories! If you have ever treasured a piece of scented cambric, think how harrowing it would be to live in the perfume factory. . . .

Such speculation is vain. Do not pity Billingsgate. I

BILLINGSGATE MARKET

hardly like to tell you because I fear you may not believe me, but—Billingsgate smells nothing! Its sense of smell is atrophied. I discovered this by the merest chance.

'By Jove,' I said, 'that's a loud fish. What is it?'

'I don't smell anything,' said the owner.

We discussed smell minutely, and I discovered that life in Billingsgate had made him immune from fishy smells. Only when he returns from his holiday is he conscious of a little something in the air.

*   *   *   *   *

Billingsgate is perhaps the most libelled spot in London. Fifty years ago you had to wax your ears. The language was awful. To-day the Billingsgate fish porters are as polite and charming as we all are.

They are the backbone of Billingsgate, for this market is worked on the most primitive system of hard transport. The Genoese galleys, which in the Middle Ages anchored near by, were unloaded in exactly the same way. So were Pharaoh's galleys, and Caesar's. These men, wearing queer-shaped leather helmets rather like stunted Burmese pagodas, carry all the fish in crates on their heads. When a man's neck 'sets,' as they call it, he can carry sixteen stone on his head. They do it every day and all day.

'Mind your back, *please!*' say the fish porters of Billingsgate.

'Shove over the hammer—if you don't mind, Jack!' I heard one say.

'Certainly!' replied Jack.

So much for that.

*   *   *   *   *

Then I walked out on Billingsgate Wharf and had a real thrill. This is where London began. It is probably the oldest wharf on the Thames. Old Geoffrey of Monmouth, who would have made a fine American reporter, says that it takes its name from Belin, King of the Britons four hundred years before Christ. Stowe thinks that it was once owned by a man called Biling. It is certain, however, that the Romans landed their furs and their wines here, and at this spot on the Thames the first imports of London were dumped, the first merchants gathered.

To the left I saw the bluish shadow of Tower Bridge. The brown Thames water licked the broad hull of a fish trawler. Crate after crate of herrings caught so far away in the North Sea were unloaded for London, and, as I passed again through the ripe, rich tang of the market, a man was buying lobsters, which, I suppose, a lovely girl will enjoy as she makes eyes at someone over the rim of her champagne glass.

Haunted ∘ ∘ ∘ ∘ ∘ ∘ ∘

DEVONSHIRE HOUSE is dead and gone. I hope that its name may be perpetuated by the new commercial building; but I do not know.

When the workmen were performing acute surgical operations on old Devonshire House I was interested to hear people, who knew the Duke quite well by his photographs, express intimate regret at this deed. 'Dear old Devonshire House!' they said. 'What a shame it is that these grand old . . .' And so on and so forth. They were wistful. They gave the impression that they knew the pink bedroom awfully well (don't you know); they that had lingered on every inch of the famous staircase. They were like people who mourned the downfall of the old home.

You see, for nearly five years Devonshire House was, in the name of charity, thrown open to the public, so that probably more people were acquainted with the geography of this mansion than with any other ducal house which has not become either an hotel or a museum. So:

'Poor old Devonshire House!'

'Yes, it looks just like a bombed château during the war!'

*   *   *   *   *

It did.

Workmen swarmed over it, stood on walls picking at it, sending it earthwards in clouds of dry, white dust. Great gashes had been cut in the sides, windows had been knocked out, the daylight shone into the out-buildings, exposing the discreet wall-paper of the servantry. The wide, walled court-yard through which swung the coaches of Fox, Burke, and the 'New Whigs' in the days when men, and many a pretty woman, plotted against Pitt, was the loading spot for builders' carts; and a place in which anyone could light a bon-fire to burn lath and plaster.

There was great interest in this patch of changing London. Not one person passing on an omnibus but remarked about it; and no wonder, for this is Piccadilly's most dramatic assassination. In the sound of the picks you could hear the voice of the new age—or the Chancellor of the Exchequer, whichever you liked! Those great houses, round which centred the wit, the beauty, the scholarship, the politics, and the art of the eighteenth century, have outlived their day. London has crept up from Ludgate Hill like a tidal wave and overwhelmed them.

Devonshire House stood, strange and incongruous behind its feudal wall, like the Lord Mayor's coach in a traffic hold-up. Great hotels and shops grew up and shouldered it, and still it stood there dreaming, it seemed, of a vanished paddock; aware, it seemed, in its gated caution, that once upon a time highwaymen rode out of Kensington with masks over their faces.

I admit that it was ugly—entirely gloomy in its grey, stiff, barrack-like way; but it did mean something—it had character. Though nobody, as far as I am aware, ever did anything splendidly bad or remarkably good in it, Devonshire House could never be neutral. The National Anthem is pretty bad music, but it could never be neutral.

*　　　*　　　*　　　*　　　*

So, as the workmen consumed their sandwiches in halls through which for two centuries passed a delicious trickle of royalties, they heard the whistle and rose heavily to grasp their picks and do some more damage. I more than once stood there, among a tangle of builders' carts, and saw visions rise out of the white dust.

What a procession!

I saw the hackney coach of Charles James Fox trundle under the portico. Burke, of course, was there too, the practical, wise Burke; for here they conspired with the Coalition Whigs to hit at Pitt, whispering and plotting with the lovely Georgiana, third Duchess of Devonshire, who enjoyed placing her white finger into this political pie. There had been a tea-party at Boston. And the French Revolution was gathering like a storm to split them. Among these crumbling stones Georgiana must have heard of that scene, one of the most dramatic the House of Commons has ever witnessed, when those two, Fox and Burke, broke their long friendship in a thrilled hush; Fox with tears in his eyes and his voice breaking, Burke grim and firm, and the House of Commons looking on at a quarrel that never healed.

George IV, as Prince of Wales, with his card-table fingers also in the Fox pie, and all the brains and elegance of that time, wits, who have been forgotten, a few, who live, laughter, music, and the flash of white shoulders, eyes above a fan. . . .

What a procession!

All this you could see in the dust of Devonshire House—two hundred years of it, duke succeeding duke; and all the time the new generations of wealth, power, and art moving up to that grey old portico.

As I passed it late one night, I wondered if there are spirits—a queer doubt to express to-day! If so, I am certain that on calm nights fit for a lady's walk Georgiana, third Duchess of Devonshire, must have visited the ruin, looking with very straight brows and considerable 'tut-tutting' at a big board on which was printed: 'The magnificent building to be erected on this site will include offices, restaurants, and flats.'

*   *   *   *   *

Poor Georgiana! Time is a queer thing, and—you, in your time, would never have believed it, would you?

About Homes in Bondage   ∿   ∿   ∿   ∿

DO you wish to feel human emotion spring from inanimate things? Do you wish to meet ghosts? Then come with me to one of London's great furniture store-houses, where a thousand homes lie piled to the roof, silent, sheeted, tomb-like.

A storeman switches on a line of lights, and we see, stretching to the distance, great pyramids of household goods, whole homes of furniture, neatly stacked and carefully ticketed against the time when a man and a woman will come to claim them. Some of the pyramids suggest Park Lane; others suggest Clapham Common.

Let us peep beneath this shroud, and what do we see: 'Good morning, Mrs. Everyman, and what can I do for you? Kindly accept this cushion as a souvenir of your visit.' There lies the gift cushion, there the once-so-loved instalment suite that was delivered in the plain van. Note the pictures by Watts, Rossetti, and others of the Victorians to whom the suburbs are so loyal. 'Love's Awakening.' Ah!

What do we see in the next tomb? Yes; here was an elegant home with a cheque-book behind it. The low satinwood dresser had a compartment like a knee desk, so that she might get close up when she rouged her lips, and three swinging mirrors in order that she might know whether her shoulders were evenly powdered before he took her out to the Berkeley. Engravings, a Japanese cabinet, a good one, a beautiful round table with a surface like that of a still pool. Little home and big home side by side. Do you see the ghosts of Mrs. Everyman and Lady Nobody meeting like sisters over their shrouded homes crying a little on each other's arms? I do. The tombs go on waiting . . . waiting.

Homes in bondage!

As we wander down the line, our eyes are caught by a doll's house, relic of some distant nursery, a child's cot, or a piece of furniture with distinct personality, and we wonder how much heartache and hope this place represents. There are people living in lodgings, dreaming of the home that they will build again one day, longing to surround themselves with loved things, to tear off the wrappings and see again those precious ordinary objects that mean so much in every life— those sentimental anchors.

Sentiment—that is the keynote. Without it, London's store-rooms would be half empty.

'Yes, sir,' says the storeman, as he pulls aside a wrapping, 'people don't seem able to bring themselves to part with things. It's mighty queer. Look at this old box, now—what would you think is inside it?'

The box is an ancient nail-studded chest with a curved lid that might have contained all the gold of Treasure Island. I hazard a guess just to please him.

'No, sir. It's just full of little old bits of cloth, the kind of things that women collect and put in old baskets because they may come in useful some day. There's bits of tinsel and lace, and pretty little cases full of red and blue beads and needles by the score. But what's the sense of letting it eat its head off here? That's what I want to know. If they've paid a penny for this old box, they must have paid fifty pounds; for it was here before ever I was. O yes, there's funny people about, and no mistake. Now if it belonged to me . . .'

As he rambles on, I examine the old box with interest. I know why it was put there; and so do you. Memories cling round it—memories so sweet that the heart revolts at the thought of burning those poor fragments.

Most people have a box of that sort. In it are queer trifles, little geometric nets on which beads are strung or sewn. Green and scarlet parrots preen themselves on half-finished trees. It is that note of half completion, as of a task suddenly put down and soon to be resumed, which makes such things so appealing. Perhaps a needle is still sticking in a corner of the fabric, waiting, it seems, for the fingers that will never come again. And when you look you see the hand that placed it there, you hear a voice and see a face bending over the pretty, unimportant thing, and it's ten to one that you are a child again on some slow, lazy afternoon of sun; and the voice is the voice of your mother telling you the same old story you have heard a hundred times as you watch her, fascinated by her brilliance, hypnotized by the growth of the brocade bird and its beaded eye: a masterpiece which fills your mind and stands out as the most marvellous and beautiful thing the world has ever seen. Clever, wonderful mother. . . .

'There's funny people about, and no mistake!' says the storeman again, giving the box a prod with his foot.

We go on. He unties the wrappings round another deposit.

All these things, he explains, belong to 'a divorced couple.' How new they are, he comments. How quickly they must have found out their mistake; no sooner married than divorced and storing their things, and chucking away good money after bad!

I peep in with a feeling that I am eavesdropping. There, piled up sideways, is the table round which this unknown tragedy of married life was acted, the solemn, stiff chairs, witness to it all, the pictures which for a little while were gathered for this mockery of a home.

'Why they don't sell it I can't think,' says the storeman.

I wonder, too, why they keep it. Neither one nor the other can bear to live with it. Then what queer sentiment, what common memory, retains this split home here in the pathetic silence of lapsed things?

We turn a corner. More avenues, sheeted, deserted.

'Some of these people are dead, we think,' remarks my guide, waving his hand towards the dim roof. 'This lot was put in at the beginning of the war. We had to sell quite a lot. Payments lapsed, and no one replied to advertisements. It is a mystery to know who it belongs to now, sir, and that's a fact.'

*   *   *   *   *

As we turn into another warehouse, we meet a man and woman. They have pulled aside the sheeting and are standing among chairs and tables and pictures. The woman comes out and says nervously:

'We've just come to see our things. The manager said that we might.'

As we enter the next compartment, we hear this man and woman talking.

'Oh, look! There it is, next to mother's writing-table. Do pick it up and let me hold it!'

There is the sound of the man walking over the stiff wrappings.

'Oh, my dear!' comes the woman's voice. 'My dear!'

We go on through the silent aisles, the storeman talkative, amusing, insensible to the drama we have met, oblivious of the longing in those few words spoken by a woman, among the sheeted pathos of a home in bondage.

Royal Satin ✎ ✎ ✎ ✎ ✎ ✎

WHEN Queen Mary was married she wore a dress which I find it rather difficult to describe, because there is a special dressmakers' language for that sort of thing.

It was low in the neck, the lowness draped with white lace. The tiny, inch-long sleeves were caught up at the shoulder with little bunches of orange blossom. The corsage curved inwards to a tight waist ending in a point, and the dress, cut away over a fine white underskirt, fell in a graceful, generous sweep to the floor. Over the front were draped trailing sprays of orange blossom. The going-away dress is a bit easier to describe. It covered the Queen from neck to feet. The collar was high, and braided like that of a mess uniform or a commissionaire's tunic. The sleeves, tight at the wrist and braided, rose at the shoulder, sharply and alarmingly, in a queer shape, known, I believe, as 'leg of mutton.' It is stately and ornate, and, in the light of modern fashion, exceedingly stiff and strange.

Men in the early thirties can just remember their mothers in a dress like this, sitting calm and lovely in a victoria with a parasol in their white-gloved hands, and a perky little hat like the entree in a vegetarian restaurant poised on their puffed-up hair. So you can't help loving the Queen's going-away dress. . . .

*　　　*　　　*　　　*　　　*

Where can you see it? Do you know? It is on view, with hundreds of other royal satins, in that beautiful and comparatively unknown museum within a stone's throw of the Prince of Wales's house in St. James's Palace—the London Museum.[1] This is a woman's museum. I cannot imagine a woman who would not be thrilled by it. In the first place, it is the most beautifully housed museum in the world. Lancaster House, which used to be the town house of the Dukes of Sutherland, is one of the finest houses in London. It makes you feel good all over simply to walk up the wide, dignified staircase that leads from the great marble entrance hall. In

[1] This was written during the reign of King George V, when the Duke of Windsor was the Prince of Wales.

the second place, the London Museum contains rooms filled entirely with royal treasures: dolls dressed by Queen Victoria, a tiny suit worn by King Edward, the cradle in which the present Royal Family were rocked to sleep, the coronation robes, intimate family relics that recall Queen Victoria, the Prince Consort, and King Edward. There are also beautiful, slightly-faded dresses which Queen Alexandra wore when she came over the sea many years ago to be the Princess of Wales.

*   *   *   *   *

Every day a few women can be found in a state of ecstasy before these cases. Sometimes the keeper, frock-coated and white-spatted and gardeniaed, can be seen conducting a tall, stately woman through the high magnificence of the halls— a woman who looks with a smile at many a relic of childhood; and people whisper 'The Queen!'

To the Londoner, this place holds more of interest than any other museum, not excepting the unfortunately entombed Guildhall Museum.

The whole history of London, dug up out of London clay and peat, is here for inspection. The finest collection of Roman pottery, found among the roots of London, is on view. There is a pot which dates from perhaps A.D. 200, on which a Londoner of seventeen hundred years ago has written: 'Londini ad fanum Isidis' ('London, next door to the Temple of Isis'). Think of it! In Tudor Street seventeen hundred years ago men worshipped the Egyptian goddess Isis, the goddess with the moon on her head, the sister-wife of Osiris, who travelled from the Nile to the Tiber, where she joined the impartial Pantheon of Rome.

There is the skeleton of a Roman galley found in the bed of the Thames: a great ship in which men came to build the first London. There is the skeleton of one of the first Londoners, lying stretched under glass as he was found, with a bronze pin under his chin and a bronze dagger at his breastbone.

Down below, in the basement, is a Chamber of Horrors few people know. Here are the great iron gates of Newgate Prison. Here in a frightening gloom are two prison cells. A wax figure, who looks as if the execution morning has dawned, writhes on his hard bed, his hands chained to the walls. Here are the manacles that held Jack Sheppard.

In another room are a series of lifelike models of old London which every Londoner should see and admire. Old London bridge, with its rows of traitors' heads set on staves, is lifelike; old St. Paul's during the Fire of London is wonderful. A mechanical contrivance gives the illusion that smoke is rolling up from the blazing church over the startled city, the windows of houses show blood-red lights, and, as you stand looking at the model, your imagination is stirred so that you can hear the cries and the shouting, see the confused rushes as citizens try to save their treasures while liquid lead falls hissing on the red-hot pavements round St. Paul's.

* * * * *

One wonders what Lancaster House will be like in fifty years' time if it keeps pace with London. Already a hansom cab is parked in the garden. Some day a motor-omnibus, and perhaps a tramcar, will arrive. There are crowded days ahead.

Among the Fur Men ᴐ ᴐ ᴐ ᴐ ᴐ

WOMEN must, I am glad to say, have fur coats. It has been so since we men set out after the ermine with clubs instead of cheque books, and splendidly have they always repaid us with a glimpse of eyes over soft furs and chins buried in the cosy rightness of it.

The result is that, all over the world, wherever hairy things creep, crawl, or climb, men are ready with guns and traps. Three times a year the pelts of the world pour into London to be distributed. Whenever this happens a large auction-room in Queen Street will provide you with the strangest sight in the City of London. You walk in through a courtyard past a man in white overalls. As I passed him recently he said: 'Hudson Bay Company selling now, sir!' and, do you know, I felt young all over! Hudson Bay Company! Shades of Fenimore Cooper! In one swift, pregnant moment I saw the white lands I used to know so well when I was at school, the driving sheets of snow, the tugging sleigh dogs, and the big, square-bearded men, with matted hair frozen under round fur hats, bending forward against the storm, urging on their teams, taking their piled sleighs to the trading post.

I crossed the courtyard and entered the auction-room. What a scene! Men who buy furs in every country in the world were present. They sat tier on tier, a good five hundred of them, looking like a full session of the Parliament of the United States of Europe. No common auction this: it was a fur parliament, a senate of seal and musquash. Russians, Poles, Germans, Dutch, French, every kind of Jew, and a good balance of English and American. If Sir Arthur Keith had been with me he would have gone crazy over the marvellous skulls and cheek-bones. It was, anthropologically, a splendid sight.

They retained their hats as they sat in the wide half-moon of the fur theatre. What hats! Here and there I picked out a round astrakhan cap, and, of course, there were fur coats. One man unbuttoned his coat. It was lined with leopard skin.

Seven men sat high above the assembly, facing it, and, in the centre of the seven, was the auctioneer:

'Any advance on three hundred?'

Instead of the nods and lifted eyebrows of any ordinary

saleroom, there was a violent agitation. To make a bid in this room a man had to create a scene. In two minutes the place looked like a crisis in the French Senate. Men desiring mink rose and shot up their arms. The three hundred pounds advanced to five hundred, hesitated, and spurted on to seven hundred. Then a man with a Central European beard rose (exposing a fine nutria lining) and carried the day. The hammer fell. At least twenty more women would have fur coats next winter!

* * * * *

So it went on. Millions of potential fur coats were bought and—not one of them in sight. They were lying in warehouses somewhere in London; but they had been carefully examined before the sale.

As it proceeded, it occurred to me how true it is that certain professions take hold of a man and brand him. There are grooms who look like horses, dog fanciers who resemble dogs, and if certain of these fur men had emerged from thick undergrowth nine sportsmen out of ten would have taken a pot shot at them. I fancied I could detect the little, rodent-like beaver merchants, the fat, swarthy seal fans, the sharp, pale-white fox-fanciers, and a few aristocratic grey men with whom I associated chinchilla.

* * * * *

The story behind it all. That was the thing that thrilled me. Behind this roomful of strange, intent men in a London auction-room I seemed to see other men, the wild, uncouth men of youthful romance, out in the savage places of the earth and in the great loneliness of forests and ice. Hunters, trappers! Though we grow old and hard and inaccessible to all soft thoughts we will never lose our love for these. It is in our blood. We have all longed to be trappers, we have all longed to blaze the trail through the Canadian wilderness, to crack the ice on Great Whale River before we could catch our breakfast, to win home at last in a flurry of snow to the log cabin. . . .

'Any advance on three hundred and fifty pounds?'

The baying of dogs in a white-sheeted world, the pine trees in shrouds; and then—silence. . . .

'Four hundred. Any advance?'

The green glitter of ice and the drama of a man fighting the elements, fighting solitude, primitive, uncouth, his mind following the minds of beasts as a fox-hunter anticipates the mind of a fox.

'Five hundred! Any advance?'

Blood over the snow and a limp body, the cracking of whips, the dog team with its laden sledge, and—all in order that you, my dear, may wrap your tall, elegant self in a lovely fur coat!

'Going, going, gone!'

Crack!

IN a high room overlooking Downing Street sit six solemn men at a table piled with books.

I recognize Lord X. and Lord Y. and Lord Z. diligently reading, saying 'Ha!' or 'Hum!' or looking grave, or reflectively wiping the lenses of their spectacles. Two attendants in evening dress, like a couple of lost waiters, tip-toe round the apartment pulling out more books from the well-stocked walls to place before their omniverous lordships. The room is carpeted with maroon felt, a few portraits in oils gaze down on the assembly with polite indifference; and there are four fire-places set in squares of veined marble. The furnishings resemble those of ideal offices in the 'efficiency first' advertisements: the inkpots are bigger and more efficient-looking than ordinary inkpots, the desks are more prairie-like in size than common desks, and the chairs more comfortable than less exalted chairs.

Yes; but what is happening? I would think, if I did not know, that a millionaire's will was being read in a country house library. A few barristers in wigs and gowns sit quietly reading as if they were in chambers. Facing the peers is a barrister standing at a little reading-desk, and, in the comfortable hush, his crisp voice goes on and on. An attendant discreetly feeds one of the four fires, pokes a second, looks critically at a third; one of the peers calls for yet another book . . . the Voice goes on and on and on. . . .

This is the highest court in the British Empire. Behind that door in the corner is, theoretically, the King. The Voice that goes on and on is speaking on the steps of the throne. This is a sitting of the Judicial Committee of the Privy Council.

Whenever that old cry, 'I appeal to Caesar!' goes up in any part of the Empire this room becomes busy. In this room the last word is given on legal differences throughout the Empire. If the courts in Australia cannot satisfy someone about his right-of-way, the trouble is smoothed out once and for all here in Downing Street. If there is a row in Canada about mining rights, in New Zealand about water supply, in India about delicate matters of caste, or even—as in a case coming on soon —about a contract for the supply of ground nuts, the Privy

Councillors hear it on behalf of the King and give their final and irrevocable verdict.

This room is the final appeal for four hundred million British subjects, or nearly a third of the human race. Legal controversies over eleven million square miles—and strangely, throughout the Church in this country—are settled here. Its decisions go to the uttermost ends of the earth. No court in the world has ever had so wide a jurisdiction.

When I walked in, the two attendants looked up curiously at me, for a strange face is a novelty. The highest court in the Empire, although it is as public as the Law Courts, seldom attracts a visitor.

I sit down in a kind of superior pew. Behind me are shelved the legal records of Canada, a library in themselves. 'Revised Statutes of Nova Scotia,' I read. 'Quebec Revised Statutes,' 'New Brunswick Acts,' 'Laws of P. E. Island,' 'Revised Statutes of Alberta,' and so on—the ideal bedside library! 'Canada,' however, is not the official title: the Dominion laws are catchlined 'North America.'

Opposite are the laws of India, Australia; and so on throughout the Empire.

*   *   *   *   *

What do litigants in distant parts of the earth think of this room? Surely they imagine the King's Privy Council sitting robed as peers in the neighbourhood of a stained glass window, trailing ermine sleeves over richly carved chairs, light falling on coronets, with perhaps the King, in full Garter robes, dropping in to see how things are going on.

Nothing of the kind! The highest court in the Empire sits in less state than a police court. There is no jury and no impassioned Law Court rhetoric. Counsel leans over his little reading-desk and talks to their lordships in a quiet, conversational voice. It is more like a directors' meeting than an Empire's appeal court. I half expect someone to rise and declare a dividend.

'And now,' says the Voice in the quiet tone of a secretary reading an annual report, 'I would like your lordships to look at page four hundred and two.'

Their lordships comply.

What strange things go on here! One day they discuss an

obscure passage in the Koran, the next they are debating the inner meaning of the Hedaya. When they deal with South Africa's Roman-Dutch law they bandy the names of Grotius and Vinnius, authorities the Law Courts never hear.

Stranger things than this happen. Did you know that in parts of the British Empire the old French law, long expelled from France, lives on, regulating men's lives. Appeals from Mauritius and the Seychelles Islands refer to the Code Napoleon! When Quebec submits its troubles to London, this room hears, like an echo from long ago, mention of the ancient Custom of Paris; and the two men in evening dress go tiptoeing round the room to look over the shelves for Beaumanoir and Dumoulin.

* * * * *

As I creep away from the Privy Council, feeling that it is one of the most wonderful places in London, that Voice goes on and on, quiet, conversational, and—the echo will be heard in Bombay.

THERE is no mystery about the making of money. The Royal Mint is exactly like any other factory. This surprised me. I had an idea that the manufacture of money must surely be surrounded by the unusual. It hardly seemed natural that this metal for whose possession we sweat and slave, lie and slander, and even, on occasions, commit murder, should be churned out by nonchalant machines no different in their general attitude towards production from those machines which cut out nails or stamp out dustbins.

It was with quite a shock that I watched a half-crown machine at work. What an ideal birthday present! The thing hypnotized me. Click-click-click-click it went, and at every click a silver-white half-crown was born, a real good half-crown ready to be spent. What a generous mouth the machine had; how casual it was. . . .

'Click-click' went the metal millionaire, shooting its lovely children into a rough wooden trough. The pile grew as I watched it. It began with a taxicab fare; the next second a twin was born; they lay together for a second before three represented a solicitor's fee, or a dog licence; in five more seconds there was a whole pound lying there. So it went on hour after hour while spectators stood by reverently, feeling that the machine was grinning as it pounded away enthusiastically producing potential ermine cloaks, motor-cars, freehold houses, and winters in the south of France.

If only the Chancellor of the Exchequer would lend it to me for a week.

* * * * *

How much easier money is to make than to earn.

The first stage in the life of a half-crown is a hot foundry where men melt down bars of silver in crucibles. These crucibles lie in gas furnaces that roar like hungry lions and give out a beautiful orange flame ending in a fringe of apple-green light.

An overhead crane runs along, picks a red-hot crucible from the furnace, and carries it to a place where a series of long moulds are waiting. The silver is poured, spluttering and

MAKING COINS, THE ROYAL MINT

blazing, into these moulds, and the result is a number of long, narrow silver bars, which are passed through runners until the five-foot strip of silver is the thinness of a half-crown.

These strips are then passed through machines which punch out silver discs with remarkable speed. The next machine gives these plain silver discs a raised edge, and the next—the machine worth having—puts the King's head on them, mills their edges, and turns them out into the world to tempt mankind.

* * * * *

While I was in the stamping-room of the Mint, all the machines were working full blast, except one, which looked like a rich relation and had become muscle bound. In one corner they were making East African shillings by the hundred thousand; in another they were turning out West African currency. The men had as much as they could do to keep pace with them. No sooner had they carried away a trough full of money, with the blasé air such an occupation induces, than a second pile was lying there on the floor like a miser's hoard.

I saw enough African money made in half an hour to buy elephants, thousands of wives, guns, horses, buffaloes, and a throne or two.

The raw material of a sultanate fell out on the floor of the Mint before luncheon-time.

I could not, however, get worked up on African money. My first bucketful of sixpences gave me a much greater thrill. There must have been at least three thousand of them lying in bran. In the shilling department they were turning out a good line in high-class shillings, and the half-crown corner became positively thrilling.

'Where's the gold?' I said, feeling slightly heady.

'Ah, where?' replied my guide.

'America?' I suggested.

'Ah—um,' he said reflectively.

Leading from the stamping-rooms are rooms where silver is polished, but more interesting is the room in which its sound is tested. I have often heard money talk, but I had never heard it sing before. How it sings!

Men sit at little tables picking up half-crowns and dashing

them against a steel boss, with the result that the air is full of something quite like bird song; only perhaps more interesting. It would surprise you to see how slight a defect disqualifies a coin. The smallest irregularity in its ring, and, flip! it is lying in the 'rejected' basket.

I half hoped they would allow staff and visitors to have these throw-outs at bargain prices; but there was no hope of this.

* * * * *

In other rooms, men, crouching over a revolving band covered with money, picked out any badly coloured coin as the silver stream advanced towards them. The next department was a mechanical weighing-room, in which wise-looking machines in glass cases put true coins in one slot, light ones in a second, and heavy-weights in a third.

As a climax I saw a giant machine that counts half-crowns into one hundred pound bags and never makes a mistake. I watched it count forty bagsful and then walked thoughtfully away.

* * * * *

'What does it feel like to make money all day long and draw a few pounds on Friday?' I asked a Mint worker.

'Oh, I dunno,' he replied, as he shook a thousand pounds through a bran sieve.

This is a merciful frame of mind.

Where Time Stands Still

LONDON is full of antique shops—places where Chinese Buddhas gaze pointedly at the alleged work of Chippendale —but, if you asked me which is the most remarkable of all, I would take you to a shop which deals only in articles more than a thousand years old.

When you enter, the centuries drop away like sand in an hour-glass. Through the frosted opacity of the door you are dimly aware of the red blur of a passing omnibus, of shadows that are men and women busying about their day's work. You hear the sound that is London; but it means nothing in here. How can it? It is a fluid unimportance called To-day and you are surrounded by Yesterday. The Present and the Future are intangible things. The Past only can be grasped and loved. That, at least, is how they think in this queer shop where Time is regarded as a mere convention; a shoreless ocean in which each man's life is just a spoonful taken and returned.

The men who wander in look mostly dull and dry, sunk in whiskers and absent-mindedness. They sometimes leave their umbrellas in the rack and say 'yes' when they should have said 'no.' They often remark on the wonderful weather when it is pouring with rain. They are probably thinking, you see, of some Grecian dawn or the raising of the siege of Troy. When you know them, and can pull them out of the Past a little, you realize that there is nothing more human on earth than the average archaeologist, because he has learned that human men and women have always been much the same, and that a little thing like two thousand years and a pair of spats makes no real difference to human nature, its passions, its frailties, and its frequent glories. In their packed minds Thebes, Athens, Rome, London, Paris, and New York, march shoulder to shoulder with nothing to distinguish them, except, perhaps, a red omnibus going to Victoria.

It is so delightful to hear them talk about Jason as if he threw up work in Threadneedle Street to go out to Australia in search of fleeces; and once an old man told me about the marriage of his grand-daughter with such remote charm that it was three days before I realized that he had not been talking about Cupid and Psyche.

*   *   *   *   *

131

However, let us glance round this shop. The first impression is that some tidal wave of Time has swept into it all kinds of articles caught up in the ruin of the ancient world of Egypt, Greece, Rome—those three great early civilizations are the chief contributors, though, of course, Assyria and Babylon are represented too.

Nearly everything you see has come from a tomb. There are hundreds of thousands of objects from the tombs of ancient Egypt. There is blue, green, and gold glass from tombs in Cyprus; there is amazing coloured glass blown by Phoenicians at the time of the Exodus, and—to come down to quite modern times—there are lamps which lit the ancient Romans to bed a thousand years ago, and Greek vases with shaggy, horned satyrs leaping round them after flying nymphs.

There are bronzes green with age, bright gold which never loses its colour no matter how old it is, shining glazed pottery which looks as if it had come yesterday from Staffordshire, save for the fact that it is finer than modern pottery and contains a rough scratched cross and the words in Latin: 'Caius, his plate.'

*   •*   *   *   *

What is the charm of it? What chains these men to the past, archaeologist and collector? Most of them are poor, for there is no money in it, and most of them are intensely happy.

Just see the way they finger a bronze that was cast when St. Paul was bearing the message of Christianity through the world. There is perhaps one part aestheticism in their love and one part association. For them an object is not only full of beauty but also full of magic; it is like a talisman that has the power to call up visions. I have no doubt that when these old men hold their treasures they can see the hosts of Pharaoh sweeping through Syria, the nodding of the plumes, the drive of arrows and all the confusion of an ancient war. They can recreate round a relic a dead empire. They feel that they possess something of the mighty personality of old times just as in millions of lives a treasured letter can call up 'the touch of a vanished hand and the sound of a voice that is still.'

In these old things the Past lives again; they release the

perfume of old loves, the violence of old ambitions, the thunder of marching troops, and the sailing of galleys over a morning world.

* * * * *

So if you collide violently with an old man who is carefully holding a little paper parcel, do not blame him for not seeing you.

You! Good Lord—*you!*

MADAME requires a gown. In a building above a celebrated street in the heart of London, M. Flair bows her to a gold couch on which are cushions of green velvet.

M. Flair has descended with dignity and charm to middle age, and everyone seems to forgive him for smelling strongly of jasmine. This apartment with the gold and black striped cushions, the dove-grey walls, the black carpet, the green jade hangings, and its scent like that of Paris is not a shop: it is a *salon*. If you pulled out a bunch of crackling fivers and offered in an honest straightforward way to pay M. Flair for one of his gowns—I mean 'creations'—he would, I imagine, appear insulted. He would much rather sue you in the usual way. He is an artist. Lady So-and-So blazons his genius along the Côte d'Azur; Miss So-and-So does him credit on the stage, so that, as he bends over Madame, cooing slightly, the tips of his manicured fingers together, there is no condescension in him. Oh, dear, no! He is a psychologist.

*   *   *   *   *

Madame requires a gown.

It must, I fear, be said that Madame has been requiring gowns for well over forty years, and, lately, requiring them shorter in the skirt, with an ever-increasing touch of spring-time over them. So M. Flair, after lightly discussing the season in the south of France and dismissing Switzerland with a shrug, whispers a word to a sylph in black and—more bowing—offers Madame a small brown Russian cigarette.

*   *   *   *   *

'Charming! delicious . . . ah, exquisite!'

These words come lightly from Madame as the grey curtains part at the end of the room, and there dawn, swaying slightly, hands on narrow hips, several visions of beauty clothed, it seems, too perfectly from their neat, sharp shoes to their tight little hats.

One mannequin is fair, another is dark, a third is petite, a fourth is tall. Each one is the perfection of her type—too perfect. As each sways up to Madame over the black carpet she gives Madame one half-smiling look in the eyes, then turns, lingers, sways a little, and slowly goes. Sometimes Madame puts out a hand and touches a gown. The mannequin stands like a piece of machinery suddenly stopped. All the time M. Flair remains with one plump hand on the gold couch, explaining, expounding, and, at length, advising. Here we have thin ice. Dangerous ice. M. Flair knows Madame's age and the lines of her figure. Madame has forgotten the first and has never really appreciated the second. This is where M. Flair earns his money. Just as he is bringing her—oh, so cleverly—away from a Maytime gown to one nearer August, the curtains part, and into the scented room glides a Golden Girl—sweet as April sun.

Ah, now we approach the comedy; now the plot thickens; now Madame permits the white ash of her slim brown cigarette to fall unnoticed on the black floor. That splendid, cunning fall of the cloth, revealing that which it professes to cover; that fine swing of rounded hips; those beautiful young arms, unmasked at the elbow, free yet from the wicked little wizened witch's face time puts there. Yes; a lovely gown! Madame looks at April and—sees herself!

M. Flair knows that the game is up. He realizes, with the instinct of a lifetime's experience, that no matter what he can say Madame will have nothing but the unsuitable magnificence worn by this most marvellous of mannequins. The artist in him wars with the business man. He feels that he should forbid it. Refuse to sell. Explain to Madame that she will not look like the Golden Girl; that she is deluding herself. Yet why?

Madame, with a woman's swift knowledge of unspoken things, says:

'So you think it's a bit too—too young?'

She appears frank, careless; but there is such a touch of hardiness in her voice, velvet over steel. It is a challenge to M. Flair to say 'Yes,' and what man would have the moral courage?

'My dear lady,' he says with uplifted hands. 'What a ridiculous idea!'

Then, when she has gone, he says to me: 'You see how it is—O mon Dieu!'

*   *   *   *   *

'Yes, but the Golden Girl,' I say. 'How did anything so beautiful happen in the world? The racehorse lines of her, the slimness, the strength. Is she one of these exiled princesses? She must stand on a pyramid of good breeding.'

'Oh, no,' replies M. Flair; 'her father was, I believe, a coalporter somewhere in London. If only her accent were a little better she might . . . the stage . . . success . . . but—O *mon Dieu*, these women who do not know themselves!'

So ends an ordinary little comedy of a London day.

I WENT into a City church the other day to hear a sermon that has been going on for three hundred and twenty years!

St. Mary Aldermary (not Aldermanbury) is an attractive Wren church tucked away on the north side of Queen Victoria Street. When I entered, I found about forty middle-aged men and twelve women. They were sitting about the church listening to a clergyman who was leaning earnestly over the pulpit talking about sin, the devil, and St. Paul. It was luncheon-hour in the City. It was also raining with ghastly persistence, and I thought at first that this congregation of fifty numbered many who might have sought refuge from the weather. A second glance assured me that this was an unworthy thought; here was an audience of devout, middle-aged City men with every mark of them of regular attendance. The rows of bald or grizzled heads were inclined towards the speaker, every word was followed with deep interest, save in one corner, where a little old man in a frock coat appeared to slumber.

'And what does St. Paul say. . . .'

The voice echoed round the church, and I smiled to think that I was listening to one of the longest sermons on record —a sermon that has been in progress for three hundred and twenty years! It happened like this.

*   *   *   *   *

There was once an ancient church in Watling Street called St. Anthonie's or vulgarly, St. Antholin's. It must have been an interesting church. It was full, in its later period, of Presbyterian fire and fury. It was also full of epitaphs, one of which I cannot resist quoting. It covered the bones of Sir Thomas Knowles, Mayor of London about 1399:

> *Here lyeth graven under this stone*
> *Thomas Knowles, both flesh and bone,*
> *Grocer and alderman, years forty,*
> *Sheriff and twice mayor, truly;*
> *And for he should not lye alone,*
> *Here lyeth with him his good wife Joan.*
> *They were together sixty year,*
> *And nineteen children they had in feere.*

Two hundred years after this remarkable epitaph, St. Antholin's became notorious as the headquarters of the Puritan clergy. The bell used to ring at unearthly hours of the morning, and all the High Churchmen in Cheapside turned uneasily in their beds and perhaps politely gnashed their teeth. In 1599 a group of citizens founded a lectureship. They gave certain property in London which was to pay for a daily lecture in the pulpit of St. Antholin's. The church became famous as a lecture theatre. Lilly, the astrologer, used to go there. Scott makes Mike Lambourne refer to it in 'Kenilworth.'

The Great Fire burned down the church; still the daily lecture went on; it was rebuilt and the lecture was continued in the new St. Antholin's; it was demolished in 1870, and the lecture was transferred to St. Mary Aldermary, where I heard it yesterday.

The sermon ended. The congregation rose. The little old man in the frock coat, who I imagined was deep in sleep, sprang to his feet and boomed 'Amen!'

'I've been here twenty-five years,' said a verger, 'and most of the people you see here are regular attendants. That old man in a frock coat was here when I came.'

*   *   *   *   *

In a solicitor's office in Cannon Street I picked up the strings of a romance that has been acted time and again in London. As the property bought in 1599 went on increasing in value, the St. Antholin lecture increased from one a week to two a week. Still the property increased in value, and funds accumulated till it was necessary to have a sermon every day, except Saturday.

'The conditions on which the lectures are to be delivered are all set down in the old deeds,' said one of the solicitors who administers the lectureship. 'The clergyman who preaches must be a rector in charge of two thousand souls, must not live more than seven miles as the crow flies from the Mansion House, and must not have a stipend of over £300.'

Some of the clergy who took up this three hundred and twenty year old sermon and carried it on for a while now wear bishop's gaiters.

So in the calm of these days the Puritanical fury of three

hundred and twenty years ago, filtered through three centuries, goes on and on and on in the City of London! If the worthy old citizens came back from the Shades they would not be able to find their old church, but the Voice they subsidized still speaks, and the property they left . . . well, they would have the shock of their lives!

THE place is generally blue with smoke and it smells strongly of grilled chops.

It is full of men: men eating and talking. Some do not remove their overcoats or hats, although the rooms are uncomfortably warm. This spot is remarkable only for the fact that it is one of the last eating-houses in London which does not cater for, or encourage the presence of, women. Sometimes a woman finds her way in, and all the men look up curiously, as early Victorians might have done to see a lone woman in a chop-house. They blink at her. They watch her covertly as she eats, not impudently, but with a slight pity, for she is, poor thing, unwittingly transgressing an unwritten law. She had no right to be there! Generations of males have marked this place out as a feeding-place, and the funny thing is that no matter how you admire women generally, and adore some individually, you feel unhappy when you see one there. You want to put a screen round her and forget her. She is all wrong there. It is like going to your tailors and finding a pretty girl being measured for a costume. It surprises and unsettles your conception of the fitness of things.

Through the smoke and the stimulating smell—which I believe is a kind of barrage put up against the feminine—move women and girls of a type quite different from the usual waitress. They resemble more the handmaids of inns in, say, the time of Sterne. They have a sharp, ready way with them, and they regard the zoo of hungry men dependent on them with the faint superiority of the ministering female. They treat elderly barristers who inquire testily for an overdue sausage rather like a school matron reproving a greedy boy.

How efficient they are! They blow down a tube and order, all at once, a sole, two grilled sausages, liver and bacon, a chop and apple tart, and never do they make a mistake in their destinations.

At first sight you might think that everybody comes here because it is cheap. A second glance shows you a curious assortment. There are celebrated barristers—the Lord Chief Justice often used to go there when he was Attorney-General—solicitors, journalists, at least one solemn editor of a literary monthly, and a floating population of publishers' readers, poets, authors, and others with business in the Street of Misadventure.

On your left, two barristers discuss a case; on your right two newspaper men whisper all the things not yet printed in a murder or conspiracy trial, and in the corner two or three men, who have not lost their undergraduate voices, argue about an unpublished novel.

'Of course, the residuary legatee is in exactly the same position as that in Rex *v.* Tolbooth, and I therefore think you will agree. . . .'

This from the left. From the right:

'The police know perfectly well who did it, but they daren't say so—yet. Of course, you've heard . . .' And from the corner:

'You can't do it with your tongue in your cheek! You must be sincere! You must believe in it, no matter how bad it is. Have you read——'

Then, slowly, peevishly, comes the inevitable Dickensian, the old man whose collars and neckties seem deathless, whose clothes have a queer cut, whose hat, while it does not actually challenge modernity, does not conform to any current mode. He is angry. Some young upstart is sitting at *his* table, the table at which he has probably eaten about fifteen thousand chops. Ancient kings must have looked like this when they caught a virile baron trying on the crown. Insolence and— worse! Much worse. An awful reminder to a man of habit! Some day . . . ah, well, that day has not come, and, until it does, he will sit at that particular table and eat his chop with his particular knife and fork. So he stands about glowering and fidgeting, the bland young man calmly eating, an innocent usurper.

But the clash between man and man is as nothing compared with the drama of a woman's entrance. Most women reach the door and, instinctively realizing that they have blundered into man's last stronghold, beat a tactful retreat, coughing slightly. Now and again some insensitive or ignorant man actually brings a poor woman there. Sex consciousness is a queer thing. Go into a telephone exchange where you are the only man and see how you like it. These women, who suddenly dawn like a crime in the unwritten convention of this place, must feel it too; but women are so accustomed to scrutiny.

Is it fancy or does an uneasy silence pass like a cloud over the babel of law, newspaper, and book talk? I wonder.

Anyhow, it is remarkable to find any place in London in which woman is an anachronism, and no doubt the day is coming when she will storm even this barricade and—then we may have more comfortable chairs and nicer tables and a change in wallpaper!

Our Roman Bath

AN American once told me in Vienna that the Strand possesses a Roman bath well worth seeing, but, being a good Londoner, I did not believe him—until I went there.

This bath, which was constructed in A.D. 200—seventeen hundred years ago—is opposite Bush House, in the Strand. Think of that. Bush House and Rome! It is in the basement of No. 5, Strand Lane, an astonishing, narrow, dingy alley that, in one step, takes you back to the darkest days of Victorian London, when lanterns glimmered in passages and 'Peelers' twirled truncheons and wore stove-pipe hats. No. 5 belongs to the Rev. Pennington Bickford, Rector of St. Clement Danes, who bought the house a few years ago to save the bath, which was—O incredible London!—in danger of destruction.

After writing my name in a school exercise book, which contains addresses in China, Japan, America, Canada, Australia (but few in London), I was taken by an intelligent young man into a high-vaulted place of red brick. What a splendid bath. How different from the bathrooms of modern London, which are tucked away in houses like afterthoughts. Even a rich man I know, who has ten bathrooms in his house, has no bath as fine as this. It is, of course, sunk in the floor. It is fifteen feet six inches in length by six feet nine inches—a proper lovable, wallowable bath, built by the only nation that understood baths and bathing.

It is an apse-headed oblong in shape, and I have seen exactly the same thing in the Roman ruins of Timgad, among the mountains of North Africa. No doubt it belonged to some rich Roman who built his villa seventeen hundred years ago some distance from busy London, so that his wife and children might enjoy the flowers of the Strand, the peace, and the river.

The young custodian took a long-handled ladle and dipped it into the clear, limpid water which for seventeen centuries has been trickling into the bath. It comes from an unknown spring bubbling from a 'fault' in the London clay.

'You'd be surprised at the visitors, mostly Canadians and Americans, who want to take off their clothes and plunge in,' said the guide, 'not because it's a Roman bath, but because

Dickens used to bathe here, and mentions it in Chapter thirty-five of "David Copperfield."'

'And do you ever let them?'

'Not likely! When I tell them how cold it is they change their minds. It's always three degrees above freezing.'

'How do you know?'

'Because I fell in once,' he replied simply.

*   *   *   *   *

I tried hard, as I stood there on the level of Roman London, thirty feet below the London of to-day, to picture this spot in its glory. It was no doubt tiled with veined marble, and the London spring water ran in over marble, and the roof perhaps held frescoes showing nymphs and fauns and Pan playing his pipes.

Signor Matania, the artist, has made a fine picture of this bath as he thinks it was when Roman ladies came there to swim without bathing costumes. A pretty picture, but— was the water ever deep enough?

'Some think it was a hot bath, and some think it was a cold one,' said the guide, 'but nobody knows. Perhaps we shall know when Mr. Bickford digs underneath, as he wants to do, in search of the heating system.'

*   *   *   *   *

I climbed up out of Roman London, and a few steps took me to the sight of Bush House and omnibuses racing past to Charing Cross.

'WHAT is the strangest thing a Londoner has lost?' I asked an official of the Lost Property Office in Scotland Yard.

'Well, let's see. Two leg bones came in last week. They had obviously been left in a tramcar by a medical student. Once we had somebody's appendix in oil; but I think the funniest thing I ever remember a man losing—and I've been here thirty-three years—was a tree-climbing bear. Alive? I should say he was alive! You ought to have seen him climb up to the mantelshelf. It turned out that he had been left in a cab by a Scotsman who owned him. This man had been abroad for a long time, and was paying his first visit to London after many seafaring years abroad. Apparently he was so excited to be back that he forgot all about his bear. He left it in a four-wheeler. He remembered next morning, and jolly glad we were, too, for, although we get all kinds of strange things in this department, it's not organized like a zoo.'

During thirty-three years in the Lost Property Office this official has seen a great change in London's crop of forgetfulness.

'Muffs have stopped coming in now,' he said. 'Once we were full of muffs; but women don't carry them nowadays. Everything else has increased, not because people are more absentminded, but because the speed of traffic has increased. We take only objects found in omnibuses, tramcars, and taxicabs. In the old days you could run after a horse omnibus and find your umbrella, but to-day as soon as you remember you have left it the vehicle is out of sight. Just look here!'

We walked down a long avenue packed with umbrellas. There may have been twenty thousand of them perhaps. The avenue ended in a room full of the more recently abandoned specimens. Here men and women were nosing round looking for their lost property. What a task! The room was stacked to the ceiling with umbrellas, all neatly docketed. They lay in racks, the handles only protruding.

When handles are round and shiny this room, which is always full, presents to the eye four walls of round and shiny knobs; when the fashion in umbrellas changes, this room changes too. At the moment it is full of originality and colour. Thousands of green jade and red coral handles jut from the walls; thousands of check handles vary the pattern. Here and there you see a dog-headed handle, a handle shaped like a bird, or a handle carved to the shape of a pierrot's head, a pathetic white face with drooping carmine lips, which seems crying to be claimed and taken home.

'Oh, I shall never find it in this forest of umbrellas!' cried a girl. 'Never! I don't think I want to. I hate the look of umbrellas.'

Another woman picked her umbrella out in the first five minutes. What an eye! And all the time girls came up to the counter, rather breathless, with:

'I've lost a lovely new umbrella on a number three omnibus; it had a dear little green handle carved like a fish, and I said to mother——'

'Come inside, miss,' said a weary official.

'I said to mother that I think I lost it when I got off at Westminster, or it may have been earlier in the morning, when——'

'Come inside, miss!'

More remarkable even than the jungle of lost umbrellas is the series of rooms packed with every conceivable thing a passenger can carry in a tramcar, an omnibus, or a taxicab. You gain the impression when you tour the Lost Property Office that some people would lose an elephant between Ludgate Circus and Charing Cross.

How do they lose full-size typewriters, gigantic suit-cases packed with clothes, gramophones, bulky parcels, crates, and small perambulators?

There are thousands of lost shoes, mostly new, some of them dance slippers bought by forgetful girls, or perhaps by husbands who were thinking of something else. There are ball dresses that have been left in omnibuses, silk nightdresses, hats, costumes, and, of course, jewellery.

The Lost Property Office looks like a gigantic pawnshop or a large secondhand store. The officials are surprised at nothing. Have they not taken care of skulls and the hands of mummies?

In another room I saw October's crop of lost umbrellas being distributed to the tramcar conductors, the omnibus conductors, and the taxicab men who found them. This happens every three months. If it did not, Scotland Yard would have to build an annexe somewhere. The finders made merry as they were given incongruous umbrellas. One large, red taxicab driver drew a neat little mincing silk umbrella with a kingfisher on the handle.

'Oh, how sweet, Bill!' said the tram conductors.

*   *   *   *   *

At the other end of the office, other conductors were handing in dozens of umbrellas and sticks: the ceaseless daily harvest of London's wonderful absent-mindedness, Most of them had wrist straps, too!

EVEN as I write, Piccadilly is changing. Eros, attended by the ghosts of undergraduates, has stepped from the pinnacle, thus evacuating the post of honour from which he has gazed upon the follies of our fathers, those wicked men who used to wait outside stage doors with bouquets before sneaking off somewhere to dine with a real actress. Ah, those must have been good days. . . .

So before the circle is squared, which seems quite unnatural, I wish to write about the flower 'girls.' Early in the morning, long before the first pair of silk stockings had been sold in Regent Street, the 'girls' dipped their violets in the Fountain and camped out on the steps. What a perfect picture they made. It always seemed to me that some unknown admirer of Phil May was secretly subsidizing them, paying for them, working, maybe, to stamp on the national mind a sharp memory of plaid shawls tight over plump shoulders, apple-red faces beneath black straw hats. In the spring they brought the first real news to the West End with their laughing prim-roses, big tight gold bunches of them; and the Fountain was a joy to behold.

'Vi'lets pennigabunch.'

That was, of course, long ago. I believe they are sixpence or more now; but the old cry from the Fountain has been remembered all over the earth wherever men have thought of Piccadilly.

The flower 'girls' of Piccadilly presented to London the most marvellous study in polite indifference. Here they were in occupation of the very centre of the world with the feminine beauty and elegance of every country always before their eyes. They remained unaffected. They were the only women in London moving in fashionable London circles who did not care a hang for the changing mode. They had sold violets to women in bustles; they had seen skirts sweep the ground, they had seen the dawn of the leg, from the hobble skirt to the knee skirt. Never once in their history did they show the instinct of their sex to imitate.

These middle-aged women who are always 'girls' have become international. American women said: 'Why, they're just sweet,' Frenchwomen thought they were almost chic,

THE " GIRLS," PICCADILLY

and sometimes a grey old man, sickened by the degeneracy of these times, would wander up from the direction of Pall Mall to buy a buttonhole just to hear himself called 'dearie,' and to know that there was still something in London that had not changed. They were Victorian London.

When I heard that Eros was to disappear and that the 'girls' were to be moved away, I had the same kind of shock that a Roman under the Empire might have suffered if a friend had moved his thumb in the direction of the Palatine Hill and had remarked: 'Have you heard? The Old Man's sacked the Vestal Virgins!'

Preposterous! The 'girls' *were* our vestal virgins—they kindled each day memory of a fast-vanishing London.

*   *   *   *   *

I found one in Piccadilly the other day. She had taken up a stand on a street refuge, from which she could command sight of her former pitch.

'No, dearie,' she said. 'Piccadilly's gorn to the dorgs, strite it 'as. Life ain't what it was, nor never will be agin with this squarin' of a plice what was meant to be a circus. It ain't right. Who'd 'ave thought we should leave the Fountain— ever. Some say we can go beck there when they've done messin' it about, but I don't believe it. I'm Mrs. Wise, I'm am. There ain't no green in my eye. . . .

'And this job ain't what it once was—not by half. No, dearie! In the old days every kebbie had his buttonhole, and no gent was dressed unless he had one too. And the drivers of the old horse omnibuses! They were rare customers—nice, pleasant men, too, who liked to pass the time of day with you and talk. Now there's no time for talk or flowers.'

She nodded enigmatically.

'Young men don't like to be seen carrying flowers to-day, but I can tell you their fathers didn't mind—and better men they were, if I'm any judge of a man, and I ought to be, seeing I've been sat in Piccadilly Circus all me life. . . .'

Then she said something that sent a chill to my heart:

'My gels ain't going to waste their lives sitting here, I can tell you. Emma going into pickles, and Maud, she's in millinery.'

This, of course, is the end! A flower girl's calling is

hereditary. It descends through the distaff side. The next generation of 'girls' are, it appears, going into commerce, and there will be none to follow on.

It is sad. If I were a millionaire, I would subsidize them and buy a hansom cab and an old pensioned cab-horse to stand there too.

*   *   *   *   *

For in the fret and change of these days the flower 'girls' of Piccadilly looked so permanent with the surge of London round them, so indifferent to change, so typical of an easier day, as they sold their flowers in that whirl of gladness and sadness, beauty and ugliness, which is the heart of London: the heart of the world.

THE SPELL OF LONDON

O gray, O gloomy skies!   What then?
Here is a marvellous world of men;
More wonderful than Rome was, when
        The world was Rome.
See the great stream of life flow by!
Here thronging myriads laugh and sigh,
Here rise and fall, here live and die:
        In this vast home.

        LIONEL JOHNSON

The Spell of London ⟡ ⟡ ⟡ ⟡ ⟡

CAN you analyse a spell? How it is possible to capture in words a thing elusive as a dream that flies between sleeping and waking?

I suppose that every man and woman in this world who has suffered the wonder of being loved has at some time asked:

'But *why* do you love me?'

The unsatisfying, conclusive answer never varies.

'Because you are You!'

*　　*　　*　　*　　*

I was walking along the Embankment one night, a fretful autumn night with a movement of clouds across a small pale moon, and I stopped before Cleopatra's Needle, wondering how I would reply if a sphinx in that magic place whispered:

'Why do you love London?'

Would I consider a moment, as if on the edge of great eloquence, and reply, as usual:

'Because London is London!'

No doubt I would. But it might not go down very well with a sphinx who had troubled to whisper. She might say:

'I am rather tired of riddles and, as I am half a woman, I would like to hear someone make love to me on this vile night with rain coming and such a cold little moon in the sky. Couldn't you try to be less vague; couldn't you begin like this: "Sphinx of London, I love you because . . ." Then you might go on and say something warming. . . .'

Woman!

*　　*　　*　　*　　*

'Sphinx of London, I love you because you have a distinct way with you, a spell, a beauty, and such amazing character. You do not give smiles to anyone who can foot a bill, as Paris does; you require, Sphinx, some considerable understanding, so much, in fact, that people often begin to love you by first hating you. There is nothing cheap and tawdry in your soul; and in that soul is knowledge of everything that can happen to a human being—all the tears of sorrow and all the smiles of joy.'

153

'Please go on. . . . Beauty?'

'Yes; you have astounding beauty. I think Whistler told you that once. In the quick mists that enchant you is the sure beauty that brings tears to the eyes: characteristic beauty, Sphinx, which is a thousand miles from prettiness; and it often happens that suddenly you shine out in glory, so it seems that a man is seeing you clearly for the first time and is rooted to the earth in cold sorrow because he can never hope to paint you. . . .

'And to go away from you, London, is often to come nearer to you in loneliness, in strange places, when a memory of how it feels to ride down the Strand in rain on top of a 'bus is like remembering something lovely about your mother. It is then that you seem to see the gulls on the Thames, all fluttering white at Blackfriars; then that you seem to feel the streets full of a life you understand—that is part of you—it is then that you seem to see the great black dome riding high on Ludgate Hill; and London appears before you more than a home: a spiritual anchorage perhaps, in which you think you would stand a chance of happiness. You sit about in strange cities thinking: "At this very minute Piccadilly is an avenue of amber lights on tip-toe with the thrill of theatres, taxi doors are snapping on a vision of silk ankles, two men in silk hats are standing in a crowd on an island, all the wide club windows are yellow, the Green Park trees are spectral white in lamp-light, and the omnibuses stand like a herd of patient red bulls behind a white gloved hand." Ah! London, dear London. . . .'

'Don't stop!'

'And you can be damnably cruel, so flint hard that when the sound of you comes through a window in the dawn a sleeper, awakening, shudders and hides his head, fearing you. Yet you may smile on him and he will almost forget that you were ever cruel. . . . I said almost, Sphinx, I hope you heard that!'

'And?'

'And then . . . well; I love you because—you are You.'

*   *   *   *   *

The little pale moon looked out of a flurry of cloud and I walked on. The Sphinx registered no emotion.

IT was a quarter to ten on a fine evening. A taxicab, cruising along Piccadilly, pulled to the kerb beside me.

'The Tower of London,' I said.

I suppose he had often been ordered to strange places at strange hours, but this seemed to surprise him, and it is something of an achievement to surprise a London taxicab driver. He looked interested.

'Right up to the gate, sir?' he asked doubtfully.

'Right up to the gate,' I replied.

We sped down crowded, glowing Piccadilly, into Trafalgar Square, along the dark Embankment, and into the deserted City of London. We rattled over Tower Hill and drew up with the grey, shrouded fortress piled behind its moat on our left, faintly white, grim, ghostly. In the shadows of the barrier gate, a figure moved; lamplight shone a second on a bayonet and picked out a sentry's scarlet tunic.

'I have permission to see "the Keys,"' I said.

A warder stepped out. 'Follow me'; and I went on to the most ghostly scene in London—the Tower, at night.

*   *   *   *   *

Imagine those great gates leaning against the stars, with here and there a little casement window gold against the black; lamplight flinging the shadow of walls over the stones —sharp black and faint grey—and through the wide arch of the Byward Tower a luminous vista of turrets and battlements lying silent like a dream of Camelot.

The centuries fall away every night when darkness comes to the Tower of London. If any spot on earth is haunted, here it is. From those eerie gateways, those unexpected postern gates, from those shadowy, machiolated walks what might not come in the silence of the night . . . what white woman wringing her hands; what sad favourite of kings. . . .

The head warder, wearing a scarlet cloak, and a black-ribboned Tudor bonnet, came from the Byward Tower carrying a bunch of keys and an old lantern, in which burned a tallow candle. He stood waiting, a splendid touch of colour in the dark frame of a gate spiked across by the bars of the old portcullis. He looked at his watch. It was not quite ten o'clock.

*   *   *   *   *

For centuries the head warder of the Tower has waited like this every night to parade the King's Keys, with curious ceremony; to lock the vast oak gates, and turn the Tower again into a moated medieval stronghold barred against the perils of the night. Few people have seen this ceremony, and when it began, and by whom, no one knows. The ritual is lost in history. It may be as old as the Tower of London.

The head warder strode off towards the Wakefield Tower, his boots ringing on the stones, the lantern bobbing at his side making a yellow moon on his scarlet cloak. Through the gate of the Bloody Tower is the guardroom. Outside this, he paused and cried in a loud voice:

'Escort for the Keys!'

There was a clatter of military boots and a thud of rifle butts as a sergeant and four men fell in. With the Keys and the swaying lantern in the middle, they moved off.

As the sentries saw the approach of the little procession with its dancing lantern, they shouldered their rifles and—ferlick-crack!—they saluted. So the King's Keys passed on into the outer ward.

*   *   *   *   *

Each sentry on the march to the barrier gate saluted as the Keys went by.

At the wicket gate, the escort halted. The warder closed the gates, the escort turned about and . . . once more the ringing of feet on the stones and the glitter of the lantern. I stood by Traitors' Gate—jet-black bars and water steps in a pool of lamplight—and watched them return towards the Bloody Tower; only this time they paused at the Middle Tower, and the two huge walls of oak were slowly moved and the great gate locked. The same at the Byward Tower. Now they approached the Bloody Tower, returning to the guard-room. In the darkness of the arch the sentry stamped on the ground with his foot and cried:

'Halt! Who comes there?'

The head warder, with the Keys and the escort, stood still.

'The Keys!' the warder answered.

'Whose keys?' demanded the sentry.

'King George's Keys!'

'Advance, King George's Keys—all's well!'

Tramp, tramp went the men with the King's Keys up the slope through the pitch black gate of the Bloody Tower to the guardroom. Here on the terrace the guard was drawn up in charge of an officer with a drawn sword. The lamps shone over the uniforms, glittered on scarlet tunics, buttons, naked steel, and high bearskins.

The men with the King's Keys stood at the foot of the steps, facing the guard. The officer cried:

'Guard and escort, present arms!'

Up went his sword hilt to his mouth, and down it flashed in salute as the rifles went flick—flock—crack in a cloud of pipeclay. So they stood a second. The head warder then took two paces forward, removed his Tudor bonnet, and cried:

'God preserve King George!'

The guard, from the officer to the drummer boy, answered: 'Amen!'

The guard dismissed; the warder mounted a flight of dim steps with the Keys, which he took to the house of the Governor of the Tower for safe custody through the night. A bell-like clock among the grey turrets . . . a sentry paced in the darkness of the gate . . . clear on the air sounded a bugle playing 'The Last Post.'

The Tower of London was locked up!

No man could now move without the countersign. Each gate meant detention if you did not know it. From the outside world of London, no man could enter unless he knew that secret password, changed each night and sent to the King each day.

As it was a thousand years ago, so it is every night when the King's Keys go by. . . .

Out into the empty gauntness of Tower Hill I went, feeling that I had fallen for a little while into some ancient dream.

'NO; there's no lift!' said an official of the Palace of Westminster (which is the correct title for the Houses of Parliament when the House is up), 'and there are three hundred and seventy-four steps up to Big Ben, which get my rheumatism something cruel when I have to go up three or four times a day.'

We stood that evening in Palace Yard and gazed upwards at the clock as critical mountaineers regard an alp before they climb it. It seemed, in my imagination, to grow higher and higher as I looked, like something in 'Alice in Wonderland.' The official then unlocked a little door in the base of the clock tower, and we ascended a narrow spiral staircase. We had, perhaps, mounted two hundred steps when, without any warning, the narrow stone tube in which we were entombed became filled with a sound so violent, so furious, and so powerful that it was terrifying—as though some horrible monster imprisoned in the tower had roared out in anger. The sound beat against my ear drums and seemed to go right through my body like X-rays. It rumbled and pounded at the stones till it seemed that they must disintegrate into dust and fall like the walls of Jericho.

It was frightening. I stood still. Theseus, I think, felt just like this when he heard the Minotaur bellowing in the darkness of the Labyrinth.

'Half-past four!' said my guide calmly.

It was only the clock above politely telling London that it was time for tea.

We mounted onward and upward.

*   *   *   *   *

He unlocked a door, and I walked into the works of Big Ben. (It is wrong to call the clock Big Ben, for that is the name of the great bell which chimes the hours; but never mind!) Was there ever such a clock? In the middle of a room, round which you could drive a two-seater car, stood a mass of wheels on an iron frame. They reminded me of a flat-bed printing machine. From this machine radiated four long steel tubes bearing the clock hands to the four round dials of Big Ben. One of the dials was visible to me: a huge round glass window bigger than the rose window of a cathedral. I could see the shadow of the fourteen-foot minute hand lying across it like a spear. I went up and measured the space between the minutes. There was a foot between each minute marked on the face of the clock. The Roman numerals were two feet in height.

'Two men stripped to the waist used to wind this clock,' said my guide, 'but now we do it with an electric motor.'

He was gazing with affection at the works, so I joined him. The big machine appeared to be asleep, except for one little wheel that went tick-tack every other second.

'Come and look at the pendulum!'

Big Ben is the grandfather of all clocks. He works on a thirteen feet long pendulum with a bob on the end which weighs four hundredweight.

'What is that halfpenny doing on the pendulum?'

'That adjusts it. Although it is so big, the slightest weight affects it, and I suppose the man who last regulated the clock discovered that it needed a halfpenny to keep it dead right.'

Suddenly the high room was filled with light: and I knew that the four faces of Big Ben were now like four yellow moons above the dusk of a London evening.

* * * * *

We mounted a maze of openwork staircases above the works of the clock, and there I saw Big Ben, the great bell, hanging with four Little Bens round him. Big Ben speaks only once an hour, but the four chimes sing the quarters and the half-hours. Big Ben is a monster. He would, if inverted, make a good public swimming bath. At his side reposes in a threatening attitude a vast hammer that weighs four hundredweights and looks like a battering ram.

And, while I waited to hear him strike five, I went up and out to the balcony round that nautical-looking lantern which is always lit at night while the Speaker is in the chair, so that absent M.P.'s may know where their duty lies. . . .

Below lay London lovelier, I think, than I have ever seen her, with an evening mist, blue and patchy, trailing in slow wreaths over her, settling down over her like a fallen cloud so that Nelson at Charing Cross stood up jet black like a cairn above the mist on a mountain top. And the streets were strings of lit lamps: long avenues of amber mellowness in which there was movement, from which ascended a dull, uniform roar of wheels. The towers of Westminster Abbey stood with their feet in a thin blue haze.

'Come quickly!' shouted my guide from the platform near the bells.

I ran down and stood leaning over an iron fence, watching the great nest of five bells, as the passenger in a ship leans over the deck rail.

No warning: and then——

Startling, hair-raising sound broke suddenly from the four Little Bens and ran round them again. Before every hour they say:

> All through this hour, Lord, be my guide,
> And, by Thy Power, no foot shall slide.

Then they stop to let Big Ben do his gigantic bit. . . .

It seemed that Big Ben gathered himself together to tell London that it was five o'clock. In a flash the great battering ram drew itself apart from the bell, and——

Bang!

It seemed to me that a howitzer had fired a shell. . . .

Bang!

It seemed to me that Big Ben was striking in my head. . . .

Bang!

It seemed to me that the tower of the Houses of Parliament could not remain erect another minute. . . .

Bang!

It seemed to me that the whole of London must surely be alarmed by this!

Bang!

It seemed to me very beautiful that it was not twelve o'clock!

*   *   *   *   *.

The hammer came to rest against the hard cheek of Big Ben, but the sound went on and on and on up there in the clock tower. It was shattering, unforgettable. I looked down into London, but no one seemed surprised. . . .

On the way earthwards in the spiral tube, I sank into an angry rumble of sound: the echoes of the great noise made when Big Ben keeps one of his many appointments with Eternity.

Among the Kings   *o*   *o*   *o*   *o*   *o*

ONE night not long ago I stood under the Arc de Triomphe in Paris beside the grave of the French Unknown Soldier.

A keen wind from the Champs Élysées whistled through the great arch, driving the flames of the graveside braziers low over the ground like streamers of wind-blown hair. There were pale flowers and shadows. A Caesarian tomb, grand and unforgettable in the centre of a beautiful city, the sound and surge of life ever near, but. it seemed to me, in spite of all, so lonely, so cold, so far from a church, like a solitary grave on a hill-top.

Westminster Abbey. . . . I stood there recently beside our Unknown Warrior, who lies not only at the heart of London, but also at the heart of England, here in magic earth, in this sacred soil, so warm in love, so safe in honour. No noise of traffic disturbs his sleep, no unkind wind whistles over him —no solitude of night. Instead, the silence of a mighty church, a silence as deep and lovely as though he were lying in some green country graveyard steeped in peace, above him a twilight in which the stored centuries seem to whisper happily of good things done for England.

     *   *   *   *   *

There were few sightseers. It was not the season. Two elderly women sat against the pillars in the south aisle making water-colour sketches of the sweep of the arches above the choir.

In the centre of the nave, free from the barriers that once hedged it, lay the grave of the Unknown Warrior—a large black marble slab, on which a long inscription is inlaid in letters of brass. From a pillar in the north aisle near the grave hung a worn-looking Union Jack. How English! Most other nations would have explained somewhere for all to see that this is no ordinary flag, that it gained those creases, which a woman's careful ironing and pressing have been unable to efface, when it covered a rude Communion table in France with the 141st Brigade of the 47th (London) Division. When they brought the Unknown Warrior through the streets, with the sombre guns booming and the troops slow marching

THE NAVE, WESTMINSTER ABBEY

to a wail of brass, this was the flag that covered the coffin;
and there it hangs unheralded in the Abbey. In its creases
you may see—ah! how many Last Suppers in Flanders
fields. . . .

*   *   *   *   *

An official guide, wearing an armlet, came up with two
Americans, husband and wife. They read aloud the inscription:
'Beneath this stone rests the body of a British warrior,
unknown by name or rank, brought from France to lie among
the most illustrious of the land. . . .' And so on to the splendid
end: 'They buried him among the kings because he had done
good towards God and towards His House. . . .'
'That's beautiful,' they said quietly, 'That's the most
beautiful thing in London.'
'Those brass letters,' explained the guide, 'are made from
cartridge cases melted down . . . cases picked up in the British
lines in France after the war.'
They went over to the Union Jack, and beneath it they
looked at a small frame, in which is the blue-ribboned Con-
gressional Medal of Valour, the gift of the people of the
United States, the highest order in their power to bestow.

*   *   *   *   *

They went away, lingering here and there under the vast
arch of the nave. I stood there thinking. There were flowers
—a few tulips, freshly pulled, and daffodils, the first of the
year. . . .
This tomb and the Cenotaph bear witness to the greatest
emotion this nation has ever felt. Children are brought here
every year; and so the memory, without the sharpness, perhaps, felt by us who lived through it, goes on with another
generation. In this way a nation keeps alive its holy places.
Wonderful to think of this unknown boy, or man, lying here
with our kings, our captains, our prophets, and our priests.
It is the first time in the history of the world that this has
happened. His fame is greater, too; he is Everyman who died
in the War. No matter how many mothers believe that he is
theirs, they are right; they are all of them right—for he is
every mother's son who did not come home from France.

Always, as long as England stands in history, this marble stone will tell the story of the only unknown man to whom the great Abbey of Westminster opened its arms, saying: 'Come in, you Unknown Warrior, among the kings and the great ones of all time, for you too are great, you too spent your life nobly, and you too are for ever holy in the memory of this people.'

*   *   *   *   *

As I went out, a thin rustle of organ music came whispering down the nave, and far off, like a voice in a cloud, sounded the echo of a prayer.

Little Tigers ◦ ◦ ◦ ◦ ◦ ◦

IN the darkness of the night the City of London, deserted and so marvellously silent, is like a prehistoric forest of stone.

Vast cliffs, which are buildings, go up in the darkness, tall, incalculable, and between lie cañons of blackness in which no footfall sounds; the small square mile within the walls is deserted. In thousands of offices sheets cover millions of typewriters. Desks, chairs, and all the machinery of livelihood stand as if sudden death had come upon their owners. Mr. Brown's old hat hangs on a peg, pathetic evidence of absent Mr. Brown. When the prince entered the palace of the Sleeping Beauty he met this same suspended animation. A sad-faced moon, peeping from a fretful scurry of cloud, pours a pale, momentary radiance on the floor, where the envelopes of the last post lie disarrayed around the waste-paper basket. Such silence! Not even the ghost of a senior partner; not even the ghost of someone asking for a rise in salary! Just grave-yard silence. Then happens that thing which would so agitate absent peach-coloured legs—the swift rush of a rat. . . .

*   *   *   *   *

This is the hour when those, to me, interesting little people come into their own—the City cats.

In the darkness of alleys, in the unlit gloom of stairways, they sit waiting. Till the dawn they own London. Their eyes, like the eyes of witches, glitter in archways. Now and again the shrill announcement of a fierce love, or an equally fierce hate, tears the silence like a knife. Little maidenly tabby, big battling ginger, slinky black mother of many families, and great coal-black tiger, they all sit and wait, hunched up at street corners or gently padding round on their little velvet feet.

Do they sit and think of the morning, when the cats'-meat man will come mewing down the road pushing his small barrow? Do they dream of this celestial visitor, the lineal descendant of the priest in the Great Temple of Bubastis, who used to feed them four thousand years ago? (They remember him, of course!) Not a bit of it! A cat never sentimentalizes like a dog. What do they think of then? Just this. . . .

Ten thousand years drop from London when the last clerk goes home. The cats are back in the jungle. They have been enduring men and women all day with a fair show of affection. Little black mother may even have exhibited her variegated tell-tale family to an appreciative typist. It meant nothing. Day is unreal to a cat; only night exists.

Out of the night, down countless centuries, comes a call—the old jungle call—and the little tigers awaken, stretch their legs, shoot out the knives in the padded cushions of their paws, lick their lips, arch their backs, and set out on their adventures. The great stone jungle of London swallows them, as the forest used to swallow them ages ago.

*　　　*　　　*　　　*　　　*

All over London comfortable human dogs lie sleeping on blankets; sometimes their legs twitch as they dream that they are following their masters on a splendid chase, or they start and awaken at a dream of food and fire, and the imagined feel of a hand—a loving hand—playing with their ears, patting their eager, delighted bodies. Dogs have travelled far away from the wolf, but the little secret cat, and his big brother the tiger, still walk through pre-history side by side.

*　　　*　　　*　　　*　　　*

Mating and death. That is what the jungle has always offered; what London offers every night to the cat people.

Romeo may crouch in the darkness, making a sound that suggests that a small dynamo is whirring away inside him, watching Juliet, who never takes her eyes from his, moving her head as he moves, retreating as he advances. Or else it is death he is after. With rocklike patience he waits by the hole on the stairs. He does not mind how long he waits. He is assisted in his vigil by the accumulated patience and enthusiasm for a kill inherited by every ordinary cat, the legacy of, a day when the forests dipped green boughs in the water. . . .

A sound? Every muscle is magnificently taut for the spring, the claws ready. His instinct tells him that his foe is there. He has only to wait and then. . . . Does he kill coldly, without emotion, or does he blaze with the red anger of a moment in

which he is obliterated and something primitive and unaccountable inside him takes control—as human beings kill?

Now! Like a black spring, he launches himself into the
darkness, there is a scurry and a fight. He almost missed!
He crouches in the dark over his victim, singing a song of
triumph that is as old as the hills. He is a complete little
savage. A hundred centuries separate him from himself as he
is in the morning, such a perfect little black gentleman tripping
along towards his milk, affectionate, almost smiling. He is
Jekyll and Hyde. So he guards his kill, giving it a push and
growling at it.

*   *   *   *   *

'Good morning, darling,' says Mabel as she takes off her
hat in the morning. 'Was he glad to see his missus again,
bless him?'

The murderer rubs his head against her knees and goes
over to Gladys, who lisps prettily and likes him a lot. Gladys
shrieks and holds her skirt tight round her.

'Oh, look—look at vat!' she lisps. 'How can he be so nice
and sweet—he's killed a wat!'

There on the floor lies Hyde's work. But Jekyll is purring
fit to burst—little two-faced tiger.

The Passionate Triangle ⚬ ⚬ ⚬ ⚬

THEY were saying good night. . . .

I thought how marvellous are lovers' partings. A man will linger, as if snatching an hour from death, as he whispers, with the tragic expression of an explorer starting off into the unknown: 'I'll see you again to-morrow, dearest.' The girl's eyes will go vague, and she will say, 'Oh, dear!'; and sigh.

These two were trying to say good night, trying to summon up strength of mind to part, when, with the speed and the silence of Fate, a thin, strident woman came up behind and lashed a big black handbag across the man's face. The blow left a pallid, bloodless patch, in the centre of which a thin red line slowly grew large; the clasp had torn the skin.

'Now I've caught you!' cried the woman. 'I'll teach you to go trapesing about with your fancy little . . . This!' she declaimed to the growing crowd, 'this dirty little rat is my husband!'

Smack!

A second time the handbag cut across his face, and the woman reeled in her forceful enthusiasm. The man was dazed. He looked round for the girl to whom but a minute ago he had represented Romance. She had fled! The third line in the triangle had wiped itself out. He lifted his arm to his bleeding face; and then his eyes took fire and he hated.

*   *   *   *   *

I stood there mildly revolted and faintly thrilled. Heat is never so devilish as cold, or, I think, so cruel: I could not feel shocked. These two people seemed like grotesque marionettes to me: unreal, improbable. I could have understood them fighting one another in private, but not with a chorus. It was the very essence of all emotional drama seen at its lowest, the plot of most plays, the theme of most fiction, boiled down to the dregs and staged in a London by-street.

I became aware that several women had gathered round the wife and were giving her the moral support of sex sympathy against the unfaithful male. She worked herself up like a dervish. Her gasping denunciation became unintelligible. Raising her voice a tone, she poured out most unexpected abuse, and the surprising thing was that she was not a common woman: she was, as the police courts say, 'well but quietly dressed,' and, at less heated moments, it occurred to me that she probably made excellent jumpers and took in the parish magazine. A taxicab driver on the edge of the crowd blanched as he listened. I remembered that a famous surgeon once told me that it is the nicest women who say the most awful things under anaesthetics.

A revolted navvy stepped up.

"'Ere, shut that, missus!' he said. She turned on him like a panther, and he went back into private life.

The husband stood there like a frightened terrier faced by a cat, rooted there by some mistaken sense of dignity, yet longing to be anywhere else.

'I'll show you!' gasped the woman. 'Take that. . . .'

The husband parried the blow and lashed out. Two men stepped between. The woman then addressed the meeting, giving a delightfully vivid account of the other woman's appearance, morals, and ancestors. It was extremely nasty.

The husband, with a pale show of heroism, tried to defend the character of his lost love, but the handbag spoilt his best bits. . . . Things began to look ugly. She took out a hatpin. Somebody went for a policeman. . . .

An uncontrolled woman is terrible as the spirit of vengeance. I watched her and wondered how many calm women boil like this yet never spill over, never show it, never allow themselves the luxury of this. How many gentle women have this tiger hidden in them?

The man, seeking advantage of a lull in operations, slunk off, his hands in his pockets, trying to look casual; she gave a shriek and started after him, and then it was that I saw the thing that tumbled me into heartache.

'Oh, mother, mother, don't, don't!' sobbed a pretty little girl of twelve, her poor, pinched face white with terror, her poor little thin hands convulsively catching at the woman's skirts. It made me sick. That child! That poor, frightened little thing dragged into this mud! What fools grown people can be; what thoughtless fools!

The tide of battle ebbed away, the man making a running fight, the woman pressing after him, harrying him, and behind went the little girl with a face like a flower hidden in her hands.

'Mother, mother, don't—oh, don't!'

I shall not forget that; and neither will the child. Quite probably those two will make it up, for life is full of fire and water, but the child will lie awake at night trembling, remembering, hiding her face in the pillow, and crying, feeling herself in the lonely misery of youth locked away from her fellows because of this ugliness, unable to size it up, her small heart drenched in horror at this glimpse of a raw world from which the fairies have gone, never to return.

To cause that suffering is, to my mind, sin.

THIS is so true of London that I must begin by saying that I am not writing about any individual, but of a type. . . .

He comes out into Pall Mall from the direction of St. James's, at about 9.30 p.m. He is smoking a cigar. His silk hat, his evening tie, his cane are each perfect. His shoes are from Jermyn Street. Observing that grey head, that clipped white moustache, that fine skull, those blue eyes in their nest of lines, bleak and cold, the Bolshevik would shriek 'Aristocrat!' and 'Capitalist!' and envy that face and that bank account. But, as a matter of fact, this old man has only four hundred a year and a certain sense of form which has never been on sale. That is all.

He walks slowly along Pall Mall, savouring the air in a quiet way, casting a frozen eye over to the young Guardsman at the gate of Marlborough House. He comes to his club, enters up the broad steps, and there he will remain hidden behind a newspaper until it is bedtime. Then he will take out a thin gold watch, which his father gave him half a century ago, compare it with the clock on the mantelpiece, snap his watch lid with an air of finality, and go home.

*   *   *   *   *

He lives in a suite of Georgian rooms in a house let out to bachelors, old and young. There is a valet on the premises. When he has paid his rent he has just enough over to keep his tailor respectful, and to procure the whisky and cigars to which he has always been accustomed. No one ever comes to visit him. No woman ruffles his smooth life. He lives alone with the antlers of the stags he shot in '75; and over the mantelpiece hangs an old pattern cavalry sword.

His books deal mostly with dead elephants and old wars. His pictures show him, young and fresh, sitting among the subalterns in martial groups taken outside officers' messes, or, older, standing with one foot on a dead pig somewhere in India, perhaps holding up the limp paw of a tiger or sitting an alert polo pony on some vast and dusty ground. That was his life.

Who, you wonder, was the lady of the Lily Langtry era in

the silver frame and the Court plumes? Who knows? She gazes at the old man all day long with a sweet and constant expression which may, of course, be misleading. His mother, perhaps, or a favourite sister, or possibly the girl who took the right turning and married someone with a real income. You never can tell; and sensible old men do not talk, except to themselves, about the women who look at them from silver frames.

*   *   *   *   *

Every evening this old man goes into his little bedroom, where he shaves and dresses, as though he were going to a dinner-party. He ties his tie as carefully as though he were dining with a woman. (Perhaps he is.) And he sits there all alone, with the sword and the antlers, eating the neat and unspectacular meal which they bring up to him from the service kitchen. Sometimes he has a glass of claret. It is good claret. He has little of anything, but you may depend upon it that everything he has is good. His guns cost a hundred and fifty guineas fifty years ago, and they are as good as ever.

Once a year he receives a letter with a Scottish postmark inviting him to join a shooting party on a friend's estate. This is the great event of his life. The whisky bottle is not replenished and he stops his cigars.

Those beautiful Purdeys' are uncased, and he devotes days to them. He sees that every inch of them is right, and he cocks them frequently through the window at unsuspecting passers-by, or whispers 'Mark over!' and lifts them towards his Adam ceiling with a promising swiftness. His eyes look bluer and bleaker. The valet comes in sometimes and finds him just sitting and smiling in his armchair by the fire. He is happy.

The guard at King's Cross spots him for 'a real toff,' and there is much unnecessary fussing round him as he and his gun-cases are shown into the sleeping car.

Then Scotland . . . and the heather; misty days, and a big, easy country house; talk and reminiscence and shooting.

He tips the gillie two pounds, and returns to St. James's to drink water for a while.

COUNSEL lean back in their seats; the juniors arrange blue papers; partisan argument is ended; now comes impartial reasoning.

Through the oak-panelled court of the Old Bailey, stuffy it seems with the reek of discovered secrets, passes a rustle of attention. Pallid faces peer from the gallery, women in the body of the court snuggle into their furs and lean forward with slightly parted lips. All eyes are directed to the bench, where the smooth-faced judge sits in a padded chair with the Royal Arms above his head. His grave face is framed by a brindle wig, his sombre robes are lightened by a touch of scarlet, and, as his arms move about his desk, there is a softness of ermine. Here is the majesty of the law, so calm, so remote, so lifted in judgment above the arena of rhetoric. He seems to collect to himself in the supreme moment of a long trial all the power and might of British justice. He looks towards the jury-box. He is speaking in a slow, mellow voice, each word weighed in the scales of value, each sentence pedantically designed to form part of the almost perfect geometric pattern of his logic.

The virtue of a woman and the honour of a man. He deals so dispassionately with passionate things. No case this about money or a dry legal argument: an invalid wife, death, gossip, the discovery of the other woman, and a house of cards falling over a man's head. Murder or not? So he goes on, smooth, deliberate, sifting things, separating good from bad, like someone sorting flowers, putting the weeds to one side, the flowers to the other.

'And so, gentlemen of the jury, I would beg you to observe . . .' So on and so on.

*   *   *   *   *

Gentlemen of the jury. Swiftly the spot-light of the drama shifts from counsel to jury-box, and, in its blaze, twelve good men and true sit up heavily, as if oppressed by words. One feels their anxiety to have done with this weariness and to hear the click of their garden gates again. What qualification have they, one wonders, to judge the passions and the frailties and to assess the nobilities that live side by side with them?

No wigs hide their shining heads, no gowns dignify their drab clothes. They sit there: twelve dullish, ordinary men. Suppose one were in the dock, caught up in the tangle of this web, how one would search their faces for a gleam of understanding; for a trace of hope! In such circumstances how sinister can an ordinary man become.

One wonders, as they lounge gloomily or place their heads on their hands, how much they know of life and temptation, what has been their greatest sin: an intrigue, a sharp business deal?

They sit there with a man's life and a woman's virtue in the hollows of their hands; and there is no sound in court but the level voice of his lordship and the turning of his crisp papers.

In the dock a worn man, caught up in the net like a half-dead fly. What is he thinking about? Is he trying to probe the minds of the twelve men who hold his fate? Or is he, under the merciful pressure of agony, caught up in some silly memory far removed from all this: some memory of a summer's day long ago; or does he rise out of himself and look down, as in a theatre, unable to realize that this poor torn man in the dock is himself, seeing, in imagination, the small black cap, the cold words that mean death?

*   *   *   *   *

The buzz of talk rises octave by octave. The jury have retired, the judge has left his seat and gone out through a little door in the oak panelling. Barristers lean back and whisper. Women, their eyes large and emotional, move their white-gloved hands in little inexpressive gestures of excitement. The verdict must be 'Innocent.' Must be! How clearly the judge put it, how well he indicated the main line of reasoning; how he, as it were, took the prosecution and tore open the argument for all to see. . . .

An usher comes in with lifted hand and cries 'Hush!'

*   *   *   *   *

The judge and the jury have returned. The prisoner is brought up into the dock again. How white his knuckles go as he grips the rails, facing the grim jury.

Very grave and unreadable. Quickly! Get it over! Finish it! Cut short the agony of waiting. Each second is elastic.

The twelve faces tell nothing. The woman in the case, with the blood drawn from the pale oval of her face, looks up as though her burning eyes would bore into the brains of the jury, and read there that which she longs and fears to hear. The verdict, quick! Anything is better than this second's delay. . . .

'Gentlemen of the jury, have you considered your verdict?'

So cold, and yet with just a tinge of anxiety, the fine face slightly flushed.

'Not guilty, my lord!'

Through the court a great sigh and an arrested wave of clamour. The majesty of the law rises slowly, and goes out . . . a touch of red on black, and the softness of ermine.

The web has broken. The fly is free.

IT was soon to be midnight.

The Strand, yellow with light and cool after a hot day, was sinking gradually to rest, as it does when the bars and theatres have closed. A nibbled gold moon swung high over the chimney-pots. Suddenly it happened! A voice high up above me said:

'Keb, sir?'

It was a hansom! I had seen it before in daylight some days previously. I remembered that a man sitting in front of me on the top of an omnibus had turned to look at it, and had made some remark about it to a friend. A hansom! Once king of the London streets, once the gondola of the Strand, and now . . . there it stood beside the kerbstones with its queer air of being wrong way up, a sedan chair slung between two huge wheels, the horse glooming in the collar, the driver sitting perilously at the back, with his long whip in a metal slot near his right hand.

'Keb, sir?'

I felt that it would be ridiculous to ride in a hansom. I was waiting for a taxicab. I thought that the last time I had ridden in a hansom was when I was a boy at school, and I remembered that it was a frosty night, and the horse sat down on a hill and kept on sitting down till we reached the level. How many Londoners of the younger generation have ever been in a hansom?

'Keb, sir?'

'Piccadilly!' I said, stepping from a foot rest to a little platform and entering this strange vehicle. The horse, feeling the weight of a passenger, was appropriately astonished. His ears went up. I heard the driver go 'Tsk, tsk!' with his mouth, the reins tightened, and we moved off smoothly, I feeling that the whole affair might turn turtle or else—fade away and leave me standing in the Strand, the victim of a vision of that old, quiet, leisurely London that has gone for ever. . . .

*   *   *   *   *

When I looked out of the window, I could see the rubber tyres of the big wheels revolving. I had, in front, a beautiful view of the horse's tail. The little doors swung to and met. I was in a cosy little arm-chair on wheels. How different from a taxicab! You can quarrel in a taxicab. You can turn your back and sulk and gloom, and even walk about and sit on the opposite seats. But a hansom. Our fathers knew something when they proposed in a hansom.

'Clip-clop, clippity-clop' went the horse up the Strand; and it seemed to me, as we entered the big vacancy of Trafalgar Square, that Nelson was quite delighted with us. I leant out, resting my arms on the little doors, smoking a cigarette in the cool night, watching the whip-lash wave in the air, not unkindly, but almost caressingly, almost encouragingly, over the horse's flanks.

Cockspur Street . . . the Haymarket. . . .

Then it was that I became aware of a faint scent in the hansom, a sweet lavender-like scent.

*   *   *   *   *

A little lid opened in the roof above me, and, looking up, I saw the driver's moustache outlined against the heavens:

'Just the Circus, sir?'

'Yes.'

The little lid closed with a snap.

Was it lavender? An odd, ghostly smell! There are times when inanimate things seem trying to tell you something, when rooms and chairs, it would seem, have a story they desperately desire you to understand. It may have been the hour, it may have been a lobster supper, it may have been just moonlight over London and the clippity-clop of those antiquated hooves up the Haymarket, but I think this relic, this last of the London gondolas, tried to tell me a story of love, lavender, and London; of a little white face behind a black-spotted veil, a little ermine cap and a little ermine cape, and a girl whose ankles had never been seen by man, who had legs only unofficially. And He, the hero, wore side whiskers and plaid trousers that strapped under his Wellingtons, and looked so, so 'noble' as he sucked the top of his ebony cane.

'You are assured of my deepest affections, Angeline. . . .

A flutter, a white hand raised protestingly.

'Fie, fie, you should not speak to me so, a helpless girl, at your mercy. It is not . . . not right.'

'Then, Angeline, may I declare my intentions to your father?'

A sigh. Eye-work. Another sigh.

'Yes—er—Montague!'

'Angeline, I crave your forgiveness for this sudden, wild ... your beauty carried me away, your pale nymph-like profile, your ...'

'Hush, sir, you make me blush. ...'

How much more I might have heard goodness alone knows, but, at this point, the lid opened and the moustache above came to view, bristling slightly with indignation.

'We've been 'ere for some time, sir!' said the voice.

'Oh, sorry. I didn't know. How much? ... Good night!'

'Good night to *you*, sir.'

*   *   *   *   *

I turned in empty Piccadilly, and listened to the ghostly clippity-clop go on into the distance, and cease.

WAPPING STAIRS. A clock struck twelve; and a high, cold moon shone over the river.

I stood muffled to the eyes in an ulster as I waited for the patrol boat of the river police which was to take me out on a night's hunting. There was no sound but the tide ebbing from the Thames mud with lapping, sucking noises. A melancholy siren gave a banshee wail downstream and was silent; round me were shadows, and lamplight pale over dreary alleyways; sinister steps led down to the exposed ooze that gleamed like polished silver in the light of the moon. What an eerie spot. I remembered every shilling shocker I have ever read. I saw, in imagination, 'the gang' creep from shadow to shadow, I heard the splash of a falling body, the swift sound of pursuit, and then, cutting the darkness, the call of a whistle and . . .

There it was! A whistle. Out of the night it came! This was not imagination. A dark shape detached itself from the dancing quicksilver of the river, and I heard the soft throbbing of the patrol boat and saw her green bow lights as she swept in towards land in the pale V of her wash, nosing the water eagerly like an otter.

'Good evening, sir!' I returned the salute as a dark form in a peaked cap rose out of the stern. I stepped in. 'Right away!' The engine purred, the boat swung round, and away we went into the mystery of the downstream reaches.

*   *   *   *   *

'Yes, crews of three men patrol the river all night long. . . . That's Limehouse to your left.'

I saw a jagged silhouette, black against the pale blue-grey of the sky. Behind us, the moon made a fish-scale pattern on the water, each wave crested with light—oily, dancing. We steered close to land. The grim wharves towered above us. Two powerful police lanterns played like little search-lights over them; pallid discs moving over the shut windows, picking out the detail, wavering over huddled, shrouded barges.

'All correct!'

Off we throbbed downstream, past a line of unemployed

barges—'starvation buoys,' the sergeant called them—moored in a line, their masts stark against the sky. We steered round the crew of a German steamer who were wearily rowing back after a night ashore.

'What's that? Ease her up!'

Out went our lights, and, noiselessly, we approached a deserted wharf.

Just like a swimming rat, we came up in the shadow, the lanterns ready.

'Now!' A steady flood of light poured over the wharf, explored the darkness of its piles. In the dazzle a huge rat, startled, leapt into the water and away. Nothing else! The keen eyes of the patrol sergeant had been deceived by, perhaps, a fluttering sack, a pile of timber that, for a second, looked like a man.

'You get so that you can smell out a river thief,' said the sergeant, laughing at his mistake. 'You get to know every boat on the river. A row boat near a barge at night is always suspicious. Do they ever fight? Lord, yes! Do you remember, Jack, that night Sergeant Blank jumped in after a thief near Deptford, and how they had a real old slogging match with the mud up to their waists!'

'Yes, and do you remember that night old Bill boarded a barge that didn't look quite right, and saw four pairs o' legs down a hatchway, and banged it down quick and sat on it and bagged the whole bunch of them? Of course, sir, you go nights with nothing happening except perhaps a body. . . .

'A body?'

'Yes; they often get caught up below water for weeks, and then . . .'

*　　　*　　　*　　　*　　　*

We were off Greenwich. We seemed the only living things on the river. From right to left bank we cruised, nosing, probing, flashing. Our lights had wavered over thousands of pounds' worth of goods lying out there in the dark of the river unwatched. Imagine miles of carts stacked with merchandise left alone all night in the streets. That is the Thames at night: an invitation to the thief. I hope the insurance companies send Christmas cigars to the river police.

Three men in a boat, with the safety of the Thames in their

eyes and in their rudder arm. It is difficult to feel romance
when the wind cuts through a blanket cloak and an oilskin,
but I felt it; the romance of these little questing crews, out
in all weathers, and night after night from dusk to dawn
safeguarding the highway of London Town, the terror of thief
and all moonlighting folk.

We turned back on our watery beat. How dead and cold
and mysterious it was! It was after 1 a.m. We passed a lone
man in a rowing boat, sweating in the bitter cold as his
cracking muscles pulled a gigantic raft of unhewn logs to
some riverside timber yard. A red lantern stood on the acre
of wet wood: and he passed on in the silence and the solitude,
a very symbol of labour. We flashed our lights over barge
after barge stacked with ingots of lead. Suddenly a shadow
rose up out of them, and we challenged. A thin wisp of a
man without an overcoat, smoking a cigarette. He was the
watchman. 'Good night!' Off we went.

*   *   *   *   *

'We're the oldest police force in the country,' said the
sergeant, as he put over the tiller and let me examine the vast
bulk of the drums of Tower Bridge. 'We were formed by the
East India Company in 1797, and merged with the Metro-
politan Police in 1839. . . . Now we're under Blackfriars
Bridge. . . .'

The Embankment swept round, its lights like a string of
pearls round the dark neck of sleeping London. . . .

As the police boat made for Waterloo Pier Station, I had
a marvellous view of Cleopatra's Needle framed in a dark
arch. The great Embankment hotels exposed lifeless frontages
to the moon, an all-night tramcar came up from Blackfriars,
and, as I stepped ashore at Suicide Station, I saw the pale
face of a poor 'sleeper-out' gazing down at us from the stone
balustrade. It was nearly 3 a.m.

But the stations of the Thames Police never sleep. Inside
was a yellow warmth and a stove. A sergeant was answering
the telephone; some detail of night life on the Thames. 'Yes,
sir. . . . Very good, sir. . . .' Far down the river it seemed
an inspector was issuing instructions that affected Waterloo
Bridge. I looked out of the window, over the dark river
streaked by moonlight, at the great bridge flung out over the

darkness, and westward, where the gold face of Big Ben shone as his cold, solemn notes chimed the hour. Moored to the pier, the patrol boat rode the tide, her green and red lights bobbing.

'So this is Suicide Station,' I said.

The sergeant replaced the telephone receiver.

'Well, I wouldn't exactly call it that,' he said with the caution that marks all good sergeants.

Nevertheless it is so. It is one of the most remarkable institutions on the river. More poor, miserable souls have jumped to death from Waterloo Bridge than from any other bridge on the Thames. Nine out of ten jump on the downstream side, probably with the vague idea in their tortured brains that their weary bodies stand a better chance of being carried out to sea.

How many Londoners know that day and night a police boat waits in the shadow of the bridge? It is tied to its moorings by a loose knot. One pull and it is free. It is a curious boat. At the stern is a roller.

'Have you ever tried to pull anyone out of water into a small boat?' asked a policeman. 'If so, you'll understand why that roller is there. Before it was fitted the rescue of a drowning person was like a kind of star turn at a regatta; now you just manœuvre the man or woman to the stern, grab hold his arms, and draw him in over the roller as easy as—well, falling off the bridge. . . .'

*   *   *   *   *

I stepped out of the little floating police station and walked along the pier. The sergeant threw open a door, and we entered one of the strangest rooms in London. It is fitted up for the reception of suicides. In the middle of the room is a bath. The sergeant turned on the tap and a hissing stream of hot water poured from it.

'That's the first thing they need!' he said.

Next to the bath is a bed. A change of clothes for men and women is handy, rolled up in neat bundles. I looked round the bare, efficient apartment, and sat down on the suicides' bed, trying to visualize the strange human stories that had ended here under a sheet; trying to imagine the tragedies averted by the swift rescue boat and the timely help in this

room, where so many times the despairing have been forced
back to life.

'Yes, I've seen some dreadful things on that bed,' said
the policeman.

The patrol boat sergeant lounged against the open door
muffled in his big blue coat. Behind him twinkled the river.

'Does a suicide repent and welcome rescue as soon as he
touches the water?' I asked.

'Not often,' they replied.

'Mostly they fight and try to get back into the water,' said
the patrol sergeant.

The three of us sat in the Suicide Room, and the two policemen swapped memories of rescues. I wish I could tell some
of the stories, but they were not quite—— You understand?

I liked the story of a sudden commotion one night. Man
in the river! Out went the rescue boat! The poor fellow had
jumped short, and had fallen in the mud: an ebb tide was
flowing. They excavated him, and carried him to the bathroom. He looked like a negro. Also life seemed to have
departed from him. They scraped him, and came upon good
clothes. This was no ordinary suicide. Gradually it dawned
on his rescuers that the man was marvellously drunk.

It transpired that he had, in a moment of divine afflatus,
and inspired by who knows what appreciation of the night
and the stars, clambered upon the Embankment to apostro-
phize the moon. When they had worked on him for some
considerable time consciousness returned; and he made the
classic inquiry: 'Where am I?'

*   *   *   *   *

I walked up the desolate Embankment, and, leaning for a
moment on the stonework, I watched the patrol boat with
its little green and red lights go up towards Westminster.
In the stern sat the patrol, shrouded to the eyes, peering,
flashing lamps, and gazing perpetually over the face of the
dark waters.

A Voice in the Night ✐   ✐   ✐   ✐   ✐

THE night was so still, so warm, so alluring. London beneath a velvet southern sky. Piccadilly empty in a mellow tunnel of gold light, save for a vague, hovering woman at the corner of Bond Street and a taxicab unloading a cargo of silver cloaks on the doorstep of the Ritz. Two men continued a club argument as they smoked a last cigar at the corner of Bolton Street.

A queer, misshapen thing, the property of the Westminster Council, hummed from a side street like some gigantic garbage beetle and cruised beside the kerb with whirring brushes. It went towards the circus; and silence came again, a portentous hush, in which the spirit of night seemed to hold its breath, waiting for something to happen in the stillness, in the darkness.

There are nights whose magic lies like a cloak over the spirit. The darkness seems always on the verge of a revelation. Something of that peace which blows through a garden at night glorifies our stone forest, as if the million denied flowers, shut for ever in the barren earth beneath the pavement, were trying to send out a ghostly fragrance; and in this peace the heart is washed clean of meanness and hard things; and any drunken beggar receives half a crown. . . .

*   *   *   *   *

I turned into Bolton Street, and, walking a little way through the square, came to a side street locked in sleep, in which one lit window shone on a second storey: a gold cube against which was etched, jet black, the twisted iron of a balcony. The window was open. The curtain hardly moved in the warm air.

As I was passing on, thinking how, at times, all the heart-ache and beauty of life can be crystallized for a wanderer in one moment before a lit window, there fell on the night, cool as drops of water, the clear notes of a piano. A woman's hands moving over the keys, softly, caressingly, and, I must confess, not too perfectly, flirting in a tired way with a bar of Grieg, wandering into chords towards a snatch of Schumann. Then silence. Then a provoking little melody picked out with one hand. . . .

I stood there feeling that soon she would slide into music, for I knew she was sitting there unable to choose, like a woman in a garden who must pick just one flower. What would it be? Chopin? Most likely. Or perhaps a foxtrot.

Then the clear notes trickled once again; and what followed was so beautiful to me, standing out there listening in the night, that it seemed for the first time in my life I had heard the Voice of London; that I had met, as in a fairy-tale, all the magic of a night stored in one moment.

Out to the darkness came a woman's voice—a soft, warm, little voice, and the song she sang was that lovely poem, written three hundred years ago by John Digby, Earl of Bristol:

> Grieve not, dear Love! although we often part:
> But know that Nature gently doth us sever,
> Thereby to train us up, with tender art,
> To brook the day when we must part for ever.
> For Nature, doubting we should be surprised
> By that sad day whose dread doth chiefly fear us,
> Doth keep us daily schooled and exercised,
> Lest that the fright thereof should overbear us!

The last notes ran on, like cool water falling, dropping into the deep pool of the night.

In the room was the deeper tone of a man's voice. The woman answered him. I walked on; and the desert of the dark London streets blossomed because of the beauty of that moment, that unknown voice in the night. . . .

* * * * *

I might lie to you, to polish a rough incident, and tell you that a London bobby stole up on rubber soles to listen to the song; that a young rake on his belated way home dashed a tear from his eye and squared his shoulders to life . . . but no; there was no one else: just an empty street in which I felt again all the aches and ideals of twenty, that sad age.

And I thought that beauty is never thrown away, never wasted, finds its mark always; and I knew that this voice, which, to me, was just a lovely expression of a magic night, might be to thousands something so poignant that the heart would overflow in the ache of it.

THEATRES have emptied, traffic has thinned, supper-parties have ended with a yawn and a thought of bed. . . .

Fleet Street is working with its coat off. The only bed it officially recognizes is that on which a paper is placed every night like a fearsome and truculent infant. Fleet Street never sleeps, and cannot afford to yawn.

For the last twelve hours the known world—and bits of it which are not known—have been flinging news at it by wireless, cable, telegraph, telephone, and luncheon tables. A relentless, doveless deluge.

Moscow has spoken after a long silence. A distinguished Frenchman, with true Gallic manners, waited till the woman he loved had finished dinner before shooting her—an event which had the same effect on Fleet Street that a sudden revolver shot would have on a man of nervous constitution. A correspondent in Peking, whom every one thought dead, has sent in a brilliant despatch; someone has interviewed a foreign Minister, and at Tunbridge Wells a solicitor's dog has swallowed a contested will. In other words, an ordinary night.

The head printer comes into the large room, in which Scottish sub-editors, in mass formation, make mincemeat of other people's work. He walks round with the air of a pirate king. Below ground, the hungry presses are ready: to-morrow's paper is about to be born.

*   *   *   *   *

It is just that moment when anything may happen: when things invariably do happen. If the dome of St. Paul's decided to fall, this is the nervy hour it would do it; this is the hour Anarchists decide to kill a President; the hour the House of Commons would catch fire—for in a few moments the first edition will come thundering from the presses. The rest of London is relaxed; Fleet Street is taut with nervous energy.

The atmosphere is like that as a great liner waits for the scheduled time of departure. The printer watches the clock; outside, in Fleet Street and its lanes and alleys, wait the empty motor-vans. In the circulation department anxious men watch the minute hand as men look up at the face of an enemy who has travelled the world to slay them. . . .

One minute late and the South Wales valley will ask for its London paper in vain.

*   *   *   *   *

The work goes on. The world is still bombarding. At the foreign desk is a snowstorm of cables. New York and Prague, Winnipeg and Berlin, Paris, Rome, and Vienna. Such variety. Some man in Washington has had a talk to the President of the United States; another in Vienna announces that a procession of unemployed men smashed a shop window.

Round the home desk the sub-editors work furiously.

In a telephone-box a man shouts over a private wire to a man in Paris imploring him to interview the Quai d'Orsay, or perhaps an actress who has insured her knees for a million francs. A bell rings! The night news editor grows one shade paler, and without a word seeks the reporters. Taxicabs quick! Scotland Yard is raiding a celebrated gambling hell. Two weary young men feel suddenly alive.

In the waiting-room a pale wisp of a man, who restlessly revolves a cap in grimy hands, offers for a guinea to tell how his brother stabbed his wife in Houndsditch.

*   *   *   *   *

Suddenly there is a roar, a deep sound that keeps its uniform tone. The machines!

The liner is cast from her moorings. Only by a miracle can that last telegram be delivered from the dock-side. And now over the newspaper office comes something of that cold excitement which fathers know when the doctor, carrying a small bag, goes upstairs. O that poignant eternity before he returns. 'A son!' and the father's breathless 'Is it—is he all right, not cross-eyed or . . .?'

The editor walks through the hive with the cool detachment of a captain on the bridge. Men intercept him with contents bills, he looks and walks on. In a carpeted, knowing-looking, experienced room, a printer puts down a warm, slightly damp, and ink-smelling copy of the first edition.

'Of a son. . . .'

*   *   *   *   *

In the cold morning streets, congested by motor-vans, walk the members of the team, the experienced and the virginal. A 'cub' reporter who fancied himself at Oxford as a writer, and during his fortnight has written fourteen thousand words (none of which the public ever saw), wakes up his wife. She rises out of salmon-pink pleats and tries to look interested.

'Tired, dearest?'

'No—my story's in the paper.'

'Oh, let me see.'

He holds her off while he describes how he went to Devonport to write up the disembarkation of the Atlantic Fleet home on leave. He describes his thousand adventures, the funny things he heard, the men he met, the presents they bought for their families. . . .

'Yes, dear, but let me read it myself.'

He unfolds the paper rather sadly, and she reads: 'Men of the Atlantic Fleet home on leave landed at Devonport yesterday.' Just that!

New to the game, she does not tell him that it is marvellous —'The most brilliant thing she has ever read.'

'Is that all?' she says. 'The milk's on the gas ring.'

*   *   *   *   *

An old hand, who has pulled off a story that everyone will be talking about in a few hours, goes thoughtfully home. He's forgotten something. What was it? Oh, yes, he had promised to take his wife to the theatre last night. . . .

*   *   *   *   *

All the time the great machines shake Fleet Street, throbbing and thundering as they pour out that rather wonderful thing built up by an astonishing organization from the raw materials of energy, enthusiasm, selflessness, and—sheer love for the most bewitched and attractive calling in the world.

THE theatre was given over to gloom and echo.

White sheets draped the stalls. A woman with a dustpan roamed with enthusiasm through the dress circle making banging noises. One or two critical men sat among the white sheets in a blue haze of cigar smoke, gazing without excitement at the bare stage on which, grouped on cane chairs before a woodland dell, were many nervous women and girls. They looked as though a charabanc had shot them over a hedge into the bracken!

'Now, then, Miss Jones!' said someone expectantly.

A weary pianist hit a chord on a senile piano as a girl detached herself from the victims in the green dell. The narrowness by which she had escaped being pretty was worse than if she had been positively ugly. Ancestors have no right to hand out the wrong mouths to girls who otherwise would be beauties. She passed her tongue swiftly over her lips, swallowed, and put on the smile which she had been practising in a mirror for days. In a confidential voice she sang:

> When I am dy-i-ing,
> Lean over me-e- . . .

'Bow legs!' whispered one of the critical men in the stalls to his neighbour.

Somehow, she faded away.

*   *   *   *   *

I looked at that pathetic, timid gathering in the dell and wished that I could make each one beautiful and brilliant; but beauty first. I thought that behind each smiling chorus in London is this saddening assembly fighting to come before the public, fighting terrible odds, unconscious of its short-comings, terribly uncritical. Some were bold with past experience, some were fresh and shy, some were the kind of girls who on the slightest provocation sing 'Where my Caravan has Rested'; and some, having passed the Rubicon apparently without a map, had, with a tense effort and a loyal rouge-pot, assembled all that was left of charm and youth with desperate gallantry.

189

A woman with a faded air of gentility about her sang a coy ballad too coyly, and fumbled with her hands when it ended in a cold, deathly silence.

'I can also dance,' she said brightly, and waited. She smiled archly and a tendon in her neck showed like a death warrant.

'Thanks, that will not be necessary,' answered a suave voice in the darkness. The pianist plugged away at the next song; and the woman looked suddenly gaunt in the strip of light falling from above. Her coyness fell from her like a cloak, and she walked away with burning cheeks.

*   *   *   *   *

Two men in shirt-sleeves walked on and removed the wood. They revealed behind, at a giddy cant, half a sultan's palace and the best part of a fountain. The girls now looked like slaves ready for execution.

A beautiful girl came forward and sang a coon song in that polite, cold-muffin way English girls sing coon songs. The men in the shadows brightened. Someone said she was a peach.

'I dance,' she remarked with a cold, superior air.

'Carry on,' said a voice.

She unbuttoned her skirt, took it off, threw it over a chair and danced; a tall yellow-legged nymph with close-cropped, tawny hair. As she danced, she smiled. They told her to report on Monday, and she left the stage without looking at the Sultan's victims; but every one of them looked at her and whispered. A few looked as though they resented her.

*   *   *   *   *

So it went on. Some, they cut short in the middle of a song; some, they heard to the bitter end. One by one they drifted away, calm, smiling, indignant, or in tears, according to temperament. It was sadder than any drama, this tragedy behind a musical comedy. I wondered how many were going out to give up, how many were resolved to try again, how many driven by vanity, how many by ambition, how many by necessity.

As the last batch walked away over the stage, there came

through their ranks a blatantly beautiful girl to a slow music of perfume. They looked at her and knew that her fur coat cost two hundred guineas; that her shoes came from Paris, her complexion from Bond Street, and that her pearls were probably real.

'I'm taking the car,' she said to one of the men in the shadows. 'And mind you're not late. See?'

An obedient voice answered.

The expelled visitors cast eloquent glances which may have said: 'It can be done, you see!' or, 'It's all a matter of luck,' or, . . .

The footlights went out. The carpenters came back with the woodland. High up in some invisible heaven a coarse voice sang:

> When I am dy-i-ing,
> Lean over me-he-he. . . .

'Well, before you die, Bill, turn off those blinkin' battens!' shouted someone.

'Righty-ho,' said the voice from the canvas sky. . . .

Then the stage became dark, shadowy, and full of impalpable, sad ghosts.

I WENT to see a Great Man in the City. He sits at a polished desk in the heart of a big bee-hive full of mahogany, pretty typists, grubby boys, telephones, and young men in pince-nez.

Behind a grille was an ancient commissionaire with a moustache in two colours, due to tobacco, so vast that, when he advanced his head towards the brass bars, large portions of this moustache straggled forth into the outside world. He looked at me with the undying eye of a sergeant-major, pushed a pad to me, stuck a huge spatulate forefinger on the pad, barked, 'Name! Business!' and then shouted, 'Tom!' in a loud voice, whereon six small boys sprang smartly to attention.

Next to the commissionaire's gilded cage was a small room with the lost air of all waiting-rooms, in which lingered several people all in advanced stages of depression. A young man, rather obviously after some job or other, pretended to look at a picture of Queen Victoria's Coronation, but really straightened his tie.

᠅   ᠅   ᠅   ᠅   .   ᠅

Through the open door I watched the big commissionaire boss his Boy Scouts and despatch them to the bank as though he were flinging a flying column to the relief of Lucknow.

In came a middle-aged man of neat, unprosperous aspect, wearing an old coat but brilliantly blacked boots. He placed a brown paper parcel on the counter, opened a book, got the commissionaire's signature, and was just leaving, when he said:

'Ain't you Sergeant B., of the Flankshires?'

'I am,' said the commissionaire with the readiness of a man who has nothing to be ashamed of in his life.

'I thought I couldn't have been mistaken,' remarked the other man, his eyes straying over the great moustache. 'You don't remember who I am, do you?'

'Was you in the gunners?' asked the commissionaire thoughtfully.

'No. My name's Jones.'

'Haven't got you,' said the commissionaire, puzzled.

'Jones!' said the other anxiously, as if the name was a kind of pickaxe that would open up the sergeant's memory.

'O Lordy!' said the commissionaire. 'I've got you now! You was Lord Blank's groom when I was his first servant in '95.'

A mutual flood of approval descended on both of them. I thought they would get drowned in it.

I found myself smiling with delight at the faces of the two old men. I hoped the Great Man would forget all about me and leave me free to sit and listen to these two hauling at their youth. An amazing conversation took place like this:

'Ravin' lunatics them Fuzzy-Wuzzies was . . . *here boy, take this up to Mr. Parkinson,* . . . and you was with Kitchener too in Khartoum, I remember, . . . *tell Mr. Patterson a lady's waiting for 'im,* . . . and do you recollect that march after we left Assouan in the heat with every fellow trying not to take a swig at his water-bottle? Blinkin' awful, wasn't it. And then them blacks, them Fuzzy-Wuzzies with their long sixteen-foot spears with trowels on the end that put the fear o' God in the cavalry, and . . . *tell Miss Snipe the lady's called from Badgerton's,* . . . and then I shall never forgit the gun-boats poppin' off at random in the river and the pot-shots that . . . *Tom! Come here. You know Gracechurch Street? Well, go on now—quick.* . . .'

That's how it went on.

*   *   *   *   *

Mr. Jones, the groom that was, expanded like a passion-flower in the glow of these reminiscences; his eyes glowed, and he used one or two improper military expressions which seemed quite foreign to his present neat but ungaudy condition.

'And did you go up with Wingate in '99?' he asked eagerly.

'Yes,' said the commissionaire, licking a stamp.

'Then you musta seen the Khalifa at some time or other?'

'Course I did. I saw him at Omdurman when he was organizing some attack against MacDonald's Brigade. You must have seen him diving about surrounded by his emirs with a big green flag waving 'an a silver ball on the top. He was . . . a proper old devil if you like, with a head of hair like a blinkin' doormat, it was, wasn't it . . . just like a blinkin' doormat. . . . *Tom, come 'ere, quick!*'

'That's right! I took my missus to the Tower of London, last Tuesday, no, last Thursday—no it wasn't, it was Monday —and they've got that green flag we captured at—what was the name of that blinkin' awful place?—hangin' up in the Tower.'

'The old Khalifa was killed, wasn't he?'

'Yes. Debrikah, that's the name!'

*   *   *   *   *

'Come this way, sir!' said an office boy.

I rose reluctantly, just in time to hear the hero of a page of English history send a youth to Cornhill.

ANY neat suburban road in London—Golder's Green or
Surbiton—and the time is 8.45 a.m.

The bright, assured, and insured-looking houses stand
smartly to attention behind strips of juvenile turf. They
spread abroad an erroneous impression of originality due to
the unexpectedness of a sudden slanting eave or the juxta-
position of Elizabethan woodwork with pseudo-Georgian red
brick. At first, it seems that each house is different; then you
realize that there are only four types tactfully arranged like
chocolates in a box to give an air of variety. Each house contains the same lounge hall, the same Jacobean dining-room
suite, the same (to all appearances) dear little wife who, now
that the weather has changed, goes out shopping in a nutria
coat.

It is important to note that, nestling beside the kitchen of
each house, is a garage containing a partially purchased motor-
car. The road glows with a proud, but discreet, prosperity.

    *   *   *   *   *

Doors open, gates click, men of forty peck their wives
swiftly and stride heavily down the path; here and there is
perhaps a wife who turns a cold cheek to her husband's farewell and watches him suspiciously as he goes; but next door
may be seen the passionate embrace of more recent partners
whose salad bowls are yet untarnished.

She says: 'Don't be late, darling!'

He says: 'I'll catch the 5.15, Popsy!'

She regards him romantically, and then whispers:

'There's a tiny bit of egg on your moustache, dearest!'

He removes it, they kiss again; she watches him go, raises
a shapely arm, smiles, departs humming 'Tea for two and
two for tea . . . a girl for you, a boy for me' . . . pauses and
looks happy. . . .

    *   *   *   *   *

Then other doors open.

From one emerges a small boy. He is dressed in grey

flannel trousers, a grey jersey with a grey coat over it and a grey floppy hat. He is five. He is the most interesting person in a road full of human cargo, for he is about to take his first step into life: he is going to a preparatory school for the first time.

His mother, standing at the door, feels silly because she knows that she is going to cry; and why? Her baby is going away from her out into the awful lottery of life. That's it. So small and defenceless he is, and so much hers. He is an open book to her, and now the world is to have its way with him. Nothing belongs to a woman so much as a child—for five years.

'Good-bye, Jack,' she says. 'Be a good boy.'

'Yes, mummy,' he replies vaguely, dropping his new pencil-box, which is all the equipment he is taking out into life.

A group of older boys wearing cherry caps pass by chattering.

'Those,' says Jack proudly, 'will be my friends.'

His eyes follow them with deep interest: a man about to take his place in the world of men.

'Yes, dear, and when you come home you will be wearing one of those nice red caps.'

'Yes, I shall be a schoolboy then,' he reflects gravely.

*　　　*　　　*　　　*　　　*

The first milestone; and he is so proud. His mother might feel conscious that his little feet are taking the first step along an alarming road; that society, by clapping a cherry-coloured cap on his vacant little head, claims him as a unit; that no doubt the gods of comedy and tragedy sitting up aloft are already regarding him carelessly, as they begin to mix that draught of experience which he must drain to the lees. Not so complex. I think she just feels a bit throaty to see him doing anything quite alone, his babyishness accentuated by his proud pretence at maturity; and, as she watches his little arrogant back, I think she feels hurt to think that soon he will be able to do without her. . . .

'Come along, Master Jack,' says nurse.

'Good-bye, my darling,' says mother; then she kisses her hand and shuts the door quickly.

*　　　*　　　*　　　*　　　*

Dusk falls over the road that so recently was a London meadow. The men come home in waves. Lights glow in windows. Behind the windows? What?

'Have some more trifle, dearest?'

'And then, Madge, I gave it him in the neck. I said, "Before I came the accounts were in a mess, and now they're straight, and I won't stand any jaw from you or anyone else."'

'Quite right, dear, the beast! . . . Cream?'

'And I made him apologize! I tell you, I made him sit up.'

'My clever husband!'

Behind the next window perhaps a woman with a frozen cheek watches the unsuspecting male, waiting the moment to pounce with a quiet but devastating:

'George, who is Phyllis?'

'Phyllis?' (Incredulous surprise.)

'Yes, Phyllis. A letter fell out of your blue coat this morning, and I couldn't help . . .'

*　　　*　　　*　　　*　　　*

And, quite near, in other rooms in this road the little boys, who have just stepped so innocently into all this life, are sleeping with passionate abandon, their tousled heads deep in pillows, their small hands outside the coverlets, and, on a chair beside the bed, three virgin exercise books with their surnames written on the cover: their first day's work!

I hope that into these rooms the fathers go reverently to look with a kind of awe at the bad pot-hooks and the A B C D and the 1 2 3 4—those first tiny scratchings on the hard surface of life.

It is very touching, very important, somehow slightly pathetic, and, altogether, rather wonderful.

A YOUNG man and a young woman marry and accept the great adventure of life as two enthusiastic bathers take to the sea in summer. Everything is so jolly and worth while. Nothing can come between them; nothing can hurt them now. 'I have you and you have me!' they say; and one of them adds: 'For always and always and always.'

Then she—or he—develops a queer little dry cough. Nothing, of course, till a definite symptom occurs; and over the unclouded firmament of two unfulfilled lives passes that awful cloud—consumption. These two young people huddle in each other's arms over the ruin of that which only yesterday seemed so glorious, so invincible, so unshakable. Where there was laughter there are tears; where there was such faith there is now only hope; where there was close association there is separation. That is the story behind every other bed in every ward of that great consumption hospital in the Fulham Road. On the other side of the road stands the peril of middle age—cancer; on this side the peril of youth, the horrible white plague.

*　　　*　　　*　　　*　　　*

It was visiting day. Through the gardens of the hospital walked young people arm in arm. It was difficult to tell which was the sufferer and which the visitor save, here and there, where a young man was holding a bunch of golden daffodils brought to brighten his bedside.

Upstairs, I walked down long corridors split up in a number of small wards, each ward containing no more than five or six beds. In all these wards were young girls. I saw few women older than the early thirties. How pitiable! Youth knocked out at the very start of the race. Unlike some invalids, who grow careless and heartsick, these young sufferers were so conscious of their youth, of their beauty. In order to welcome husbands, sweethearts, and parents they had put little touches of vanity to their toilettes; a new blue ribbon threaded through a nightdress, a new lace cap, a touch of pink at a sleeve . . . heartrending, small vanities. . . .

A girl, who might have been Rossetti's 'Blessed Damosel', sat up in bed with her fine-spun, red-gold hair falling over a marble neck and shoulders; and, every time the ward door opened, a flush mounted to her face and the rich curve of her mouth deepened in expectancy; for she was waiting for some-one. Beside her bed was the photograph of a small child.

* * * * *

'How cheerful they seem, how anxious to laugh and to be petted!'

'That is always the way,' said the doctor. 'A consumptive, even when dying, believes that he will get well; and the strange thing is that, here and there, a hopeless case does recover. People who have been sent away from here to die in a home have sometimes recovered instead. Some sudden change takes place . . . one cannot say how it happens.'

* * * * *

Gradually the wards filled with visitors and flowers. Little tables were buried under cascades of daffodils, primroses, violets.

Young husbands sat on the edge of beds holding the pale hands of young wives, talking, laughing, whispering. Each bedside was a little patch of sacred country on the wrong side of love.

Suffering is bad enough to watch at any time, but when the sufferers are young, when their eyes sparkle with life, when the bed-clothes drape the young curves of their bodies, and when their whole attitude denotes a capacity for life and happiness, the sight is ghastly.

In one ward I saw the meeting of four young couples. Four young wives with the seeds of disease in them sparkled as their husbands came in with flowers to tell them the news since last visiting day; the thrilling unimportances of life outside in the great, free, healthy world. And, in a corner, a beautiful pale young girl, lying on her side, pretending to read a book, watched. She was too young to have a husband to meet her: life had cheated her even of that.

In the men's wards, it was the same: wives visiting husbands. More pathetic, perhaps, because here it was the woman who was alone in life while the man was chained to a bed, denied his natural part in the struggle of life, his cross of suffering weighted with anxiety for her; and she bravely putting up a good fight, smiling and trying to hide her heart.

Here is Youth crucified. . . .

*   *   *   *   *

If you know anything of human nature, there is no need for me to tell you of the plans, the hopes, the dreams that are born each week when young people in love, and separated by the white plague, hold hands in the grim whiteness of a ward.

It must take courage to launch a dream on the sea of eternal hope when a woman sets her teeth and determines not to let you see the cough that shakes her body when you are not there; but, let us hope and pray, that now and then some dream wins home to harbour.

THE room has heavy double doors. As you approach, your guide puts a finger to his lips, makes a face at you, and tip-toes in, you after him.

You are now within earshot of millions of homes. Every vibration in this room is being broadcast by wireless. If you sneezed or hiccoughed, millions of people would think: 'That's not Beethoven; what *was* it?' and you would be led out in disgrace for behaving at 2 L O in a manner unbecoming an officer and a gentleman. As a matter of fact, the tip-toe air, the atmosphere of nodding and mouthing, has a curious effect on you. In most of us there lives a queer little devil who sometimes urges us to fling an egg into an electric fan, to throw an omelet at a solemn person, or otherwise to behave publicly in a Chaplinesque manner. Some vague undergraduate god seems daring us to outrage the proprieties. In 2 L O you have to grip yourself hard in order not to make a sudden noise and pull the leg of the world.

So you occupy your mind by looking round.

*   *   *   *   *

The room is thickly carpeted in green. Some woven material drapes the ceiling to condense the sound. A pianola stands in one corner, a grand piano in another, a string orchestra occupies the centre of the floor. The musicians are so quiet. They are longing to make little toots and tinkles that precede melody. Now and again an anxious player cannot resist the temptation to emit a little ping-ping on a violin (or a little pong-pong on a 'cello), but all the other musicians turn and look at him as if he has committed a sin; and he swiftly puts his fingers over the strings.

Opposite, like a great, open mouth, is the microphone in a box. It looks rather like a superior gramophone. Suddenly a smart young man in horn-rimmed glasses detaches himself from the grand piano, where he has been whispering into someone's ear, and, walking up to the microphone he says, in a cheery, jaunty way, one hand in his trousers pocket:

'Hallo, everybody! London calling the British Isles . . .!'
You cannot help smiling. It seems so far-fetched—a joke!

Is it really possible that this young man, standing before a little cabinet in London, is heard in Belfast, in Aberdeen, in the far misty hills and valleys of Wales? He is apparently not a bit impressed by it. He calls the British Isles in just the same tone of voice he would employ if he met you in the street: 'Hallo, old dear, how are you?' He takes up a programme, and has another word with the Grampians:

'In two minutes the Symphony Orchestra will play the Pilgrims' Chorus from "Tannhäuser."'

He strolls away from his old friend the British Isles and goes back to the piano. The conductor takes off his coat and hangs it on a chair. Somebody looks at the clock, nods, the conductor gathers his musicians with an upward movement of his hands, down comes his baton, and right out over the British Isles crashes the solemnity of Wagner.

* * * * *

Upstairs, I enter another room in which men are pumping Wagner over telephone wires. It is like a telephone exchange. Little black ebony honeycombs stand round it, labelled Newcastle, Aberdeen, Birmingham, Manchester. Coils of cable droop down the walls. There is no sound but the clicking of plugs in black honeycomb.

'The music is amplified here and put over ordinary telephone wires to other towns, where it is sent out by wireless.'

'Is there any delay? Does Aberdeen get it a fraction of a second later than Kensington?'

'Not one fraction of a second. When Lord Blank spoke recently in London, people in Aberdeen heard him a fraction of a second before the people at the back of the hall! Sound travelling through the air is delayed: electricity is instantaneous.'

A man gave a little touch to a plug and—Manchester was probably delighted.

* * * * *

In the artists' room sit, or walk, the men and women who are about to face the invisible lions. Some are composed; some are obviously nervous. One man with a high brow is anxiously reading his lecture, another is chatting nonchalantly

in a ripe baritone voice to a friend. A pretty young girl in a
silver evening wrap moistens her lips and, nervously clearing
her throat, gazes all the time at a song she must know by
heart. The door opens.

'Miss . . . er . . . will you kindly . . .?'

Her time has come! I want to hearten her. It is obviously
her first broadcast. I want to say:

'Cheer up! All their crystals have gone wrong to-night.
Every cat's-whisker is on strike.[1] Just sing to yourself!'

Then a high and comforting official goes up to her and, in
the most fatherly way, gives her the secret of this strange
new art:

'Don't worry,' he says. 'You'll be splendid. Don't think
that millions are listening. Do remember that you are not
singing to a massed audience, but just to one man and to one
woman sitting together in the evening over their own fireside.'

She smiles gratefully, and then goes out quickly to keep
her appointment with—the British Isles!

---

[1] Broadcasting was in its infancy when I visited the B.B.C. at Savoy
Hill in 1925, and it is interesting to compare the humble surroundings
of 2 L O—as London was then known—with the later magnificence of
Broadcasting House. In those pre-valve days, the listener sat with
ear-phones strapped to his head, and tuned in by probing the facets
of a small metallic crystal with a thin wire, known popularly as a
'cat's-whisker.'

NO one ever sings an ode to the unknown, undistinguished houses of Camberwell, and suchlike places, which year after year crumble and vanish to the sound of the pickaxe.

I was walking along a mean, crowded high street, a mass of jangling tramcars and skidding omnibuses, when I came to an old house which stands a few yards behind the shop frontage, and a little to one side, as if it were trying to turn round and forget that the fishmonger lived next door—the old snob!

The last thing that can happen to a house was happening —men were hitting it with pickaxes. The displaced bricks fell in a cloud of white dust, exposing a gaunt, ragged hole through which could be seen a faded bedroom paper: pink rosebuds tied with blue ribbon.

There are such houses all over London, standing in a decayed, alien atmosphere among hundreds of cheap, vigorous little shops. They are the local eyesores.

The spearheads have been snapped from their railings, the few yards of garden have become disreputable, the windows have turned black, and over the walls has crept that unpleasant eczema which afflicts old houses, giving to them an appearance of confirmed disease.

* * * * *

When the last tenant dies—for it is impossible to think of anything so lively as a removal—these old houses often become lodging-houses, and sad faces peer from behind the grey lace curtains. Occasionally a young actress alights on them for a week, like a butterfly which has mistaken a dustbin for a flower. The next stage is a garage, which either fails or succeeds.

If it succeeds the old house is eclipsed by petrol and oil advertisements. It is reconstructed. Green pumps appear in the front garden, so that you would never guess that behind all this coming and going the ancient house lives on.

In the event of failure, the house just glooms vacantly, standing behind its rank garden like an old aristocrat so sad, so ill, so miserable that he has even given up dreaming of the old days.

Yet, no matter how many windows are smashed, how many
tin cans find their way into the garden, how many timber
merchants use the stables as a storeroom, there is always an
air of quality about such old houses; they suggest, as they
shoulder a greengrocer on one side and an undertaker on the
other, that a relic of a finer civilization is lingering in the last
agony.

So might a Roman villa in Saxon London have stood among
the wattle huts of a less advanced people.

*   *   *   *   *

Bang-smack went the incessant picks, and the dust flew
high. . . .

I thought that in 1800 Mr. Timothy Snapper, merchant of
the City of London, must have been proud of his country
house lying back among the fields of Brixton, lonely and not
too grand, but—just grand enough for a man who might hope
to be Lord Mayor and perhaps Sir Timothy Snapper, Kt., J.P.
That Corinthian portico; that spacious flight of steps. A good
house. And every June day, as he rode down to the City on
a steady brown mare, he wore in his button-hole a rose
plucked in the garden.

No doubt he, and his Jorrocksy friends, often reined up
below the portico and drank a glass of sloe gin and ate a slice
of damp, sticky plum-cake before they went off to the meet
of the local pack. . . .

The tramcars became blocked in a long line, the omnibuses
piled up, the wagons, with their steaming horses, came to a
standstill. Bells rang, motor-horns blew. A hawker threw
up his head and howled for old bottles.

*   *   *   *   *

I thought that naturally a young man once rode over the
fields to the old house to see Miss Emily Snapper—a good-
looking young man in a tight claret coat, tight trousers
strapped under his boots, and hair so well pomaded that it
brought the antimacassar into fashion for the protection of
drawing-room chairs.

'Dearest nymph. . . .'

Emily *was* rather nymph-like in flowered soft muslin,

girdled under the arm-pits, and falling in folds to where her little toes peeped out. In the garden among the roses (where now the oil and colour merchant dumps his drums) this young man dropped on one knee and asked her to marry him.

She, of course, said 'Ask father,' and father said 'No'; so obviously they ran away; he very noble in a claret coat and Hessian boots, she pale and timid, her hands in a muff and her lovely, scared face under the great arch of a bonnet that tied with a large yellow bow beneath her chin.

Did Timothy relent and leave them the old house when he died of port? If that old house could speak, what would it say?

*   *   *   *   *

There was a much bigger hole now, and more bedroom paper showing, more pink rosebuds and more ribbon. I wondered how many generations of lovers had looked through that window and had seen moonlight soft over the fields; and how many babies, their pale, blue eyes wide, had through it taken their first look at life.

Bang-crack went the picks.

And the white cloud rose higher.

SHORTLY after noon many unusual people arrive in Leather
Lane, near Holborn Circus, to turn an honest penny—sometimes sixpence.

Two negroes, wearing silk hats and morning coats, erect a
little trestle and unpack a bag which contains small paper
packets. A young man dressed like a chef wheels into position
a barrow on which lies a sack of potatoes. A jazz band appears.
Various seedy-, and several prosperous-looking, men lurk in
the lane, holding carpet bags or old attaché cases. They are
all waiting for that stroke of the clock which will release on
Leather Lane, from office, workshop, and factory, a flood of
clerks, typists, machine hands, artisans, and hundreds of
fluffy-haired workgirls who, walking arm in arm, contrive at
the same time to eat apples or ice cream wafers.

On both sides of Leather Lane stretch booths from which
the fruit lover can buy bananas or oranges, from which the
connoisseur of old bed knobs, rusty keys, or stray lengths of
iron piping can recognize many rare specimens, from which
the sweet-lover can purchase everything from milk chocolate
to apples soaked in toffee, from which those who desire fish
can buy kippers while they watch one of the most loathsome
sights in London: the decapitation of live eels and the head
that refuses to die.

Ting! The luncheon bell! Leather Lane prepares to give
its daily *matinée*.

*   *   *   *   *

The street is crammed with people. A two-horse dray
delivering acid in big glass bottles is hopelessly marooned.
Men shout. Crowds collect round any merchant who seems
interesting or amusing.

The two negro doctors settle their silk hats on their heads
and begin to talk. No symptom is hidden from them. They
are realists. As their words strike home, men and women part
with tuppence and take a little paper packet. The jazz band
plays with remarkable skill. The chef takes a potato from
his sack and begins to peel it with a small instrument which
clips on a knife. He does a brisk trade. The most unlikely

looking people exhibit an interest in his commodity: solemn old men, young men. They are told that their wives will bless them for their kind thought.

A little man with a muffler round his throat shows how easy it is to paint a penny silver. Ice cream is being sold in quantity.

   *   *   *   *   *

A large crowd surrounds a young man who has a humorous, intelligent face. He is trying to sell a gyroscope top. He does it like this:

'Now, look here! You insert a string like this, which doesn't require the genius of a Leonardo da Vinci, does it?'

He stops and looks at the rows of stolid faces.

'Now does it? No. All right.'

He demonstrates his top. No one buys. He looks round, smiles, and remarks with a fine sarcasm:

'Do you know, I often think I'll go to the Zoo, but, then, I say to myself, "Why should I do this when I can look at Leather Lane?" D'you know that after you've all done standing round here with your mouths open, and your pockets closed, this place is covered with apple-cores and monkey-nuts. It is, really! Why should I go to Regent's Park, I ask myself, and—echo answers why? . . .

'To resume. This top is a marvellous invention. . . . You observe that, when I hold the string like this, it retains its equilibrium—as the scientist would put it—but why I, an itinerant street vendor should use such terms I cannot say, and neither, I suppose, can you. Now those of you who have read Herbert Spencer will possibly know. . . .'

This young man earns his shillings!

   *   *   *   *   *

Before two o'clock men are bearing all manner of things away from Leather Lane. They have found the nut, screw, or bolt that will 'come in useful some day,' they have discovered their imaginations touched by the sudden beauty of painting a penny silver or buying a half-crown box of Turkish delight for fourpence ('flavoured with the jasmine of the mystic Heast').

Then the bell rings. The luncheon hour is over; over is that short ramble among bargains, that glorious uncertainty beside a tray of junk, that harmless half-hour beside a dusky doctor. . . .

The men of Leather Lane, having made their short, swift raid on spare pennies, pack up their trifles and depart whistling.

Sister Anne　　*o　　o　　o　　o　　o　　o*

IN Bloomsbury there is a captive lady. I have seen her.

She sits at a window in a tall, grim house, too near the roof to be the owner and not quite high enough to be the maid. She reads a lot, I believe, and thinks more than she reads, for whenever I see her she has just looked up from a book, and is gazing down into the rather too consciously respectable square with eyes which may, or may not, see the life that goes on there.

She reminds me of Sister Anne of the fairy-tale turret; only she is a much older Sister Anne, with a something about her that tells me how long ago she renounced all hope of seeing a horseman come spurring down the road to rescue. She is the lady of the bed-sitting-room . . . 'a gentlewoman in reduced circumstances.'

'Bed-sitting-room, with use of bath.'

*　　　　*　　　　*　　　　*　　　　*

There are thousands in London, in every great city, and in many of them a woman is sitting 'like Patience on a monument smiling at Grief.' It is good for us now and then to know hard times, but it is tragic to fall into that hopeless category among those who 'have known better times.' Sister Anne has known better times, and that, I think, is what she is always thinking about when she forgets to read and sits looking down into that too self-consciously respectable square.

'I remember when my dear Henry was alive,' she always says, if you listen long enough; for that is the burden of all her thought. Dear Henry, however, died and left her stranded. He either crashed on the Stock Exchange, or she discovered that everything was mortgaged, and she turned to face life alone—imagine beginning life alone at fifty—in a bed-sitting-room 'with use of bath'!

There is little that Sister Anne can do. What can a woman who has been nursed all her life learn at fifty? Sometimes, I think, I have seen her steal into Bond Street shops trying to look like a customer. She unwraps a brown paper parcel and takes out embroidery; for her mother fortunately taught her to be 'clever with her needle.' They give her a few shillings and some more work. Out into Bond Street she goes, still trying to look like a customer, for, you see, she has the pride of the poor and the shame of 'having known better days.'

'Poor thing!' they say in the shop. Or perhaps: 'Do you remember when Mrs. X used to drive up in her carriage?'

*   *   *   *   *

In the bed-sitting-room in Bloomsbury are those few things which she managed to snatch from the creditors and the auctioneer; a silver frame, that looks so alien in a tawdry room, from which dear Henry gazes out with the blithe and dashing expression so characteristic of his more prosperous day. A chair or two; a carriage clock: useless knick-knacks which look as queer in that nakedness as the strange things the sea leaves when the tide goes out. . . . Sometimes there is a photograph of a child who, had he lived, would be a man now, capable of picking his mother up from the humiliation of a bed-sitting-room.

*   *   *   *   *

In the winter, when coal is dear, Sister Anne leaves her turret and spends the day in the rest rooms of the big Oxford Street stores, writing innumerable letters, reading magazines, and watching other women; remembering things about the other half of her life.

Or she haunts, like a ghost, those parts of good hotels where there is no danger of being handed a bill. The porters and the clerks know that she has no appointment in the lounge or the writing-room. Sister Anne just sits there because it is warm, and because it is what she was once accustomed to do before dear Henry escaped from this life.

London is cruel to the lonely.

As long as you have a pound note to squander, you find a friend. When the last penny goes, and you are too proud to exhibit your poverty, Solitude and Memory perch on your window-sill like birds of ill omen; and you grow inward and talk to them; and people think you are talking to yourself.

*   *   *   *   *

So whenever I walk through Bloomsbury and see Sister Anne's refined white face at a window, I wonder why some of the altruism that runs waste does not trickle in her direction.

How much happiness a Bed-Sitting-Roomers' Club would bring into the world I am not prepared to say, knowing a little of human nature. But it always seems to me that if Sister Anne could, without any loss to her dignity or any hint of that kind of charity which thrives on the enjoyment of pitying, be drawn away from that lonely window she might learn how to smile again—as she did before poor, dear Henry, with characteristic dash, flung his widow at Fate.

The 'Junior Turf'   o   o   o   o   o

AGAINST the trees of the Green Park, which it matches exactly in colour stands on the edge of the roadway the Junior Turf Club. It is fifty years old.

Ah, how the old men in club windows prick up their ears! (What a pretty girl Nellie was till she opened her mouth! An English rose with thorns for a voice!) How those solemn old men smile to themselves and remember a day before 'Ta-Ra-Ra-Boom-de-Ay,' when they used to wait outside stage doors with bunches of roses—how naïve our fathers were!—and watch dawn break over the Green Park to the cheering scent of sausage and mash and—well; the Junior Turf Club knew them all, knew Debrett and Burke's Peerage from page one onwards, and the Gaiety chorus from Alice right through the alphabet.

But times are changed. Years ago the Westminster Council said that, if the Junior Turf desired to hand out sausages to the nobility and the frivolity, it would have either to pay rates or shut its doors; and the people who lived over the way said that, although they loved life and laughter they hated them in the middle of the night, so the Junior Turf Club, being only a cabman's shelter—but the most famous shelter in London—pulled itself together and decided to keep its sausages within bounds; which is legal and proper.

*   *   *   *   *

I passed by recently and looked in.

Taxicab drivers, following an ancient custom, can eat roast beef at any time of the day or night. It was 11 a.m., and the ribs of beef were on the table.

The Junior Turf always smells hearty. There is a pre-cocktail era relish about it. Just to smell it in the middle of the night was to feel hungry. I say 'was,' because when it ministered to exhausted humanity London was a city without a night club. The Junior Turf, standing so modestly on the edge of the road hard by the Ritz, is the humble parent of all the gilded dens which add to the expensive boredom of our times. It is the grandfather of Ciro's and the Embassy.

'Where can I get something to eat, cabby?'

'You come along o' me, captain.'

That—so bad old men tell me—is how it used to go on. And the old cabby, scenting a meal at the expense of his fare, would whip up the horse and make for the Junior Turf.

There, in the tiny box, or in neighbouring cabs, would be gathered a distinguished company drawn together in the dead of a London night by a passion for bacon and eggs or toad-in-the-hole. While all London was a black desolation, the little green Junior Turf shone like a good deed in a hungry world.

It is whispered that, now and then, a beggar by the park rails would peer into a cab in those old, far-off days and see the bearded face of a royal prince who, homeward bound after a late party, had stopped at the Junior Turf for a cup of coffee which a palace could not provide at 3 a.m. Of course this may be a rumour. . . .

*   *   *   *   *

'Can no one tell me the history of the Junior Turf?'

All the taxicab drivers were young men. To them, it was just a shelter, and the memory of old days just a scandal. But I found an old driver who told me he had driven a horse cab forty years ago.

'All sorts I've seen there!' he said. 'It isn't allowed now. In the old days everybody knew it. I couldn't tell you all the "nobs" I've driven there in the middle of the night. . . . In recent days the man who loved to eat in cab shelters was the late Sir Ernest Shackleton.

'He liked us and we liked him. He used to bring down great big books of photographs, and talk all night sometimes about his travels. He was a rare sportsman. When we got orders to serve no more food, he was that sorry that he had a little table made that just fitted into his taxicab, and he'd drive up in the night, and insist on his sausage and mash, sitting there in his cab and talking to us. . . .'

*   *   *   *   *

'But the old days were the times, sir! Everybody liked the old London cabby. We were a bit rough and talkative, but there was no harm in us. Nowadays the London taxicab driver isn't too popular, because when the young ones joined the mechanical transport during the war a lot of pretty tough customers got licences and didn't play the game.

'You can't blame the public for giving the taxicab driver a bad name. But that's dying now. Most of the rough sort have gone, and the boys have come back; and I don't think you'll find a better crew of fellows anywhere. The public don't forget the war-time driver, and I don't blame 'em, sir.'

I looked up at the Junior Turf Club, no longer a haven, no longer (let me say in a loud voice) a generous distributor of midnight sausage, no longer a romantic oasis in the darkness of a sleeping city in which you might find a yawning beauty, a crumpled peer, a prince, a pauper, or a rake.

'OH . . . blow! Another ladder!'

Miss Jones hits her Remington savagely and swears that she will never again buy good stockings. That's what comes of wearing her best pair of non-stop silk on a week-day. If she had been Lady This or Lady That, lounging about in a motor-car all day, she expects that her lovely pair of crunchy ones would have lasted for years; but just because she was nearly run down by an omnibus at the Bank and had to jump for her life . . . oh, blow! (I may remark that when you are trying to dress like a duchess on seventy shillings a week a ladder is a tragedy.)

So, when the typewriters are sheeted, and silence falls over the City of London, Miss Jones takes an omnibus to Bagdad to repair the damage. She crosses Piccadilly, walks up Shaftesbury Avenue, turns leewards up Rupert Street, enters Little Pulteney Street, and right opposite is Bagdad-in-the-West, known to thousands of girls who walk in fear of ladders as Berwick Market.

*　　*　　*　　*　　*

Berwick Market was patented in Bagdad and Jerusalem centuries ago. In sun or rain the shop awnings come down and meet the canvas roofs of a continuous line of street booths, so that when you walk on the footpath you go through a dark tunnel of canvas, just like an Arab *souk*. If all the Jews in Berwick Street would wear long false beards one day, it would be possible to take a photograph which any short-sighted traveller would swear was Jerusalem.

A glorious colour is given to Berwick Street by thousands of silk stockings. Every shade of sunburn is there, from the boiled shrimp to the colour of a brunette spending a holiday in Jamaica. Those stalls that do not sell silk stockings sell other necessary, and unnecessary, female garments with true Oriental candour. (Berwick Street is the one proof this age possesses that the corset is not quite extinct.)

*　　*　　*　　*　　*

As Miss Jones goes thoughtfully through Bagdad, sharp dark eyes realize that she requires silk stockings. If Joan of Arc went to Berwick Street in full armour, they would think the same about her.

'Now, miss, four and six a pair, any colour! The very same you pay ten shillings for anywhere else! Look for yerself. . . .'

Miss Jones goes critically onward, neglecting the soft blandishments of ripe young Rebeccas and the advice of their smart younger brothers. As she proceeds, she sees dozens of girls like herself, who have chinchilla minds and coney incomes, carefully picking over stalls burdened with every kind of attire, smart, flashy, and slightly elegant.

Miss Jones toys a moment with quite a good white fox fur that would look so nice with that snuff brown coat and skirt of hers; but it's far too much! She sees a tea-gown with the authentic plainness and simplicity about it that tells her it began life in higher circles.

'Now, that's a snip, miss. Just your style!'

She moves on to her particular stall.

Her hands dive into silk stockings neatly packed in long cardboard boxes, lying in peachy heaps, and waving limp, distorted legs as they trail unhabited from the roofs of stalls. Ah; the right smart shade, the right subtle tint; not that cheap pink, or that common reddy brown!

'Six shillings!'

'Four and six,' says Miss Jones, who knows the price to a penny.

An argument inseparable from Jerusalem or Bagdad follows at once.

'Then five shillings and sixpence to you, miss.'

'Four and six,' says Miss Jones coldly and with hauteur.

'Be a sport and split the difference—five bob!'

'I said four and six, and I mean four and six,' replies Miss Jones.

Contemptuous looks pass, and Miss Jones, with a faint shrug of pretty shoulders, walks quickly away; but not far! Although she has not travelled in the East, she has instinct.

'Miss, one moment! Take 'em. They're the last pair!'

        *   *   *   *   *

Through the dim gloom of Bagdad-in-the-West walks Miss Jones with the comforting knowledge that, on the morrow, a close observer, regarding her, will find her irreproachable. ('Ooh; what a lovely blouse!' Impossible; she just owns the omnibus fare home to England!)

HE is one of life's little insincerities. You have not seen him for years; you have, in fact, forgotten his existence, and he yours. Suddenly, from the mystery of a London crowd, he springs at you with an overjoyed expression and two out-stretched hands. At first you think that a stranger has mis-taken you; then, vaguely, you remember him. His eyes are shining with delight, and you instinctively withdraw from this overpowering affability, feeling that, in a comparative stranger, it is almost indecent.

'Well, well, well!' he gurgles, breathing all over you. 'If it isn't dear old Henricus! Put it there, my boy!'

You have no alternative. A dog would bite him, a child would run away, but you, being a full-grown man, are forced to stay and play out the farce to the end.

* * * * *

'How are you, Jones?' you say, inwardly congratulating yourself that you have got his name right first time.

'In the pink, old dear, in the pink!' he replies (he says everything twice); 'Jove, I'm glad to see you; I'm glad to see your dear old face again!'

You wonder why. You are not glad to see his. You do not dislike him, and you do not like him: he is just one of millions outside your life; yet he behaves as if he owned the corner seat in your heart.

You endure his attitude, feeling mildly hard-hearted and wishing that you, too, could join with him in being pleased. Are you misanthropic? Yet you cannot let yourself go; some shrewd .instinct tells you to keep your mouth shut because you realize that he is insincere; a glad hand merchant, full of what the Americans call 'blaa.'

'I'm doing marvellously . . . marvellously!' he rejoices, hitting your shoulder heartily. 'I've just bought a brand new forty-five horse-power Flick and I'm off to France next Monday with the wife and kids. Going down to Monte, and then probably Italy. Have a cigar?'

'No; I never smoke them!'

'A cigarette? This side. They're a special kind of Turkish I have made for me!'

He looks at you intently, hits you on the chest, smacks your shoulder, and tells you that you look ill.

'Look here!' he cries. 'Why don't you come with us?'

*　　　*　　　*　　　*　　　*

This friendliness is staggering. You are divided between wonder at it and horror at the thought of being alone with him for a day. You point out that you have work to do and certain responsibilities. He waves them away.

'Nonsense, my dear old thing! Snatch a fortnight, snatch a fortnight!' he says airily. 'By the way, you've met my wife, haven't you?'

You say that you think you have. There is a pause. You try hard to fill it with some innocuous remark before he invites you to go and stay with him for ten years.

'Jove! I shall never forget that speech you made at the dinner,' he says moistly. 'I often sit and think about it. It was dashed good.'

'When was that?'

'Do you mean to say you've forgotten? And old Brown, the chairman, and Robinson, who—by the way, Robinson's dead!'

He peers at you sadly, expecting you to burst into tears; but you cannot remember Robinson. He might just as well become emotional about Julius Caesar. Oddly enough, you half like the man. What a hard-hearted fellow you are—selfish, self-centred. What right have you to drop old friends? He seems to represent a forgotten world which is aching for your return. How terrible to be loved; and not to love.

*　　　*　　　*　　　*　　　*

'Come to dinner to-night?' he flashes at you.

This sobers you. You fend him off. You say good-bye, but he comes back, as if unable to leave you.

'Have you heard this one?'

You say 'Ha, ha,' and try to laugh. He lands a farewell hit at you and departs. You go on, congratulating yourself that you are alone again; but you are not. He is at your side.

'Look here,' he cries urgently. 'If you *do* think you can snatch a fortnight, ring me up.'

'I will,' you say.

'But you don't know the number.'

'No; of course not.   What is it?'

'Here's my card!   Now, don't forget!   We expect you!
Don't let us down!   We won't hear of a refusal!   Good-bye,
old dear; it's done me good to see you!   Good-bye; and, look
here, if you see Brown at any time . . .'

*   *   *   *   *

Eventually he goes.

You walk on with the certain knowledge that he has by
now forgotten you.   You wish you had agreed to invade his
holiday just to see the effect of the shock on him.   You also
wonder what would have happened had you asked him to
lend you five pounds.

I WONDER how many among the thousands who walk down
Monkwell Street, near London Wall, every day of the year,
know the story of the Man with Two Lives? Tucked away
between warehouses and offices, is the hall of the Worshipful
Company of Barbers. I entered the courtyard and rang the
bell.

'I want to look at the screen,' I said.

'Come in.'

I was led through an admirable hall into a much decorated
early-Stuart court-room that escaped the Fire of London.
In this room, built over a much earlier hall, the barber surgeons
met to discuss medieval shingles and Tudor appendicitis.
The surgeons grew too clever for the barbers and were separated by Act of Parliament in 1745.

The screen I had come to see was standing behind the door.
There are millions of screens in the world, but I think none
has a history to compare with this; as you shall judge.

*   *   *   *   *

In the year 1740 the body of a notorious criminal was cut
from the gallows at Tyburn and sent to the Barbers' Hall for
dissection. I think the company were granted four bodies a
year. A member of the company accepted the body, and was
preparing it for the post-mortem when he was startled to
observe signs of life, very slight, very uncertain. You can
imagine how, torn between astonishment and professional
enthusiasm, he set to work to make that 'dead' man's heart
beat again. When he had worked over the body for some
time, it became obvious that the hangman had been cheated.
The criminal was alive.

His heart gained strength, the blood began coursing through
his veins, and, at length, his eyes opened. What a situation
for both men! The criminal in that second when his brain
awakened, still packed with last-minute reflections, his ears
still hearing the shouting of the mob that had seen him at the
gallows, must have imagined himself in heaven or hell. The
anatomist, too, must have suffered a shock; he had given life
back to a criminal. What should he do? What would you

have done? Would the man belong to the law, or to your sense of humanity?

Sitting in the dissecting room with the man who was officially dead, the surgeon decided that this resurrection must be kept dark. He was forced to inform the other anatomists who were ready with their knives. He told them. They agreed that the poor wretch had atoned for his sins, and that they would have to stand by him in his rebirth. They fed, clothed, and hid him, and, one dark night, when he was strong enough to travel, they gave him money, wished him luck, and shipped him to the Continent.

The man who had been hanged departed gratefully.

One wonders, for details are scarce, if he left a wife to mourn him, or children who thought him dead.

*   *   *   *   *

The story does not end here.

Years passed by. One day there arrived at the Barber Surgeons' Hall a richly decorated screen. It was from the man who had been screened. It appeared that he had begun a new life under a new name, had made good, and was a rich and influential merchant in the Levant.

'It's a wonderful old screen,' said my guide.

'Indeed it is,' I replied.

I found it more interesting than Holbein's picture of Henry VIII granting a charter to the company, a picture which Samuel Pepys tried to buy after the Fire of London for two hundred pounds, because, as he naïvely admitted, it was well worth a thousand pounds. How much it is worth now it is impossible to say. The Prince Consort was so fond of it that he used to visit it frequently, and he even persuaded the company to send it to Buckingham Palace for a month. A royal commission inspected it later, and tried to decide whether its life in the atmosphere of the City was injurious to it. They hung in the room specimens of colours for many months, but when no change took place they decided that it would come to no harm in Monkwell Street.

There is a story that Robert Peel admired it so extravagantly that he wanted to sleep on the table in the court-room, so that it would be the first thing he would see in the morning.

*   *   *   *   *

But give me the symbolic gift of 'the man who was hanged.' There are few such human relics in the world. It stands there, its paint still vivid, a testimony to the queer ups and downs of human life, a proof that while there is life there is hope, a faded sermon from another day telling us that, no matter how bad a man may be, he sometimes seizes a second chance and takes a grip on life.

Under the Arch ✑ ✑ ✑ ✑ ✑ ✑

IF you wish to feel your heart touched one moment and to rock with laughter the next, come with me any Wednesday evening to a gloomy railway arch off the Camberwell New Road.

Fifty men, women, and children sit on wooden benches in the gloom, facing each other across the rough stone floor. Each one of them holds a cat or a dog. Some of them nurse sacks full of indignant wriggles. Each one has a story. Prince swallowed a needle, Jenny was run over by a brewer's dray, Alf's tail won't wag, something queer has happened to Beauty's left ear . . . see how it droops! This is Sister Mabel's Free Dispensary for Animals of the Poor. Here come all the comedy and tragedy that can happen to a dog or a cat in Camberwell. . . .

It is a poor place. Just a railway arch. It is as poor as the animals it helps, yet for four years it has been famous all over South London. A surprising little smiling woman, known to every cat, dog, goat, donkey, and canary in Camberwell, opened this place of healing four years ago, with the help of Lord Hertford, and, ever since, Sister Mabel has been smiling benevolently, looking at her bankbook and believing in Providence.

*   *   *   *   *

A silver-haired man with a fine face stood under a gas jet in a tiny room—Mr. Murt, the 'vet.,' who for four years has crossed London every Wednesday to give his services free and to put in a week's work in four hours just because—well, there is something in the eyes of a suffering animal that grips the heart.

One by one the people sitting in the adjacent archway entered the tiny consulting-room. A girl came in: a handsome grey-eyed girl.

'What's the matter with Chum?' she asked, lifting a collie to the table.

'Mange,' said Mr. Murt promptly. 'Now take this ointment and cut off his coat and . . .'

A dramatic change came over the girl. Her arms went round the dog. She might have been acting for a film.

15   225

'Chum, Chum!' she said. 'Your lovely coat! Isn't that rotten?'

She looked up from the mangy fur, and two tears fell.

'He won't let anyone but a policeman touch me,' she said. 'He's my guardian, he's my . . .'

Chum licked her hand, and two more tears fell. Then, swift as a flash, she smiled and wagged her finger at the dog.

'You bad boy,' she cried, 'you've caught this from your wives! Serve you right, Chum! Didn't I tell you to keep away from the girls?'

'Are things always as funny as this?' I asked the 'vet.'

'Oh, that's nothing!' he said.

*   *   *   *   *

In came a ragged old woman wearing a black straw hat and a sack round her waist. She had no teeth. She emptied a sack, which she carried, on the table. Out came a large, injured-looking black cat.

'He's getting better!' shouted the old woman with the vigour of the stone deaf.

'Yes, he is!' yelled Mr. Murt in her ear.

'How I've persevered with that there medicine!' shrieked the old woman.

'Go on with it!' bellowed the 'vet.'

Then the old, gnarled hands picked up the cat, and the old eyes grew tender. 'There, there, Tibby!' she shouted, in what was meant to be an intimate whisper. 'You'll soon be well!' and I knew that the big black cat was the only living thing on earth that this poor woman had to love.

I watched this for an hour: pups run over by motor-cars, dogs with mange and distemper; and always such love, such tender looks, such tail waggings from the dogs, until:

'Please, mother says will you have Arfur killed, 'cause the lady upstairs says she'll turn us into the street if he don't stop barkin'.'

Arthur, a nice little fox terrier, stood there with his head on one side, so pathetically unconscious of crime, so pleased with life, and—so near to death.

'You can't kill him?' I said.

'We do our best not to,' said Mr. Murt. 'We have a register of those willing to take dogs. We keep these poor little chaps and try to find them homes, but if we can't . . . it's better than having them kicked about the streets starving.'

*   *   *   *   *

'What's that queer sound?' I asked.

It came from an inner room: a regular beat like a muffled engine. I went in. Six big galvanized boxes with glass lids stood by the wall. From one of them came this strange sound. In a corner lay a pile of poor stiff little corpses, cats and dogs: the unwanted, the maimed, the victims of street accidents. I looked through the glass of the box from which the sound came. Inside was a small black spaniel, unconscious, his legs running, running into death, his claws hitting the tin sides of the box regularly, growing weaker and weaker and weaker.

Run over, maimed! A weeping child asks: 'Please will you make him well again?' and the 'vet.' looks from the child's red eyes to the dog's eyes and knows that nothing can be done. They must say good-bye.

*   *   *   *   *

'I dream,' said little Sister Mabel to me, 'of an animals' hospital here some day where I could do so much more.'

'And if I were a millionaire,' I replied, 'I would take out a cheque book now and make your dream come true.'

A breathless girl came up with a pink-nosed bull-pup.

'Please, Sister,' she gasped, 'mother says will you kill it 'cause she's got too many children.'

Sister Mabel picked up the fat white pup, which licked her neck, and she called for the list of 'dogs wanted'—a book of life and death.

BEHIND the counter sit (unusual sight) policemen without helmets. They are writing. They write with that diligent expression common to all literary policemen.

Facing them, crowding round the counter, are men and women of a strangely varied kind. No other room of this size in London holds so many different types. This is the Aliens Registration Office in Bow Street Police Station, and the walls are lined with a card index packed with foreign names. Here are known the name, home town, business and address in England of every foreigner in this country, their wives, their families, and all manner of intimate details. Every time a foreigner leaves London he has to tell Bow Street about it, and, when he returns, he has to inform Bow Street that he is here again. (And this is the country that once held open house to the world!)

*   *   *   *   *

The crowd seeking registration contains men and women who are obviously alien; swarthy men, sloe-eyed women, and olive-skinned children—Slavs, Japanese, a stray Chinese, talkative Frenchmen, whose square black beards hide their ties; plain, middle-class Frenchwomen, hand-in-hand with big sons in sailor suits. Others present seem remarkably English till they talk in German or Scandinavian; some hail, without doubt, from the land of the Stars and Stripes.

'See here!' says an American, 'I'm back in London!'

He pushes over grey papers bearing his photograph.

The policeman turns round, pulls out a drawer in the wall, picks up a card, and says:

'You left Stratford-on-Avon last Wednesday, didn't you?'

'I guess so.'

Wonderful system! Here is a net spread out over the country to catch the undesirable.

'It's a darned nuisance,' says the American, 'all this hokum.'

'Well, you see, sir, it's necessary,' replies the constable. 'We know you are all right, but some people want watching.'

'I get you. The innocent sufferin' for the guilty.'

228

'That's it.'

Bang goes the Bow Street mark on the papers, and the American walks out with the freedom of London in his pocket.

*   *   *   *   *

A pretty girl comes in and breaks into attractive French-English. She is excited. She wants to tell the story of her life. Bow Street is a cold, unemotional spot, and the young police officer allows her to empty her heart completely before he asks her a few pointed questions:

'So you're a governess!'

She waves her hands and leaps into explanation. The policeman sighs heavily.

'Don't go off the deep end again, miss,' he pleads. 'Are you, or are you not, a governess?'

They straighten that out. He stamps the necessary documents, and off she goes. The policeman then, with the calm of a granite statue, turns to register a Pole or a Dutchman. He is used to the whole world.

*   *   *   *   *

Sometimes a test case in patience arrives.

This proves that the London policeman is the most considerate and helpful policeman on earth.

An Oriental, with narrow startled eyes in a large expanse of yellow face, comes up and makes queer noises with his mouth. The policeman reaches the conclusion that he is speaking either Japanese, Siamese, or Chinese. He scratches his ear with a pen and looks thoughtful.

'Where do you live?' he asks hopelessly.

The alien returns a blank stare.

'Live!' shouts the policeman, who believes, like so many, that if a foreigner cannot understand, it helps to shout English at the top of your voice.

The mystery man shakes his head.

'Live!' repeats the policeman. 'Sleep, then?'

He places his hands together and puts his cheek against them, closing his eyes. This electrifies the applicant.

'Huggleboff!' he says brightly.

The policeman ponders.

'Say it again slowly!'

'Huggleboff. . . . Huggleboff. . . .'

'Bill, where's Huggleboff?'

The policeman is forced to consult his colleague. Their worthy faces peer at the foreigner; they persuade him to say it again and again, only to descend deeper into doubt. After half an hour's work the foreigner has a brilliant inspiration, and pulling out a much-thumbed map of London places his finger promptly on Hammersmith.

'Well, I'll be dashed! Why didn't you say so?' asks the policeman.

*   *   *   *   *

So the mental wrestling match continues. The room fills and empties every fifteen minutes. In the corner remains an exhausted policeman and a man making funny sounds that seem like:

'Hikklegobble.'

'Bill,' says the policeman to his friend, wearily but kindly, 'we were getting on a fair treat and—now he's said that!'

Bill looks sympathetic; and comes over to help.

SHE was sitting on a doorstep near Ludgate Hill. It was bedtime.

A late Liverpool Street omnibus came down Fleet Street full of people anxious about the last train to Ilford. In another hour the best part of eight million people would have locked their front doors and have sought rest in the security of their own homes. . . .

This woman was alone on a doorstep; her roof the cold night sky; her bed, stone; her covering, a thin white mist like a winding sheet that was slowly creeping over Blackfriars from the river. At first sight, she resembled a vague bundle of rags hunched against the door, lying in the shadow with grey hair escaping from an incredibly ancient bonnet that had once been rather rakish. Round her shoulders was a torn and dirty plaid shawl, and her boots had, when they were young, belonged to a man. Lying in a bar of light cast from a street lamp was a thin, claw-like hand, deformed by rheumatism, brown, horrible; and also pathetic, because it had outlived the plough to which it had been set.

* * * * *

Who was she?

I suppose every man who lives in London has at some time or other asked himself this question as he sees Nobody's Women lying in doorways, trying to snatch a moment's sleep on an Embankment seat, stretched full length on the pews of merciful St. Martin's crypt with white hair on a pile of prayer books.

An abandoned woman, old, ugly, and helpless, flung on the scrap heap, is the most hideous of all Nature's jokes.

Perhaps forty years ago some man compared her eyes with stars and thought her shoulders—those shoulders leaning now against cold stone—the most perfect beauty on earth as they peeped from a thin gown. No doubt she once inspired all the good in a man—or all the bad. And now: Nobody's Woman. . . .

What stories lie behind each of these lives: stories of bad luck and bad character; stories, no doubt, of supreme self-sacrifice, trust, faithfulness, and betrayal. If it were only possible to flash a light back over the lives of these failures what would we see? In some we would be able to forecast the end, no doubt; in others the end, by contrast with the beginning, would horrify us. We read in the 'Thousand and One Nights' of beggars who become princes and, in a night, descend again into the gutters, and we think this a marvellous romance: yet here in London, as in Bagdad, the ups and downs of life lie tossed about street corners for anyone to see.

Dull, mercifully comatose, Nobody's Women drag themselves about the streets at night looking for a place in which to rest their unwanted bones. Sometimes you see them creeping like ghouls round the galvanized tins which the restaurants put outside in the streets in the small hours of morning, digging into the foul rejections of other people's dinners with poor, claw-like fingers which once—who knows?—were lovely and white round the stem of a champagne glass.

*   *   *   *   *

The human heart so often outlives the body that I wonder how many of these old wrecks tossing about the world are already dead to feeling, untouched by humiliation; for it is possible for a human being to be dead to everything but memory. I wonder how many live with the knowledge that the dream is over, yet eternal; that the present is nothing, the future nothing, the past the only thing of which life cannot cheat you.

I have heard so many strange things that it would not surprise me to hear a voice from the rags cry: 'Go away, with your sentiment and your speculations, you fool; I have once been happy. I was once beautiful. I was once loved. . . .'

*   *   *   *   *

The hair lay in thin wisps, that brown, wrinkled hand lay listlessly in the bar of light; and the rags stirred uneasily against the stone.

I went up to salve my conscience, to make myself feel comfortable at the cost of half a crown, but, when I drew near, I realized that it would be cruel to do anything; for she was asleep.

Gold Watch Men ✍ ✍ ✍ ✍ ✍

IT is a well-known maxim in certain walks of commercial life that, if you can wait long enough, a mug will always arrive on the scene.

The three men near the door, who were trying to look like the general public, bore a strong racial and family resemblance to the auctioneer. They edged up when I arrived; and I could feel the mental telepathy go from head to head—'The Mug, bless him!'

The shop was in a condition of delirious altruism. Posters inflamed the little side street with news of incredible bargains. I received the impression that wrist-watches, gold cigarette cases, and safety razors had been having a race down the hill of reduction and had collapsed together in a heap in the window.

Looking beyond the little table drawn up in the shop door, behind which stood the auctioneer, I could see shelves dominated by simpering china shepherdesses and sweet-faced china dogs. There were also several bronze men who had evidently lost their trousers in an attempt to control runaway horses.

'And now,' said the auctioneer, 'will any gent give me a bob for this fountain pen? 'S'worth ten shillings!'

There was a sticky pause. Then:

'I will,'' brightly responded the fattest relative.

'You're a sport! Gimme a penny!' said the auctioneer, throwing the pen towards his relation, and accepting in exchange a penny on whose well-worn surface Britannia and King Edward were dizzy with passing to and from the auctioneer all day long.

*   *   *   *   *

In fifteen minutes I was sorry for the fat man. His pockets bulged with gifts: cigarette cases, fountain pens, pen-knives, cigarette holders, safety razors; and still the fish were not nibbling. It was becoming rather unpleasant. The auctioneer contrived to make me feel ashamed. He started to give the fat man things in the most open-handed and embarrassing way: somebody trusted him, somebody was a real sport, but, more important than anything—somebody trusted him!

"Ere, put this in your pocket! When a man trusts me, I stand by him.'

A briar pipe flew through the air.

(I stood watching such a silly china shepherdess who was engaged in the act of curtseying in my direction. I remembered that, when I was a small boy, I used to scatter handfuls of ground-bait into the water before angling for little fish.)

The family were beginning to hate me, and I wondered whether they would have the honesty to say: 'Oh, do go away and let's have a quiet smoke!' Then I became aware of a certain access of briskness. A man with a droopy moustache was standing next to me. He offered a shilling for a pen. It was given to him for a penny. A man and a woman joined us. The man wanted to buy a pen, but his wife whispered, 'No, no, don't you!' The auctioneer, hearing this, seemed cut to the heart. With a generous gesture, he asked the man with the drooping moustache to accept this second pen as a gift, because—he never could resist a good sport!

*   *   *   *   *

'And now, ladies and gents,' said the auctioneer, mounting a rostrum, 'here is something worth buying. It's my last lot to-day!'

He placed on the table a woman's glittering gold wrist-watch.

I admired the way he kept things going. The crowd was just like a herd of deer. You can coax a herd to you, but, one sudden movement, and it is off to cover. We were like that.

Still; things were looking pretty bad. The family ran up the bidding to eleven shillings. The man with the moustache offered twelve shillings. A fresh-faced young man in front offered fifteen shillings. I had not noticed him before: he was obviously a little too anxious to buy the watch. He turned round to cast a swift look at his rival, which I thought a rather inartistic action. Then this young man ran up the bidding to eighteen shillings. People pulled themselves together and left. The party was breaking up.

With consummate skill, the auctioneer held the man with the drooping moustache; he reminded him of the two pens worth one pound which had cost him one penny. Two more shillings and the woman's rolled gold wrist-watch was his!

One pound and worth ten! Come along now! The little man wavered, was just about to bid, then, thinking that either the watch or the woman was not worth it, shook his head and walked out. I admired the sporting way the auctioneer took his defeat. He knew that there was no other buyer, so, casting a quick glance at the young man, he sold him the watch for a crumpled pound note. Very pretty!

* * * * *

I walked slowly down the side street and into the main road. At the corner the fresh-faced young man was talking to a girl.

'It's nice, isn't it?' he was saying.

'Oh, but you shouldn't have!' she replied, holding the frightfully gold wrist-watch to catch the sun.

The Children's Ward ⚬ ⚬ ⚬ ⚬ ⚬

ON the top floor of the Charing Cross Hospital is the children's ward. A fat Teddy Bear stands in smug cheerfulness by the door. Marigolds shine in a slant of sun as though self-illuminated. Each cot contains a small child.

Some are asleep, their heads lost in white pillows, a picture-book flung aside on the bed, small fists clutching the sheet as if in need of something to hold in this first unfair conflict with life. Crazy temperature charts hang by each bed, up and down like the plan of a switchback railway. The sister walks softly to a cot, places her cool hand on damp curls, gives a swift glance to the chart, and sighs; or smiles and passes on. In many beds children are playing quietly with bricks and dolls, or sitting up with wide eyes, singing little songs to themselves, or proving their recovery by pretending to hide beneath the clothes as we approach.

*　　*　　*　　*　　*

I stop at the bedside of a girl of eight. The bedclothes outline her slim little body. Her skin is pure pink and white; her hair, spun gold with a deeper blush of brown in it; her eyes green-blue as the sea at Capri. Someone's lovely little daughter. She smiles as we come up, and ceases to build bricks on her chest with such white hands.

'Sister,' she whispers, flirting her sea-green eyes wickedly. 'Sister, I do love you. . . .'

The white arms are raised as the sister bends down. The body moves slightly, instinct with affection, urgent with a desire to love and be loved, and the arms go round the sister's neck and the hands play a minute with her hair.

'What a beauty,' I say, as we go on. 'When she grows up she'll——'

'She'll be a cripple,' says the sister quietly. 'Spinal.'

*　　*　　*　　*　　*

We enter a ward inhabited by small brownish babies, who sleep with their tiny faces screwed up and lips moving. Now and again they make queer indefinite movements, a kind of

236

boneless writhing. I bend over them and smile; for it always seems so funny that these strange little things can turn into men and women, grow whiskers, and become grandfathers . . . then the sister says one word and I draw back in horror, for this is one of the most ghastly rooms in all London.

'But we call it "wasting disease," ' she murmurs.

The sins of the fathers and the mothers. As I look at those poor babies I think that I would not only call them by their real name, but that I would also show them to all young men and women. This is a black sin. A man's life is his own to make or break, but this stream of other lives, tainted at the source of life, handicapped before birth, and going on and on branded by impurity, is a crime the soul shudders from.

'And science must keep them alive? That seems unfair to them and to the world.'

'Thou shalt not kill,' says the sister. 'Thou shalt not kill!'

*   *   *   *   *

In another room, jolly little babies of all ages roll and tumble round their cots, pulling themselves up solemnly and subsiding fatly, vaguely annoyed or thrilled by the law of gravity. Babies are of two types: the batter-pudding kind and the little old man kind which enter the world looking like their own grandfathers.

'Curious things happen here,' says the sister. 'What do you think of this little fellow?'

He is two months old, and resembles the oldest inhabitant. His chin juts out and his nose is large. The only thing he requires is a small blond moustache and a pair of pince-nez and he could then put on a bowler hat and go out into the world. I told the sister that he could get a job anywhere as a collector of rates and taxes. That type. A smart little man.

'Well,' she said, 'he's a poor little fellow, and he doesn't know the trouble he's caused. He's the exact image of his father, and his father cannot see it. He thinks he looks like someone else. He's separated from his wife because of it.'

'But this baby is like a family portrait,' I say.

'Of course he is,' she replies indignantly. 'And if that wretched father came in now you could hardly tell them apart. The fool!'

*   *   *   *   *

A woman sits beside a cot in a quiet ward holding the hand of a baby. The child turns and twists in a troubled sleep and whimpers piteously. The woman is poor; her hands are grimed with work.

'That's her seventh child,' whispers the sister. 'They are to operate in a few minutes. Something wrong inside, and we don't know what it is.'

And the woman with seven children sits there, a symbol of Motherhood, grieving for this little child of hers as if it were the only one, worn with sacrifice, torn with pity, raw with love.

A doctor comes in, soothing, kind.

'Don't worry. It will be all right. Really. Trust us.'

He beckons to the nurses; and the woman kneels down and buries her tired face in the bright hair on the pillow.

*　　　*　　　*　　　*　　　*

How unconscious are the London crowds outside of all this so near to them, always with them; this tall building ploughing its way through suffering like a splendid ship at sea.

TWO men with earphones strapped to their heads sit in a tall white tower at Croydon Aerodrome. When they are not speaking on a wireless wave, receiving telegrams, writing figures in ledgers, or poring over maps, they can look out of the windows and watch the big Paris air liners swoop out of the sky. The green Surrey fields behind the landing ground rise to a ridge on which, far off, the Crystal Palace holds two giant candlesticks in the air.[1]

This is the Control Tower of London's Air Port. It is the ear, eye, and voice of the aerodrome. There is nothing else like it in the country. Pilots above the clouds in the Channel pour their troubles into the ears behind the headphones, and voices from this white tower go out into the sky, soothing the worries of airmen in bad weather, helping them, leading them home. On a cork table is painted a map of Europe. One of the men is always busy sticking little coloured flags on the map.

'Look!' he says. 'These are the aeroplanes now flying. This Goliath has just passed that Handley Page over Hythe. That flag in mid-Channel is a French machine coming over with a cargo of silk stockings. This blue flag is the Cologne 'plane. . . .'

'Passed Lympne!' whispers the man next to him; and the aeroplane-spotter picks up a little flag and takes it out of Kent into the sea.

*   *   *   *   *

. I pick up a headphone and strap it on. Nothing happens. Everybody, it seems, is happy in the sky. There is no fog, there is no wind, there are no complaints. Then, suddenly:

'Hallo, Croydon?' cries a cheery voice. 'Hallo? A passenger in my machine is very troubled.'

'That's the Cologne pilot speaking from the Channel,' whispers one of the control men.

'He's very troubled,' says the pilot, 'because he's left his passport with you at the aerodrome. Now, can you send it

[1] The Crystal Palace was burnt down in November 1936, ten years after this was written.

on at once to the Dom Hotel at Cologne? You can? I'll tell him. Thank you.'

Before the man driving the Cologne air-liner cuts off I think I heard him sing a cheerful little song away up there in the sky above the Channel; but I cannot be sure!

*   ⁂   *   ⁂   *

One of the clerks writes out a note about the passport, and a messenger climbs down the perpendicular ladder with it and goes off among the old army huts below to deliver it.

I look round the control tower, admire the hundred gadgets it contains, admire the map with two pieces of string hanging to it, which is one way of finding a lost 'plane. (I wish I could explain why.) Then one of the control men turns a switch and hundreds of red lights spring out, deep ruby in the sun-light, crowning the tops of huts. He turns another switch and ground lights come to life. I realize how thrilling this tower must be on a stormy winter night with a cold pilot buffeting about in the sky and the rain lashing the windows, and a plaintive voice coming out of the clouds, asking for light— and more light—and news of the wind down below. . . .

*   *   *   *   *

The telephone bell rings. The restless traffic controller of the Imperial Airways is on the other end of the wire. He is a man who counts his 'planes more carefully than a hen mothers her chickens. If one lags behind, he gets nervy and wants to know all about it.

'What's happened to the cargo machine that left Zurich this morning?'

'Signalled Lympne half an hour ago,' is the quick reply.

'Thanks, she'll be here in no time.'

A man with a pair of field glasses moves round on the out-side platform and says something that sounds nautical. I look out and see far over the Surrey hills a dot in the sky. He has spotted the Paris 'plane. The men write in their books. She is up to time.

In a few minutes she comes roaring over our heads, making a wide circle, going off, it seems, to the Crystal Palace; then she turns, skims back over the aerodrome roofs, and comes to earth, her fat-tyred wheels churning up the dust from the grass. She is big and brown, and along her body runs a strip of plate glass, through which I can see a row of excited faces, a girl's pink hat, a man in a tweed cap. . . .

She taxies to her landing place. The mechanics run to her. The pilot heaves himself up in his seat, raises his goggles, and steps out in a belted leather coat, groping for a cigarette. Men run up with steps. A young man comes out of the aeroplane with a camera, the girl in the pink hat appears and stands smiling in the doorway as he takes a snapshot of her. Then she steps delicately out upon the earth.

She does not notice the tall white tower that brings liners home through the sky, and the tall white tower does not notice her, for—it is chatting with a pilot half-way to Holland.

16

HE was only a little fellow and he was tired.

Every now and then he would rub his sleeve against his eyes and yawn. It was dark. It was also cold, and he had no coat. The London traffic thundered at intervals past him along the street, but he took no notice of the waxing moons, that are headlights, or the splendid scarlet omnibuses charging out of the distance into the distance. He was leaning his thin body against the open door of a public bar, gazing through it into that warm yellow cheerfulness in which his parents were putting away considerable quantities of beer.

Now and then he would forget that, for legal reasons, he had been told to 'keep outside.' His feet would stray naturally from the dark into the light, a yard or so only; and he was over that threshold, his pale, tired face watching—a poor little creature capable of getting everybody into an awful row with any passing policeman.

*   *   *   *   *

At such moments his mother would put down her glass with a 'drat that child' thump, and would dart to him and take his thin little shoulder in her convivial hand, saying:

'Now go on, Alf, keep outside, can't you? Outside, you understand!'

Unquestionably, Alf went back outside, a frail black silhouette that no one noticed: back to lean against that door, to be jostled by people going in and people coming out, to rub his hand across his seedy-feeling eyes, but not (so marvellously do children accept circumstances) to wonder for one second why on earth he had been born to stand outside an unpleasant place that makes parents either hit or kiss one another.

Poor Alf.

*   *   *   *   *

I felt sorry for Alf.

I remembered that, when you are as small as he, things have a way of etching themselves on your brain in fine, deep lines. Grown-up people think you do not notice things; but you do. Nothing escapes you. Grown-up people think you are a child, whereas, to yourself, you are just as mature as they are, only in a different kind of way. They are big and strong and incomprehensible; you are small and weak and clear-minded. Your world is more logical than theirs; at times they seem insane: they do such silly things.

All you can do is to remember and think, and worry and wonder . . . wonder. . . .

* * * * *

A thin woman left a perambulator outside the public-house as she went inside to 'have one.'

Alf stole over to it and looked inside at a fat baby deep in sleep. In this baby's hand was a paper bag which evidently held sweets. The sight appeared to revive Alf slightly. He looked round. He looked inside the bar. He looked up and down the street. Then he put forth a hand and took the bag. He took a sweet and replaced the bag carefully. The sweet bulged in his cheek. Then it did not bulge. Alf looked towards the innocent child, his morality on the ebb. He stole up again and took two, then he felt it was a pity to do a thing by halves —he took the last and put back the bag.

I forgot my omnibus as I watched him.

I wondered whether he was conscious of any moral lapse or whether it had seemed to him the only right and proper thing to do. I felt that if at Alf's age I had spent many evenings waiting in the street outside a public-house I would probably have done exactly the same thing; and who would be to blame?

The thin woman came out, looking stronger, and removed the scene of the crime. Alf exhibited no outward signs of relief as the perambulator with its comatose victim departed into the dark. . . .

* * * * *

Mr. and Mrs. Alf came out of the bar in a jocose mood. They lingered with an acquaintance.

'That your little boy?' asked the acquaintance.

'That's the nipper,' remarked Mr. Alf proudly.

'He's a good, quiet little chap,' said the acquaintance. 'Why, my Bert hardly gives you time to 'ave a quick one, he's that restless.'

'Alf's a good boy,' said his father heavily, giving the pale little face a playful slap. 'Ain't you, Alf . . . a good boy,' he repeated reflectively.

Alf did not deny this. He just looked up with that peaky little face at the parents who were letting him grow like a weed in a garden. Then they all went homeward.

Poor Alf. . . .

IT is 4.30 in the afternoon, that sluggish time when the City of London, the bulk of its work done, begins to think of tea-cake.

In a large building near London Wall a well-lit room that knows no tea-time, no luncheon interval, no dinner-time, no Sunday or Bank Holiday, is just getting into its stride. A steady slacking of typewriter keys, staccato drumming from queer electric instruments, the plopping of leather cylinders as they fall from pneumatic tubes into wire cages compose the metallic medley that never ceases day or night. More than seventy men and women sit at desks, ranked row on row, bent and intent; for they are serving the great Atlantic cable. For three thousand two hundred miles it lies like a swollen serpent on the bed of the ocean, while messages of wealth and ruin, of hope and despair, of friendly greeting and commercial agreement flash along the mysterious length of it. The room is the receiving and transmitting office of the Western Union Cable Company.

Now see one of the most marvellous things in London.

A young man sits at a desk watching a little inch-wide strip of paper run from a complicated looking box over a metal strip. An uncanny little metal pointer, one end vibrating in a tiny pool of green ink, the other moving rapidly over the paper, traces a queer endless pattern on the strip, rather like a fever patient's temperature chart.

As the young man watches the niggling pattern, his brain is busy translating it into words, and his hands—which often tap out seventy words a minute—put down the words on a typewriter. He is receiving a message from New York. That steady motion of the metal pointer, as of an invisible hand using a stylographic pen, is the work of a man three thousand two hundred miles away in the United States. There is no interval in time. The very second the man in New York taps his keys the pointer in London traces its green message; and the other man at this end of the sea serpent bangs it out on a typewriter. Most of New York's remarks seem to read like this:

VZONFGTY   MKJHNBGR   LOKMNZZDR
HGTRDFGTERR.

I suppose somebody understands.

*   *   *   *   *

Down one side of the room are the desks of the banks, the big commercial companies, and trusts. They are chattering away to New York like starlings. It is 4.30 p.m. or 11.30 a.m. in America. While London is tired and tea-timeish, fresh young America with its coat off, the juice of the morning grape fruit still upon its lips, the first bootleg cocktail[1] a good hour and a half off, is receiving the result of London's day's work.

Suddenly a whole colony of machines sing a chorus. Something has happened on Wall Street! How they chirp and chirrup and then stop. How temperamental this room is; how sensitive to the swift neuritis of finance. Listen! Clatter, clatter, clatter! Someone, perhaps, is a millionaire; someone else broke. Instantaneously the little machines blurt it out like a lot of women at a tea fight, singing their eternal song of pounds and dollars. Then the London machines join in as our Stock Exchange replies. . . .

Once at school I saw a doped frog's heart beating: a little red pumping thing. Here in this room I seem to see the heart of finance beating, pumping out its daily nourishment to the million arteries and veins.

* * * * *

I watch a girl with shingled hair send a message to New York as easily as if she were playing a foxtrot on a pianola. It is timed 4.34. She sends it. It is at once in New York. The clock stands at 4.35! One minute to cross the Atlantic! She takes up an electrically regulated time punch, stamps it, flings it in a basket, and—goes on flashing things over the Atlantic.

I have a vision of millions of Babbits chewing their cigars, tearing open envelopes, profiting by their contents, buying, selling, losing, gaining, putting on coats, and taking chorus girls out to lobsters, while all the time throughout their day (part of which is our night) the little spitfire machines snap their fingers in Wall Street.

* * * * *

How typical of civilization. Each age piles up its marvels and becomes dependent on them. Where was all this fifty

---

[1] The Americans were drinking secretly and illegally when this was written. The Prohibition Act was repealed on December 5th, 1933.

years ago? What consternation would fall to-day in the City of London if this room were blotted out. Yesterday's miracles are to-day's platitudes, yet much more: they are to-day's necessities. Imperceptibly life changes, is readjusted because of them. How many London businesses would smash if it still took three weeks to reach New York?

'And this is not the end,' says an official. 'There's no doubt that some day soon we shall be speaking to the States. We are always improving, speeding up. Look at that!'

I see a typewriter working away furiously in a corner with a kind of devilish deliberation, and—no human hand over the keyboard. It is comic in its efficiency, in its air of I-don't-make-any-mistakes; in its solemn self-satisfaction.

'Who,' I ask, 'is working that?'

'A man in our Amsterdam office!'

*   *   *   *   *

As I leave the room, there is an outburst from New York; a sharp fusillade in reply from London. I go out thrilled by the human brain, wondering if it will lead to the stars and the moon, or whether it will all end with a strange, savage man picking up a telephone insulator from a lonely ruin and wondering dully what it is, thinking that perhaps it might make rather a wonderful pendant on his wife's necklace of chipped glass.

On a Sunday ✒ ✒ ✒ ✒ ✒ ✒

EVERY Saturday, Gladys covers her typewriter, pats her hair, pulls her hat over her ears, and abandons the City of London to cats and caretakers.

What a gloomy, lonely spot it is on Sunday. Leave the main omnibus routes, on which there is a thin trickle of traffic, and you plunge into street after street, lane winding into lane, empty, lifeless. Can this be the same City of week-day drive and thrust, of charging wheels and urgent feet? Life has gone from it as completely as a tide goes out to sea. Look! In that little road, famous for five hundred years as one of London's thronged streets of commerce, there is nothing but a grey pigeon nodding quickly as it picks up oats dropped from the nose-bag of a carter's horse on Saturday morning.

Desolate London! The tall warehouses gaze blankly at one another on each side of the narrow road. It is almost a city of the dead. Not quite: it has a strong 'back-on-Monday' look about it: there is a vigorous promise of return over the locked warehouses and offices.

The last act of Phyllis, before she went home on Saturday, was to pin a big sheet of brown paper over the hats in the showroom window; and surely that is Mr. Jones's alpaca coat hanging up there behind the closed door; and note how neatly Mr. Robinson placed his big cloth scissors beside a pile of serge on the counter, which you can see quite plainly from the road.

*   *   *   *   *

The next street is the same, and the next, save for a big ginger cat enjoying the rare experience of sitting on the kerbstone.

'Hullo, cat!' you say, glad to have found something alive in the City of London.

She blinks her amber eyes at you once or twice, and looks away, as if occupied with higher thoughts.

'Thinking about Confucius?' you ask, and she blinks again, and says as plainly as a cat can look such things: 'Go away, and don't spoil the only peace this City ever enjoys!'

'Nice cat . . .' you begin, but she casts a look of hate at you and, rising slowly, walks wearily away.

Down the street you go, thinking how different it looks. Some merchants have emptied their windows, as at the menace of an invasion; others have left them as they were on Saturday —a kind thought, for it gives the City police something to look at during their lonely walks.

One is looking now. He is solemnly regarding silk stockings on cardboard ankles.

*　　*　　*　　*　　*

In another deserted street, you surprise three cats sitting together looking up at something. They slink off with a guilty air as you advance. You wonder what they were watching. You see a milk-can hung well out of their reach on a door handle. Strange! Does the milkman still go jangling through the City of London? The door opens. A man in the early stages of dressing comes out in carpet slippers and a cap, takes a look up and down the street, unhitches the milk-can and prepares to retire.

'Do you live here?'

'Yes,' he says grudgingly, really meaning, 'What's it got to do with you?'

'How many miles do you have to walk for a pint?'

He smiles. You have hit his great grievance. He becomes human and tells you a few of the sorrows of a caretaker's life. 'Yes; it's lonely living in the City of London, and you can't leave a bit of food in this particular house because of the rats, and, if you were to let the milkman put the can down on the step, there wouldn't be a drop left, and the places where you can get a drink on week-days are shut on Sundays. . . . Still, it's quiet, and, for them that like a bit of peace, living in the City isn't too bad.

'And there's always plenty of churches for the wimmen. . . . I was just lookin' for my missus when you came along, sir; regular church-goer, she is. Good morning, sir. Ah, get away with you, you great big sandy thief. . . . That's the one, sir, that ginger cat! Some day he'll bring a ladder with him. . . .'

*　　*　　*　　*　　*

The church stands at the end of the street. A tall sycamore leans from the few square feet of churchyard left: a lovely, colourful thing, in this greyness of stone. It is one of the old churches that Wren rebuilt after the Fire of London. You go inside; it is half full of men and women, but mainly women. The voice of the clergyman drones on and on, the sunlight slants through the stained-glass windows. Here the life of the old City of London is continued. This has not changed.

You go out again, down more silent thoroughfares, until, at St. Paul's, a flood of life meets you, and the omnibuses come charging up Ludgate Hill almost as though it were Monday.

YOU can wander London for twenty days speculating on the motives which sway men and women; on things that go on in the brain behind the mask, never knowing for certain, just guessing; but on the twenty-first day a little deed, a stray word will swiftly illuminate the mystery of another life; and you will know. . . .

He sat on a wooden box outside one of those ramshackle eating-houses round Covent Garden. A huge cup of coffee was on his knee, and in his great, grimy hands was a slice of ham hidden between two paving-stones of bread. He was a tough fellow with a blue chin. His greasy cap, pulled down over his eyes, did not enhance the charm of a face like that of a battered bulldog. His figure was that of a heavy-weight champion who is getting heavier.

Round his feet were tomatoes that had fallen by the way-side, also fragments of cabbage and the tissue wrappings of oranges.

* * * * *

A few feet away, on the edge of the kerb, stood a young man with a high crop of brittle hair, who, holding a cap to his breast, opened his mouth in a song which even the adjacent barrel organ could not entirely suppress. The big hulk sitting on the box was his only audience; and it was obvious that the audience hated to be sung at. When the big man was not glaring murderously at a punctured tomato, he was glaring at the vocalist, as if at any moment he might spring up and transform him into a punctured tomato.

The songster appeared blissfully unconscious that he was standing on the edge of death. . . .

> I per-hassed by your whi-hindow
> When the mo-horning was red . . .

—declared the young man; while the other regarded him with a baleful eye that suggested that, if only he had been aware of this, he might have sat up for the singer with a gun.

* * * * *

I wanted to see how things would end, for the audience was becoming restive. I lingered at the shop next door.

In the spri-hing I bring you vi'lets . . .

—began the tenor sentimentally. The other lifted his eyes slowly. He looked as though his contribution to the autumn would be the thickest ear in London. Then he brought from his pocket a bottle and poured neat brandy, I think, into his cup and drank it at a gulp. He began to look at the singer meditatively, critically, almost with interest, as a man chooses a target. His eyes were slightly red, and I realized that he was not sober. This had the makings of a real murder.

All the time sentiment flowed from the harsh throat of the unsuspecting youth.

*   *   *   *   *

Song followed song generously, until at last the singer looked up to the sky and began what I instinctively knew was his *tour de force*. It suited his unfortunate voice:

> Ten dirty little fingers,
>   Two dirty little hands,
> Ten dirty little fingers
>   That have broken all commands.
> What would she do without them?
>   A mother understands. . . .
> Bless his little heart and soul,
>   And dirty little hands. . . .

Now it was coming . . . now . . .! The big man rose with a livid face. I cannot report his remarks. Among other things, he told the songster to shut his regrettable mouth and go to a place where it is too hot to sing. He stood over the thin youth like a mountain, with his arm raised. Then he crumpled . . . he was certainly not sober . . . and, fumbling in his pockets, took out a coin and gave it to the young man. That, I thought, was indeed strange, even though he were drunk. He lurched away and came into slight conflict with the kerb. . . .

A girl who had come out of the shop said to another girl: 'He's still on the drink, poor feller!'

Why 'poor feller'? He was a great drunken bully. I asked them why.

'Well, you see,' said one, 'he lost his little boy last week

. . . run over by a van. He was only five, and ever such a dear little chap!'

*   *   *   *   *

I went on over the littered pavements, and that voice seemed to fill the heaven:

> Bless his little heart and soul,
> And—dirty little hands!

Mayfair's Cottage

THREE hundred years ago there was a cottage in Mayfair: and nothing else: no lords, no ladies, no rich Jews, no gouty old men in arm-chairs; and not one solitary butler.

And in this cottage, which was Mayfair's only mansion, lived a shepherd, who used to look after the cattle during the annual fair in May. When he was not doing this he had time to look out over the wilderness of Hyde Park towards Kensington, where there were robbers and highwaymen, and, in another direction, he could see, across green fields and hedges, Charing Cross, an upstart village, and, beyond it, the hill of Lud, on which the great City of London sprawled and smoked on quiet evenings. If Mr. Shepherd, Mayfair's one inhabitant, wanted a new pair of trousers (which probably never happened), he had to tramp miles to London to buy a pair, and when he reached home again he no doubt sighed, and picked a few blackberries in Park Lane and said to his wife: 'That be a wicked city, wife, and it's good to be back in the country!'

*　　　*　　　*　　　*　　　*

The fields have gone, the blackberries have gone, everything that made Mayfair nice and restful has gone, but, miracle of miracles and marvel of London, that shepherd's cottage still remains. I found it in Little Stanhope Street. It is squeezed in behind Park Lane and a huddle of mews and garages. 'The Cottage, 1618 A.D.' is written over an oak postern gate, from which hangs a brass lantern. I opened the gate and went in.

I was in a tiny garden. A jackdaw in a wickerwork cage with an open door sat with a cheerful expression on a perch. Small blue countrified flowers grew in a border. Ivy hung from the walls of the cottage. I was as surprised as the boy in H. G. Wells' story, who, opening a green door in a wall, encountered the garden of the Hesperides, where golden apples hung from trees and girls played with leopards on the grass. This Mayfair. Incredible!

A man came out of the shepherd's cottage. He was Brig.-General R. S. Stronach, who owns thousands of acres of Sutherlandshire as well as the most romantic little town house in London. We went over and talked to the jackdaw.

'Yes, he flies about,' said the general. 'But he never goes far. His only adventure was when he flew into Lord Curzon's bedroom round the corner and perched on the bedpost. Lord Curzon looked up rather surprised and John looked at him, and they made friends. When I went round to bring John home, Lord Curzon wanted to keep him. By Jove, he did!'

*   *   *   *   *

Inside, the shepherd's cottage looks like every good American's dream of heaven: soft light on old oak, intelligent furniture, good pictures, gleam of old brass and pale shine of pewter.

'This,' said General Stronach, 'used to be a blacksmith's forge.'

It is now the most picturesque dining-room in London: a beamed roof with tool marks in the wood, a great red-brick hearth, a flagged floor, a long refectory table, a grandfather clock, tapestry, and mellow family portraits.

'Can you hear London?' asked the general.

'No. I can hear only the year 1618 A.D., as promised on the gate outside.'

'It may surprise you to know that I can remember horses being shod in this room. I didn't mind that; but when they began to make tin pans I decided to add this forge to the cottage.'

*   *   *   *   *

We went out into the small flagged garden. It was just as though some magician had picked up an old country cottage and had dropped it into the heart of London. We talked about Shepherd Market, which lies at the back of the house. On the other side of it once ran the brook from which Brook Street takes its name.

The wind rustled the ivy. John put his head out of his cage and made a vague remark. I felt as though a ghost had risen up out of the London soil saying: 'This is what Mayfair was like once before grandeur went to its head. . . .'

I had the fancy that perhaps when the general goes away to Scotland to kill salmon the ghost of Mr. Shepherd, the pioneer of Mayfair, comes on moonlight nights to lean on his crook and wander contentedly round the house to which Time has been so kind. Why not? Perhaps if there is any shortage of butlers in the immediate neighbourhood, it may be due to the fact that, during those rare evening moments when a butler is not butling, a flock of sheep have been seen coming up Little Stanhope Street to fade, as in a mist, towards the little postern gate in the corner.

'Well, there's nothing like it in London,' said the general.

'There is not.'

'There is not,' repeated Lord Curzon's friend, with a wise shake of his black head.

I went out through the little postern gate, where a man said, 'Taxi, sir?'; and a Rolls-Royce glided round the corner containing the large, exotic apple of some Hebraic eye.

The Engine Driver ⚬ ⚬ ⚬ ⚬ ⚬

EIGHT P.M.

In ten minutes the ordinary man leaning far out of the engine cab will see the flutter of a green flag. He will turn swiftly to the gauges and levers above the roaring furnace, there will be a gusty burst from the low smoke stack; and the giant locomotive, with its chain of coaches, will glide smoothly from the gloom of a London terminus towards the other end of England.

Such a powerful poem in steel. The oil gleams green on its axles, the long body, built for eighty miles an hour, crouches over the metals in concentrated strength like an heraldic beast, swift and lean in line as a panther, strong and masculine as a stallion. It sways through the outer suburbs and roars out into open country, where little hares sit up in the corn and lollop away in alarm from the scream of this sudden, unaccountable monster that eats up miles as a scythe eats grass. Darkness finds it still thundering through tunnels, thudding with a rattle, as of musketry, over river bridges, flinging the length of its yellow tail across the night like an earthbound meteor.

And the ordinary man, now black with grime and sweat, gazes with narrowed eyes over the track, the lives of four hundred men and women in his soiled hands; and his eyes looking for the green lights against the sky which beckon him on and wink in a flash as he goes by to the song of his thunderous wheels:

> Bring 'em home, bring 'em home,
> Don't be late, don't be late.
> Clear the road for the night express. . . .

    *   *   *   *   *

In the body of this flying thing, Romance, Comedy, and Pathos have corner seats. Wherever there are men and women are these three.

I suppose every one of us has some time in his life played each part in a train, setting out on a romantic journey, on a silly journey, on a pathetic journey. No one has ever guessed. We sat huddled in our corner locked away from observation, masked with our human faces, cloaked by human speech which is so often designed to say the things farthest from the heart. We might be on the way to the turning-point in our life with the same expression that we should assume on the way to Broadstairs for the weekend. Only when we are nearly dead (or on our honeymoons) do we unconsciously give ourselves away in a train!

Have you ever dipped a net into a pond to draw it forth teeming with life, which you have dumped in another place? A train is like that: a netful of human emotion in transit. Each life temporarily dominated by an intention, each person animated by some definite desire, to get somewhere, to see someone. . . .

That young man in the corner? Is he aching with every revolution of the wheels because SHE is at the other end of the journey and Time has become an elastic band pulled out by two giants? (Or is he going to Bradford to sell collar studs?) Down the corridor in an empty first-class carriage are two honeymooners. He has shaken himself like a dog and has carefully picked up each tiny crescent of confetti and hidden it under the mat. She is thinking of home, and the wheels sing to her:

> You've done it now, you've done it now;
> He's rather a dear, but you've done it now. . . .

The train rockets into the darkness; and they kiss.

*　　*　　*　　*　　*

There are placid people, dull people and interesting people. You look at them wishing that their heads were transparent so that you could see inside and discover the motives working them, pulling them over a thousand miles from one place to another. Now and then you hear without asking:

'My daughter's going to have her first baby, and so I'm going to be with her. . . .'

'I hear it's very bracing. My doctor told me that I really ought to go to Switzerland, but I can't afford it. . . .'

'I haven't seen him for ten years. His ship comes in to-morrow. . . .'

Little flashes like that, rare but illuminating.

*　　*　　*　　*　　*

Wait till the journey's end. Then, and only then, do the
zzles work out:

'My dear, I don't want to alarm you, but she's terribly ill.
fact . . .'

'You mean—I'm too late?'

'Yes.'

Just that. Or this: a girl waiting on the platform and a
ung man, trampling on porters and passengers as he forges
s way to her, his eyes seeing only her.

'I thought I'd never get here! Didn't sleep a wink all night!
ou *do* look lovely. . . .'

*   *   *   *   *

So they split up and merge themselves in the life of another
wn, but few, as they pass, look at the ordinary face in the
gine-cab, so black with coal and sweat, or at those grimed
ands which held their lives through the swift thunder of
e night.

EVERY day people go to see the historic frescoes in the Royal Exchange hard by the Bank. How many, I wonder, notice the more interesting dado of faces below the frescoes?

Young, lanky boys working near the Bank, too poor or too careful to spend money on luncheon, go to the Royal Exchange from noon until one to occupy the wooden benches and bring out from their pockets bulky brown paper bags. The sandwiches which mother, or the landlady, cut at 8 a.m. are there consumed, so that soon, whichever way you look, you see bulging cheeks and rhythmically working jaws.

Round the Royal Exchange walks the grey-haired Elizabethan constable in his watchman's dress—green-caped coat, gold-braided hat and stick—a venerable official, who by virtue of ancient custom has the right to arrest evildoers within the City's walls. But I think he would always tell a policeman.

'Yes,' he says, drawing a hand down a silver beard. 'Yes, they make a terrible mess with their apple cores and their monkey nuts, their silver paper and their brown paper bags; but it's nice for them to have their quiet place to eat in, isn't it? Boys just starting work in the City, you know.'

*   *   *   *   *

Now London does things just as a matter of course which make you proud of London. In Berlin, or any city not so sure of itself as London, poor, grubby little boys, red at the wrist and with no money, would not be allowed to seek sanctuary in one of the most historic buildings in the City; a building which, although it now has outgrown its purpose, did, in its day, help to lay the foundations of commercial London.

When Sir Thomas Gresham gave London her first Royal Exchange in the reign of Elizabeth, the court—still paved with the Turkish hone stone of the first building—was crowded, not with little boys and humble clerks, but with the merchant princes of Tudor London.

On those stones was unfolded that chapter in London

THE ROYAL EXCHANGE

history more thrilling than any fiction of the Spanish Main, when the merchant adventurers of London, their minds dazzled with the romance of a widened world, formed companies to sweep the seven seas and bring the riches of the earth to London Town. The South Sea Company, the Guinea Company, the Royal Africa Company, the Turkey Company, the Canary Company, and many more—only one of which remains, the Hudson's Bay Company—began the greatest trade boom England had known.

In this Royal Exchange was the first common meeting-place the merchants had enjoyed, the first Bourse; the telegraph office before the telegraph was invented, the Fleet Street before there was a daily page of City news. It pulled commercial London together, gave her that unity which enabled her to profit by the Netherlands wars and knock out Antwerp as the centre of commercial Europe.

How much talk there must have been of the new sea route to India, of the amazing Americans, of the new colony of Virginia, of the mysterious white lands of the north not yet known as Canada, as these great soldier-merchants sent fleet after fleet of London sails slanting over the seas of the world. . . .

*   *   *   *   *

And the Royal Exchange, having done its work well and truly, sits in the heart of London with the traffic on all sides, the telephones in every office, the little messages ticking themselves instantly under the Atlantic into Canada, the United States, South Africa, Australia. Throughout the air go messages that link continent to continent, hemisphere to hemisphere. . . .

When you pass by the Bank, look up at Gresham's grasshopper on the campanile of the grey old mother of London trade, and remember that, while she stands there full of past glory, she is not too proud to open her arms to that character very dear to London: the young boy just beginning his career in the City. . . .

Munch-munch go their jaws from twelve until one. On each knee is a folded magazine . . . a tale of pirates and dead men's gold. They do not hear the thunder of the wheels, the sound of life outside; for in their ears, I think, is the sound of wind in a sail, the ring of a grappling iron, the hoarse cries of a boarding party.

They go out, full of fiction and ham, unconscious that the greatest story of all was in the stones beneath their feet.

The Mild Giants

EVERY morning they come straining with a great clatter of hoofs over Blackfriars Bridge, pulling a lorry piled with boxes. One is a big bay with a white blaze; the other is a big black with a star on his forehead.

Above, among the boxes, sits a little wispy creature with a greasy cap over one eye, a stumpy pipe sprouts from the ragged moustache which covers a weak mouth.

He is the master: the triumphant declaration of the power of mind over matter. Like most London carters, he is a good master, a kind and considerate master. Between him and his two mild giants exists complete understanding; a mutual confidence, built up in years. He knows them; they know him.

If you or I were to drive this lorry over Blackfriars Bridge on a crowded morning, when there is not more than half an inch between wheels and a policeman's notebook, our inexperience would communicate itself by way of something more subtle than the reins; and we would end up the centre of a crowd.

*　　　*　　　*　　　*　　　*

They pull up over Blackfriars Bridge, harness jingling, great bodies steaming, and go slowly along New Bridge Street to a warehouse in a narrow lane off Farringdon Street, where the master backs the lorry against the kerbstone so that his two giants may relax. As he clambers down from his pyramid two faces turn, one with a white blaze, one with a white star, both inexpressibly mild and patient. A great hairy hoof paws the pavement impatiently.

'Aw' right, aw' right; don't get the wind up!' says the master. 'I'm a-comin'.'

He walks round with two nose-bags half full of oats. The great heads nozzle him, the huge forelocks wave as the heads move, and the velvet-soft dewlaps twitch in eager anticipation.

He straps on the feed-bags, and the two mild giants of every London morning stand peacefully eating. If it were possible to put a finger on the happiest moment of such dull lives, no doubt this would be the time. They eat until the oats diminish and the bag has to be flung high in the air. . . .

*   *   *   *   *

The dog offers man friendship; the horse unquestioning service.

These lumbering giants of the London streets are painfully beautiful in their complete subservience. They are not pathetic, because they have no self-pity; they have never known anything but labour.

There may have been a day when, as long-limbed colts, they ran over green fields, but the memory has surely been obliterated by their fate as beasts of burden.

All day long they stand relaxed against the kerb hardly moving for hours, standing in that dull, ordained servitude with their great heads drooping, the sweat dried black on their bodies, waiting, waiting, waiting as hour succeeds hour for that moment when the master will mount and the reins tighten, telling them once more to strain against the weight.

There is, to me, no lovelier sight in London than a rough carter making much of his horses; no sight more worthy of punishment than the brute who swears at them and jags their mouths. But this is rarely seen. If you keep your eyes open in the narrow lanes of the City, you will, on most days in the week, interrupt a conversation between a carter and his giants:

'Go on with you, you blinkin' old flat-footed good-for-nothin'. . . .'

The big head noses the master's greasy waistcoat. Something of the affection in this familiarity finds its way into the patient head. A dumb animal sometimes looks at a man in a way which should, no matter what that man has done in his life, provide him with a passport to heaven.

*   *   *   *   *

The afternoon wanes; the last box is unloaded.

'Gee-up!' says the master.

The two mild giants settle into their collars and go out into the gathering dusk of the streets, over the bridge to stables. A night; and then to-morrow the same early dawn, the same load, the same servitude. . . .

As I see them go, heavy, patient, clumsy, yet, in some way, magnificent and grand, I hope that a large tract of paradise is set apart for them—a green heaven in which no lorry is ever seen.

In the streets of London they have earned the right to some friskiness and a sense of joy—and, perhaps a worse heaven could be devised for the carter who loves his giants than a seat in sunlight from which, with a pipe always packed with excellent shag, he might observe their elephantine gambols over lush meadows.

WE were together in a smoking carriage. The woman was elaborately unattractive, but her husband was stone blind. He sat in his corner like a bloated idol, his huge hands on his knees, his head and neck rigid, his sightless eyes gazing directly in front of him towards the wife he could not see. They had been married a long time, for their wedding rings were old and sunken in the middle-aged plumpness of their fingers.

'Would you like a cigarette, dearest?' she asked.

'Yes, darling,' he replied.

She took his cigarette case from his pocket, tapped the end of the cigarette on the case, put the cigarette in the man's mouth, and lit a match for him. He patted her hand an instant.

'Thank you, dearest,' he said.

It is not usual to hear middle-aged people talk like this. I watched them. The woman was oblivious of everything but her idol. His bow tie had been perfectly tied. She had done it. The blind man was scrupulously neat. She, on the other hand, was untidy and tastelessly dressed. I wondered whether she would have dared to wear stockings of biscuit-coloured wool with *suède* shoes if the man could have seen them. Her bottle-green costume was unbrushed, and her hat was old and unbecoming, and her gloves, which were good, gave the strange impression that her hands belonged to another and more elegant woman.

'Such fields of golden flowers, darling!' she said, gazing at the sightless eyes.

'In the grass?' he asked.

'I'm sure the sun's too hot for you, my love; let me pull down the blind.'

'Thanks, dearest.'

After an hour or so their endearments began to get on my nerves. I felt that the carriage was full of pastry. I began to count the various 'darlings' and 'dearests,' wondering if they could pile up two hundred love notes before Ipswich. It cloyed.

The woman looked at her watch and unstrapped a handbag. She brought out two little medicine bottles and a measuring glass, poured out a dose, and, sitting beside the rigid old idol, whispered: 'Time for your medicine, sweetheart!' She brushed the cigarette ash, which had fallen on his waistcoat, and, obediently, he swallowed his mixture, then held up his head for her to wipe his mouth. He patted her hand, and her unattractive face positively glowed with devotion, so that I knew instinctively that the poor old idol was her lover, her husband, and her child rolled into one helpless human being.

The woman was happy. Time, which causes most women to gaze anxiously in a mirror, meant nothing to their love. He could not move a step without her. He was helpless, out of the race, as alone with her in the very surge of life as if the sound of the world were the thunder of surf breaking on the shores of some desert island. On this tragedy had been built a happy married life. I looked at the man's huge frame and wondered what difference, if any, sight would have made to them—sight and the freedom for him to join in life arrogantly, to escape from this sweet solitude of sightlessness. . . .

'Would you give me a match?' said the woman. I gave her one, and she lit another cigarette for her idol. We got into conversation. I wanted to find out the key to their lives. How long had he been blind? I made him tell me without having to ask so intimate a question. He had gone blind just after their honeymoon, fifteen years since!

*　　*　　*　　*　　*

'Wouldn't you like to change sides, dearest?'

'Dearest' said that he would. She helped the big frame to move over, fussily taking his shoulders and pressing him back in the seat she had vacated.

'That's better, darling!' said the idol.

He smiled towards her voice. Behind those blank eyes was a picture of her fifteen years ago, when he loved her most, a picture of her engraved there during their honeymoon. If all married men could carry this remembrance! I wondered, if his sight came back, would he recognize her now? I closed my eyes: she certainly had a lovely voice, velvet with affection and joy in service.

I left the train at a little country station. The old idol sat bolt upright and rigid. She was feeding him with a ham sandwich . . . an ancient god receiving offerings from a priestess! The train went on, taking with it the happy Man Who Had Not Seen His Wife For Fifteen Years, on, on, on to their lifelong honeymoon. . . .

The Last Farm ✎ ✎ ✎ ✎ ✎ ✎

THE farm is, naturally, one of the few things which, to London, spells romance, peace, and innocence. If you could run a convincing farm in Trafalgar Square, you might make a fortune by letting stockbrokers in at five shillings a time to lean over the pig-sties. (Smocks half a crown per half-hour.)

So when I took the tube to Highgate recently to examine the last farm in the four-mile radius, which was advertised for sale as a site for flats, I realized that I was engaged on a romantic adventure. London's last farm! In its passing I read the whole history of London:

> Here herbs did grow,
> And flowers sweet,
> But now 'tis called
> Saint George's Street.

Perhaps somebody, centuries ago, wandered sentimentally among cowsheds in Pall Mall, and wondered what the world was coming to.

*   *   *   *   *

'Fitzroy Farm? Never heard of it!' said the taxicab drivers at Highgate. They held a conference, the result of which was that I was taken through this mountainous region to the very edge of Ken Wood, where a sloping path led down to a gate on which was written for the warning of vanished cow-herds: 'Beware of the dog'. It was not good grammar. There were two dogs with extremely pink throats. 'Good old fellows . . . there . . . there,' I said, with the hopeless air of a man blowing a kiss to an earthquake. A woman came out and locked the dogs in the stable; and I was free to examine London's last real farmstead.

*   *   *   *   *

Gaunt bars with tarred beams, blistered and patched, stood round a big, cobbled yard. There were cowsheds in which I visualized Tess-like maids sitting on three-legged stools singing. There were stables empty, granaries desolate, and a big gate through which the hay-wains lumbered once with their fragrant loads. Nothing but a derelict ship seems so dead as an empty farm. No thick boots striking the cobbles, no stamping in manger and stall, no creak of wheels, no cluck of hens . . . only two dogs, the last guardians of the last farm, on guard against—London!

I sighed as sentimentally as any stockbroker, and went round the farm buildings into a little fairyland.

'Used to be Lady Southampton's shooting-box over a hundred years ago,' said the woman. 'At least, so I've heard.'

I picked a cluster of red currants and ate them reflectively, looking at a quaint little thatched house with eaves like an old hat low down over a head, such a Grimm's fairy tale of a house. It was empty, like everything else. Ivy glistened on it. A line of hollyhocks stood to attention. There was a bed of flowers. Opposite, at the end of a rough lawn, was a pool of water. It was covered with a scum of minute weeds so that its unbroken surface resembled green ice. Trees grew out of it and dipped their boughs into it, to be at once lost to view in the placid green ice. I walked round the old house. It seemed so simple and full of peace, and so old, as if it had grown up out of the soil without any help from man. For an instant I hated London for killing it.

I ate some raspberries, and watched a bee wrestle with a flower, thinking, as I stood there, of the flats to come, of men rushing out to business, of wives, of children, of geysers, of cold mutton, of alarm clocks, of pictures by Watts and Burne Jones and Rossetti, of men who test gas meters, and of plumbers and their mates.

'It's very old,' said the woman.

'It's very beautiful,' I said.

'Gr-r-r-r-r,' growled the dogs from the stable, as if, in me, they had scented the enemy who had done this thing.

* * * * *

Out of such murder has London been born. . . .

A butterfly flew out of Ken Wood, flickered into the garden, and off into Ken Wood again. I heard a motor-horn in the road above; and was surprised. I admired the sunlight lighting up red and white flowers in a mass. I watched the queer insects skating over the green ice of the pond, the occasional rise of a bubble that told of life below the weed. I looked at a little window hidden in the thatch, and I thought of the eyes that had looked through it into green fields for generation after generation, and how wide they would have grown had they been told that some day London would stretch out its stone fingers and pluck this farm as a hand plucks a flower.

'That's your car, sir.'

There was a violent rude honking from the path above. Confound it! London calling!

I pulled a white rose from a burdened bush near the porch and placed it in my buttonhole.

The next time I go there I expect there will be gramophones.

I WENT over to Bankside when Blackfriars Bridge was a tangle of lorries and carts, to find an old house which I think must have been pulled down years ago. An hour's search led me to a policeman and a man in shirt, trousers, and cap; and somehow we began to talk about Queen Elizabeth, with the result that I forgot all about the house.

I want you to picture us standing in the early morning in this dingy street, full of the sound of scrap metal being hurled about and boxes being shot into barges. A policeman, a man in shirt and trousers, and myself earnestly discussing the Virgin Queen. We were standing beside Cardinal's Cap Alley, the site of the infamous Southwark Stews, for centuries the legendary home of vice in London. I would like to describe ancient Bankside, its theatres, its bull baitings, its bear fightings, its pleasure-gardens, and its whited houses with signs painted on them, its thieves' kitchens, its 'Clink,' but we should never finish; and it is all in the histories.

The few old houses, which have not become warehouses or wharves, stand facing the river, as they always did. There is no wall at this part. Over a pile of rusty scrap metal, disused cog wheels and the ugly entrails of dead machines, I looked across the dancing Thames to the piebald beauty of London rising high in spire and dome, dominated by the sturdy bulk of St. Paul's. (If ever you wish to paint an unusual picture of St. Paul's or to take a novel photograph, do it from this spot by Cardinal's Cap Alley.)

*   *   *   *   *

'I dunno where that house you're wanting can be,' said the man in shirt and trousers, scratching his head, 'and I've lived here for thirty years and more.'

The policeman put his head on one side and tried to look helpful. I glanced along Bankside, thinking that all places in which people have been extremely wicked have a certain lure. Although this haunt of dead gaiety is now a street of wharves, it still wears an experienced air: a stray window, a door post here and there, pull you up sharply.

'The house I want has underground tunnels,' I said, as a fisherman casts out the ground bait.

'They mostly have,' replied the policeman.

'I've got a cellar,' said the man in shirt and trousers, 'where thousands, millions, are supposed to be hid. The times I've been over that cellar with a hammer, and never a sign of a blinkin' bob!'

We all agreed that it was hard luck, but worth while sticking to. You never know, do you?

*   *   *   *   *

'You see this place used to be the Stews . . .' began the man.

'That means houses of ill-fame,' explained the policeman, gravely, as if he were reading a charge sheet.

'Yes, awful,' replied the man. 'The goings on 'ere in the old days was something dreadful. There was a feller called Cardinal Cap, who had a house full o' wimmen just here.'

We all looked revolted, and the policeman sniffed and remarked darkly like a Calvinist:

'Well, he would have, wouldn't he?'

I smiled, because the real facts are these: 'The Cardinal's Cap' was the name of the most notorious house in the ancient Stews, from which the alley takes its name, and not, as some writers have said from the connexion with the old religious house of St. Mary Overy. The man was right about the house, but there was no Cardinal Cap.

Here it was that Gloriana, most unexpectedly, entered the conversation.

*   *   *   *   *

'See these three houses,' said the man, 'that's where Queen Elizabeth used to bring her young men.'

I was profoundly shocked. So was the policeman.

'It's right,' said the man dogmatically. 'She used to row over the river and land just there, and they'd have dinner in these three houses, which were only one in those days.'

He then described one of Gloriana's visits so vividly that I began to feel that he must have been there. So did the policeman.

'So old Walter Rayley's been there,' he said.
The man nodded his head.

*   *   *   *   *

I was silly enough to spend the afternoon in the Guildhall Library trying to discover if there is any record of Elizabeth's visit to Bankside other than her journey with the French Ambassador on May 26, 1599, to see a baiting of bulls and bears; but no. I think scandalous Bankside, true to its character after all these centuries, had just awakened to take a kick at Henry VIII's daughter to pay him out for shutting up the Stews by Royal proclamation and the sound of trumpet.

It was such an eye-witness's account. Was it garbled history, an old legend, or merely the penalty of having had red hair?

I give it up!

The Girl in a Box ～ ～ ～ ～ ～

SHE sits in a box dressed in black, and no one ever sees her arrive or leave.

She possesses in a marked degree that air of calm superiority assumed by mathematically minded people. When she looks you in the eye never flatter yourself that, in some remote corner of her exact mentality, exists a spark of appreciation; for she is thinking automatically 'fifteen and ninepence ha'penny from one pound is . . .' Bang! There before you lies four shillings and twopence halfpenny! She is the Girl in the Restaurant Cash Desk. All round her every day flutters the curious life of a London restaurant. It is one of those gold and marble places which flatter while they feed: chop-house prices in the Palace of Versailles.

*   *   *   *   *

The girl in the box looks out over an army of moving jaws. A steady trickle of Puccini from the corner, where a shock-headed Slav sways with his violin, helps to increase the noise made by civilized people when they nourish their bodies. Tinkles of glass, plopping of corks, clatter of plates, and the metallic undercurrent of the knives and forks, the whole symphony clouded by tobacco smoke and whipped by a steady accompaniment of bass and treble voices trying to go one better than Puccini, is the atmosphere over which she presides like a priestess.

Has she imagination? What does she think as she watches the hungry feed themselves?

Does she, I wonder, ever reflect what a queer thing a restaurant is. Along among the animals we human beings make a social function of feeding. I can never decide whether it is an upward or a downward step. It is not a pleasant sight. In fact, to the girl in the box the spectacle of hundreds of men and women of all shapes and sizes stoking themselves with fishes and roasted birds and animals must in time become repellent. A dog and a cat have greater delicacy. They hate you to watch them eat. The dog slinks off with his bone, and the cat feeds delicately wherever her food is. Do you know why this should be so?

I think the dog was always a pariah. He had to steal his food and get away quickly before someone threw a stone at him. Perhaps that is why to-day he drags his food to a corner of the carpet, although there is no one to interfere or hurt him. The cat, of course, hunted and killed and crouched down and filled herself on the spot.

*   *   *   *   *

Men and women, on the other hand, must have developed the restaurant habit in the jungle. The desire to eat together is older than legend. If it were not so, how could we bear to see the beautiful women we love—who, even, occasionally marry us—lifting beefsteak to their mouths? Had we not lost the horror of this surprising sight in ancient orgies, we should surely fly from it in loathing.

*   *   *   *   *

This, I imagine, does not worry the priestess of the cash desk. What interests her is the personal drama. Sometimes she betrays her human origin by forgetting to spike a bill and allowing her eye to rove pointedly towards a particular table. What does she see?

A man and a girl. Nothing unusual you think. He is at his best. His jokes are going down well. She is mooning at him with that you-really-are-the-most-charming-man-I-have-ever-met look in her eyes, and he, intoxicated by his temporary pre-eminence, leans towards her and gazes at her as children sometimes look at cream horns. You have the impression that beneath the table their feet may have flirted, for she goes flicker-flicker with her eyelids, languishes, and eats an olive she did not want.

But the girl in the cash desk seems annoyed. She is siding with an absent woman! She has so often seen that cream-bun look in the man's eye and always, until recently, directed to a nice girl in grey. She followed the romance, as women do, through its early stages. She guessed that evening he ordered a bottle of Möet and Chandon that an engagement ring was about to appear, and then, yes; she was right!

*   *   *   *   *

No doubt she gloated over them as day by day they steadily consumed bits of cow and sheep, and, of course, she never knew what the row was about. All she saw was the girl in grey pushing a fried sole from her and refusing to eat, and the man gloomily prodding his *entrecôte* and quarrelling with the waiter. Another woman, of course! She'd never trust a man with hair that colour or eyes like that! Many a time he looked at *her* when he should not, but she, of course, pretended not to see.

Now the drama is in its third act: the other woman has turned up! Little cat! Potted complexion, too, and what elbows! She spikes a bill savagely. Will it all come right again? Will the girl in grey ever return? Who knows?

'Seven and tenpence. . . . Two and two change. . . . Good morning.'

And the girl in the stage box turns again and watches life.

Behind the Window   ✍   ✍   ✍   ✍   ✍

IN that mean London street the small shop stands with a certain air of authority, due to the fact that the world's problems break out like a daily rash on contents boards. 'You may telephone from here,' says a tin plate over the door.

I went in to telephone. It was a tiny, dark shop that suggested in a melancholy manner that steak and onions had recently passed that way. I rapped on the counter. There was a quick movement across a glass window, through which was revealed a dark sitting-room behind the shop.

A young woman came out smiling. She was good looking. Her hair was beautiful, her hands were rough, and her mouth looked as though a hard word would not be possible to her. She was a surprise to me, because it was just the kind of shop in which you expect to find a large man in shirt-sleeves who lost his razor last month.

'There's the telephone box!' said the young woman. Then: 'Oh, lor', Mrs. B., fancy seeing you! Alf *will* be glad!'

Mrs. B., who had entered on my heels, was a neat, bleak woman of the kind that harbours an unquenchable enthusiasm for funerals. The young girl departed in excitement. My number was engaged, so I sat down on a chair in the shop and waited.

*　　　*　　　*　　　*　　　*

'He's coming!' said the young girl, returning.

'How is he?' asked the sorrowful woman.

'Bad,' replied Mrs. Alf. 'But ever so cheerful. It's wonderful. "There's millions worse off," he says; and I suppose he's right!'

'When was he took worse?' asked the visitor avidly.

'Six months gone. After he came out of hospital we thought he was cured, and he got a good job round at Morrisons. Then all of a sudden . . .'

'You've been a good wife . . .' began the bleak woman.

'Well, who wouldn't have been?' asked the girl indignantly.

'I don't know so much about that,' said the visitor. 'There's many a girl promised to marry a boy in 1914 who didn't

278

marry him in 1919 when he came back wounded, you take
my word for that.'

*   *   *   *   *

There was a shuffle from the back room. A young man
came slowly into the shop leaning on a stick. His eyes were
bright and sunken in his skull. His smile seemed the only
live thing about him except a cough. On his waistcoat
was the Mons medal. I looked at him and said to myself:
'Gas!'

'How are you?' asked the melancholy friend.

'Not so bad,' said the man, trying not to cough. 'There's
millions worse.' He smiled. 'You must be glad to be alive
these days,' he added.

A child came in and bought a pennyworth of red sweets.

'What we should do without the shop I don't know,' said
the little wife, with a laugh.

'Yes, that's a fact; we're very lucky to have the shop,'
agreed Alf, smiling.

A fit of coughing seized him suddenly, he waved his hand,
and went back slowly into the dark room.

*   *   *   *   *

'Poor feller,' mused Mrs. 'Gloom.' 'You don't have a very
gay life, do you?'

Just for a second I caught the passage of something terribly
sad across the face of the young woman.

'Sometimes,' she said, in a low voice, 'when I see girls
going past to the pictures-house I feel I'd give anything to
put on me hat and go out for a bit, but I daren't leave him
alone. "There's only one thing I'm sorry for," he says, "and
that's you." . . . When he talks like that he makes me feel
that ashamed I could cry.'

'Well, well . . .' said the visitor with a sigh. 'Take a plum!'
She opened a bag. 'Go on, help yourself!'

'Don't think I'm grumbling,' said the wife, 'because I'm
not. If I could go back, there's nothing I wouldn't do the
same all over again, and that's straight!'

*   *   *   *   *

'Yes, it's a lovely day, isn't it?' said the little wife as I bought a newspaper. 'Just like summer again!'

Through the window in the wall I saw the hand of her young husband groping along the mantelpiece to find something—the thin, sallow hand of a man of eighty.

* * * * *

'There's millions worse off,' I whispered as I went out. A gallant gentleman in a side street.

The Rotter

'YOU rotter!'

Six schoolboys, with their coats off and their white shirt-sleeves rolled above their elbows, stood in the Green Park and shouted the shrill taunt. One held a bat, one a ball, and another was putting down the stumps; and all looked in the direction of the Rotter, who was walking slowly away.

The Rotter was small—smaller than any of the six—and his tumbled hair fell in a brown cascade over his forehead. His sturdy legs, with their knobbly, scratched, and not too clean, knees, were in wide grey flannel shorts, and he had just put on a little flannel jacket with gilt buttons. Ah, that jacket! One of life's final gestures. You can temporize and fool people and play with a poker face as long as you like, but there comes a time when, up against it, you make a final gesture of resignation, and unmake it you cannot—except at the sacrifice of all dignity, all manhood, all self-respect. . . . You put on your jacket, snap your fingers, and walk away. Finish. The boats are burned!

'You rotter!'

Again the taunt came clear over the grass. The Rotter dug his small fists deeper into the pockets of his little grey bags, his mouth sagged and his rounded face, so between baby and boy that you could see what he was like in his perambulator, and also guess the kind of youth he will be in ten years' time, looked bitter; and his eyes glowered. He was in that rage of childhood that knows no caution, no reservations, no cunning. He would like to turn back and fight on the grass, fight in a blind, whimpering rage, dig his nails into them, bite their ears . . . But they were so big and powerful, and—there were six of them!

'Ca-ad! You're a ca-ad!' came a sing-song thrust.

The Rotter and Cad stepped sturdily over a small rail to the gravel path, walked round a fat wood-pigeon, and went on towards the lake.

*   *   *   *   *

What had happened, I wondered.
Had the Big Six bullied him until he had revolted? Had

they refused to let him bat, or denied him bowling? He may have been in the right or in the wrong. As I followed his small, indignant figure down the path, I didn't care; for he had all my sympathy. We have all been the Rotter. We have all at some time put on our jackets and said 'It's finished,' and we have all flinched at the yelp of the gang coming down the wind.

Trivial, everyday sight, I know!

But, say what you like, this little fellow, walking away with dignity, the absurd dignity of the very small, was the essence of all drama: struggle, man against men, defiance; a splendid rebel.

* * * * *

Something was going on in that tousled head. I could feel it fairly buzzing.

When he judged that he could look round without appearing to exhibit any interest in those others, he turned, left the path, and walked up to a tree, peeping round it towards the scene of his difference. He wanted to know how they were getting on without him! And what did he see? Did he find his enemies prostrate with grief, did he see them standing forlorn round the stumps weeping, crying, 'Now we've done it, now we've lost him; won't somebody go and ask him to come back?' Alas, no! Poor little Rotter, he saw a game of cricket in hearty progress; things were as they would have been had he never been born! This is one of the tragedies of defiance!

Had I seen less clearly into his young heart, I might have been one of those well-meaning idiots who go up and ask: 'What's the matter, my little man; what did they do to you?'

No. Never!

As he turned away from the tree, and the sight of that unconcerned group of which so dearly he wanted to make one, something of his defiance left him, and he became, not a hero, but just a poor little boy with nowhere to go now, no one with whom to play. He walked slowly, aimlessly from one to the other side of the path, and, in time, I passed him. Two enormous tears were rolling down his cheeks, and he was sniffing hard to keep back others.

But I was glad to see that the Rotter's shoulders were set, his hands well down in his pockets, and his feet unwavering in direction: away from compromise or surrender, going on into solitude where there was no bat, no ball, no soft green grass.

Turning of a Leaf ◦ ◦ ◦ ◦ ◦

THEY sit in well-bred isolation, turning the pages of old magazines.

Many are old, a few are young; men and women. Outside, beyond the chastely curtained windows, the traffic of Harley Street goes maddeningly past, as though there were no illness in the world. A damnably happy butcher's boy perched on a high cart whistles the mutton on its way, a limousine spins shopwards, a brisk, cheery man who has chops for breakfast (and looks as though he sings while he eats them) strides by with his chest out carrying an attaché case. What zest! What a lucky number he has drawn in the lottery of life. Wealth, Fame, and Blood count for nothing on the other side of the window-pane where those others, the prisoners in the Bastille of a specialist's waiting-room, regard the freedom and gaiety of a world peopled by the physically vigorous.

*   *.   *   *   *

In the high, finely proportioned room the captives of ill health wait with a show of indifference for that call to the knight of the knife and the medicine bottle.

Such splendid masks. They could be crying like children who have not learnt to hide feeling, or they could be discussing symptoms with the freedom of sufferers gathered at a clinic, but instead they preserve their privacy and their dignity and go on reading that 'Violet Lady Tooper is playing in the women's finals at Cannes.' That queer pain at the heart may be nothing—or everything. They will known soon, perhaps. Meanwhile there is such a thing as a *panache*. The magazine leaves tremble as they are turned. That is the only sign. No; not the only one! The door opens, but, before a frozen-looking manservant can murmur a name, every eye in the room looks up questioningly. A woman rises and goes out. There is no sound but the turning of a leaf. . . .

*   *   *   *   *

The sun-brown elderly man in a check suit is a colonel in the Indian Army. He has come half across the world to find out what betrayal his splendid physique has played him in the prime of life. He does not realize that he is reading a fashion magazine, for the fear of ill-health waters the blood of men who have always been strong. When he faces fire across the specialist's desk all that funk will go. He will be slapped reassuringly on the back, no doubt. If not, he is the kind who makes the drama of Harley Street. He will take his medicine and walk out with his chin in the air.

The young girl with the seeds of disease is there, pale and handicapped, and rather lovely with the mark of those doomed to suffer. The man is there to whom this visit and a probable operation mean a ghastly hole in a small bank account. But his doctor shook a weary G.P. head at him, and said: 'I would rather you saw Sir Quite Blank. He'll tell you right away, and—we might as well know!'

Yes, *she* is there, too, of course, Dolores, Lady of Pains, with all the symptoms of every known and unknown disease. What interest would she have in life if the enthusiastic pursuit of new anxieties deserted her? How carefully she hoards her fears. The frozen-looking manservant tip-toes in. Will her ladyship come? In the sanctum Sir Quite Blank glances at his appointment book, and smiles. Here she is again, that hearty hypochondriac! How the extremes of human nature meet in this room! A man has just left with his death sentence. What balance a man needs to close the door on the sublime and open it on the ridiculous, giving to each the same suave attention.

'Oh, dear Sir Quite, I've just raced back from Nice to see you. That cure, you know. . . . I'm afraid . . .'

She fixes on the specialist the avid eyes of one whose hobby is illness. She collects mysterious aches as some people collect stamps, rejoicing over a rare specimen. Perhaps subconsciously all she needs is sympathy.

'She ought to have had two children ten years ago,' thinks the specialist, as he sends her to Contrexeville. She gushes out, and he presses a bell. In the waiting-room the poor care-driven man buttons his coat with trembling fingers, and a quick little picture forms in his mind of a wife and children waiting for the verdict.

*　　　*　　　*　　　*　　　*

Down Harley Street whistles the butcher's boy. His girl jilted him last week and his employer sacked him yesterday, and he whistles out of a sad heart. Life is a pretty rotten affair. No girl, no job! He stops whistling: it isn't decent. What right has he to whistle? His face shines like a red apple in autumn, his blood courses through his healthy young body.

What a tragedy life is, he thinks!

Simple soul. . . .

DO you desire a crowded hour of life on a Sunday morning? Then come with me to London's unknown Petticoat Lane in the West.

We leave behind us the prosperous, stately Holland Park Avenue, Notting Hill, and plunge into roads at the back which have socially declined. They are deserted; sunk in Sabbath calm. But suddenly at Sirdar Road, at Bolton Street, at Crescent Street, we come on a great crowd that packs the roadway tight. This is 'Rag Fair,' a street market that lasts only for a few hours every Sunday morning, but until the clock strikes twelve the entire district is flung into a commercial ecstasy.

You cannot see the stalls for the crowds which press round them. The road is a mass of slow-moving men and women. The tenement houses on either side vie with the stallholders in an attempt to make money. On each flight of steps is a pathetic array of worn-out articles, neatly arranged, but so old and useless that it seems to you children must be playing at shop.

Yet this is the work of grown-up men: those torn babies' shoes side by side, those intimate but ragged garments, those battered hats stuck on the railing spikes, those awful pictures of little girls in frilly frocks cuddling huge collie dogs and— essence of commercial optimism—that photograph of someone's grandfather! He stands jauntily beside a bamboo table on which is an aspidistra; and he has a gold Albert and white side-whiskers.

'Fourpence,' says the man who is selling his ancestor; then quickly, to your back, 'tuppence!'

Can anyone, you wonder, be so alone in this world that they would live with someone else's tuppenny grandfather?

*　　*　　*　　*　　*

From time to time, householders on the top step take out their clay pipes and thoughtfully arrange old bicycle wheels, vague bits of wood, nails, shoes, and bound copies of the 'Sunday at Home,' while, from upper windows, women, surrounded by their young, gaze down upon the weekly excitement.

Now and then an unshaven and thirsty-looking man dashes down the steps hauling at an ancient perambulator. His wife looks down on him as a dame might have regarded her own true knight as he entered the lists at a tournament, for— if father manages to sell the pram there will be beer in a large jug. . . .

The stallholders harangue the mob, humorously, violently, insultingly, or with a grave attempt at superiority. Petticoat Lane in the East is Jewish: this Petticoat Lane of the West is English. Here is rough costermonger wit, an Elizabethan ribaldry and frankness, no Oriental subtlety, no sly cleverness.

'Give the wife a treat once a year,' shouts an old man standing behind a barrowful of combs. 'Give the old girl a treat. . . . Give 'er a comb that won't ketch fire and burn 'er blinkin' 'ead orf. . . . Look at this . . .!'

Dramatically he strikes a match and holds it to a celluloid comb. It flares up. He holds the flames to the combs he is selling, and nothing happens. This seems to impress the crowd. With fanatical enthusiasm, he quickly grabs six combs of different sizes and yells: 'Sixpence!'

There are outstretched hands offering money!

*   *   *   *   *

As you go through the crowd, you observe barrows which are really Harrods and Selfridges reduced to the lowest common denominator. They contain a multiple assortment which no man could invent. One stall offers a bottle of pickled onions, a broken stove, an odd satin slipper (left foot), a lithograph of Queen Victoria holding a sceptre, two pairs of combinations, and a set of stags' antlers.

Is anything in the world too old and useless for commerce? How can there be purchasers for pieces of knotted string, old elastic tape that refuses to be elastic, broken decanters, odd gloves, and Chaplinesque bowler hats?

'Here is the produce of the cocoa bean,' declares a plump little man with a sweetmeat stall. 'The pure, unadulterated mixture of sugar with the cocoa bean!'

He carefully tears aside the silver paper from a packet and holds it to the crowd, as if showing them a miracle. (There is always a dramatic moment in street salesmanship: the moment when, after hypnotizing your victim, you drive home a great truth and take his money.)

'If,' says the fat man, arriving at this critical moment, 'you are this afternoon going to see your dearest friend in life'. . .'

Here he holds up the packet of chocolate and gives it an appraising slap.

'If you are going to see this friend, you can take with you this packet with absolute impunity.'

No one laughs. Before him are rows of stolid faces. A young man pulls himself together and buys a packet, whether or not because he is relieved at the thought of feeding his sweetheart with impunity I cannot say!

*   *   *   *   *

A pale woman, who carries a pale baby, gropes among the debris of a stall. She disentangles something from a grey, dirty decoration in which it is caught up; a pair of infant's shoes mixed up with that which was once a wreath of orange blossom. She buys the shoes, poor little tattered second-hand shoes that have already served their purpose. . . .

A few yards away on the main road purr the limousines of Holland Park.

Back Gardens ∘ ∘ ∘ ∘ ∘ ∘

FOR fourpence halfpenny you can have an exciting peep into, roughly, ten thousand lives by buying a ticket at Fenchurch Street and sitting in a train drawn by a keen little elder brother to Stephenson's 'Rocket.'

I know few things more provoking than the back gardens of London. It seems a rule in certain crowded streets that the front of a house must be as glum as the face of a poker player. You must never be able to tell from the front of a house what is going on inside. But the back of the same house casts off restraint.

The back windows and the back gardens are allowed to tell you almost as much as an old matron who has had ten children will tell you over her third glass of gin.

First of all there are marvellous underclothes. Some districts send their garments to the laundry in secret—no one knows what the person next door wears underneath; in others these facts are blazoned in an almost boastful fashion; and it is always washing day.

Sometimes you see a woman with her mouth full of pegs pinning a sheet to a line, and sometimes you observe a dog that has suddenly gone gay walking across the garden wound up in somebody's shirt; and you hope he won't be found out!

*   *   *   *   *

Then how much character each little strip of garden spells, as you go by.

Most are just dreary dumps littered with the debris of ancient enthusiasms: the odd bicycle wheels which Bill found in the rag market and bought, first, because they were sixpence each and, secondly, because they looked vaguely useful; the wireless contraptions erected with American intentions, and the semi-naval masts put up in who knows what romantic nautical longing?

These masts are, to me, one of the mysteries of the London back gardens. In what fit of seasickness have they been erected? They are somehow pathetic. They tower above barren cabbage patches as if some ship has sunk there with all hands. Do their creators derive comfort from them? Do they ever run up dramatic signals on them, or do they just lie in bed (trying hard not to see the gasworks) in an attempt to catch them against the sky, believing them to lean over the green bosom of the deep?   I do not know.

*   *   *   *   *

In the chaos of crowded buildings, which is offered swiftly to the train, you can pick out a yard full of scrap metal. Everything that can fall, or ever has fallen, from machinery seems to have found a dishonoured grave here. Every kind of cogwheel lies in rusty confusion with all manner of mechanical entrails whose technical names might baffle an expert.

There are always gloomy men with sacks who keep on adding to the loathsome pile, as if, behind it all, is some restless mind demanding more and more with, perhaps, the eventual intention of mounting to heaven on old tins.

The melancholy pyramids rise to a great height—a cemetery of dead machines; but over it broods, not the peace of a cemetery, but the contempt for past service which is the peculiar horror of all scrapheaps.

*   *   *   *   *

Windows.

They flash past, showing things. It is like dipping swiftly into a dozen novels in a library, receiving a hint of a plot here, a sentence there. . . .

Hogarthian women, their sleeves rolled up, eat heartily in one window. It is probably bacon. You wish that you might be invited to share it, to find out why they are laughing; but the train takes you on to little dwelling-rooms turned into horrid, tiny factories in which numbers of women are bent over sewing machines, pedalling away in a desperate race, their pale faces, old and young, close to their work.

This is an unpleasant sight; they look like captured animals in those small, mean rooms.

Larger factories, with hundreds of young girls in overalls packing something. They wave gaily to the train and laugh.

A man in the next carriage puts his head through the window and waves back from unadulterated gallantry. He can never surely hope to meet these girls, yet, in a swift moment of romantic enthusiasm, he feels compelled to respond. A born serenador, no doubt, a knight born out of his due time, ripe for every kind of errantry and trouble. . . .

Then, a face in a window, just looking dull and stupid. That is most provoking of all—a dull, listless face in a dull, bleak frame.

Behind it—what? Tragedy? Comedy?

An unknown face with a blank expression—thinking, perhaps, an immortal loyalty; thinking, perhaps, a great hate; thinking, perhaps, that sausages are too dear for breakfast.

Out-Patients

THE place smelt faintly of ether and disinfectants and that vague mixture of clean odours common to hospitals.

A policeman, mopping his brow, stood in a passage holding his helmet by the chin strap. He had just appeared with the limp form of a girl over his arm. Several sad people waited about: a woman who had fallen down in the traffic, an old man who had hurt his hand in the door of a railway carriage, and a girl who had fainted in the street.

I looked through a door into a snow-white room where a man in a white overall was deftly bandaging the head of a woman, snipping lint, twisting the bandage with practised fingers, now and then speaking reassuringly to his patient. Near him a girl with auburn hair, far from one's idea of a woman doctor, was bathing a hurt arm, her hands moving expertly among many bottles which stood beside her on a glass shelf. There was a sudden commotion. A noise far down the passage. Two policemen entered carrying a man. Knocked down by a taxicab! He was hurried into a vacant room, a doctor rushed up, the door closed. . . .

*   *   *   *   *

Here is a new aspect of London: London the blind beast that tramples on her children, London the heartless piece of machinery that catches humanity in its wheels, mangles it, and passes on. Every day it happens, every day policemen come in holding a helpless girl or an old man, every day the rush and roar of London means for someone a calm doctor in a white overall snipping lint, murmuring, 'Don't tremble, don't worry; you're all right. You've had a marvellous escape!'

*   *   *   *   *

I went into a long, tiled room with a floor like the deck of a battleship, scrubbed till the wood looked like grey linoleum, and, in this room, were nearly a hundred men and women, sitting in pews as if waiting for a church service to begin.

This was the out-patients' department, the most dramatic

spot in a hospital. Here the man or the woman waits to learn whether that queer ache in the back means a temporary break with life, a white bed, and an operating theatre, or—blessed words—'nothing to worry about.' A bell rings! A pale little woman looks round to see if the time has really come, swallows hard, rises, and passes through a door to learn her fate.

I fear to enter a hospital because I hate to see suffering. It is cowardly, it is wrong; and it is something we should fight against. But, once inside, I hate to go away. Here is courage, here is humour, here, I believe, is true beauty: the beauty of the human spirit putting out its loveliest flowers. Where is ugliness: in a beaten body? Yes. But have you seen the eyes of sufferers? Something shines there. In a hospital, which, you might believe, would break your faith in life and bring you to regard human beings as organisms in various stages of decay, you touch the soul of man.

Say what you like about the medical profession and its shortcomings, a doctor's is the most noble calling a man can follow. He may be incompetent, he may be helpless, but he is never out when suffering knocks at the door. . . .

I slipped into a seat beside the out-patients. Quiet middle-class folk most of them. Some stolid, some waiting their turn with trembling fingers, some ignorant and terrified, like poor animals cornered, not knowing what is to happen to them, and just quietly waiting. Humour? Oh, yes! There is always a little worm of laughter gnawing a sore heart:

'My sister 'ad the same pain as you've got,' I heard the inevitable Job's comforter remark with a sniff. 'And she, pore thing, just faded away, she did. Worn down to a point, she was.'

The other woman looked towards the speaker with eyes in which fear and dislike seemed equal.

'P'raps my case won't be so bad, let's hope.'

'I expect it's the same,' replied the intolerable Mrs. Job. 'Low down on the left side like a knife jabbing. That's it.'

'It isn't my side; it's my leg.'

'Oh, I beg pardon. I thought you said habdomen.'

*   *   *   *   *

In a small room, a specialist, who charges rich people big fees for his brains, was giving his services to the poor. The patient, unclothed, stood before him. Medical students stood around following his diagnosis, taking notes, and greedily gathering his whispers.

His uncanny, sympathetic hands moved over the body searching, searching, his fingers feeling the flesh, as if drawn by the magnet of disease. I looked at him bent over the naked, living body, listening to the heart, swift, keen, concentrated: a symbol of that enviable happy warrior who fights in a splendid cause. . . .

When in the frenzy of war a man saves the life of a comrade, his country pays him the high tribute to courage. Here in London these V.C.'s of the X-ray and the lancet and the test tube, often unknown to science or fame, and often careless of reward, go over the top every day of their lives to rescue a fellow-man from the death that creeps towards him.

On the way out the little woman in black came from her ordeal, ah, so changed. She went out into the surge of London, an empty shopping basket over her arm; and there was something about her that made me think of a caged bird, released, going up into the freedom and the beauty of the sky.

Dog and Cat ✆ ✆ ✆ ✆ ✆ ✆

THE narrow lane, lined with eating-houses, storerooms, and offices, possesses a cat colony which for sheer variety is unsurpassed—probably unequalled—by any other street of the same size in London.

It has long been my ambition to catalogue them, to probe with the zeal of a Rouge Dragon Pursuivant into delicate questions of ancestry and intermarriage; but this I shall never do, having only one, fully-occupied, life. The colony is almost incredibly complicated, so that only the cats'-meat man, who dawns like a good deed in a noisy world each morning, can have any intimate knowledge of it. Strange, attractive females appear from time to time, licking their lips at their little hour of life, causing, no doubt, a flutter of excitement, of scandal, all of which passing, life resumes its normal calm. Now and then I notice suspicious importations in dirty shades of ginger (always an outcast colour) slinking past under the unwinking eyes of the established natives. Some of these visitants take root, some depart. All the time dynasties rise and dynasties fall in the refreshing shade of the fried fish shop; and no one knows.

* * * * *

There was a crowd in the lane yesterday. All kinds of people joined it. The carters, and the men who unload things from lorries, remained loyal until human flesh and blood could stand it no longer; for a Londoner may be able to resist wine, women, and song, but he can never resist a crowd. When I arrived, it looked like a first-class street accident, or a spectacular dive from a top-floor window. I expected to hear them all press nearer crying, 'Give him air!'

In the centre of the ring was a space, and in the centre of the space was the smallest cat on earth, the youngest inhabitant of the lane. He was black, and his eyes, not long open on the world, had that milky blueness of extreme infancy. He was ruffled, and, generally speaking, he looked as innocent as a reporter just down from Oxford.

Facing him, with his head on one side, looking as though he had just apologized and couldn't add anything, was a big, experienced fox terrier. He was the first dog this kitten had ever encountered, and he was much worse than anything it could have imagined. This small cat thought that he had stepped right out of the cradle into the grave.

* * * * *

The crowd were delighted; the crowd smiled.

They saw, without realizing, probably twenty or thirty thousand years assert themselves with unerring rapidity in this just-born cat: it turned itself into a small black pot-hook and faced the dog. 'Now open your mouth and spit, and get your claws ready, darling!' said millions of dead-and-gone cats in his ear. And this he did with great success, except for the fact that no sound came from his small pink mouth.

A marvellous tiny ball of instinct. Just imagine how a human baby would walk down the throat of the first lion it met. How have we managed to survive?

The dog blinked his eyes and looked away as if he had seen something regrettable. After all, it was only a cat! He looked again. The youngest inhabitant, who was rapidly packing the education of years into minutes, sensed that this hereditary enemy was thinking along the wrong lines; and he actually took a step forward and opened his mouth.

'Ha, ha!' said the crowd.

'Poor little thing!' said the girls.

'Leave it alone,' said the man. 'It knows its way about all right!'

And, before this small spiteful thing, the big dog backed with a 'sorry-I-intruded' expression. It was a victory for heredity!

Behind this scene I seemed to see thousands of years full of cats being chased up trees by dogs, thousands of dogs being scratched by cats, piling up the race memory, perfecting the technique of resistance, establishing an ancient law of prudence.

* * * * *

The dog walked down the lane with a casual air—a masculine air of not having been mixed up with anything connected with cats. The cat withdrew to normal proportions, and slunk off with a feminine air of having sent some man about his business.

The crowd scattered.

The work of the world was resumed.

HE rises every morning with military precision, boils his shaving water and shaves. He is eighty-two. Most of those he once knew are dead.

On the shelf in his little room are books: a Bible, 'The Horse in Fact and Fiction,' 'Cavalry Tactics,' 'India as I Knew It' (by Lieut.-Colonel Cuthbert Blunderbus, V.C., C.M.G.), 'Religio Medici' (how did that get there?), and an Army List for the year 1885. Near his books is a rack containing six blackened pipes and a tin of navy-cut.

The old man opens the door and finds, on the step, a loaf of bread, sugar, and tea, and he potters round his room, perhaps toasting a slice of bread or watching the kettle as he slowly prepares his solitary breakfast. A woman of thirty looks from a picture frame on the mantelpiece as if she would like to say 'Poor darling, let me help'; and her eyes, it seems, follow him round and watch his old fingers fumble with canister lids and spill the thin trickle of sugar from the bag. He does not see her. His rheumatism is worse to-day.

*   *   *   *   *

He dresses carefully, puts on a gloomy black cloak that hangs behind his door, and a gloomy black hat to match, and walks out through grey cloisters to chapel, where Christ crucified hangs in the shadows over the altar.

He returns to his little room, ties his tie more carefully, puts on a felt hat at a distinct angle, takes an umbrella under his arm, and fixes a gold-rimmed monocle in his eye. When he moves you notice the breed, the good lines, the thin flanks, the spindle legs, the spare, whipcord old body, the way he puts his feet, the set of his shoulders, the manner in which his worn clothes sit on him.

With a clubman's nod to the porter at the gate, he passes out under the arch of Charterhouse: hat cocked, monocle set, shoulders squared.

*   *   *   *   *

There are sixty of them; sixty old Colonel Newcomes, who have fallen on evil days, 'gentlemen by descent and in poverty' runs the old rule, 'soldiers who have borne arms by land or sea, merchants decayed by pirates or shipwreck, or servants in household to the King or Queen's Majesty.' The Charter-house—a good deed that took root in London three hundred years ago—gives them a pound a week, a black cloak, a black hat, rooms and food in hall. All that it demands is that they attend chapel once a day.

* * * * * *

Seven long white tables stand in an oak-panelled room, a rich, ancient hall; and into this room troop the sixty old men who have know better days. Sixty old men with the ghost of old authority over them, dead fires in their eyes, in their hearts what? Pride, I think, and tradition.

See how they sort themselves out. Is it imagination, or has old age stiffened their natural prejudices a little? Do some hold themselves aloof, clinging, with the tenacity of age, to a relic of superiority? Those two childish old men who shout into one another's ears and, from time to time, glare round the table! They are always together. They were at the same public school.

They drift off slowly after luncheon by ones and twos. Some go out, no one knows where. A few sign the book in the dining hall, notifying that they will be out until midnight: such a spidery announcement of a night out! One of them, who is over ninety, rests most of the day, so that he may be strong enough to go down to his club at night, the club he has always known.

Most of them, however, just sleep or read, or they walk, leaning on two sticks, beside the green grass in the quadrangles, or through cloisters and under grey Tudor archways into quiet, cobbled courts where there is a richness of Elizabethan brick, a wine-dark creeper over old stone, and an air of peace. The ancient quiet of the old monastery still surrounds these Carthusian monks. A beautiful ante-room to paradise. . . .

* * * * *

At eight o'clock the curfew sounds over Smithfield from the bell tower of Charterhouse.

Sixty times the bell rings, each note a human life, once for

CHARTERHOUSE

every old man in Charterhouse. Once it rang nearly seventy times, and the ancient brethren rose up out of their chairs in alarm, cast aside their pipes, and peered out from their windows anxiously, wondering what disaster had followed them even into harbour. Seventy! That would mean a curtailment of privileges! Sixty furious old men were only soothed when it became known that the bell-ringer had a bad cold and, sneezing violently between his pulls, had lost all count of the curfew.

That does not often happen. The curfew of Charterhouse keeps faithful count of its sixty brothers, and, in their little cells, they listen, knowing that some night it will ring only fifty-nine. . . .

One by one, the lights go out. Stray fingers of moonlight touch veined hands lying outside coverlets, fall over grey lined faces, find that place on mantelpieces where a woman in a picture frame looks out into the darkness with eyes which seem to say: 'Poor darling, if only I could help!'

The Last Tube ⌒ ⌒ ⌒ ⌒ ⌒ ⌒

THE golden chain of the last tube swings through the black O of the tunnel. Above ground London is silent. The monster is wrapped in sleep, but Piccadilly clings to consciousness, as if unwilling to risk a nightmare. A slow taxicab skims the kerb, a policeman shakes a shop door, men with waterhoses stand shooting a young Niagara over the tired road. . . . A new day has just been born. Another twenty-four hours of possibility, of time, in eight million lives for good or bad. . . .

Down in the tube station, where the last train swings in with a protest of brakes, there is nothing to indicate the hour; yet it is vividly obvious. A rat, unseen by most of the waiting passengers, has just gone like a flash from the porters' room to its usual hiding-place beneath a seat, on which so innocently sits a girl. If she knew . . . if . . . ! A big, lollopy rat so near those sandy legs!

A pale thrill goes round the waiting crowd as the train comes to a standstill. They are like people who have lost all interest in life. They are dull, tired, listless. The men seem to be smoking pipes or cigarettes just to keep awake. The girl with the sandy legs has thrown off all coquetry—she is just herself, a poor, tired little scrap of humanity.

'Move along there, please!'

That 'please' after midnight strikes me as a pretty good tribute to our polite Virgils of the underworld.

* * * * *

The nightbirds blink and revive in the amber warmth of the carriage.

What a puzzle the man opposite will be until the end of time! We survey each other with that faint distrust born of this unnatural hour. What are we? What business, or pleasure, kept us at the heart of London when all good people should have been a-bed? We gaze at each other like stuffed owls. When we have done that, we read a stale newspaper.

There are solid, reliable-looking men with black bags: printers, telegraph men, or otherwise members of that army which works by night. There are two young men in evening dress, each different—the one an elegant young rake, the

302

other dolled up for an occasion in evening clothes not often aired in public. At Charing Cross in steps a musician and a young fellow who looks as though the upper half of him was dressed at 8 a.m., and the lower half at 8 p.m. He wears patent leather shoes and dress trousers, with a lounge coat. He carries a brown paper parcel. He is a waiter. What do waiters carry home in the small hours? Fragments of the feast? Tips?

A 'huge negro enters. What is he? A prize-fighter? A leader of a crook gang? No, madam, he is the picturesque person in the baggy red and gold costume who at dinner made your Turkish coffee and shook rose-water on your hands.

In a corner a regrettably elderly man dozes in the untidy manner of one assisted to this by the grape.

Some go out, some come in.

A girl is standing. The dozy man awakens, and, with the courtesy of a Raleigh placing his cloak in the mud, rises heavily, and extends his hand in what would have been a graceful gesture, had it not carried away the hat of a little man sitting next to him, who glares with the fury of a lifelong abstainer forced to inhabit a world full of Bacchic satyrs.

'Madam!' begins the inflated man impressively, thinking of something beautiful to add, something poetic and flowery that fills his soul, but finds no doorway through speech; then, baffled, he sways twice, licks his lips, and ends lamely: 'Sit down!'

      *   *   *   *   *

She sits. He stands, holding a strap and gazing, as if from the top of Mount Everest—from the crest of his inflated imagination—at his fellow-passengers. Then, as if suddenly stricken with a great truth, he says in a loud voice to everybody: 'Isn't it per-perfectly remarkable?' He pauses, and everybody listens. What is perfectly remarkable? He stands arrested in his portentous attitude, one admonishing finger outheld. Then, dropping his voice to a stage whisper, he says:

'We're all . . . going . . . home!'

His great truth appeals to everyone. The pale, tired girl, who has forgotten to be coy, smiles, the solemn men in black coats smile, and, encouraged, the man goes on:

'Home,' he says heavily, with a hint of tears in his voice, 'swheetest word in the English language. . . .'

The train stops; and the lecturer promptly sits down in the lap of the man opposite, and is ejected.

'And why,' he goes on, 'are we going home? Why?'

He turns to the little teetotal-looking man, whose hat he knocked off at the start of his performance.

'Why are you going home, sir?' he asks politely.

The little man stiffens, and looks dead ahead.

*   *   *   *   *

'My friend here,' explains the straphanger to the entire compartment, 'is going home—the swheetest word in the English language—because there was nothing left in the decanter and they turned him out into the cold street. Isn't that awful? Isn't that a tragedy?'

'Camden Town!' shouts the conductor, wondering why everyone is smiling.

'Good night,' says the lecturer, raising his hat. We see him raising his hat to the conductor (and to anybody else who is looking), and so we leave him in an attitude of polite regret on the empty platform of Camden Town. . . .

*   *   *   *   *

The last tube rushes on beneath sleeping London and then out into the open, where the pale light of a new day will soon creep up into the sky.

THE NIGHTS OF LONDON

The full streets beckon: Come, for toil has burst his bars,
And idle eyes rejoice, and feet unhasting go,
O let us out and wander the gay and golden night.

LAURENCE BINYON, 'London Visions'

The Nights of London

NIGHT in London.

We are off again on more adventures. Before us lies the mystery of dark London, of London under the glow of lamps; London under moon and stars; London under fretful, dull skies. Before us, also, lies danger—the awful danger of repeating a story that has been well told already. You must leave this to me and hope for the best. I promise not to drag you through that inevitable night on the Thames Embankment or the equally ancient night in a doss-house. I will try to take you as little as I must in the well-worn footsteps of other night-errants. I may not do half so well. I do not know; for the night of London is a dark puzzle in which it is possible to find almost anything.

When night falls over London ancient and primitive things come to our streets; for night is sinister, dramatic; it brings with it something of the jungle. Beasts of prey and great cities alone in nature remain awake when darkness comes; the one in search of death, the other in search of an extra hour of life.

The very quality of the darkness in a great city like London is itself a study. The darkness of Pall Mall is different from the darkness of Bishopsgate; the lights of Piccadilly are different from the lights of the Edgware Road. And the men and women who move slowly through the streets of London at night, complex in motive, freed from work, moving for once at the bidding of their own wills, their faces bloodless in the pale stream of lamplight, gliding past in waves, a concentration of all those unknown things that have made great cities since Babylon a mystery and a heartache.

*   *   *   *   *

No man, I think, can say that the words 'Night in London' leave him entirely unmoved. To the student of human nature they act like a whip on the imagination, for night in London is a brief period of infinite possibility. Dickens placed strange people in strange places, but Stevenson placed strange people in ordinary places, and thus enlarged the possibilities of romance and gave life a new terror—or a new thrill. No matter how often life proves to us that pale ladies in deep sorrow (and limousines) do not glide to the pavement edge and whisper, 'Follow this car and save me!' yet at night we are almost persuaded that adventures in which fate has cast us as the hero lie just round the next corner. This rarely happens; but it explains why some people get into trouble at night!

There is in the heart of the darkness an allurement that calls, promising that somewhere in this respite from day is a release from routine, telling us that the world is free to us.

* * * * *

Night life is the last social habit to be developed by a city. It is only since the growth of the West End, the invention of gas and the establishment of a police force that London has had the opportunity, and, incidentally, the audacity, to plunge into the night.

Roman London must have been deadly dull after dark; Saxon London duller still. The curfew, which announced the official night of Norman London, must have acted as a damper on any gaiety that happened to survive the Conquest. The law of the Middle Ages assumed that any man who walked the streets at night was bent on evil; which was probably true. Tudor London developed a little patch of vice and villainy on Bankside, but it is not until the Georgian Age that we observe the first Nights of London. Beyond the walls of the City the West End with its squares had grown up; and it is in this new London that we see for the first time the night hawk sitting behind the yellow windows of St James's Street staking his estate on a throw of the dice.

I suppose no age devotes itself to nocturnal gaiety till its women dress for dinner. Mrs. Dick Whittington, I am confident, had no evening gowns. She wore her best gown trimmed with miniver indiscriminately at noon or night; for a 'riding' along Chepe or for a State banquet. In the Georgian Age, however, white shoulders flashed through the tinted dusk of Ranelagh and Vauxhall. In the new West End the torches of the link men grew pale in the dawn as a tired beauty was borne in her sedan chair from a rout.

The night life of the Georgians was the effervescence of a privileged few. Behind the wildest party was always the old London problem of getting home, complicated in that age by the solemn thought that Dick Turpin might be waiting with his pistols cocked behind a hedge in Mayfair. Still, that did not deter them: our forefathers contrived to have a good time by candle-light.

The lights of London grew brighter in the next century until they blazed on a boiled shirt in a hansom cab. We are now almost in modern times. The London of the Georgians had been naughty; the London of the staid Victorians became wicked; that, at least, was her reputation; and they say that where smoke is there is generally fire. Night crowds, made up, not of lords and ladies, but of ordinary Londoners, filled the Strand, for years the most famous street in the world. It handed its supremacy to Piccadilly almost in our own times, and fell into position as a kind of connecting link between the staid old City on the hill and the giddy young West End.

Old men who drink port have told me, when warmed up, how beautiful London was at night in those days of side whiskers and plaid trousers and Ouida. They have described to me the unforgettable sensation, unknown to this age, of waiting outside a stage door with a bunch of flowers. The Georgian night was sustained by port; the Victorian by champagne: this was the age of Clicquot. A series of sharp explosions and a barrage of corks went up in the Strand restaurants every night as grandfather leaned single-mindedly towards his favourite ballet girl.

Nowadays the nights of London, through which we shall journey in the following pages, are free to all men. The cheap restaurant, the tube train, the omnibus, have packed the West End at night. The desire to extract just a little more from life than Nature intended, confined during the eighteenth century to the quality, and, during the nineteenth, to the man with money, is now shared by the millions of London. The bright lights call them night after night, if only to saunter for an innocent hour in the slow, exciting crowds.

This, then, is our stage. It is an interesting one. By day we can say that London obeys a master; by night she is her own mistress. She is not bound to stay up after dark; in fact the doctors say it is unwise.

*   *   *   *   *

Something more.
Among the eight millions which are London are thousands

of men and women who sleep by day and work by night in order that we may eat new bread for breakfast, drink fresh milk, read our newspaper, and be in the position to slip unwelcome letters behind the clock before we begin a new day.

How often do we think of those children of the London night—those work-o'nights—who sleep in hushed homes with blinds closed against the daylight and sally forth at dark to perform work that upholds so much easiness in our lives?

What manner of people are those owls of London, and how do they like living behind the back of the sun?

I will go through the silent streets of London and discover them to you. I will describe them and their opinions and their tasks; for those are our companions in London of whom we know little, of whom we think less. . . .

But look, a little half-moon lies over the Thames. The stage is set. Let us go into dark streets.

TWO o'clock in the morning at the Bank. . . .

Arc lights burn over empty streets. It is so cold, so quiet. The Lord Mayor of London asleep behind the Corinthian columns of his dark, island house; the lieutenant in charge of the Bank Guard (soothed by traditional port) asleep opposite behind the eyeless frontage of Soane's stone money-box; the constables of the Royal Exchange asleep in their suburbs, their cocked hats on the bed-posts, their silver, Elizabethan beards above white sheets . . . dreaming of Gloriana, perhaps, who made them, or of scrubby little office boys, who live on apples and leave the cores to plague their lives.

This is the Bank: the busiest scene, by day, in London; by night the most desolate, most forlorn. A forest at night has a hidden life; even the Sahara and the Libyan desert seem to pulse with a queer vitality under the stars, but the City of London, made by man and deserted by its creator, dies each night. Dead as Timgad, it seems; as uncanny in its shuttered trance as some lost city of old times discovered standing in silence under an indifferent moon.

I stand by the Duke of Wellington, gripped by the silence of this so recently crowded stage, feeling in some small way the horror of being the last man left on earth.

A black tom-cat of great girth and dignity comes from Cheapside into Poultry with an air which suggests that he is the managing director of London, Limited. He alone treads roads which a few hours since would have meant annihilation; leisurely he comes, as if savouring the solitude, as if purring in the silence. He stands a moment lost in thought, and then slowly crosses the road—Cheapside to his tail, the Royal Exchange to his whiskers, the Bank to his left, the Mansion House to his right—the only living thing in the core of London's sleeping heart.

In the desolation of the Bank at two a.m. he is an event.

'Puss-puss,' I whisper.

He considers me and rejects me in the manner of cats. What right have I to be messing about in the coverts scaring the quarry? He walks to the Royal Exchange, and is lost round a corner. I wonder whether he will hunt the rat over those stones from Turkey on which London found her fortune.

A taxicab spins across from Queen Victoria Street; one of those curious unbalanced motor-sweepers releases its brushes and hums beside the kerb in Poultry, going slowly on into the lamplit solitude like an ugly garbage beetle.

*   *   *   *   *

I meet a policeman in Cornhill; another one in Gracechurch Street.

London must have appeared like this during the Great Plague; silent locked buildings and dead avenues. A square mile of solitude where once was such throbbing life, where London behind her wall lived and slept, married, died, and was buried. There can be no such things as ghosts, or the empty City of London would be full of thin, mistlike clouds every night, clouds with faces in them, peering, wondering.

Who could resist going on past the Monument to London Bridge?

London Bridge deserted, twin rows of lamps over the dark river, and—such a heart-catching beauty of London lost in a faint night mist, picked out with pin stars of light, the Thames in movement round the jutting piers, barred with gold fish scales of lamplight, and, to the right, a great splendour of grey spires, and dark stones. . . . London asleep! No sound but that of a stray, petulant siren downstream; no movement in all London but an approaching red tug light on the Thames, the rush of lit water and a sudden puff of steam from the Cannon Street railway bridge; a white cloud lit with red flame for an instant and then lost.

This is the time to see London, to love London, to make promises to London, to pray to London, to plead with London; for London now, grotesquely, seems all yours in loneliness, for once in the twenty-four hours harmless, unable to hurt or bless . . . lost in a dream.

*   *   *   *   *

I go down Lower Thames Street, where the cats are all in love, sitting crouched low, face to face, whirring inside with savage sonnets, advancing, retreating, eye to eye. I come to the Tower of London, which lifts grey walls and bastions in the night. One small window only is lit; a tiny square of gold high up in a turret. The mind fastens to it. I think of a knight hurriedly arming in the stone room and his horse ready below; I think of a yeoman warder with neuralgia. Such a speculative little window in a London night!

I creep to the wicket gate and peer in at the sleeping Tower of London. A shadow at the gate moves. I see the light run on steel:

'Who goes there?'

The Tower is awake: that is the discovery of a City night! The Tower is as it always was: a fortress locked with a password, locked by the King's keys, slipping back into medievalism every night prompt at ten.

'Who goes there?'

In the voice of the sentry at the wicket gate is the Voice of our London coming down, with a touch of indignation, over eight hundred splendid years.

THE last train had flung its golden chain into the tunnel. Piccadilly Station was closed. The moving staircases were not moving, the lifts were not lifting, the 'Book Here' signs were all lies (for you could not book anywhere): and over the ninety-six miles of tube track was a silence as of death. It was almost one a.m.

I stood in the desolate Piccadilly Circus Station watching a musical cleaner sweep up the litter of a day's tube crowd to the tune of 'Yes, Sir, She's My Baby.' Such a queer litter: reams of silver paper, bits of biscuit, chocolate, cigarette packets, envelopes, the heel of a white satin dance shoe, and —unspeakably disreputable and riotous—an old umbrella that had snapped somewhere. I thought of the things you see on the floor of a monkey's cage in the Zoo.

It was sad and lonely. The advertisements, to my weary eyes, were insolent; the thought of drinking vermouth was in itself intolerable; the idea of spending a holiday in Scotland loathsome.

*   *   *   *   *

Two whistling bill-posters arrived with a ladder, a bucket, and a roll of paper. They went to the edge of the platform.

'Is the juice off yet, Bill?'

'No,' replied Bill. 'Gimme a fag.'

They waited. A group of workmen, carrying leather bags from which protruded the blunt noses of large hammers, stood together at the platform's end, their attention divided between the acetylene lamps, which they carried, and the railway lines. This interest in the lines is characteristic of all who inhabit the tube stations when the last train has gone by. Men look at the rails as a dog looks at a sleeping cat—a will-it-bite expression. A foreman climbed down to the track, fixed a metal shoe to one conductor rail and a thing shaped like a small doll's house to the other. Immediately the doll's house became illuminated by twelve electric bulbs—the juice was still on!

He gave a respectful glance at the track and climbed back into safety.

A young man hurried down the platform towards me.

'Good morning!' he said briskly. 'I'm from the engineer's department, and I'm going to take you for a walk through the tunnel to Leicester Square. Shall we get a move on?'

'The—er—juice,' I began thoughtfully, 'is still, apparently, active, and lively . . .'

'Oh, that's all right,' he said heartily as he leapt down into the death zone. 'So long as you don't fall across the conductor rails, you know. . . .'

I hate being brave; I hate these situations from which it is not possible to retreat with self-respect. Jumping down beside him, I walked on in a manner which would have given Agag, who came unto Samuel 'delicately,' a number of useful hints.

*   *   *   *   *

You may not realize that when the tubes cease work the current is switched off in sections. As each section becomes 'juiceless,' gangs of men waiting at the stations set out to examine every yard of the one hundred and seventy-one miles of track on the Tube and District systems. It is probably the most important four hours' work during the London night. Every nut, bolt, screw, lamp, wire, signal, telephone, disc, sleeper, key, and rail is hit and prodded and peered at; they even go over every yard of the great iron ribs of the tunnels. They wander on like explorers in an Egyptian tomb; and this resemblance is intensified by occasional mosquitoes which live in this even temperature all the year long.

I did not see one. I am told, however, that gangers who go to sleep often awaken bitten; but as a stray ganger is the only brightness in the life of a tube mosquito—for they never penetrate to the richer potentialities of the stations—who shall grudge them an infrequent happiness?

We walked on through a gloom lit by small flasks of *crème de menthe*. We came to a straight stretch of track on which the rails converged to a point, and over this track swarmed men with hammers. The tunnel boomed with their knocking.

'The juice is off!' said the engineer, promptly walking on the live rail. I looked at him, silently abhorring the over-confidence of all mechanically minded men. Not to be outdone in courage, I lifted a foot gingerly and gave the rail a kick;

then, as I still appeared to be in existence, I boldly stepped on it with both feet. Apart from a second in which I experienced all the pangs of electrocution, there was nothing to report except a faint feeling of foolishness to be walking along a thing which any madman breaking into the power station could have filled with death in half a second.

We chatted to the repair gang. We collected one of the oldest night workers in the tube, Mr. Parsons, who waved a white acetylene lamp in our faces and became technical to the engineer.

These men love their tunnels; they take a pride in keeping every nut tight, they tell you in the same tone of voice that men say 'the wife's not very well,' that water is still leaking slightly through the iron joints by the 'dead end.'

'What,' I asked Mr. Parsons, 'is the most extraordinary thing you have found in a tube tunnel?'

'A dead 'un,' he replied bluntly.

*   *   *   *   *

Our arrival at Leicester Square was supremely nightmareish.

There stood Leicester Square Station as we all know it: advertisements, clocks, lights, indication boards and—not a soul on it. We limped in a leisurely way, now on the rails, now on the sleepers, talking in loud echoing tones about Mr. Baldwin's voice as heard over the wireless, the prospects of television and the mummy of Tutankhamen. We stood looking at desolate Leicester Square as two archaeologists might regard it in two thousand years, if London, by that time, is lost and ruined. A gang of men emerged from the opposite tunnel with a brazier and many hammers.

They swarmed like rats over the rails.

'By the way, I have seen no rats,' I said.

'There are very few,' replied the engineer.

'I suppose this hammering is going on everywhere?'

'Over one hundred and seventy-one miles of track,' he said.

*   *   *   *   *

They unlocked Leicester Square for me and I came out under the mild scrutiny of a policeman into cold, empty streets.

THREEPENCE. I gave it to the conductor at Ludgate
Circus and left the omnibus at Limehouse. If I had paid fifty
pounds for my ticket, I could not have travelled farther from
the London that most of us know. The West India Dock
Road is as glorified by darkness as the native quarter of an
Oriental city; its meanness is swallowed up in shadows; the
jutting lamps in dark side lanes leer adventure; the lit windows
near the roofs of rickety houses hold a sordid promise of thrill;
and I sniffed the air hopefully for the unforgettable pungency
of opium, but found only the unforgettable pungency of
fish and chips.

The pavements were barred across by light falling from the
windows of eating-houses and cook-shops. In these shafts of
brilliance, Chinamen passed me without 'brushing' past me—
as in the best literature—and I wondered, as I gazed at their
frozen faces and their live slit eyes like the eyes of animals
looking from a cave, whether such masks conceal drama or
only mild domesticity down Limey-housey-Causey-way—as
they call it.

A lascar shuffled past; a group of three vague Asiatics turned
suddenly into a side alley. I wanted to follow, to find out if
these stories are true. I had half a mind to break my tryst
with the dock police, but, without warning—I came face to
face with high spiked gates, and before me lay the docks
at night.

*   *   *   *   *

'There's a bit of a river mist,' said the police inspector,
handing me an electric torch, as we stepped out into pitch
blackness.

Now the docks are one of London's great thrills by day,
and by night they are one of London's great pictures.

In this lonely land of darkness, full of titanic shadows, where
huge ships lift themselves into the night like mountains, you
realize the startling variety that one great city can hold. Here
is a new London within half an hour of St. Paul's: a London
of dramatic gloom, tramping night patrols, shadows like men
and men like shadows, the whole place tinged with the grim

romance of labour on the Seven Seas, and vivid with the feeling of ships at rest, the water licking at their anchor chains.

We turned a corner of a shed. The dock-side cranes stood straddle-legged like queer Martians in the darkness. Three yellow portholes shone in the side of a large West Indiaman. We stepped over a coil of rope and were talking of something when, suddenly, the inspector stopped in his tracks and flashed a moon of white light into a corner. In this darkness a man stood blinking in the torchlight.

'Hallo, sir!' said the man.

'So it's you, is it?' said the inspector. 'What's up?'

The man gathered himself to tell us what was 'up'; and in this he was entirely successful, for he had developed the gift of fluent expression. His problem was whether the great big blinkin' teak ship would blinkin' well put out at this time of blinkin' night and collide with his blinkin' barge in the fog.

We made reassuring noises, but he was not to be interrupted. It was something he had been saving up all alone in the darkness of the dock, and he was glad to unburden his soul. . . .

It appeared to him that if the blinkin' people responsible for the unloading of London cargoes could blinkin' well tip their ships upside down and empty the stuff on the wharf in five minutes and load them again in five minutes they'd be off again to blinkin' Jamaica before you could say Jack blinkin' Robinson, and, strike me pink . . .

Before either of us could do this a melancholy 'moo' sounded in the mist: the deep moo of a doubtful siren. It electrified our blinkin' friend. He called on all the deities who safeguard the barges of lightermen; and leapt at random into the darkness. . . .

*   *   *   *   *

The millions of pounds' worth of goods which the world sends to the Port of London are guarded through the night by young men in blue. They have a nasty habit of looking like the end of a shed and suddenly stepping out with an 'All correct, sir!' to their inspector. They step back and melt into the shed again.

'All the rum that enters England comes here,' said the inspector, flashing his torch on an army of vast barrels lying stacked in rows.

'Thirty over proof,' we read on them.

'We can store four million gallons of it,' he said. To a sailor, this must be one of the most impressive spots on earth.

*   *   *   *   *

'There's precious little thieving in the docks these days,' said the inspector. 'We know every hole and corner of them. It may seem impossible to you, but we know every coil of rope and every brick that's left lying about. The river "rats" who used to pilfer have turned their attention to stuff lying out on the Thames, and the Thames police are kept busy with them. We don't often get a thief here.

'It's a funny thing the way people give Limehouse and Wapping a bad name. I suppose it's the writers that do it. You've no idea how mild and quiet people are down here, except for an occasional scrap when the pubs close. I know a pal who married a girl from Brixton, and when she had to come and live at Wapping—oh, my, wasn't there a business! She thought—well, I don't know what she didn't think. But she goes about at all hours of the day and night, and nicer, better-mannered people she says she never met—even in Brixton. She's a good deal safer from being insulted than she would be in the West End; and that's the truth. . . .'

*   *   *   *   *

Outside the dock gates, three brown men were explaining to the police in some unknown language that they desired to sleep in a ship that night, and through the gloom of the West India Dock Road drifted those furtive, suspicious figures with hunched shoulders and yellow faces and a walk that is almost a shuffle.

Opium?

Or fried fish?

I must find out one of these nights.

Under Waterloo Bridge

LEAVE Piccadilly, its epileptic lights, its feverish, lost air of searching for something that it will never find, and go down to the Embankment on a clear night. In the cold purity of this stillness the spirit is lifted and soothed. It is good to be alone in the night; it is good to feel sharp wind on the face; it is good to see the Plough flinging its clear symbol over a powdered sky . . . the dark bridges spanning the river; the only silver ripples from the moon; the oily golden ripples from the bridge lamps that shake and waver like swords beneath the waters.

The Thames at night is the most mysterious thing in London. So much part of London, yet so remote from London, so cold, so indifferent, so wise; for there is nothing about London that the Thames does not know. . . .

'Yes,' said the young police-sergeant. 'Waterloo Bridge has always had a kind of fascination. I suppose because the stone seats make it so easy to jump from. Many a time we've sat here watching people trying to make up their minds to jump, but, of course, we didn't know this till we'd fished them out and they had confessed that they'd been sitting there hour after hour trying to work up enough pluck.'

Against the windows of the little police pier known as Suicide Station, there was a steady, dark movement: the movement of the Thames going out to sea. Through the final span of Waterloo Bridge we saw, framed in that black arch, a pastel of blues and blacks: the near lights of Hungerford Bridge, the more distant lamps of Westminster, the slow glide of a lit tramcar in the emptiness of the early morning.

I know of few more dramatic places in London than the Suicide Room of this police raft: the bed ready, the bath ready, the cordials ready, the little dinghy with the rubber roller at the stern, its nose pointed to the dark arches.

'Of course, since the bridge has been under repair things have been quiet, and, in any case, there are not half so many attempted suicides in the river as there used to be.'

I looked out at the steady, dark movement of the sinister, indifferent Thames.

*   *   *   *   *

'A cigarette?'

'I'll smoke it later. . . . Of course, some come to themselves as soon as they touch the water. In fact, they mostly do—I suppose dying isn't nice once you start doing it! On the other hand, now and again they don't. It's generally the women that don't want to be saved; for when a woman makes up her mind to do a thing . . . I remember one night in summer . . .'

The chug-chug of the patrol boat sounded and ceased outside. We looked through the window and saw it and its shrouded crew of three rising and falling on the ebb tide.

'I remember one night in summer we heard a splash, and we were out in a second. She was a good-looking, nice-spoken young girl, but she *did* want to die. I've never seen anybody that wanted to die so much. She fought us and told us to go away; what right had we got to come interfering with her private affairs?—and all that sort of thing. She struggled so that it was a job to get the stern of the dinghy round to her. Have you ever tried saving anybody in a small boat? No; well, unless you grab 'em right you swamp the boat. Anyhow, we got her in, and she gave us a piece of her mind, sitting up with her hair all down and looking lovely—a treat she was. . . .'

He paused and looked earnest.

'When we got back,' he said, 'it was three o'clock in the morning.'

He stopped as if expecting comment.

'Well, why not?'

He leant forward earnestly, and I could tell that something serious was coming:

'Well, you see, the lady from Bow Street who undresses female suicides was off duty.'

'But the poor girl was half dead. Surely in a case like that . . .'

'No; she wasn't half dead! Only shock. I told you it was summer. You can't be too careful, you know. How did we know that she wouldn't get nasty for having her life saved, and complain that she had been treated disrespectfully?'

I tried hard not to smile. I could see his problem. I could also see his earnest, solemn face, anxious that I should see that problem.

'In addition to which,' he continued, 'all us fellows on duty that night were unmarried!'

21

Harder than ever, I tried not to smile! I was conscious that
this was the best police story I had ever heard. I was torn
between admiration for such fine feeling in a force often
accused of callousness, and amusement at thought of the
problem which confronted three young bachelors on a London
morning.

'What did you do?' I asked.

'Well, we had a kind of consultation. She fainted. Something had got to be done at once; and none of us wanted to
take the responsibility. Then we remembered Old Sam, who
does odd jobs about the station. We went outside and found
him. "Sam," we said, "you've been married, haven't you?"
"Yes," he said. "Why?" "This is why," we said: "There's
a young woman got to be undressed in the station, and it's
you who've got to do it." "All right," said Old Sam, "I will." '

'And he did?'

'He did.'

'Is that the end of the story?'

'Yes.'

'Did the girl complain?'

'No, she didn't.'

'Why did she jump in?'

'I think,' said the young sergeant, tapping the cigarette on
the desk, 'it was love. It mostly is with women.'

And he nodded towards the bridge that casts a varying
shadow over Suicide Station.

*   *   *   *   *

I glanced back from the Embankment and saw the Thames
heavy with the secrets it has carried to sea these thousand
years; and in the sky was a remote half-moon lying on its
curve in a ridiculous and careless attitude, as if London did
not mean anything.

A Jungle Night

YOU think that you know the Zoo. You have laughed at the bear who paws a bun through the bars; you have watched the whiskered sergeant-major faces of the seals as they bark for fish; you have seen the sleepy cats in the lion house, and you have, of course, noted the contempt in the tiger's amber eyes for you and all mankind.

Now I will show you the real Zoo; I will show you a Zoo that no one in London knows or suspects; I will show you a Zoo that lies in Regent's Park like a patch of primeval jungle older than Adam—the Zoo by the light of a full moon. . . .

The keeper unlocked a small wicket gate, and we went in. A white terrier called Bess, who adores a night rat-hunt more than anything in the world, ran ahead and became lost to sight. The moon, clear of clouds, rode above the spectral, black trees. A green wash of light fell over all things, casting shadows so black that a child might have tried to pick them up and carry them away; cold, green winter moonlight.

It was at first quiet. The only sound was the tap of the keeper's stick on the path.

*   *   *   *   *

'What is that?'
'A lion,' said the keeper.
The call came in the night so differently from the daytime howl for meat; a wild, hot huskiness of two notes. It was an uncanny, savage hoarseness that vibrated in the night. It was difficult to locate: now it seemed to the left, now to the right. It was the kind of cry that would inevitably have drawn you into that lion's jaws had you been trying to escape from them. There was a shuddering attraction about it, too. . . .

'Listen—she's answering him!' said the keeper. 'He's calling to a lioness!'

Through the night came a softer, shorter cry. We crept up quietly and saw them. He was sitting in the moonlight on a high rock—the magnificent, perfect savage—his great head in the air; she was crouched against the bars in the next pen, slim and slinky, watching him, then looking away, taking a walk and slinking back again to sit and admire him against the yellow moon.

She answered him from time to time through the bars— poor Thisbe!

'What do you think they are saying?' I asked the keeper.

'I don't know,' he said.

But I do! It was this:

'My dear,' he was saying, 'I would like to make love to you with newly killed meat, for the moon is full, and this is the time the deer go down to the salt licks. My paws are full of moonlight. They itch to tear something—for you, of course. How long is it since you tasted warm meat?'

'Don't talk about it, dearest! I feel like killing, too! I would like to feel my body crouched against something not quite dead . . . you know that feeling, that rich, purring feeling. Br-r-r-r-r-o-o-o-f-f-f!'

A savage love song under a cold moon in Regent's Park.

*   *   *   *   *

A cloud scurried over and the light faded. There was a soft, furtive movement in the dark. Three feet away, close to the bars, crouched two leopards, their bodies pressed against the earth, their tails moving slowly from side to side like yellow snakes. I saw their unwinking eyes fixed on something beyond me, on Bess, the white terrier. Whenever she moved they moved with horrible intensity; the desire to kill was in their noiseless scrutiny; every nerve in their bodies gathered in this desire.

In the next pen a tiger was crouched to spring; in the next a leopard lay full length on a rock and gazed up at the moon, his green eyes alight. The moon had brought the jungle into Regent's Park, and over these cages brooded the ancient instinct to stalk and kill, to tear and rend and fight. Such dear, sleepy cats by day; by night such murderers! I stood lost in a delicious horror. London was ten thousand years away.

Regent's Park was a little patch of country from the very dawn of time. It had nothing to do with London; it belonged to the heathen moon. In the air was the old law of tooth and claw. It was not horrible; it was exciting. I was surprised to find myself thrilled as if the moon, that had whispered the call of the wild to these beasts of prey, had also touched some ancient memory in me; something that could fear these creatures yet admire them, as the hunter admires his quarry.

'Am I,' I asked myself, 'at the very secret of existence—this machine-like lust to exterminate—whence comes the brain and muscle to survive?'

The great cats lay in wait . . . unblinking eyes watched our every movement; tails hit the earth.

We came to a bare tree shaking in the night wind. It was covered with dark objects like rooks' nests.

'Funny,' said the keeper, 'how the racoons refuse to sleep in the warm house we made for them, and climb that tree every night.'

I looked up and saw these little people, their tails twisted round the bare tree branches, their noses warm in their fur, fast asleep in the air, rocking this way and that across the moon. The instinct of their tribe. The whole of Regent's Park seemed to be given up to race memory . . .

Even as I thought it, there rose on the air the most blood-curdling cry that ever came from the throat of man or beast. It went into the night like the essence of all ache and agony —a banshee wail. And it seemed to me that all the creatures became silent to listen, for it went on alone in the night, horrible, frightening.

'The big grey wolf!' whispered the keeper. 'He's going to howl for the moon. If we stand still, we shall see and hear something in a minute!'

We stood in the shadow of a tree and saw him fling back on his haunches, lift his shaggy throat, and pour into the night all that was in his wild heart. . . . 'Ooooh,' he howled, 'Ooooooh to be running in green moonlight to-night, hungry in the snow, with the feel of the pack at my heels. . . .'

His cry was inexpressibly terrible, that long-drawn moan known in Scotland as the 'death howl'—a cry that dogs make when something old and sweetly miserable stirs in them, and they forget the fireside and the bone buried in the garden. It wavered on the night air, beginning as a whine, rising to crescendo, and falling through every variation of ache and agony into a sudden bitten-off silence.

'Now you wait!' whispered the keeper. 'That will set them all off. Don't move. . . .'

The old grey wolf lifted his head again and opened his lean jaws, and this time he sang on and on, picking up his howl as it fell, and casting it back to the moon. And the song he sang was the song of a running scent and the swift, savage joy of a pack in full cry. . . . There were pine forests and moonlight in his song, snow drifted against the trees and ice on rivers in a lonely lost world far from Regent's Park. It was a call! The note of exile in it almost brought tears to the eyes; the savagery in it made a cold mane stand up on the spine. He called and he called with his gaunt muzzle lifted. Then . . .

There were furtive, silent movements in the cages, little soft springings to earth and in each patch of moonlight in each cage sat a wolf.

The old wolf gave them the note, and they lifted up their voices in the old song. Then he ceased, but they went on and on. The little white foxes sat up and yapped; the lumbering hyenas came into the moonlight and joined the chorus; the jackals whined and barked.

'We remember,' they seemed to howl in chorus. 'We remember what it is to run free in the light of the moon. . . .'

'Yap-yap!' yelped the little white foxes, pushing their black noses through the bars. . . . 'Yip-yip!' sang the small brown jackals; and the wolves, without ceasing, bayed the yellow moon. . . . My mind went far from London. I remembered standing one night of the full moon beside the Nile listening to the jackals in the Valley of the Dead challenging the dogs of Luxor from the opposite bank of the river. The dogs went wild with rage, and the little jackals sat out on the sand in the moonlight and barked back at them. All night long it went on until the mad moon faded.

*   *   *   *   *

'What do you think of it?' asked the keeper.

'Marvellous!' I whispered.

I wish the British Broadcasting Company[1] would give this blood-curdling chorus to London on the night of the full moon. How it would chill the blood of Golders Green. I would also like to have a dog's opinion. It would be interesting to see

[1] The British Broadcasting Company was formed into the British Broadcasting Corporation on January 1st, 1933.

how he would behave if awakened from the warmth of a fire
by his ancestors.

We walked towards them. The chorus stopped at once.
Grey bodies leapt back into the shadows. All except one.
'Don't touch this animal' was written on his cage.

He dropped his voice and looked ashamed. (I did not
know that a wolf could look sheepish!) He rubbed his
rough sides against the bars and made the crying noise
that collie dogs make when they want you to rub behind
their ears.

'Old fellow!'

He whined in delight. I scratched his back and he danced
with joy. I rubbed his nose for him and he said, 'Thank you,'
just as any dog would say it.

'To-night he feels like being petted,' said the keeper, 'but
to-morrow night he might feel like taking off your hand.'

Perhaps the moon had gone to his head.

*   *   *   *   *

We went on, and came to an island lifted above a pit. In
the centre of the island were rocks and caves. The moonlight
fell over it, making a miniature world of it.

"Seventy Madras baboons live there, but they are asleep,'
said the keeper.

But he was wrong. A queer little old man's face peeped
at us, round the rock, and a queer little old man hunched out
of the cave and came limping along with his big arms. He
sat down on the edge of the island, hugged his stomach, looked
up at the moon, scratched himself, and said something in a
loud, harsh voice.

At the sound of his voice, the whole tribe appeared in the
mouth of the cave, incredibly weird and manlike. They
peered with their whiskered faces and they stood bunched
together in the narrow opening.

'Come on—it's only men!' the old baboon seemed to say
to them.

They advanced in great disorder, rather timidly and slowly,
and it seemed to me as I watched them in that pale light,
fascinated by their uncanny little human faces, that I was
seeing something that had happened long ago, before the first
bludgeon had been discovered.

The little old man gave a curt nod to the moon, chattered something at us that sounded like an oath, and walked back over the moonlit rocks. The tribe retreated before him. The glimpse of history was over. . . .

* * * * *

Wild in the air above the homely trees of Regent's Park sounded the song of the wolves. The moon looked down, and the light, that brings the jungle to London once a month, lay over stick and stone—an even, green magic.

'TWENTY-FIVE years ago,' said the stage door-keeper, 'you ad to be a regular pugilist on this job, and you needed a ouple of first-class chuckers-out to help you through the vening. You just take a look out now, sir, and tell me what ou see. . . .'

It was eleven-thirty. I pushed against the bar of the stage oor and looked on a dark alleyway between a high wall and he entrance to the gallery. There was no one there. That is he story of the modern stage door: *there is no one there.*

'Twenty-five years ago,' continued the stage door-keeper, you could have looked through this window and seen, at the nd of the passage, a row of hansom cabs waiting, and round he door here would be standing what we used to call the tage-door johnnies dressed in evening clothes, some of them n long black cloaks, and all of them holding bunches of flowers nd black canes with silver tops. . . .'

'Our fathers,' I said reverently.

I suppose he would have confirmed this had he not been alled to the telephone.

'Now it's *their* fathers,' he remarked, returning to the onversation.

'Whose fathers?' I asked.

'Why, the fathers of the chorus girls, of course. If it isn't a ather, it's an aunt. They call and take them home.'

'Times change,' I said.

'They do,' he agreed. 'You wouldn't hardly believe the number of golden quids I've taken through that door just to un up with a note. There was one little fellow whom the girls ised to call the "Rat," but his real name was Lord Whortle-berry. He had a lisp, and he was awful sweet on Harriet N——, and he used to hate waiting, but was frightened that ne of the other johnnies would go off with her. "Tell Hawiet o huwy," he used to say, and she used to say when I told her, 'Tell the Wat to go to hell." And one day I did tell him, and ne went off with Harriet's chum, a lovely girl of the name of Gubbins. There was a fair old shindy, and in less than a week Harriet had married him. "If it hadn't been for you, John," he said once when she called here for her carriage, "I'd never lave left the chorus, and I don't know whether I ought to give you a fiver or a thick ear." I winked at her and said, "Well, my lady, if you takes my advice . . ." '

'Trrrrrrng!' went the telephone.

The promotor of dynasties answered it.

*   *   *   *   *

The door behind the keeper's box opened, releasing that lively scent of peardrops that fills all theatres. Two plain maidens stood waiting. The stage door opened, and a meek middle-aged face with a wispy, mouse-coloured moustache appeared:

'Come along, girls,' said the face.

'All right, Dad,' said the girls.

They went.

'That's how it is now,' said the stage door-keeper. 'Mind, I'm not saying it isn't better, but—it's not so exciting!'

A young man's head appeared out of the night:

'Miss Robinson ready yet, John?'

'Not yet.'

The head shot back into the outer darkness.

'Now that's the nearest thing to a stage-door johnny we've got to-day,' explained John. 'He's the fellow Miss R.'s engaged to. He sits in the pit three nights a week—or the gallery if he's broke—and waits to take her home.'

The door leading to the cold stone steps that mount to the dressing-rooms was flung open and out came a lovely long-legged vision in an inadequate kimono. She put twopence down on the janitor's desk and, taking up the telephone, demanded Brixton.

'Is that you, Mum? What's for supper? Steak and kidney? Well, it's not very, but—never mind. I'm bringing Mr. de Courcey Potts home for supper. Don't let Dad see him if he's a bit—you know? S'long.'

The vision faded upwards in flying kimono.

*   *   *   *   *

Through the door burst a number of pretty young girls chattering of last trams and trains.

They disappeared down the empty alleyway.

Then from the dressing-rooms came a pale masculine flapper

about twenty-five. He took up the telephone and spoke
ith the voice of the spurious Etonian:

'Hallo, old dear. Courcey Potts speaking. I can't come
ong to-night; I'm going on to supper somewhere. So long,
d darling!'

'You wouldn't think he was a chorus "gent," would you?'
id the door-keeper.

*　　　*　　　*　　　*　　　*

The sound of feminine chatter rose round the stage door.

'The gallery girls,' said John.

Gallery girls. They have replaced the johnny. They
ursue their favourites with schoolgirl heroine worship.
own came the 'star.' She plunged into their adoration and
isappeared among them in the direction of a taxicab.

One by one, the lights went out.

The stage door stood with an experienced air, as if conscious
f the glamour it had cast over the Victorian Age; as if aware
hat in the stately homes of Old England . . .

'Good night, sir,' cried the stage door-keeper, his boots
inging on the empty flagstones.

Night in Hospital ❀ ❀ ❀ ❀ ❀

WHEN you pass a London hospital at night think of this. . . .

The wards are darkened. The nurse goes tip-toe over the polished floor between the two white, shrouded ranks. It is quiet. Now and again she passes a bed, congratulating life in general that the occupant is sleeping, only to find two wide-awake eyes fixed on her in the dimness: eyes that follow her hungrily, anxious that she shall not go and leave no focus for thought; eyes which plead not to be abandoned to the horror of a darkness in which the sore mind plunges like a ship at sea.

Night turns sleepless people into frightened children. The nightmare of the sleepless is more terrifying than the nightmare of the dreamer; for awake we make our own grotesque hell consciously, and there is reason in it.

Of all the agonies suffered by London in the night I would place first those waking nightmares of the hospital ward when a man or a woman, lost to companionship, waits miserably for the first streak of dawn.

'Sister, speak to me, say *something* to me. . . .'

Is there a more pathetic cry in the night of London?

There come moments in all lives when we can touch beauty and godliness—unconsciously, perhaps, and as a matter of course—and this moment in the life of a hospital nurse comes in the darkened ward when her hand, stretched out over the white sheet, has the power to lead a soul out of torture into the mercy of sleep.

*　　　*　　　*　　　*　　　*

Grim humour and heartache follow each other through the wards at night. . . .

It is that 'nerve' period between eleven p.m. and four a.m., the time when human vitality is at its lowest, when the tide of life so often ebbs. And the nurse sits there watching over every kind of possibility.

The large man with d.t.'s has just called her up and asked her to remove the snake from the bunch of bananas that grows over the foot of his bed; the delirious patient has just stripped off his clothes and expressed a desire to run down to Brighton for a bathe; and in many a bed there are sighs; and sleepers turn restlessly as though that Angel of the Small Hours is passing down the ward.

Now drama! In the next ward the nurse goes to á bed. The signs for which she has been ordered to watch are there. She must act at once! In a second she is speaking to the doctor on duty. He comes quickly to bend over the bed. Here and there heads on pillows turn to watch as the sleepless ones dimly sense this battle going on about them in the night: this splendid fight waged night after night in hospitals when skill and science mobilize against death. Yes; it is touch and go. An immediate operation is necessary. Relatives must be warned. The police in the district in which they live are instructed to awaken them.

A Harley Street surgeon picks up the receiver by his bedside, and into a brain dull with sleep is borne the knowledge that he must go out at once to fight with his mind and with his deft fingers. Being a man he may say 'Damn,' but, being a doctor, he never says 'No'; and over him, as he hurries into clothes and into the waiting motor-car, is something more splendid than you will find in London all night through. Harley Street may bleed the rich, but the specialist often gives his knowledge to the poor.

A clock strikes three. London is asleep! In the brilliant light of the operating theatre the surgeon, sharply awake in every nerve, picks up an instrument and bends over the body of a young girl whose life seems gathered in the points of his fingers. The actors in this drama, hurriedly assembled from sleep, stand shrouded in white garments. . . . Silently, efficiently, they go about the white room; and there is no sound but the sharp tinkle of metal on glass and the noise of liquids boiling. . . .

The clock strikes the half-hour.

'Yes, she will live,' they tell the relatives. 'She will live.'

*   *   *   *   *

Down in the casualty ward is comedy.

Night casualties arrive in a centrally situated London hospital in three waves: the before eleven o'clock casualties, which represent the final kicks delivered by London before bedtime on her careless, or unfortunate, children; the after eleven o'clocks, mainly due to strong drink and the staircases;

and the after three a.m. casualties from Covent Garden and night workshops, which represent the first kicks delivered by London at the opening of a new day.

I say there is comedy. There is the comedy of the policeman who thinks he has brought in an epileptic, and discovers that his patient is just an ordinary drunk; there is the tragicomedy of the old crook, who summons up more symptoms than any hypochondriac in order to occupy one of the few casualty ward beds for a night:

'Then I comes all over dizzy and I can't stand, and the pain at me 'eart is just like a knife twisted.'

How many young doctors new to night casualty work have cheated a deserving case out of a bed by giving the old Embankment hand the benefit of the doubt? And the news of a soft-hearted hospital doctor flies round homeless circles like an arrow from the bow.

*   *   *   *   *

Then . . .

'Make way there. . . . Tip up your end, Bill. . . . Mind that doorpost!'

On the stretcher is a girl, deathlike, on whose face rouge and powder are grotesque. The forms of the policemen who have brought her through the London night bulk largely in the narrow passage. The young doctor and the nurses are bending over something red wrapped round her throat.

'Yes, we got him,' say the police. 'He didn't know what he'd done. He cried like a kid. . . . Bow Street. Has he killed her?'

The door opens. A nurse comes out white-faced, wide-eyed. The door closes. The drama goes on. . . .

In an hour or two dawn comes to London in a wave of pearl-pale light.

I DINED in a West End hotel, exchanged a silk hat for a cap in the cloak-room, and in half an hour was enjoying one of London's strangest contrasts—Limehouse.

As I walked on through dark streets, it seemed impossible that the restaurant I had left, with its elegant women, its discreet string orchestra, its air of assured comfort and well-being, could exist in the same world with these gloomy avenues, like a slum in hell, through which shivering lascars shuffled, hugging the shadows, while Chinamen peered with mask faces and sharp eyes from dim doorways.

I am not attempting to add to the romance of Limehouse, because there is no romance there; only squalor, and the pathos of poor, frightened odds and ends of humanity whose lives are spent in the bowels of ships, whose pleasures consist in being stranded for three days in London, Yokohama, or Jamaica while their ships unload. It cannot matter to them where they are, for all their gambling dens are the same, and they go from ship to den and from den to ship. They are modern galley slaves, and their eyes are either sharp and shifty or sad and brown, like the eyes of monkeys.

Before the war, Limehouse had a Chinese population of twenty-five hundred. To-day its population is two hundred and fifty. An Order in Council of 1916 made it an offence to smoke opium. Since then Limehouse has gone to pieces.

*   *   *   *   *

The squalor of Limehouse is that strange squalor of the East which seems to conceal vicious splendour. There is an air of something unrevealed in those narrow streets of shuttered houses, each one of which appears to be hugging its own dreadful little secret. As you go on through them, past hunched figures who give way before you, it seems that, at any moment, you might stumble on the key to the mystery; that you might open a filthy door and find yourself in a palace sweet with joss-sticks, where queer things happen in a mist of smoke.

On the other hand, you would not be surprised to know that such things have never been, for Limehouse—that dirty tentacle which the East has flung into London—exerts that spell of provocative mystery which is the gift of the ancient East to the youthful imagination of the West.

*   *   *   *   *

A gigantic negro, who had smoked his cigar to the band, leaned in a doorway. He rolled his eyes at me and moved aside. He lifted a hand to his cigar: there were only three fingers on it. I drew aside a curtain of old sacking and found myself in a narrow hall, bare as the hall of an empty house. On the banister was a card bearing two Chinese hieroglyphs stating that the game of fan-tan was in progress.

Every other house in Pennyfields bears this sign at night. This short street which links the West India Dock Road with Poplar High Street is the Monte Carlo of East London.

In the gaming-room—a mean, shuttered apartment at the back of the house—twenty coloured men were bending over a table in front of a blazing fire, watching the board with an intensity which linked them with the International Sporting Club. The banker, a little Chinaman, whose face looked like a handbook on smallpox, had that far-off expression which you will see on the face of all croupiers, as if in close communion with the gods of chance. His eyes took in every face in a flash. He saw me and his eyes flickered in surprise; but he never ceased play.

The gamblers put shillings on the numbers one, two, three, or four. The banker took a fistful of small buttons and counted them in fours. The uneven number remaining after he had counted his last set of four determined the winners, and he paid those men who had put money on this number. Long before he had reached his count, when yet there remained under his hand a confused pile of buttons, the keen eyes of the fan-tan fans had sorted them, spotted the result, and their hands were ready for the money.

I wondered what would happen if the bank went broke; and I judged the distance to the door!

*   *   *   *   *

Half the players were Chinamen, but not the Chinamen of romance. They wore soft hats and collars and ties. Some of the teeth present suggested to me that opium is still smoked.

There were four or five stumpy brown West Indian niggers and one coal-black coon with the thickest lips I have ever seen. They looked like two grey pneumatic tyres.

He was a champion player. I saw him win sixteen shillings in ten minutes.

'You're a lucky player,' I said to him.

'I guess ah'm a good speculator, suh!' he replied with a perfect Charleston accent.

'Where do you come from?' I asked.

That was my one mistake. The gambling den's attitude towards me changed in the most swift and subtle fashion. They were willing to tolerate my presence, but not my questions. I quite agreed with them. It was an unforgivable break.

'Come over in the teak ship, suh!' he said resentfully.

Two Chinamen slipped out.

Dozens of mild, brown, monkey eyes were fixed on me. I smiled. They smiled. They nodded their heads and the smiles broadened. In their smiling politeness I read the thought: 'We do wish you would go away, because we don't know who you are and we don't particularly like you.'

I took the hint.

The big nigger at the door asked for a match to revive the last half-inch of his cigar; and he took one with his horrible hand.

*   *   *   *   *

I went into six other dens in the space of twenty yards. They were all the same: a front room in which melancholy lascars and Chinamen were painting out the hieroglyphs on pucka-pu cards; a back room in which they were crouched over the swifter results of fan-tan.

Such silence in den and in street; the uncanny silence of people who do not think as we think, whose ways are not our ways. The silence grips you, almost persuading you that behind it is something which you are always on the verge of discovering; some mystery of vice or of beauty, or of terror and cruelty; something more than those mild, monkey eyes bent on piles of shillings. . . .

The red omnibus at the corner of the West India Dock Road took me back to London for threepence; and I came home with the belief that, if all the things written about Limehouse are not true, they ought to be!

PICCADILLY is empty. That throbbing pulse of London life is stilled; a lingering, painted woman stands on the cold corner of Regent Street, and two policemen walk slowly towards Leicester Square. . . .

It is the time when the taxicab cruising softly by the kerb from the darkness of the Green Park becomes the most dramatic thing in London. The omnibuses have stopped; there are no tubes. Through the dark, unnatural streets quests the taxicab, linking lover to lover, crook to crook, criminal to criminal. It is a drama on wheels. At any moment a figure may materialize from the deadness that is London, and a lifted finger or a raised cane will call the taxicab to swifter motion, turn its bonnet towards Houndsditch or Park Lane.

The man at the wheel sits like a blind knight-errant of the streets at the service of good or evil. . . .

He does not know the whys and wherefores of his small-hour pilgrimages—the surprising places he may be asked to visit do not excite his imagination; for it is all in the night's work. He rescues a damsel in cold distress and takes her to Curzon Street; he picks up an unsteady man and takes him home to a furious wife in Hampstead; he meets a suspicious couple and deposits them in a snug little suburban villa; he carries a cheery, honest, hail-fellow-well-met character to a deserted mansion. . . .

He picks up the odds and ends of London and tidies up the empty streets; only now and then, when a King's Counsel rises in court and says: 'Gentlemen of the jury, you will hear the evidence of the taxicab driver who was chartered by the prisoner in Piccadilly at two a.m. on the night in question'—only then does the taxicab driver emerge as the genius of the London night whose hands steer tragedy through dead streets.

Blind knight of London. . . .

    *   *   *   *   *

It was warm and cosy in the cab-shelter. Now and again the moon of some passing headlight would wax and wane through the frosted glass of the windows. The place smelt of sausage and mash, gunpowder coffee, damp overcoats and sawdust. It was blue with smoke, and as fuggy as a French bedroom.

The taxicab drivers sat in their coats, their caps pushed back on their heads. They ate sausages (and anything else that was ready), and they drank coffee from thick cups.

The London taxicab man is a fine fellow. He suffered badly during the war from the reputation of a bad type of driver who had the instincts of Dick Turpin; but with demobilization that kind of man was weeded out of the business, and to-day the taxicab man is a credit to London. He is an interesting fellow to talk to, for he holds so many secrets of London. There is a fine conspiracy of silence in the profession: a driver never splits on a fare. Doctors and taxi-drivers never tell.

'Though it's surprising how some well-known people go about London not thinking that we recognize them . . . the places I've taken some people to who wouldn't like it in the papers—pass the matches, Bill!'

(You can have all the elegant conversation you like, but give me the queer, disjointed, half-expressed confabulations of policemen, taxicab men, bargees, and others who move about London at strange hours. . . .)

'Only once a fellow killed himself in my cab. . . . I picked him up outside one of the big clubs along Piccadilly late at night, and he seemed a bit queer. I thought that he'd been having a drop too much. He gave me an address in Bayswater, and when I got there he didn't get out, and I hadn't heard a sound. I thought he was asleep—I hadn't seen his face then—and when I shook him a revolver fell out of his coat.'

Nobody seemed interested. They sat round, chewing and swallowing.

'The funniest thing that ever happened to me in that line,' said a driver, 'was when I picked up a fare in the Haymarket one night, a lady she was by the look of her—but you can't tell one from the other these days, can you?—and, when we got half-way where we were going, she tapped on the window and I slowed up. "Driver," she said, "I wish you'd take care of this for me," and she handed out a little pistol no bigger than my pipe.'

He took a great gulp of coffee.

'What did I do? Well, I didn't know what to do! What would you have done? I didn't want to tell a cop because there's no knowing what mightn't have happened, so I just went on and when she got out she asked me for the pistol. "Look here, miss," I said, "you let me throw this 'ere away or you may get into a mess." She went up in a fine rage. "Don't be insolent," she said. "Do you suppose I want to shoot myself? It isn't loaded, but I've borrowed it in case burglars break in as I'm living all alone—and I don't like the feel of it!"'

*   *   *   *   *

Then they began describing in broken sentences the strange places to which they had been ordered at night—places they had not known of before, places that suggested even to their matter-of-fact minds that 'something was going on. . . .'

'That was a funny job I had the other night I was telling Jim about. A bloke in a silk hat comes running up to me in Regent Street at about one-thirty and tells me to go to an address in Hampstead as quick as lightning. When we get there we turn up a long, dark drive and come to a big house with all the windows barred—one of those barracky places that they are turning into flats. There wasn't a blinking sound. The fare hammered on the door and nothing happened. I got down and gave him a hand, but the place seemed to be empty. Then we heard a dog bark—one of those little lap-dogs by the yap of it—and then another one; a deep bark that I knew was a big dog. The fellow got very excited, and started running down the steps and looking up at the windows, but there was no light. And the dogs went on playing hell. . . .

'Then they stopped and a window in a shrubbery lit up. We ran down a side path. The window was a kitchen window; it had bars down it, and on the other side of it was a girl who had just got out of bed. She had put a pink silk thing over her nightdress, and under one arm was a Pekinese barkin' fit to bust, and standing beside her looking through the window was the biggest bloodhound you ever saw. My fare went up to the window, which she opened, and said something to her. I tried to hear what it was but couldn't, but she seemed to be giving him a proper old telling-off. . . . He got back into the

cab and I dropped him at Regent Street, where I found him!
Now what do you make of that? I call that funny, I do!'

*   *   *   *   *

Through the silent streets of London they go . . . at any
moment Comedy, Tragedy, Mystery may come to the kerb-
stone and lift a finger to them.

Cabaret ⟋ ⟋ ⟋ ⟋ ⟋ ⟋ ⟋

WE must not miss a fashionable London cabaret.

It is ten p.m., which used to be considered fairly late. The place is empty because it is too early. Three or four couples move timidly in each other's arms over the small dance floor under the critical Italian eyes of an army of relaxed waiters. Nothing happens till midnight; but Sutton, Kensington, Manchester, and Liverpool have contrived to form a thin crust of humanity at the inner circle of tables. Beyond this circle hundreds of little gold chairs wait to be sat on; hundreds of white tables stand ready for oysters and plover; hundreds of glasses are waiting for their champagne.

We admire the 'niceness' of the English girl and the pinkness of the young man who is in love with her, and we wonder how life will go with them and how dull they will be in time. A middle-aged man, who should deny his tailor nothing, glides round with a young girl who possesses the eyes and mouth of a chartered accountant. We wonder if his wife cares.

Corpulent elderly people, who fifty years ago would have been at least resigned, hug each other like bears and bob defiantly in the direction of their old age. The band whines and whinnies and underneath it is the steady rhythm of Africa. We chase away the feeling that we are watching something happening long ago in a forest clearing as we gaze round for somebody to dance with; because nothing is funnier than the act of dancing until you become involved in it. . . .

*   *   *   *   *

It is now nearly midnight.

In one hour and a half the atmosphere of the room has changed. It is now packed with people. All the little gold chairs and the little white tables are occupied by the after-theatre crowd. Social self-consciousness has been replaced by social curiosity. The slightly-warm front row turns and regards the quite-cool back rows with furtive interest. Here and there above the olives and the Martinis and the lobster mayonnaise are well-known faces; faces which most mornings gaze upon the British Isles from the newspapers.

Look at Lady X! Age is the last thing that matters about

her; she has that marvellous American poise; she makes all the 'nice' girls of twenty-five look pale. The girl in shell pink who appeared quite interesting at ten o'clock is now toneless as we watch Lady X leaning, her fine lips slightly parted, her experienced eyes narrowed as she inhales cigarette smoke nervously and quickly dabs the cigarette to death with a flicker of diamonds on white fingers. . . .

The band throbs, the audacious saxophone blows out little velvet-lined sentimentalities which are surely in league with French vineyards. The lights go down. The small floor becomes a mass of moving people. There is a clatter of plates, a popping of corks, a great hum of talk; and the waiters go swiftly over the thick carpet, bearing food which, at this time of night, would have killed the toughest Victorians stone dead.

We of this syncopated period may have poor souls, but our digestions are ahead of history.

    *   *   *   *   *

Midnight!

The band stops and the lights go down; the cabaret is due. A London night is about to close on an adequate vision of lovely women.

'It costs us fifty pounds a week in silk stockings,' whispers the producer in the darkness. 'Can't allow one ladder in this show.'.

The curtains at the end of the room part, there is an encouraging burst of melody from the band, and out glide a crowd of genuinely lovely girls dressed in musical comedy pyjamas. They look like a box of selected peaches in a Bond Street fruit shop.

'Well, I've seen a few shows on Broadway,' whispers an American, 'but this bunch beats the band!'

They sing. They dance. They go. The dim crowd of white shirt fronts and the faint blur of white arms move restlessly in applause. A delicious girl comes out and dances round the room, her short skirt brushing the inner ring of tables. Turn follows turn. It is a thumbnail revue. It is clever, it is pretty, but it would not matter much if it were neither, with a chorus like a box of picked peaches. It is strange how the idea of feminine beauty changes age by age; it would be amusing for the producer to contrast his essentially modern, shingled, lamp-post chorus with a chorus of the kind that drove our fathers to the stage door thirty years ago.

The peaches mass for the finale. They crowd towards the tables and point fingers round at the white shirt fronts and the white shoulders, singing: 'Keep it up . . . keep it up. . . .'

The revellers applaud discreetly and with great decorum; as long as it is perfectly good form to keep it up they will carry on. This is not Parisian: it is merely an acquired habit: something that grew up out of London's post-War restlessness; out of London's passionate determination to resist the temptation of going home. The lights flood the room, the dance band gathers itself and leaps into fractured excitement; the floor fills. . . .

*　　　*　　　*　　　*　　　*

Outside it is cold, an old man is selling matches, the Thames is dark under a clouded half-moon, and the night becomes a reality.

The First Edition ◦ ◦ ◦ ◦ ◦

IT is that time of night when the wives of newspaper men—
that noble army of martyrs—having placed Daddy's slippers
before a stoked-up fire, have retired to dream that they have
been sensible and had married the rich brass-founder, who
ceased work prompt at five—as all married men should do.
Poor Fleet Street wives! It must be like marriage with a
bigamist. How difficult when children ask: 'Who is that man
who comes here to sleep?'

*　　　*　　　*　　　*　　　*

In Fleet Street it is zero hour: the first edition is just going
over the top into a new day. The omnibuses have ceased
running and the arc lights, hanging overhead across the street,
illuminate an empty road bright with the lit windows of the
world's 'London Offices.' Behind these windows, men are
pumping news into Adelaide, Winnipeg, Washington, New
York, Berlin, Paris, Dublin, Liverpool, Cairo, and Hong
Kong.

Groups of cloth-capped men wait in alleyways. They
stand about furtively like hired assassins met on a dark
occasion; drawn up to the kerb-stone are motor-lorries and
vans. In a few minutes the newspapers, warm and damp and
smelling of hot ink, will come pouring from the great presses,
folded and counted. Then will begin that nightly race to the
stations where the mail trains spread the daily snow-storm
of information and opinion over the length and breadth of
the British Isles.

Fleet Street at this time is the only live street in the City
of London; yet it looks so quiet, so different from the Fleet
Street of fiction, which is always 'shaking' like a wet retriever.
No difficult operation is so quietly performed as the production
of a newspaper. You might walk down Fleet Street at midnight and never guess the madness and frenzy behind it; in
its most hectic hour it seems a street of secrets, a street
hugging to its breast the 'beats' of to-morrow.

Only when you turn down an unpromising alley do you hear
the treble scream of a metal cylinder as it meets the trimming
knife; only then do you smell the important smell of a matrix
turned silver: only then do you glimpse, in a well-lit yard,

ranks of waiting lorries and a crowd of men standing before
an ominous open door . . . beyond, in a mauve light of mercury
vapour lamps, are big machines almost ready to tell to-day
about yesterday.

    *   *   *   *   *

In offices, centrally heated by the cigars of dramatic critics,
calm young Scotsmen in horn-rimmed glasses, who since four
p.m. have heard the whole world speaking at once and have
rejected (or 'spiked') or accepted (or 'sent-up') its varied
remarks, lean back and put down their pencils. In twenty
minutes the ship will be launched, and nothing on earth can
catch the first edition—if St. Paul's fell down, if the House of
Lords caught fire, if the franc went back to par, not a line.
. . . Oh, ghastly thought. . . .

The tape machine and the post office pile up the agony;
the mound of events grows higher; the sub-editors go through
it listlessly as clerks handle cables when the liner is 'cast-off'
from the dock side. Still, you never know. . . . Hell! A young
man at the foreign desk casts a look of terror at the clock and
dives out with a telegram in his hand!

'Yes?' asks the night editor, with the coolness of a doctor
at a childbirth.

'The Emir of Karaheesh has been shot by his favourite
wife!' cries the young man.

'Really?' says the night editor. 'Rush page one.'

He touches a button. Another young man comes in.

'Oh, Robinson, when you were at the Foreign Office did you
ever meet the Emir of Karaheesh?'

'I was with the British Mission to Karaheesh, sir.'

'Then write ten lines—no more, mind—for the second
edition on the life and the habits of the Emir. I suppose you
never met his chief wife?'

'No, sir.'

'Ah, what a pity. . . . Never mind!'

    *   *   *   *   *

A fire engine runs up Holborn.

A vague street lounger, smelling of remote beer, stands
panting in the waiting-room.

'British Musheum's on fire!' he says, holding out his hand
for ten shillings. 'Heard it from a cop on Ludgate Hill.'

The night news editor looks at him sadly and goes to his telephone. He then calls a reporter.

'A boarding-house is on fire in Bloomsbury,' he says. 'You have fifteen minutes to get two lines in the Stop Press.'

(Who ever appreciates the gallant agonies of the young men—often delicately brought up and well educated—who fight by night to get two lines in the 'fudge'?)

*   *   *   *   *

Hark!

There they go! They start slowly, grindingly, accelerate in two seconds, and reach a deep, uniform roar—the machines! The first edition is flicking through their oily entrails; and the men waiting in the street outside crank up the lorries. It seems as if a sudden fresh breeze has invaded the newspaper office as the throbbing machines go pounding on; for this is the sound you never, never forget when you marry a newspaper —the voice of your first wife.

In the editorial room a group of men recalls Rembrandt's 'Lesson in Anatomy.' On the operating table lies the first edition. The editor, in the centre of eager heads, marks this and that, deletes here, amends there. A young newspaper is the only birth on which men immediately hold an inquest.

*   *   *   *   *

Then Fleet Street in the early hours, St. Paul's riding high above the City, and little lost winds pulling at street corners. . . .

Men go home through the Street, which Mr. James Bone has so rightly called the 'village street'—the street of the village pump—and, as they go home, some, in this tired, sentimental hour, think of the dreams lost there; and the dreams that almost came true.

Here it is that Dick Whittington would have come to-day to snatch the bright promise of glory, that seems to hang— quite invisibly—somewhere between the 'Griffin' and Ludgate Hill. . . .

A lorry changes gear and dashes on to Euston like a dispatch rider. Beneath the ground the great presses throb and pound . . the voice of Fleet Street, the voice of Power, the astonishing thunder of the Press.

A Lost Day   ◦   ◦   ◦   ◦   ◦   ◦

IF you roam Piccadilly at night looking lonely and innocent, you will meet various well-worn characters; young men who overdo a careful Oxford accent, and eventually suggest a game of cards; three men who are dying to 'let you in' on a good thing because they took a fancy to you right off ('only it needs capital, old boy'); twinkling, middle-aged men with an over-stressed man-about-town air who hint that when you 'know the ropes'—and they would not mind showing them to you this very night, being at a loose end for once—'when you know the ropes, old fellow, Paris isn't in it!'

Unclean people! They make you want a bath!

There is the little vampire with the hard mouth, and the big eyes and the cheap scent, who slips an arm through yours and, finding you soft-hearted, tells you the story of a country vicarage—one of Piccadilly's oldest stories—and, if you can forget Charles Garvice and believe that you are hearing these details for the first time, she may swagger off with the Treasury note on which her poor heart is set.

There are, however, other chance acquaintances of a London night who have no mean motives. They just want to talk; and some day I would like to make a book of all the unsolicited stories I have heard from strangers in Piccadilly.

*   *   *   *   *

The young man wore the hat of a genius—an old felt horror, with a stained band and a limp crown, the battered survivor of a thousand riots and revels.

It was this hat that interested me as I sat opposite the young man in a Piccadilly café. It interested me because it could not have looked more out of place with the rest of him had it been a Life Guard's helmet. It was not the kind of hat this type of young man wears—it was the hat that goes with soiled shirt cuffs and a soul. This young man was, with the exception of his alien hat, a prosperous, rather smug, business man from, I judged, Bradford.

He was drinking beer, and, when he lifted the glass, his hand trembled. Every now and then he looked at me, wishing to speak, but he thought better of it, and looked away quickly like a dog that has not made up his mind to wag his tail. He had a simple face, and he looked round the smoky café, its drinking, laughing crowd, with rather wide, surprised eyes. Two girls sitting at the next table had summed him up as 'soft' and were giggling. Then he spoke to me.

Yes, it was getting colder. Probably freezing. Colder in London than in the north. . . .

His accent was faintly provincial. He leaned forward:

'Would you, sir, have a drink with me?'

I said I would. We went on talking.

* * * * *

The young man put down his glass.

'See how my hand trembles,' he said.

'I know,' I replied. 'Your nerves are bad.'

'As a matter of fact,' he said, in a low, matter-of-fact voice, 'I have been dead for twenty-four hours. I am terribly worried about it.'

I thought at first that he was probably mad; but his eyes reassured me.

'To-day's Wednesday,' he said. 'The last thing I can remember is Monday. I can just remember going to bed on Monday night, and I woke up this morning in my hotel in Paddington, and, when I looked at the newspaper, I saw it was Wednesday. What did I do yesterday? I think I may have been out and about, but—I don't remember a blessed thing! I was so dashed drunk on Monday night that my brain was a blank for a whole day.'

The mild young man laughed in a half-ashamed way.

'On Monday,' he went on, 'I came to London from —— to attend a wedding. I didn't know anybody there save the bride and bridegroom, and afterwards I went round London drinking. I put down an awful lot, and mixed them too. I then remember getting back to my hotel. That was Monday night. I awakened this morning feeling a bit dizzy; and it's Wednesday, isn't it? What I want to know is: where was I yesterday?'

'Perhaps you were in a kind of a trance,' I suggested.

'I thought of that. But when the chambermaid brought me tea this morning she said nothing. The hotel people said nothing. If I had been in a trance yesterday the hotel would have brought a doctor to me.'

'Why don't you ask them what happened?'

'I don't like to. I'm ashamed; and, besides, look at this!' He picked up the battered felt hat.

'Well, what about it?'

'It isn't mine. I don't know whose it is. I found it on the bed-post this morning! Now it seems to me that, although my brain was dead all yesterday, I must have got up as usual, dressed, shaved, and gone out. Where? Goodness only knows! I have been wandering all over London to-day, trying to think things out, hoping that my memory would come back; for it's awful not to know. And this hat! It's a terrible hat, isn't it? I've been so worried that I've not bought a new one! I feel somehow that if I stick to the thing I may remember something of yesterday.'

'Has anything like this happened to you before?'

'Only in France, when I was knocked out.'

He looked at his watch.

'I've got to get over to Paddington,' he said. 'I'm going home. If ever you are in —— do look me up.'

He gave me a business card. He got up, smiled in a puzzled way, and went out into Piccadilly Circus.

*   *   *   *   *

I thought how unpleasant it must be to know that you were about London for a whole day with a dead brain covered by an ominous hat.

'Sir Percivale'

'SIR PERCIVALE' comes thundering up through Kent, the night Continental boat train behind him, his lean, lithe one hundred and twenty-nine tons flung out over the track like a running leopard; and he sings as he runs:

I'm bringing you home,
To England, to England,
I'm bringing you home,
To London, to London . . .
Bringing you home, bringing you home, bringing you home. . . .

The line of his lit Pullman cars is like a string of pearls flashed through the hop-fields, whipped through the night against the Pilgrims' Way; and he comes so regularly, and goes so swiftly, that only the newest born rabbits at the edge of woods dream of showing their little tails at him. He is not as heavy as the 'Caerphilly Castle,' or as famous as the 'Flying Scotsman,' but, to me, he is a poem in steel, for, in the roar of his wheels, if you know him well, is the most lovely song in all the world: a song of olive trees and roads in Spain, the sun on ripe oranges, the camels humping in from deserts with the date harvest, snow on Lebanon, dawn on Carmel, the moon caught up in the palm trees on the beach at Haifa, and the little tunes played on flutes by boys beside the Nile. . . .

* * * * *

He stands in Victoria covered with the sweat of his run, his six-foot-seven driving wheels moist with green oil, his great connecting and side rods silver with effort, his pistons bright, the flanges of his bogie wheels white as new shillings. . . .

(Women go to the Customs and declare the Paris *lingerie* in registered trunks, the crowds kiss and go, the last taxi disappears. . . .)

A squat little shunter departs with the Pullman cars; and 'Sir Percivale,' with a mighty snort and a puff of sudden steam, backs his long leanness out of Victoria into that place where all engines go at night to be fussed and washed and patted and bathed and made ready for new miles.

* * * * *

'Hi, Bill, here's the Continental!'

In the smoky darkness of the vast Locomotive Beauty Parlour—one of the largest in the country—a grimy mechanic runs to the huge turn-table and places it in position as 'Sir Percivale' swings in over the points with a low escape of steam, that sounds like the whinny of a horse in sight of oats. He sinks on the turn-table with a noise like a house falling, and the great circle revolves with him as sweetly as a roulette wheel, leading him to a track that will take him to the repair sheds.

Far off the repair sheds expose roof lights in a steam of damped furnaces. There is a sound of released pressure and hammers.

'Sir Percivale' puffs slowly on, the men who have brought up the boat train lean out of the high cab. Cleaners run up.

'The old gal's running a treat . . . puffing her head off!'

(I shudder to hear 'Sir Percivale' called 'old gal'!)

The fireman and the driver climb down, oil cans and leather bags in their hands. The driver walks to the great wheels and opens a little oil box and snaps the lid again. I watch his competent hand on the smooth flank of his giant.

'She's a fair treat!' he says to the old cleaner; 'you should have heard her humming up to Shepherd's Well. . . .'

They rake out the furnaces, they board the engine, they wash, they wipe and polish, as fussy as a bunch of ladies' maids.

On parallel tracks are other locomotives: 'King Arthurs,' heavy goods, 'mixed traffic,' humble suburbans, and little tanks. They take their places in the sheds in the order of their going forth again. All night long they arrive or leave; all night long the giant turn-table revolves in the darkness, bringing them home or sending them out on the road—to the south, to the west. . . .

*   *   *   *   *

'Here's the nine forty-five from Exeter!'

A shadow like a moving cathedral looms into the shed, bearing a yellow lamp.

'Make way there; tell Clapham I'm coming!' says a sharp escape of steam, and there is a grinding of wheels and a few heavy puffs.

'There goes the engine of the fish train. Picks up the Grimsby train at Clapham and takes her on in the night!'

Among the sleeping, sleek giants is, here and there, a roar of re-fired furnaces, in many a cab the stokers work in a red glow like shovelling devils, one eye on the coal stack and the other on the rising gauges. . . .

'Good-bye, you lazy slackers!' cries the engine of the Southampton night mail. 'I'm off with the King's mails! If you've any news for the next Cunarder, look sharp about it!'

'Pretentious ass,' growls 'Sir Percivale,' with his last inch of steam. 'I take the mails to France, and if we're late we're "for it". . . . Southampton? Where's that? All down hill from Litchfield! How would he like to catch the boat over a switchback of one in a hundred . . . up and down to Dover? . . .'

'And I also take the newspapers . . .' toots the night mail in farewell.

'Pah!' growls the big Continental, 'you may take the divorces, but I take the divorcees!'

'I don't think you're quate nace!' says the Streatham local, with a stiff look about her mid-Victorian smoke-stack.

'Hear, hear!' whispers the Orpington tank. 'This boat traffic makes people positively . . . well, positively!'

'Sir Percivale' cannot retort; for his last steam has gone.

*   *   *   *   *

'No two engines alike . . . not two, sir, and I've been driving these last twenty years. Like women they are! They want fussing. You may make 'em in the same shed to the same design, but they come out different. Now 4040 is a proper old devil. I used to take her to Bournemouth every night, and this one, made the same year, runs like a sewing-machine, she does . . . like cream she is, soft and smooth. . . . Right away, Alf!'

With a prolonged hiss and a stealthy movement of connecting rods, the great 'mixed traffic' backs out over the points, turns the table, and, with the green signals calling in the London night, puffs slowly out to take a train to Devon.

THE Chinaman was frightened.

His face registered no emotion, but his hands trembled.

'No smokee opium, John?' asked the plain-clothes inspector. 'No opium upstairs, eh?'

The little eyes gazed from the blank yellow face. No, he said, in high-pitched protest, he had never smokee since policeman say it was no good—oh, one, two, tlee years long ago—and, oh, yes, he had been to the police-court once for having a pipe and having friends who liked to smoke it; but not now; oh, everything allee-lighty now. Honest. John no liar. . . .

The inspector flashed his torch on a dark, forbidding stair-case, and expressed a firm determination to invade the upper regions. John was most upset. He assured us that nothing in the world could be more allee-lighty than his upstairs; but the inspector was not impressed.

First he took a glance round the basement of the queer, rambling, low-class café; room after room full of strange foreign men who backed away from us like a herd of startled deer. Some were clever at fading through curtains of sacking. One moment they were there, the next they had gone: a curious slinky business! There was an atmosphere of something suddenly stopped. There were swift chinkings as if piles of silver had been swiftly pocketed. It was pretty obvious that in this foul unfurnished den John made a good living from the rabble of foreign men who come to London in ships.

'Now upstairs with you, John!' said the inspector.

For one second John looked as though he would give any-thing for a long knife to twist in us; and the next he was all whispering humbleness before this rude invasion, back bent, hands spread, and over him the humility of an exile 'up against' the steel wall of an alien law.

'Allee-lighty,' he sighed, with resignation; 'allee-lighty!'; and it seemed to me, the way he said it, that he was quoting Confucius.

* * * * *

I have inferred once, and I repeat, that Limehouse is the most overrated excitement in London, but when on the spot

ou can forgive most of the luscious things written about it,
or it has atmosphere; it is a dramatic theme that just howls
or a plot: a stage that cries for a drama. . . .

There was no light on the stairs. We went up by the light
f the inspector's electric torch, hanging on a shaking banister,
tumbling up the worn treads. Cobwebs and dust gave the
place a mothlike mustiness. Like everything else in Limehouse, it was dreary, sordid, dirty, squalid. The soft moon of
he police torch stimulated the imagination; one felt oneself
on the track of Fu-Manchu; but by daylight how entirely
nauseating it must be!

We stepped out on a dim landing with rooms leading from
t. We opened a door. The inspector flashed his light over
a chamber that looked ten thousand years older than the
omb of Tutankhamen, for dust had been falling for years
over boxes, over a broken chair, over a collapsed table. The
little window was boarded up with wood.

'You see?' said the inspector. 'You see?'

The yellow light wavered over the tell-tale window.

The next room was the same, and the next: dark, musty
horrors. In one was a dirty old iron bedstead without a
mattress. No one had been to Paradise on it with a pipe for
a long time; for each wire was thick with dust like a fall of
soft brown snow.

'Allee-lighty,' whispered the voice. 'Allee-lighty, sir?'

'It is all right,' whispered the inspector, 'for you can smell
the stuff ten miles off.'

I was bored, and I felt sorry for the deprecating voice that
followed us whispering in the darkness.

'Hallo, John,' said the inspector. 'This room's locked!
Open it!'

John looked as though he might refuse.

'Open it!' ordered the inspector, raising his voice.

'That is my room!' whimpered John.

'Open it!' repeated the inspector, with just a hint of hand-
cuffs in his manner.

John drew a key from his pocket and fitted it into the
padlock.

*   *   *   *   *

The room was lit by electric light under a pink shade. A
fire blazed on the hearth; an electric radiator assisted in the

uncomfortable warmth. It was a bed-sitting room, intimate, cosy, clean, comfortable, and refined. Indifferent pictures in heavily gilt frames covered the walls, a good carpet covered the floor. On a table, in the centre of the room, was a large bunch of grapes on a plate. A crowded sideboard bore a silver tray piled with biscuits and dates. Beside the tray were wine glasses and a bottle of Sauterne.

I took it in slowly, hit in the eyes by the crazy contrast to the decayed morgue of a house. The rest of the house was dead; this room was brilliantly alive.

I looked at John as he stood resentfully with his hand on the light switch, and knew that this room was his whole life. To make it, he screwed money out of his compatriots and the sweepings of the Seven Seas in the dirty dens downstairs. So obviously was it his whole life that I felt I had no right to invade it, to bludgeon my way into a man's inmost secret. What right had we there, gazing as if at an animal's cage? I looked at John, noticed little refinements in the room, and felt that his eyes were as old as the world.

'Very nice, John,' said the inspector.

John made no reply.

Something moved. From beneath the bed walked a Pomeranian dog. He stretched himself and yawned at us and sat down before the fire. Then light broke over me, and I began to notice all over the room evidence of a woman: a neat pile of laundry at the foot of the bed, with three or four pairs of silk stockings on top, beside the hearth a pair of shoes, in the centre of the crowded mantelshelf the picture of a young English girl smiling. I looked again at the incalculable little wrinkled creature with his lean, monkey-like hand on the light switch and shuddered.

'Right. Lock up!' said the inspector.

The light flashed out, and only the firelight remained to light the secret, playing grotesquely with the shadows in the live room of the dead house.

,   *   *   *   *   *

'All you can say,' said the inspector as we went through the dark streets, 'is that they treat that kind of girl better than many a white man would. They do, generally speaking, make good husbands. I believe it's going to rain. . . .'

IT is eight p.m.

The cinema at the corner has digested its uncritical queues. The billiard saloon is packed. Young men and girls enter the dance hall. Crowds gather for the second house of the music-hall. The lit streets are full of a vague excitement, an alluring restlessness, and, through them, pass young people with books beneath their arms. They are ordinary young people. They look exactly like those who have gone to the cinema and the dance; but, if you could see inside their heads, you would, perhaps, observe a different point of view.

They arrive at a tall, ugly building situated in the centre of all the excitement. It lifts uncurtained windows into the darkness. They cross an asphalt playground and enter a place which, by day, is a London County Council school and, by night, a kind of monastery in which gather those pilgrims who have set their feet along the stern roadway of ambition. Twenty years ago it would, I suppose, have been called a night school, but to-day they call it an evening institute. It is one of about three hundred established in every part of London by the London County Council.

It is curious that London does not know the most interesting things about itself. It is possibly a penalty it pays for its size. I wonder how many young people who grouse about the lack of opportunity in their lives know that, for a fee varying from 3s. to 15s., they can receive a year's instruction in almost any subject from book-keeping to foundry work, by way of Greek literature and dressmaking. Knowledge and the power to rise in life have never in the history of the world been offered to young men and women on such easy terms.

There is nowadays no excuse for any young Londoner to bewail opportunity; the opportunity is there for him to seize —just opposite the dance hall and the picture theatre!

*   *   *   *   *

You enter a room in which young men in the twenties are sitting at school desks, notebooks before them. The walls of the schoolroom are decorated with the coloured carrots executed during the day by a younger generation. A barrister stands before a blackboard lecturing on commercial law. The students work in the City during the day, and come night after night to study the subject that will give them a 'pull' over the other fellow when the time comes.

In the next room tiers of young men and girls pore over Spanish primers. A pretty little girl holds her shingled head in her hands and reads in Spanish. The master pulls her up from time to time. It is all very much in earnest: a school that means to learn at all costs. A girl comes in and says she's sorry she's late. She sits in the front row, takes out her books and pulls off her gloves. On her finger is a new wedding ring. You look at her and admire her, knowing how difficult it is for a young wife in a small home to do much more than run round the gas stove and wonder if the steak and kidney pie is burned again. . . .

The evening institutes contain hundreds of independent young wives who work in the City and pay fifty-fifty towards the home, and carry on with their studies at the institute, or else continue them as a hobby. Often, of course, a perambulator runs right across their talent, and—the Temple of Knowledge loses a priestess.

*   *   *   *   *

In the next classroom . . .

> *At dawn thy voice is loud—a merry voice*
> *When other sounds are few and faint. Before*
> *The muffled thunders of the Underground*
> *Begin to shake the houses, and the noise*
> *Of eastward traffic fills the thoroughfares,*
> *Thy voice then welcomes day.*

The girl stands in the centre of the floor and recites W. H. Hudson's poem to a London sparrow. Round her in a half-circle sits the class. She ends. The elocution teacher calls for criticism. The class pitches into the reciter. She did not stress this word or that, she did not give full value to that phrase or this. The teacher then pours balm on the hurt mind, and another student rises and recites, and runs the gauntlet of discussion.

These young people are not going on the stage. They are

learning assurance and the ability to express their ideas in public. Some of them will, no doubt (via Shakespeare and Milton) lead directors' meetings to victory in the splendid future.

'You cannot wonder that I am an optimist,' says the head master, 'for more young men and women are working to advance themselves every year; in spite of the fact that every year outside attractions increase. It takes courage, after a hard day's work, to come here night after night.'

'Self-discipline too.'

'Exactly. And the kind of courage that develops character.'

You pass room after room, each with its small, intent class.

'It is wonderful to think that every night this goes on all over London,' says the master, 'not only in commercial institutes like this, but in technical ones, in laboratories and workshops, art schools, and so forth. Forty years ago the night schools taught under ten thousand pupils; to-day the evening institutes of the London County Council are attended by one hundred and twenty thousand.'

* * * * *

You go out into the busy streets where the omnibuses mass at the junction, where the crowds, free for a few hours from duty, move in search of amusement and excitement. You remember the quiet class-rooms, the young heads bent over books. You feel that perhaps London's proudest boast should be that, when night falls, she opens the road of Ambition to all those of her children with the grit and the nerve to take it.

'MY dear!' he says.

'My dear!' she says.

Wonderful the way lovers meet in London every night as if the world had been born again that minute. You can see them 'under the clock' at Charing Cross, at the Piccadilly Tube—the meeting place of love and £ove—and you wonder, generally speaking, what she can see in him, how she can tolerate the way his tie rides up over his winged collar, and the cow-like glassiness of his eyes when he comes towards her in the crowd; such an ordinary little fellow.

'Where shall we go?' says Romeo.

'Mother says I must be in at ten,' says Juliet.

'Right-o. Let's go to Soho. I know a little foreign place where . . .'

It is Friday. In Romeo's pocket reposes the weekly packet containing four pounds in Treasury notes. Going to Soho will cut an awful hole in one pound, which, in terms of knightly hardship, represents, according to the Arthurian reckoning, the meeting of a knight with one dragon and two giants in an enchanted grove.

They link arms and cross Piccadilly, where the red and the green and the gold lights wink; and they go down Shaftesbury Avenue, their souls suffused with the warm desire to link their fate with a furniture instalment organization.

Marriage seems to them the one reality. Everything else is just playing at living. Romeo aches to escape from his lodgings; Juliet longs to escape from her home; and, to both of them, the act of putting a Yale lock into the door of a red brick box represents a shattering victory against the mighty forces that keep people apart. Romeo has dreamed of going home and finding her always anxious to greet him, her soul on her lips; and Juliet has dreamed the slightly more practical dreams of women: how far ten pounds in the post office will go towards a white satin dress, new shoes and stockings, and things like that. It would be nice to be alone in her own home . . . no eternal nagging . . . no 'Now mind you're in at ten sharp, my girl' . . . no sisterly backbitings and cattiness! Why can't people be happy together and kind to each other? Marriage is the way out. . . .

(Ignorance and lack of imagination have been responsible for more fearlessness in the face of danger than all the calculated bravery in the world!)

*   *   *   *   *

'Drink? What shall we drink?'

'A small lemon!' says Juliet.

'Come on. Let's have some wine!' whispers Romeo. One line in that wine list sticks in his imagination: 'Marsala, 3s.'

'Let's have a bottle of that!' he says, putting his finger on it.

The waiter droops off in a pale contempt.

They drink the golden error in large draughts, like lemonade, and discover each other's feet beneath the table. It is that time when people like Romeo and people like Shakespeare feel that words are just bundles of old sticks snapping. He leans over the chicken *en casserole*:

'I love you!' he whispers huskily.

'Sssh!' she replies. 'Someone'll hear you.'

She receives an impassioned hack on the ankle.

*   *   *   *   *

'Dangerous the ways boys and girls fall in love and rush into marriage, isn't it?' says a reflective person at a near table. 'Look at those two. What is he, do you suppose?'

'Rather sweet, don't you think?' says the woman quite tonelessly.

'In a way—yes. They ask so little of life, knowing so little of it, therefore they may get more out of it than most of us. I believe they are the happy people. He will be quite happy all his life in a rut . . . can't you see him wheeling a perambulator on Sundays and clipping the front hedge . . . and she'll be happy round a gas cooker, rather damp about the forehead, but—frightfully happy!'

'Awful, isn't it?'

'I wonder. Nothing piles up more misery than an imagination!'

*   *   *   *   *

Romeo pays his bill, and, through a rich mist of marsala, comes the fact that he has paid away thirteen and sixpence.

His mind automatically visualizes next Thursday as a cigar-etteless day. (He owes his landlady fifty shillings!)

Through the star-spangled London night they go, hand in hand, on top of an omnibus. It begins to rain; but that is all the more wonderful because they can pull up the oil-sheets and cuddle closer.

'When we're married,' he says reflectively, 'I shouldn't be sur-prised if I got a job with Wilkin's for four pounds ten shillings.'

The woman answers him.

'You stay where it's safe, dear.'

He does not recognize the ancient voice, being intoxicated with complicated emotions:

'D'ju remember when I spoke to you at the corner by the Plough?'

'Cheeky! I noticed your eyes then! I wouldn't have taken any notice if I hadn't—straight! Oh lor, here we are! Come in for a second and speak to Mother—please do!'

They pause half-way down the dark road and say good night. All their sacred moments are spent in streets, on the tops of omnibuses, in public parks. . . .

'You do, don't you?'

'Course I do, silly. . . . Come on. It's after ten.'

    *   *   *   *   *

Juliet's family is gathered in the kitchen: Dad in shirt sleeves and carpet slippers reading a newspaper, Mother knitting a vague object, Phyllis manicuring her nails, the bottles and pastes spread out on the table round a half-full bottle of invalid stout. In the middle of this Juliet is like a strayed fairy.

'So you've come at last, miss,' says Mum. 'Good evening, Alf. Where've you two been? Soho? Hear that, Dad? Soho! Wasting their money. I should think you want some-thing to do. Take a look at yourself in the glass. I wouldn't like to come home looking as if I'd been pulled through a hedge backwards.'

Mother gazes acidly at Romeo, who, acutely indignant at the injustice of her insinuation, smiles feebly and makes some remark about the high state of the wind.

'You're a nice pair, I must say!' remarks Phyllis maliciously, polishing her nails with a gory-looking piece of white plush.

'Shut up, sis!' says Juliet, and the air is brittle with female repression; invisible swords seem to be swinging. Romeo twists his hat in his hands and says that he must be going. Insincere smiles follow him to the door.

'Just like her to take up with a soft ass like that!' He knows what they will say. . . .

'Oh, I love you, I love you!' cries Juliet behind the bead curtain in the hall; and he feels her mouth trembling. She buries her head in his shoulder and clings; then, suddenly, she pushes him away as a bar of light falls and a voice cries:

'Now, you love birds!'

*   *   *   *   *

He goes through the London night unable to analyse the situation, unable to see ahead, unable to detach himself and look down on himself and his motives and actions, conscious only that he loves her and that the night is more gracious because she lives, and that the stars above the chimney pots are not more lovely than her eyes above a golden glass. . . . Thirteen and sixpence! That must stop, that wicked waste of money! Life is serious . . . now!

The moon above London hides her face, having heard all this over and over again.

Omnibuses in Bed · · · · ·

THE last omnibus goes down the road with its weary cargo.

'All change!' cries the conductor at the end of the journey.

If you did not obey him, or, rather, if you were able to remain in your seat, you would be carried at high speed into one of the busiest scenes in the London night. You would arrive at one of the many L.G.O.C. depots[1] which, between them, put four thousand red omnibuses to bed each night and make them fit to rise early in the morning to take London to work.

Holloway Garage, so they tell me, is the largest garage in the world. The distance covered each day by its scarlet inhabitants is twenty-five thousand miles, or, as they point out at Holloway, 'once round the world.' Holloway has two peculiarities: a new day does not begin at midnight—as everywhere else in London—it begins somewhere round about five-thirty a.m., when the first omnibus trundles out into the dawn. Monday is never Monday until this happens. The second peculiarity is that Holloway does not know the meaning of the word 'omnibus'; they call them 'cars.'

*　　　*　　　*　　　*　　　*

The clock strikes twelve! The entrance to Holloway Garage is congested by 'cars' standing two by two. Their engines run, the lights shine over empty seats, the conductors look along the queue with a Tottenham Court Road and Oxford Street expression, anxious to hand in London's pennies and the unused tickets, the drivers lean over the steering wheels, tired after the race home. They come from every part of London. You look at their indication boards and see that they have been gathered from Crouch Hill and Norwood, Highgate and Crystal Palace, Shepherd's Bush and Camden Town.

The engines throb. Slowly the queue advances inch by inch into the night nursery of the red fleet.

*　　　*　　　*　　　*　　　*

Hark! Far down the road—that melancholy, empty Holloway Road—sounds an approaching omnibus. You do

[1] The London General Omnibus Company was incorporated in the London Passenger Transport Board on July 1st, 1933.

not notice it because two hundred engines are running; but the natives do! They hear that lone 'car' coming along, and they go out into the road to look for it, because there is something in the sound of it that tells them it is an invalid.

It limps up and joins the crew.

'What's wrong, mate?'

'Only the blinkin' engine blinkin' well conked on the hill and . . .'

Omnibus drivers do not love their machines, as ships' engineers and locomotive drivers love theirs, possibly because an omnibus driver's life is a daily philander with three or four different 'cars,' and abiding love, as everyone knows, has its roots in steady companionship.

The driver dismounts, casts a look of hate at the bonnet, and goes on to relieve his feelings on an official 'running report.' Mechanics come up and investigate the case. A marvellous man called a 'shunter'—who is a kind of super London omnibus driver—takes charge. (The difference between a 'shunter' and a driver is merely that whereas a driver can drive his 'car' with the space of tissue paper between his wheels and the wheels of the next 'car,' the 'shunter' can take an omnibus backwards through a drapery store without upsetting a pin.)

The invalid is taken to hospital. No crime is greater for a No. 3 than a show of temperament on the Crystal Palace Hill. That is a contemptible 'let down.' So the Bad Boy of Holloway stands in disgrace with the mechanics groping at his entrails, his wheels covered with bits of Brixton, his indication boards dirty, his floor thick with tickets; and, when they find a bag containing half a pound of pork pie on the top deck, all the Golders Green omnibuses veil their windows and look down their radiators in horror.

*   *   *   *   *

As the queue advances into the juvenile Olympia, men attack them outside and inside. The outside men fill up the oil and the petrol tanks, the inside men sweep out thousands of tickets. Then comes the murder gang.

They advance wearing gas masks. They carry syringes filled with perchloride of mercury. If any measly or mumpish child has travelled during the day this is the time the germs die. The 'car' then moves to a watery siding, on either side of which is a shower bath. Jets of water spray over the chassis, the windows, the top deck and the wheels. Cleaners polish the indication boards, the 'shunter' takes charge and insinuates the 'car' into the one, and only, position in the scarlet jig-saw from which it can make a graceful exit in its due order at five-thirty a.m.

* * * * *

It is interesting to 'board' an omnibus in the great nursery where they sleep and, sitting on the front seat, to take a look round at the red fleet at rest.

They stand, hundreds of them, berthed in the darkness. I do not know any assembly as typical of London except, possibly, a parade at Scotland Yard or a battalion of the Guards. The red omnibus is as characteristic of London as the blue policeman. Paris is a city of lunatic taxicabs and clumsy, single-deck Molochs like pirate sloops; Berlin used to be the city of the broken-down droshky; and other capitals have each their own mode of movement, but none, I think, is quite so spectacular as our four thousand scarlet two-deckers. They, with pillar boxes and the Household Troops, provide that subtle touch of colour which we love; that line of scarlet against the silver-greyness of our Portland Stone

It would be an artistic calamity if the L.G.O.C. painted its 'cars' black: it would change the look of London. . . .

And, sitting on top of a sleeping London omnibus at two a.m., is the ideal time to write. I will have one some day in a garden. All our best thoughts arrive on the tops of omnibuses. Sometimes one's whole life seems to have been spent on them in the Strand! Lacking these red monsters, what a wilderness London would be: north would not know south; Peckham Rye would be sundered from Camden Town, and Norwood would be to Colney Hatch as the Cape is to Cairo. The taxicab is an incident in our lives; the omnibus an institution.

In spite of it, the omnibus is not a lovable thing. Drivers never call it 'Kate' in secret or stay overtime to play about with the magneto. It has become the modern London gondola without enriching London with any romance. It is true that there is an awful mystery about those long-distance omnibuses, which go through the streets bearing the names of foreign places unknown to man, awakening the ambition to travel, and planting fear in the hearts of the timid. Perhaps those lost Londoners who disappear from home might be discovered living quietly at Ball's Pond or under the promised oak at Honor. . . .

'Are you all right up there, sir?'

'Yes. I'm having a wonderful time!'

'Because we want to shunt her!'

'I don't mind.'

Who knows all the marvels of London until he has been 'shunted' at two a.m. in the largest garage in the world, whose wheels never leave London, yet go right round the earth once a day?

'SIR IVAN, I think you will agree that Munchausen's theory on the pancreatic juices is—shall we say?—a trifle out-dated!'

Lady Anaemia Gasp crumbles bread with thin fingers, and looks up with those bird-like eyes, which have sought health in Bath, Aix-les-Bains, Cannes, Vichy, Contrexeville, Harrogate, Wiesbaden, Marienbad, and that awful place in Italy where they put you in a nightshirt and take you into the bowels of a steamy earth.

The pink candle-light glows over shirt fronts, which conceal a little mild indigestion, over faces on which self-pity and fear have etched fine and expensive lines. The silver shines into polished mahogany, as if in still water. There sits Mr. Adolphus Quinsey, a famous neurasthenic who fears death every night (he owns much slum property), Mr. Green (liver), another distinguished invalid, the Dowager Countess of X (old age) and Jane Lady Boreington, who possesses more harmless symptoms of approaching death than any other woman on earth. What a curse money is.

An interesting party.

*   *   *   *   *

The great Sir Ivan, one of the world's foremost medicine men, sits at the head of his table and thinks, as he dips the tips of his fine fingers into the finger bowl—who knows? What a fortunate thing that people's insides have not kept up with evolution? Lady Boreington's liver, for instance, has been worth a thousand a year for six years, and Mr. Green's kidneys are positive gold mines. They never die, these people who believe themselves marked down by the archangel; if they did, of course, nothing on earth could stop them. They linger richly on; which is all to the good. . . .

Sir Ivan was always too handsome to become an ordinary G.P. Not for him the rush to help humanity into the world at the behest of frenzied fathers; not for him the small twoseater and the complicated secrets of a garden suburb. No; early in life he developed the ability to pat a neurasthenic palm in that manner which, when accompanied by a deep, soothing and intensely masculine voice saying: 'Dear lady,

don't worry, we will soon put you right,' makes rich women
sing a man's praises from Dan to Beersheba and even farther
—New York, for instance.

(Few things are more important in the psychology of
success than the praise of the right kind of women at the right
kind of dinner-party.)

If you went to Florida or to Florence you would find some
women ready to say with a gasp of ecstasy:

'Sir Ivan! That man is a marvel.'

And the funny thing is that they may be right.

    *   *   *   *   *

As you sit and watch him, you wonder how much of the
charlatan and how much of the great man is behind that
commanding, smooth, clean-shaven, noble exterior. Great
men are rarely handsome. Providence rarely hands out
brains with beauty; and then there is usually something fishy
about it. So you sit fascinated by Sir Ivan, watching him, as
he methodically washes his grapes in a silver bowl, feeling
that you are looking at a physician on a stage. He looks too
good to be true. If you met him in an omnibus—which is
not likely—you would at once say: 'That man is a great
doctor.'

Personality is the most marvellous thing in human affairs.
While Harley Street wonders, generally speaking, how to pay
the rent and is too superior to join heartily in an epidemic,
Sir Ivan gathers round him his faithful adherents, linked
by that encouraging eye of his, that beautiful voice, those
mesmeric hands. You reflect that it is unnecessary for him to
know anything about medicine; that such knowledge is almost
a sad reflection on a man who is otherwise such a perfect
gentleman.

'Oh, of course, Sir *Ivan* . . .' say his colleagues in the profession, with a wan little smile and the accent on the Ivan.
'Oh, of course, Sir *Ivan.* . . .'

They infer that the man is a witch doctor, but that attitude,
which seems to come under the head of medical etiquette, is
to be expected. Success always breeds spite. However, they all
call him in when heaven is at the other end of the stethoscope.

    *   *   *   *   *

Into this shaded dinner-party comes a young girl.

She has a notebook in her hand. All the guests look up and smile; for she makes their appointments for them. But she sees no one. She is agitated.

'His Royal Highness,' they hear her whisper.

Sir Ivan rises. He apologizes. He is very sorry, but duty calls him. Outside sounds the insistent call of a telephone. You look at him and feel sure that he is a real doctor. Some power has come to him. He looms above the lit tables, exuding confidence in the highest degree. You feel that if you were dying and he came into the room it would be like having a lifebelt thrown at you.

He smiles, he thinks he may be back soon, he hopes his guests will play bridge upstairs, he bows, he goes; and, with him, goes the life of the party. Unless someone makes a move soon, the conversation will turn to symptoms.

*   *   *   *   *

'His Royal Highness passed a good night, and there is no immediate danger.

'(Signed) SIR IVAN SMOOTH'

His disciples read the bulletin in the morning. Of course, there is no danger. Sir Ivan! That marvel. . . .

The 'Spring Onion'   ∘   ∘   ∘   ∘   ∘

'LET'S go on to the "Tadpole" or the "Spring Onion" . . .'

Every night in London there are people who 'go on.' They 'go on' because, like gamblers who cannot stop playing, they are wound up. They want that 'something more' out of an evening which is not there. Experience tells them that all they will get out of 'going on' is the feeling that they are wearing someone else's head the next morning, but— never mind—French sunshine bottled in 1911 is shining over their illuminated souls; and the 'Spring Onion' may be 'amusing.'

It is late. Piccadilly is settling down, its sound muted, its wheels fewer, its crowds less dense; and over that small triangle of disillusion, formed by Shaftesbury Avenue, the Charing Cross Road, and Leicester Square, is a dreary reluctance to go to bed, and the suspicion that many have no beds to go to. The beggar leans against the wall holding out a thin, hopeless hand, containing one box of matches; big limousines go by with lights that glow on grey cushions, furs, and white shirt fronts; little sharp harpies walk the pavements, while shifty, seedy young men in groups stand about, as if lost or waiting for a leader. It seems to you that the clean tide of life has ebbed, leaving this queer driftage on the shore. . . .

The 'Spring Onion' is a night club. Night clubs in London are of two kinds: clubs to which people go to spend money and clubs to which they go not to spend money. The 'Spring Onion' is that kind. As you leave your hat and coat, there trickles down from some distant place the throb of a trap-drum and the tinkle of a piano. You enter a room full of people.

At first sight, they look dangerous. You might think that they are waiting for the dope to take effect; a most unjust assumption, because they are only bored. A thin girl with a corrugated back leans forward, observing, through a monocle, the movement of dancers in the next room. Now and then someone waves a hand to her, and she replies with a thin smile and taps the ash from her cigarette. A young commercial traveller from Sheffield sits opposite, believing her to be a vampire. Three young men with alcoholic puffiness at the eyes sit and talk together in loud voices, two or three smartish elderly men laugh loudly with their partners; in odd corners sit the evening dress explorers, the people who have 'gone on' in the hope that the 'Spring Onion' might be 'amusing.'

Amusing!

They glance round, and conclude that they are in Bohemia. Quite a number of people hold the same belief.

'Almost like Paris,' says a stockbroker's wife, as a young man with long hair goes by.

There are few things in Paris so honest; this is not a side show for trippers; it is a perfectly genuine home for lost dogs.

The atmosphere of the 'Spring Onion' is one of unrelieved sadness. It gets you at the heart. The louder they laugh and the longer they dance, the more it gets at your heart; for fifty per cent of the 'Spring Onions' do this night after night, month in and month out, because they are lonely and hate the thought of going back to furnished rooms. For a few shillings a year they can belong to the 'Spring Onion,' and forget, in drink at a reduced price, that achy something at the back of their minds.

The clock goes round, and some of them give it the quick, spiteful glance reserved for enemies. Only one-thirty! Oh, dear! Too early to go. Waiter!

They order poached eggs and whisky. They do not want the eggs, but, after a certain hour, eggs chaperon whisky.

So the small hours drift by.

The normal eyes of those prosperous merchants who have 'gone on' watch the scene without appreciating its essential pathos. They wonder dimly how much wickedness is behind it all; they feel that these people could not endure this dullness every night unless . . .

A pink-faced young visitor, who has been mixing champagne with poached eggs and whisky, and feels himself filled with a pagan beauty, decides to put things to the test. He approaches the thin, pale girl, and says:

'Shall we dance?'

She adjusts her monocle and regards him slowly:

'We will not,' she replies.

The pink-faced young man retires, wondering why everybody looks game and won't play.

*   *   *   *

Under an elaborate pretence of cheerfulness, is not the 'Spring Onion' the Club of Lost Dreams? Are there not people in London—in all great cities—who dare not be alone with themselves, who must seek company from loneliness, from things undone, from opportunities missed, from that demon which sits on guard at a man's conscience, making him cry: 'Go away! How dare you say I am second-rate? You know I have never really had a chance!'

*   *   *   *   *

'Then,' say the people who 'went on' next morning, 'we went to the "Spring Onion." Extraordinary crowd . . . oh, yes; *most amusing*!'

YOU, who are possibly bored with the Berkeley, may care to dine with me at 'Charlie Brown's,' just outside the gloomy gates of the West India Dock, East. . . .

We go into the bar to have a gin and Italian. It is full of ships' officers discussing the traffic of the Seven Seas. Through the folding panels of the bar, designed to hide the guilty face of the drinker from the barmaid, we see, opposite us, men of the lower deck drinking beer, as they also discuss the traffic of the Seven Seas. More people meet unexpectedly in 'Charlie Brown's' than in any other spot in London. We admire their sunburn. (A ship has just berthed with rum from Jamaica.)

However, we merely notice these people and forget them; for we are in a peculiar bar. It looks like a junior branch of the South Kensington Natural History Museum. Queer stuffed creatures, presented to Charlie Brown by the mercantile marine of every nation, hang from the walls, crown the eminence of cupboards and repose dustily on the top of cabinets. Prominent among them is an unfortunately born calf with three times the normal allowance of legs. There are snakes in bottles (and, I am sure, someone's appendix), Chinese gods, Japanese ivories, African assegais, French bronzes, and, hanging from the ceiling, a long, dusty pipe which, sooner or later, someone will tell you 'is the pipe Billie Carleton used to smoke round the corner in the Causeway.'

'Dinner's ready!' says a charming girl from the bar.

We go into the dining-room.

The room has a wooden roof. From this roof hang more curios. The bar was merely an introduction to this. Our eyes have time only to appreciate an albatross speared to the wall, and someone's skull hanging from the ceiling, before we are led to large plates of roast pork and apple sauce. We sit at a table occupied by men with clear eyes and stubborn chins: young men round whose lounge-coat sleeves is the ghost of gold braid. (A ship's officer can never disguise himself.) At the head of the table is Charlie Brown.

Now suppose you were a stoker in Shanghai and you said: 'I know Mr. Baldwin and Mr. Winston Churchill,' no one would pay any attention, but if you said: 'I know old Charlie Brown,' someone would at once stand you a drink—which would be the highest compliment one man could, in such circumstances, pay to another. Wherever ships go over the seas, in whatever harbours they rest, you will find someone who knows Charlie Brown.

Mr. Brown, who is sixty-seven years of age, is short and muscular. He has the figure of a man of thirty, the instincts of an artist, looks like a retired gladiator, and wears a peek-a-boo shirt and collar cut low at the neck to give him air. He ran away to sea when he was a lad, but hated it so much that he came home and settled down. Then he developed the collector's instinct, and started buying beautiful things. His clients, with no real appreciation of Charlie's tastes, began to present him with bottle-nosed sharks and parrot-faced fishes, and shrunken human heads from the Cannibal Isles; which accounts for the queer appearance of the public rooms.

No man with a tinge of feeling could refuse monstrosities carried at great personal inconvenience from the other end of the world.

*   *   *   *   *

Charlie Brown explains his exhibits as we dine:

'That lifebelt up there came from the first German ship captured in the War . . . that skull is from the South Sea Islands. You wouldn't think the albatross was snow-white underneath, would you? It is! They say an albatross can crack a man's skull with its beak.'

We gaze round at the dusty marvels. We avert our eyes quickly from things in bottles—from a small mummified baby in particular—and we appreciate the childish happiness of the tough fellows who brought these things across the sea to Charlie.

'That,' says Charlie Brown politely, 'is, I have been told, the pelvis of a lady.'

We look up and see a dusty bone hanging from the point of an antler.

There is so much else to see that we do not dwell on this pelvis as we should, or speculate whether it ever walked down Bond Street. . . . 'The pelvis of a lady.' What a perfect title for a modern novel!

'And now,' says Charlie Brown, 'if you've quite finished, I'll take you upstairs.'

*   *   *   *   *

Here is probably the most surprising room in East London. In an ordinary front sitting-room Mr. Brown has crammed the results of forty years' acute collecting. Ivory and bronze are his passions.

An embarrassing display of Chinese and Japanese ivories stands packed in the room on tables, in cabinets, on shelves. There is a remarkable Louis XIV cabinet with painted panels, an eight-hundred-year-old Chinese cabinet, an Elizabethan prayer-book bound in faded embroidery, statuettes, cut in the finest ivory, of fishermen going out with cormorants to fish in the Chinese manner.

'Everything nice I see, I go after!' says Mr. Brown, as he wanders round the room touching his treasures with the loving fingers of a collector.

He points out objects which the London museums would like. (Until a collector can do this he is a mere beginner.) We sign a visitors' book containing many famous names (which proves that fame is not always made in, but always spreads to, Mayfair); and then we take our leave.

*   *   *   *   *

In the bar downstairs, the tankards are replenished. The worthy fellows pour beer down knotted throats.

Some, no doubt, pledge themselves to bring Charlie back from the next voyage a pig with two heads, little guessing that, when Charlie leaves his Barnum and Bailey dining-room, he goes upstairs to enter the rarefied regions of art, to stand with his head on one side before a fifteenth-century statuette of Joan of Arc, and become quite a different Charlie Brown. . . .

Life is a queer, unexpected business, and 'Charlie Brown's' at the gate of the docks strikes a keynote.

FIRE!

The scarlet escape roars through the London street to the urgent clang of its big brass bell. You have a second's glimpse of a man crouched over the wheel; 'riders' manning the escape; faces tense under burnished helmets; the long backward sweep of the rescue ladder; and you hear the crisp roar of an engine with the power of sixty horses in its voice.

It is pale blood that does not tingle to this, the swiftest, most heroic pageant of our streets. It always seems to me, as the red cars cleave their clamorous way through still traffic, that I have seen a chariot and its heroes thundering to the Siege of Troy.

Come with me to the head-quarters of the London Fire Brigade; and we will look behind the scenes of this drama. The time to go is at night, for it is then that, out of the silence of London, may come from anywhere the cry for help; at any moment that old enemy of London, the little red flame that licks and flickers, may leap up and illuminate the stage.

*   *   *   *   *

Brigade head-quarters, in the Southwark Bridge Road, reminds me of a battleship. There is a fine disregard for steps. Men swing down brass poles as sailors swarm down ropes, they shoot from the top floor to the bottom in a second. The men in blue look like marines; they have the competent, rough-and-ready smartness of seamen; the same humour.

A perpendicular ladder with brass-bound rungs leads to a kind of quarter-deck, and, beyond, is the most watchful room in the night of London—the telephone room of the G.H.Q. Fire. Men in uniform sit before the switch-boards. One is waiting for calls from London's 1,670 street fire alarms; another waits for the call from fire bells; a third has the general public's calls; a fourth is in touch with the other sixty-two fire stations in the County of London.

On the wall hangs an extraordinary map of London; it is London in terms of conflagration. Sticking in it are cork discs, which represent the exact position, at that moment, of every fire engine and escape in the London area. A young fireman stands beside this map and keeps it up to date, so that the chief officer, coming in at any moment, can see, at a glance, how every fire-fighting machine is employed.

'Where's fifty-two and three?' says the superintendent, giving a quick glance at the map.

'Small fire in Chancery Lane, sir,' replies the map keeper.

As you look at this map, and turn to this room with its listening firemen, you have an impression of astonishing watchfulness, unsleeping, tireless.

'Could you have put out the Fire of London?'

'Well, it wouldn't have started had we been in existence then. We should have nipped it in Billingsgate.'

Downstairs there is a card-index room like no other in London. Each card bears the name of a well-known building, and on it is written the recipe (in terms of engines and escapes) necessary for its preservation. The whole of the great Oxford Street drapery stores are tabulated here; you can look through the cards and see how much water power, and how many ladders, are necessary on 'the first call' from Jones and Brown's!

'Yes, something happens nearly every night.'

In 1925 something happened 7,476 times! Those were the fire calls answered. The actual fires put out in London last year were 5,168.

* * * * *

You cannot talk long to an experienced London fireman before he tells you stories of the air raids, that dramatic chapter in the history of the brigade which should be written up and put on record.

'We could hear the Zepp unloading far off, as we crawled in on hands and knees. A sheet of plate glass came down and cut the brass comb off my mate's helmet, as if it had been butter! I remember that night well, because that was the time I smashed my shoulder. . . . I felt myself falling. I was in a cistern full of water and printer's ink. I found my electric torch. There were two dead bodies in the cistern. The bomb had flung great slabs of concrete about as if they were cardboard. One slab had blocked the stairway. On the stairway, huddled together, piled on top of each other, were about thirty men and women, dead—killed as they tried to fight a way out from the fumes and the fire. I found a baby with its clothes cut from it—not burned, but cut—so that when I picked it up they fell apart. Its body was not even scratched. . . . Oh, yes, it was dead. . . . Nothing could have lived in that room when the bomb hit the concrete.'

Each profession or trade has its jokes.

'You'd laugh like anything to see a new hand on his first real job meet a bit of live electric wire! It's our great joke to push a fellow under it so that it catches his helmet. He's wet through, of course, and that makes it worse for him!'

'What does it feel like?'

'Well, at first you think an elephant's kicked you under the jaw. That teaches you! You watch out for hanging wire after that.'

* * * * *

Down in the station is the drama. . . .

The scarlet escapes stand, bonnets to the door, rugs over the radiators, and beside each 'van'—as they call them—the 'watch' sleeps on camp beds. This is the first escape on duty. The men sleep fully clothed, their big boots beside the beds, ready to step into, their helmets on the 'van.' The same with the engines.

What happens when the call comes? The men in the look-out room receive it and press a button. The lights leap up over the engines and escapes, the fire bell rings, the men leap from bed into boots and jump to the 'van,' the driver starts his engine, a pipe-clayed rope, that hangs above the driver's seat, is pulled, the doors swing open, and, with a clang-clang-clang of the bell, the first escape on duty is out in the London night.

Two seconds!

And more behind! The next 'van' and engine are ready.

'Better be soon than sorry,' is the unofficial motto of the brigade.

The men sleep wrapped in brown blankets, like troops bivouacked on the eve of battle. Every night, and at any moment of the night, the dim station may blaze with light and sound, calling them from sleep to an inferno of flame, with a house reeling against a scarlet sky and, high up above the smoke, a life in peril. . . .

They sleep, but always on the eve of battle.

THE first night of a new play.

A second act has fulfilled the promise of the first. Over the theatre is that electric tautness, that marvellous feeling that every word is 'getting over' to the still rows of bleached faces in the darkness.

The author, who for an hour sat in the shadows of his box with the impression that he was about to witness a child of his sacrificed on a heathen altar, now sits confidently in the front, the glow of light on his boiled shirt front.

A friend has just whispered that the libraries are making a 'deal,' and that old So-and-So is ready to bet that 'the show will run for a year.' The author nods. That means that he will not only be able to pay all his debts, but that he can also go to the South of France, and never, never again have to say he is out when a man calls with an overdue account.

Wealth. Even in his preoccupation with his play, he thinks how wonderful it will be to have not only enough to be miserably comfortable—the competence which illuminates unattainable desires—but wealth.

Those much better plays, which no one would look at yesterday, can now be unloaded one by one. Funny place, the world!

* * * * *

But the audience care nothing about him at this moment. Their sympathies are centred in a woman who moves across the stage in a beautiful gold dress. She is a beautiful gold woman with tawny hair and long arms and fine hands: a new star.

She is struggling at cross purposes with life, and, in this struggle, all the watching faces see mirrored their own tussles with life, so that they have taken sides with her against the other forces in the drama. Things are real. While they ache for her success, and try to believe that virtue always beats vice, they can see only her failure, so heavily are the dice loaded against her.

She is not pretty: she is beautiful. Unsophisticated young men in the pit have already claimed her as their ideal, the unattainable. She for whom the world would be well lost. They do not analyse the spell that has been cast over them.

Here and there a callow youth wishes that he might be brought into some heroic adventure on her behalf; a burning house from which, forgetting that he weighs only seven stone, he would swiftly and masterfully carry her; or a knightly rescue from a cynical man in well-cut evening clothes and a monocle: a rescue involving a fight, with those eyes looking on watching for his safety.

She drops her eyelids and her voice. She concentrates the drama of the act into one swift second. The curtain falls. The storm breaks loose.

'Come round and meet her!' whispers the author. His eyes are damp with unexpected happiness.

*   *   *   *   *

The dressing-room smells of scent and an electric fire.

An elderly suppressed-looking woman, wearing a neat apron over a black dress, moves round the room with a pair of silk stockings over her arm: those same gold stockings. A kind of overdue happiness lights up the elderly woman. She walks in the reflected glory of success. She is the 'dresser.'

Three or four pink, elderly men perch themselves on various sofas, and, when the door opens, as it does frequently, you can hear the muffled sound of the orchestra, feet pattering up stone stairs, and the hollow tramp of scene-shifters.

The men spring to their feet as the lady of the play comes through a side door, wearing a pink silk wrap edged with pink fluff. From the pinkness, comes a long bare arm; and she shakes hands. She seems smaller, and your eyes fix on her eyelashes, which are stuck together with grease paint.

'Billy, get me a drink, a very weak one!' she says.

The kind of man who is always discovered sitting on a chintz sofa, leaps up and obeys.

Acting is a marvellous thing, you think, as you watch her, no longer the romantic lady of a dream, but herself: a rather ordinary young woman. Unless you knew, you would never guess that she could be a heroine.

'I'm famished,' she says. 'And I've had indigestion all day. I had kippers for breakfast.'

Her court make sympathetic faces. The elderly woman

comes in with a gown over her arm and a pair of shoes. Outside somebody is shouting. The curtain is rising. . . .

* * * * *

To the stage she comes again, radiant, cool, elegant. Her lovely voice falls on a hushed house. Each movement is followed by hundreds of eyes, each small gesture of fine hands.

You sit there, unable to believe that things are quite so real as they were: wondering if she had two kippers, or only one.

'STOP messing abaht! Hit him!'

The cry rises from the crowded seats of the boxing booth. There is the same tone in it that told the gladiator in Rome to plunge his sword in the body of his opponent and—let them get on with the Christians! Stalls and circle are 'full up.' Eyes smart in the smoke of cheap cigars. Lights, green and spluttery, hang over the ring, and, in the pool of these lights, two East End boys are trying to fill each other's head with stars.

Their naked bodies are pink with the rash of the blows rained on them. Their hair is straight on their wet foreheads like the hair of Japanese dolls, their mouths sag, and their movements are becoming slightly vague: the brain and the nerves are not working together.

The fat seconds with their punched-in noses give twisted smiles, in which contempt for the clumsiness, and admiration for the stamina, of these young fighting cocks appears more or less evenly mixed. They are tired of swabbing them down at the end of each round, weary of inviting them to part with any teeth which appear superfluous; and they, like the fight fans, would be glad to see one or the other stretched on the floor.

Round fourteen!

It is curious, at times, to notice, when two boxers reach the last gasp, that the subconscious mind functions even though the brain may feel like an underdone omelet.

Smack-smack-pat! goes a quick punch on the jaw of the thinner boy, and, more by good luck than skill, he lands a blow on the other's nose which sends him reeling among magnificent constellations. Then, as this thin fellow recovers he flashes an incautious glance over the crowd as if in search of something, wipes the dank hair out of his eyes with a glove, and lurches to the attack. Just a second's lapse from concentration, but enough to show you that some part of him, which yet remains unmashed, is thinking of somebody or something outside the arena!

You have not far to look! Midway in a row of intent enthusiasts, a girl sits. She has evidently put on her best hat. She does not move. She just sits with wide eyes, watching;

and she is watching the thin youth. Every time he lands a crack at the other lad, she tightens her hold on her handbag; every time the other boy lands a crack at him, her lips part and her eyes go wider. . . .

'Stop messing abaht! Hit him!'

At that wild roar of the bored crowd she moves her shoulders and looks at the man next to her, as if she would like to say:

'Shut yer mouth, you great ugly brute! How'd you like to stand up to that?'

She is anxious. It is difficult to say whether she wants her boy to win at all costs or whether she would like him to lose in order to have him out of it.

Round fifteen!

There is some booing.

*   *   *   *   *

The two fighters square up.

They hug one another in sheer weary desperation until parted. Then they reel and stagger together. Their arms shoot out, and each one receives a blow on the point of the chin. The crowd looks on as if it would like to take a hammer to them. Suddenly the stockier man goes to pieces.

The girl half rises in her seat.

'Oh, Jim!' she cries. 'Smash him one—*now*!'

Jim, at the sound of her voice, makes as though he would turn; as though he would dearly love to describe, in her general direction, a gallant gesture with his glove, as though he would, if the flesh were not so weak, place his thickened lips in a smile. In that second the smaller man comes up and deals a beauty, which stretches Jim flat.

'One, two, three . . .' they count over his body. Then he rises. His pulverized face looks angry. He discovers his opponent in the semi-darkness, in the mist in which he moves, and slowly, deliberately—for they are both half-dead with fatigue—he gets one in between the eyes. The other lad falls, crumpled, done for. They count him out!

The crowd sing a facetious song. They carry off the body. Jim limps down, as if in a dream.

'Gentlemen, I now announce Battling Jones and Blue Peter!' cries a man in a dinner-jacket, as two heavy-weight fighters stride into the ring and smile down on their partisans. The crowd howls with delight. This is the big scrap! That other sparring match is already forgotten. . . .

*   *   *   *   *

Outside in the night, the boy called Jim is carefully counting half-crowns by the light of a street lamp.

'I can't see too well! You count 'em, kid!'

'Thirty bob!' says the girl in a voice that means money is money. They both look pleased. Over the swollen face of Jim spreads, in parts, a wrecked smile.

'That's a bit of all right, ain't it?' he says, pocketing the money. They link arms, and, as they go off into London, it seems to you that there is about her the pride of all women for whom men fight in tourneys.

I SET off on a romantic adventure the other night.

He is to be married in the summer, and he is building a small house in a northern suburb which he wished me to see because I have followed every stage of the comedy which has led to this, now running with the hare, now with the hounds, on his side one day, hers the next—but generally on hers. . . .

We came—after living on an omnibus for hours—to a remote, lost district on the edge of London where the roads, still glutinous with country mud, have lately received that accolade of civilization—lamps. The little houses, pink, gabled and garaged, march down hills, which, but yesterday, were wet fields full of cows and marshmallows. There are hundreds of such roads in outer London now; the edge of that lake of life which, since the invention of the steam engine, has overflowed from London, linking village to village in one labyrinthine network of streets.

These houses, so new that they have not lost an air of having intruded, as if still apologizing to dead thistles, stand with a coy, bow-windowed surprise at discovering themselves so swiftly 'desirable' and 'freehold'; so soon drilled to stand shoulder to shoulder, like red grenadiers on that recently wet field.

*   *   *   *   *

It was ten p.m.

We walked down the 'avenue,' admiring the saffron, the blue, the pink curtains in the lit windows of drawing-rooms—so bridal, cosy, and intimate. (Mothers-in-law may have been inside, but there was nothing to suggest it.) We caught glimpses of chintz walls, brass lanterns swinging in 'lounge halls,' and, once, we heard a piano and a little pale voice declaring that she was less than the dust beneath his chariot wheels. It was all so new and experimental, and it would have been terrible to know that hate had any place or prospect behind that saffron glow.

'You're quiet,' he said.

'Yes,' I said. 'I feel two hundred and twenty years old.'

Then, half-way down the hill, we came to a place where the

armies of occupation ceased. Here houses flung dark gables into the night. Their windows were blind and unborn. Over them was written the word 'Sold' in red type. Past the empty houses, and at the bottom of the hill, we reached a series of excavations; beyond was the wet field with a white mist over it; all the stages in the history of colonization in one short road! Up from these ragged walls and dark pits, Pompeian doorposts rose against the sky; there were foot-high mantraps and duckboards over the mashed cocoa of unturfed gardens. We searched until we came to an extensive ruin.

'This,' he said, 'is ours!'

We leaped a ditch in the dark.

'Here,' he said, in the showing-off voice that comes naturally to people who are building anything, 'is the front door!'

I saw two posts in the mud. We then came to a wall.

'The fire-place will be over there,' he continued, striking a match, 'and you walk out here into the lounge hall, which is going to have a decent stained-glass window. Over there—where they've left that galvanized tank—we have the dining-room, and outside will be a loggia and the garden. It's difficult to grasp; but you'll be able to imagine it all.'

I thanked him for this flattery, and he gazed round with the eye of a seer.

'We mean to do this room in blue and saffron,' he remarked.

I stepped out of a puddle into another, and began to feel that I was locked in the grip of a great natural force—as, indeed, was true. He roamed about in the dark, visualizing his home.

'In a few weeks,' he said, 'we shall be able to go upstairs.'

I looked 'upstairs'; and the stars were smiling.

*   *   *   *   *

It came over me, standing there in the cold dark in this unborn home, that there should be some office in the Book of Common Prayer for the blessing of such places. 'Forasmuch as all mortal men be subject to many sudden perils, and ever uncertain what time these shall be met. . . .' It might begin like that before calling down upon these brave places all that is kind and lovely in life.

'What are you doing?' I asked him.

'Burying a shilling in our front door—for good luck, you

know. But I must jab the mortar down, or someone will find it and buy beer with it.'

I also took a shilling and rammed it well down into the mortar.

'For Babs,' I said. 'She'll probably need the luck more than you. We can't tell yet.'

       *   *   *   *   *

Then we went out into that inhospitable road, which was all the history of man's struggle with wet fields, and we saw on the crest of the hill—for it was nearly eleven o'clock—the little saffron windows snap into darkness and higher saffron windows leap to light. The brittle stars winked and moved, knowing everything, having seen everything. At the top of the hill I heard a small baby crying; but I don't think my friend did.

'KUNG-HI!'

In the dark arch of the doorway, a Chinese lad, who shivered in his thin serge coat, bowed and smiled, whispering 'Kung-hi!' ('I wish you joy!') as I went in across a courtyard to the guest-room in the lodging-house of Ah Tack in Limehouse Causeway. It was eleven-thirty on February 12, and I had been invited to see the Chinese New Year in; for the end of the Twelfth Moon was near.

Ah Tack's hidden little house is the Ritz of Limehouse to all Chinamen who sail the seas to London. They lodge with Ah Tack between voyages. Queer fish hang in the kitchens, and pallid chickens, killed in a peculiar manner and instantly boiled; also quantities of pork. There are turkey's tongues dried and powdered, a mixture which the Chinese believe is good for consumption. Ah Tack's is half empty now, because there are fewer Chinese crews about, but time was when he was always busy. Many of his guests have no money, but that does not worry him, as it would worry the manager of the Ritz. He just smiles and looks impenetrable—which means that his expression does not alter—as he folds his hands and says:

'You come again, perhaps next year?'

And his penniless guest replies:

'Most assuredly, and then most honourable debt will be discharged.'

Off he goes. It may be years after, but the bill is always settled—now and then by a relative of the debtor. A strange hotel for a strange people. They seem to have such a marked sense of the realities; they seem to go through life with a waiting-room air, as if conscious that they possess a return ticket to Paradise. . . .

I crossed the courtyard and entered the room. In all London there was no stranger scene.

Six or seven Chinamen sat smoking on chairs round an ordinary kitchen range. At the end of the room was a shrine which extended from the floor to the ceiling. It was made of red wood, and the central feature was a picture of Confucius. The sage sat in crimson silk, gazing at this Limehouse kitchen, philosophizing above his thin, black, drooping moustache.

Before him burned two tall garlanded candles. On either side
of the candles were white flowers in vases, plates piled with
oranges, washed and polished, and a big plum cake.

This room is the only temple of Confucius in London. On
weekdays, the shrine is used as a kind of sideboard; and the
cat sleeps on it in a basket. Sometimes a Chinaman will put
down his cigarette and sit before the altar, shivering and
muttering things to himself—or Confucius—oblivious, apparently, of the cat and the empty beer bottle, which would take
our possibly more trivial minds from God.

'Good evening,' said Ah Tack. 'I velly glad you come.'

He was in shirt sleeves, which are the badge of his office, and
he wore a black velour hat. He introduced me to his lodgers.
We bowed stiffly, and smiled. Then Ah Tack took up a
pewter teapot and poured out a drink for me into a wine cup.
It was neat whisky.

You must realize that it was, I take it, an emotional occasion.
The Twelfth Moon had but a half-hour to its wane. We sat
watching the clock and sipping the fire water. The candles
burned with a steady yellowness that brought out the crimson
in the robe of Confucius. The cat walked in, took one look at
the lit shrine, and went out again. The Chinamen began to
talk in that clipped sing-song, which I find most difficult to
follow. They talked about New Year's Eve at home in China
. . . shops closed for three days . . . lanterns in all the houses
. . . cakes and fruit and flowers . . . Chinese crackers that went
bang-bang-bang and covered the floor with soft red paper.
New Year's Eve: the day that all Chinese debts are paid.

Ah Tack rose, as if sad memories stirred within him, and
poured himself out another neat whisky.

The door opened, and two wizened little Chinamen came in
as silently as blown leaves. They drifted up to the shrine and,
whispering, accepted a drink. The clock ticked on. . . .

I began to feel (as Ah Tack solemnly toasted me every two
minutes in neat whisky) that I was assisting at the service of
some decayed priesthood: at a ceremony which had lingered
on from remote ages. Scenes like this must have taken place
early in Christian times, when the last priests of Thebes
gathered to celebrate the resurrection of Osiris, hardly knowing the meaning of the things they did, giving utterance to
the death rattle of a faith. It was like that.

It was uncannily solemn and deliberate. I wondered what

they were really thinking, these expressionless exiles. I wished something would happen. I wished that they would show some animation. I watched the clock anxiously, feeling that, when midnight struck, something remarkable and dramatic would occur. Perhaps they would pray before the shrine. . . .

*   *   *   *   *

It was five minutes to twelve.

The cat came in, very annoyed at being kept up, and attempted to reach Confucius. Ah Tack went round with the alcoholic teapot. (I think we all looked fairly swimmy about the eyes.) Then midnight. . . .

'Happy New Year,' said Ah Tack, rising and removing his velour hat.

'Sin-hi . . . Sin-hi!' cried his guests, which means 'May joy be yours!'

Then Ah Tack advanced to the altar and took a knife. His guests put on their hats and sat down. Someone put coal on the fire. I sat watching Ah Tack's priestly back moving about before Confucius, and it occurred to me that it would not be in the least surprising if he suddenly offered up a sacrifice. These composed, deliberate faces affect one like that. Nothing would be surprising. He waved the knife in the air, put it down on the altar, and came towards me:

'Have a mincey pie?' he said.

I took an admirable mince pie; and so did everyone. It was full of anti-climax.

*   *   *   *   *

Ah Tack shuffled to the shrine and began burning brown paper.

'What are you doing?'

'Making good luck,' he said. 'Much good luck.'

On each piece of paper was written a sum of money. He gave thousands of pounds to the flames, sacrificing, I suppose, to the God of Fortune.

After bidding everyone good night and a happy New Year, I walked out into the cold, dead streets of Limehouse, feeling that I had been to a secret society that was on its last legs and in urgent need of subscriptions.

I WAS finding my way to Blackfriars from a region of warehouses on the other side of the river, and the tramcar was empty. It was about ten p.m. The conductor was singing down below, in a deep and penetrating voice, as he stamped his cold feet on the platform . . .

> Yes, sir, that's my baby;
> No, sir, don't mean 'maybe';
> Yes, sir, that's my baby now.
> Yes, ma'am, we've decided;
> No, ma'am, we won't hide it;
> Yes, ma'am, you're invited now . . .

It was a singular voice—deep, full, ripe, and rather wild. He had a great sense of rhythm, and the stamping of his feet kept time to the dance tune. I was certain that he was having a good time all by himself on the platform, as the tramcar spun on down the dark roads, on either side of which warehouses frowned with an air of locked strongholds. In a few moments he came jingling upstairs into the empty car still singing . . .

> When we reach the preacher I'll say . . .
> *(Where to, guv'nor?)*
> Yes, sir, that's my baby;
> No, sir, don't mean 'maybe' . . .
> *(Threepenny, sir?)*
> Yes, sir, that's my baby now. . . .
> *(Blinkin' cold, ain't it?)*

'You,' I said enviously, 'seem almost horribly happy.'

'Happy?' he cried in a cavernous voice. 'What's the good of being anything else? We shall soon be dead. We all go the same way home. I've got no blinkin' reason to be happy; but I can't help it.'

'You are happy in spite of yourself?'

'Yes, and I've just had a rare old ticking off, too.'

'Why?'

'Whistling. You wouldn't hardly believe the dirty tricks the public serves you at times. I suppose some crusty old bloke was trying to read his paper and the tunes I was whistling got on his nerves. Well, why couldn't he have told me so?

I'd have stopped! Instead of which, he goes home and writes a stinking letter to the Tramways Department giving my number and complaining that I upset the whole car.'

He swung his satchel round till the pennies rang together indignantly.

'That,' he remarked loudly, 'was not true . . . in fact, it was a rotten lie. I never have upset the whole car—not the whole of it! Often people say to me, as they get off: "Well, I wish I felt like you do!" and once, guv'nor, I had the whole car whistling! I did—straight! And what do you think got em? "Marchin' to Georgia." It's a tune, that is! Know how it goes? . . .

Bring the good old bu-gle boys, we'll sing ano-ther song.
Sing it with a spi-rit that will start the world a-long.
Sing it as we used to sing it fif-ty thousand strong
   WHILE WE WERE MARCHING THROUGH GEOR-GIA.

'Great, ain't it? Got a swing with it! Better'n all this fox-trot muck that you whistle just because you can't forget it! When I told the missus, she said, "Joe," she said: "if you don't watch out you'll get the sack"; and I believe she was right!'

*   *   *   *   *

I looked at him and realized that he had a certain quality. He was small and stockish, and his issue coat was made for a much taller conductor. He was one of those people who give you an impression that he ought to be on the music-hall stage: he was like a caricature of his calling.

He had a likeable personality, a gentleness of eye and the gruff voice of the giant, which is so often imprisoned in small men. I had a vision of him in his right environment; a little, slightly pathetic figure in the spot light of a stage singing to a hushed theatre. . . .

'People often say I'm rude,' he volunteered, 'especially old ladies. And I'm not rude; it's the way I speak; I can't help it. Wish I could! Might be an inspector! But if I was to say, "Tickets, please"—just like that—somebody'd write up and complain about it. Straight they would!'

A girl got in and sat down.

'Where to?' bellowed the little man.

'Elephant,' she replied.

'You're only going the wrong way. Do you mind?' boomed the conductor in his terrifying *basso profundo*.

The girl looked a bit frightened and rose.

'Wait till I stop the car!' he shouted gruffly. It was a kind thought, yet the passenger appeared offended. I realized that the little man was one of those people born to be misunderstood, fated to suffer for a manner over which he had no control.

'It's not often I can have a word with people like this,' he said, 'and I like talking. You're not an actor, are you?'

'No,' I replied, 'I write.'

'Do you?' he said surprised. 'I should think you need a head to write. I've often thought I'd have done better at something else. It's not much of a life running up and down stairs punching tickets. I don't like doing it. . . .'

'Then why do you do it?'

'S'truth!' he cried, with deep feeling, 'I've got three kids! How many blokes are in the wrong job because they've got kids? Millions! And glad to be in any job! 'Course it's worth it! I got three fine kids: laugh and whistle all day long, they do: just like me. My missus says that between us we shall drive her barmy; but that's only her way of putting it.'

I smiled at the lost artist, and saw him at home tumbling about and acting, putting all the vitality, which he might have flung across the footlights, into a rough and tumble on his kitchen floor. . . .

*   *   *   *   *

We swung in over Blackfriars Bridge, and the delicious curve of the Embankment lights swept on into the dark.

A new audience stood waiting innocently in the tram shelter, some for the stalls; some for the gallery upstairs.

'Good night and keep smiling!' I cried.

'Can't help it!' he said. 'Yes, sir, that's my baby. No, sir, don't mean "maybe"; yes, sir, that's my baby now. . . .'

His song was suddenly cut off, as an inspector emerged from the shadows. I heard his deep voice encouraging his audience to 'hurry along there. . . .'

I found myself smiling and, quite surprisingly, cheered-up.

I THINK the grandfather of good journalism, Daniel Defoe, remarked that nothing gave him a more vivid idea of London's size than the daily business at the Customs House. There was, of course, no G.P.O. when Defoe lived. I would give anything to show him round King Edward's Building, E.C., at about 6 p.m. any night of the week, for here the size of London leaps at you until your head goes round. . . .

It is nearly 6 p.m. All over the City of London those little enamelled discs—'Next collection, 5.30 p.m.'—have been removed from the pillar-boxes. The big evening mail has gone. It is the boast of the Post Office that letters posted before 5.30 p.m. in E.C. are delivered in the London area the same night. It is the rush mail of the day: a mail that comes in like a white avalanche, is stamped, sorted, broken up and sent out at once to flutter like an evening snowstorm over London.

In a long, high room one thousand three hundred men grapple with the '5.30.' As you enter, you push through an army of postmen who have just emptied the pillar-boxes. They are handing in their enamelled discs and the keys which unlock the boxes on their 'walks.' (A policeman calls his patrol a 'beat'; a postman calls the same patrol a 'walk.')

You go on into the most quietly efficient scene in London.

Wide, travelling bands, covered with letters and postcards, empty a stream of correspondence into baskets. They come fluttering down from the post-boxes outside the G.P.O. As soon as a letter is posted, it moves on and falls into the stamping-room.

Men carry the baskets and pour them into the general mail that lies like a view of the Alps on a series of long tables. It has come from pillar-boxes in office and street. The letters are arranged with the stamps all facing one way, and are passed through a machine that goes click-click-click, stamping one thousand items a minute, writing 'British Goods Are Best' on the stamp, and adding a circle containing: 'London, E.C. (the date, the year), 6.15 p.m.'

'But this is a 5.30 mail! Why do you stamp it 6.15?'

'Collections are stamped three-quarters of an hour later than the pillar-box time because we discovered that some people got up to all kinds of trickery. At one time it was quite common for people to hear the result of a race sharp on posting-time, write out a bet and rush to the pillar-box, and, afterwards, produce the postmark as a proof that they made their bet before the race was run! Things like that!'

One stamping-machine deals only with official matter. Is there a more melancholy sight in the G.P.O. than one thousand long buff income tax letters being rushed out with indecent haste to the, as yet, unsuspecting public?

The mail, stamped, passes on down the room in a steady stream, where it is joined by another stream of letters from dozens of provincial mails that happen to arrive at the same time. It is 'broken up.' It is sorted. Hampstead's letters go into one department. Norwood's into another. Park Lane's into a third; and so on. Postmen in the E.C. 'walks' come along, take up their bags, and go apart to sort the mail in the order in which they will deliver it. They make little piles, each pile a different street, arranged numerically. No two postmen sort their letters alike. They know their 'walks,' and they know the peculiarities of them.

'Why do you put letters for No. 32 crossways on those for 46?'

'Well, you see No. 32 has moved to 46, and the housekeeper at 46 takes them in for him. No. 3 in C—— Street has a brother at No. 104. He's ill and has transferred his business to his brother, who takes his mail. Now, see this! This is what makes a lot of trouble to us postmen. "Mr. Jones, Splendiferous House, E.C.1." Now Mr. Jones has a little office in the roof, but he won't put "Room 510" on his note-paper, because he wants people to think he owns the whole blinkin' show. Till you get to know these people with large addresses and small offices, you spend hours finding them. But you soon get to know them!'

* * * * *

Past the crowd of sorting postmen (who seem to be playing some obscure card game by themselves), you go to the last scene of all. Outside, in a great yard, the Royal Mail vans await the first bags for the district offices. They are flung in, checked, the doors bang:

'Right away, Bill!'

And off goes the red van with income tax notes, letters beginning, 'Sir,—We are surprised to learn that the enclosed account . . .'; letters beginning, 'Dearest,—It seems a century since I saw you . . .'; letters beginning, 'With reference to yours of the 18th ultimo . . .' (millions of those!)

'Have you any statistics about the 5.30 mail?'

'We have,' says the official, bringing out a book.

'An average posting every day for the 5.30 at this office is 146,395 letters, 3,983 postcards, 5,715 registered letters, which with newspapers, packets, etc., makes up a daily total on one collection of 260,280. But that is not the heaviest mail. Every week the 7.15 a.m. delivery in the City of London totals 6,642,700, and in addition . . .'

'No more figures, please! They cease to mean anything!'

'And, remember, this is only one office.'

*   *   *   *   *

Upstairs, you enter the region of foreign mails. Men are sending a few hundred thousand letters to Cuba, to Egypt, to small republics in South America, whose names remind you of geography primers. In one corner of this room, the whole British Fleet is mapped out in little boxes, each box the name of a battleship.

'Admiral's Letters' is a big sign over this department.

'The admiral,' it is explained, 'being a big pot, has his letters delivered in a special bag.'

Downstairs again.

The clock strikes 7 p.m. A change has come over the big room. The white flood has ebbed. You have to walk two hundred yards to catch sight of its tail disappearing into the sorting boxes. Outside is a roar of motor engines and a slamming of doors. Postmen are shouldering bags and marching off into the night. The great room in the G.P.O. has digested the '5.30' prompt to the minute!

Then . . . click-click-click . . .

The stamping-machines all sing together. The busy One Thousand Three Hundred form up behind the tables. The revolving bands again shower their burdens into the baskets, hundreds of bags are again emptied on tables.

'That's the 6.30 just beginning!'

The tables are suddenly white once more. In a secluded

corner, a man, who combines the eye of a hand-writing expert with the mind of a detective, shuffles the casualties of the night mail:

'Mr. Jones, London.'

He flings it wearily into a box marked 'Blind.'

* * * * *

And the white avalanche of the 6.30 moves on through the machine.

The Thames: Two a.m.

'ON a June night,' said the sergeant, 'this job is all pie, but, just now, unless you wrap the oilskin round your back—excuse me, sir, that's better—you're liable, if you don't mind me saying so, to catch a chill on the liver.'

The patrol boat of the river police shot out of the black shadow of London Bridge and nosed, like a swimming rat, to the Southwark side, where warehouses and wharves go down to the water. The sergeant sat in the stern, a river policeman beside him, and the driver crouched amidships over his motor, interested in the chug-chug-chug that told him whether it was running well or badly. The navigation lights bobbed and danced as we rode at full speed across the wash of a tug. . . .

'On a June night,' repeated the sergeant, 'it's just pie, this job, lovely and cool with sometimes a moon round as a soup plate over the Houses of Parliament, so bright that you can see to read the paper. It's true that bodies are worse in June, but—there's always something, isn't there? You can't have everything all your own way, can you?'

He gave the grappling irons a push with his foot; and they responded with a gruesome rattle . . .

To our left, the great drums of London Bridge, like the bastions of a fort, thrust their wedges into the swirling eddies of the river. The Thames is still strong here, as it was when old London Bridge was a place for wise men to pass over and fools to pass under.

What an aloof river is the Thames! It 'keeps itself to itself.' It never joins in things, as, for instance, the Seine joins in the affairs of Paris. Modern London has not tamed the Thames as some cities tame and domesticate their rivers: it is a melancholy, primitive streak in the character of London. The Embankment civilizes it for a few yards, but the essential wildness of it crops up at Westminster, where, it seems, bulrushes might grow on the slightest provocation, and, east, beyond Blackfriars, where the gloomy buildings stand with their feet in the water, looking much as Thames-side buildings have looked since Augusta.

Yet, if you would know London, it is necessary to sail at night with the patrols of the river police, for it is then possible, in an impersonal drapery of night, really to see London: an experience that cannot happen by day. All you see by day is a muddle of roofs and streets and spires. From the old unchanged Thames at night, the outline of London looks much as it always has looked, and, by slightly closing your eye, you can see first Augusta, then the Conqueror's London, then the London of the Middle Ages, then the London that disappeared in the reign of Charles II: each passing across your imagination in a dark, exciting procession.

*   *   *   *   *

It was past midnight as we chugged towards Wapping. We nosed round the hulls of tall ships, shining our lanterns over them.

'Bananas and tomatoes!' said the sergeant, indicating a galleon.

We came to another one:

'German! Full of reparation goods!'

We swam in under the shadow of Limehouse, every second revealing a narrow slit of riverside that seemed staged for a dramatic crime: steps awash in the tide, a cold lamp shining over them, and, at the back, shuttered houses. We crisscrossed to the other bank, and came to a queer fleet at anchor:

'The smallpox boats,' said the sergeant. 'They are always fitted up ready to take patients down to the isolation hospital in the event of an outbreak.'

They were queer, old-fashioned craft, with tall smoke stacks and paddle wheels. Lower down the river we came to another flotilla. It was made up of Thames tugs, about thirty strong, riding at anchor side by side. • This is where they hull when their day's work is done.

'Lights out!' whispered the sergeant suddenly. 'Let her go!'

He had seen something! The little boat shot ahead over the water. We overtook a man in a small rowing boat.

'Where's your light?'

'Got no matches!'

'Got your papers?'

'Yus.'

'Let's see 'em!'

Heads in peaked caps bent over the papers in the moon of an electric torch. More conversation about lights.

THE CLOCK TOWER AT NIGHT

'Right! Let her go!'

Off we sped again.

'Can't be too careful about people who move in the river without lights,' explained the sergeant, 'but thieves aren't as bad as they used to be. There was a time when they'd have untied a loaded barge and walked off with it!'

We sailed round clusters of barges laden to the brim, lying together out in the stream with no one on guard. Then we turned and ran with the tide back to London Bridge.

* * * * *

One of the loveliest glimpses of London I have ever seen is that which unfolds itself at night through the jet black arches of Blackfriars Bridge . . . the pin points of the Embankment lights curving round to Westminster across an oily expanse of Thames, the lights wavering in the water, and, in the background, grey and sleeping, the tall buildings of the Embankment . . . a little oblong yellow tramcar moving slowly in the darkness. . . .

We shut off the engine and drifted. Someone arose and flung out a thing like an anchor that splashed and sank. Then he threw out something else:

'That first is the drag, and that other is the trip line.'

And there you must leave us—for it was not nice, in all that loveliness of London by night, to be drifting with the tide dredging, and talking about a lost woman. . . .

Big Ben struck two; and his great yellow face was like a friendly moon in the darkness.

THEY dine with the blinds up. Beyond the yellow oblong of the window is the darkness of the Bloomsbury square. Beneath skeleton trees cats have their loud love affairs.

The major dresses for dinner. He enters the Victorian room, making blustering, throaty noises, and spreading a full-blooded heartiness, due to an expensive-looking complexion, inherited, with a series of mortgages, from his family. He takes his seat beneath 'The Monarch of the Glen,' and the critical eye would find an aptness in this; for he himself is the monarch of this glen, the arbiter of its fluctuating manners, the focus of its social aspirations—the star turn of the boarding-house.

Some people, knowing that his income from all sources, with the exception of the Turf, is two hundred and fifty pounds a year, would be inclined to laugh at his grand manner and put him down as a silly old snob. We will not. When an exile tries to re-create the atmosphere of his native country in a strange land, no one calls him a silly old patriot; the major, exiled in the wilderness of poverty, is merely trying to remain true to his blood. He is not always successful, except in the evening, for a dinner suit generally acts on whatever breeding there may be in an Englishman, just as it seems to obstruct the decent instincts of certain other nationalities.

During the day, the major has vague dealings in saloon bars with foxy little men who live on horses, and, at such moments, in his seedy bowler and his faded, pre-War, over-cleaned basket-weave lounge suit, you might mistake him for some not too honest camp-follower of Chance. In the evening, however, he reverts to his instincts: he is the perfect gentleman —Major Gorey-Goreish, D.S.O., of the 5th Royal West Blankshires (Princess Augusta's Own).

* * * * *

One by one, the chairs are occupied. There is a clatter of plates. A small, sour girl, who seems to have been weaned on disillusion, emerges from a Japanese screen bearing a trayful of steaming soup plates. She rests the tray on her knee, as she unloads soup to the people whom Fate has brought together in Bloomsbury.

'Pea soup again!' whispers a shaggy young man at the end of the table.

He looks across for approval to a pale girl with a sleek brown head; but she takes no notice. Stuck-up lot in this place!

'And when I was A.D.C. to Lord Bloodsome in '95,' booms the ripe voice at the end of the table, 'I met the Crown Prince in Ceylon, and he said to me . . .'

'Could you lend me fourpence, you dear old top . . .' mimics the shaggy young man to his neighbour, with a furtive glance at the major.

'Really, how interesting . . .' remarks a faded widow as she crumbles bread with fingers which look somehow naked. Her diamonds went one by one years ago, after dear Arthur's creditors had been partially satisfied. Bloomsbury is full of faded ladies with omnibus clothes and a Rolls Royce air, who, after flinging possessions at the creditors of their husbands as one throws things to a pack of ravenous wolves, escape into discreet poverty with a carriage clock and a photograph of the Italian garden.

* * * * *

A young American 'Commercial' looks round at the well-bred derelicts and finds his worst suspicions of the effete English more than fulfilled. A lot of silly old snobs! He could buy them all up and write them off on his expenses as 'car fares'; and no one would know. A bunch of bum failures without a dime between them, dressing up for dinner and talking about the foxes they killed years ago. Gee, they cut no ice with him! What a bunch of stiffs!

The shaggy young man, who has just come up to London from the provinces and is doing quite well in the City, is inclined to agree with the American, with whom he has discovered a spiritual affinity. 'Unmatey' gang, that bunch of the major's—probably he isn't a real major! Every time the young man smartly pierces a piece of Gorgonzola, and marvellously introduces it into his mouth on the point of a knife, he discovers the major's baleful eye on him. It is as if someone has whispered 'Bounder!' And he is not a bounder; but he hates to be made to feel inferior. He is annoyed by the major's ability to make his hands feel red and large. . . .

'Punk lot of goats, ain't they?' whispers the American.

'Yes; listen, now we're going to hear for the twenty-third time since last Friday that ruddy story about Lord Dash and the wild pig!'

'Gee, this is just fierce! Doin' anything to-night? Let's get clear of this and go up west.'

*   *   *   *   *

In the middle of the table a young man, who is supposed to be something in the City, looks on at the tragi-comedy, taking no sides, seeing both so well. (It is almost a pity to spy on them and put them in his play.)

He is amused by the arrogance of the young hustlers as he is by the arrogance of the major with his aura of caste. The young men are going up the ladder of life arrogantly; the others are coming down in the same frame of mind. They cling pathetically to old things. Their 'air' is a barrier of self-protection erected against a social abyss. Having a tradition, they owe more to that tradition than to themselves, which explains the sting in the genteel poverty. They are also malicious, full of suspicion, soured by disaster and made mean by having so little—watch their faces when they are playing bridge at threepence a hundred! And, with it all, they are extraordinarily gallant.

Night by night goes by, and the card tables are brought out. One by one, the people who have known better days steal off to bed. What dreams come to Bloomsbury every London night no man can say; but it seems reasonable to suppose that the cats in the square often awaken faded ladies from Italian gardens to a grim little bed-sitting-room where a carriage clock ticks in a patch of moonlight.

THE man next to me was smoking a hearty little cigar. He may have been a plumber or a gasfitter or a carpenter; he had carried with him the careless atmosphere of one accustomed to bang about homes with a hammer.

'This is going to be a bit of all right!' he remarked, waving the stump of his cigar towards the stage.

Round us curved the gallery of the 'Old Vic.' It was packed with men, women, and children who had paid fivepence to hear *Aïda*. Most of them were artisans, a few were labourers from the Waterloo Road district, and many were young girls and boys with more brains than money. There were three or four plump matrons sitting together eating cake, as they waited for the curtain to rise.

'I remember this theatre thirty years ago—and more,' said the man with the cigar. 'Regular blood bucket it was in them days. A couple of murders in every act, and dead baronets all over the stage, and the gallery trying to throw things at the villain. . . . Now, of course, it's a real theatre. You get something to think about here. . . . Shaw's clever, of course, but he doesn't touch your heart. I like Yourip-ides. And I like opera, although I couldn't abide it at first. But I stuck to it; and now you can't keep me away. . . .'

The lights were lowered. Instantly the full theatre was hushed, and there fell a dead silence of people who have come with the grim determination to extract each hard-earned pennyworth of enjoyment or instruction.

Radames stepped forward and sang that sweet cruelty to tenors, 'Celeste Aïda'; and I could see by an undulating glow that my friend was beating time with his cigar.

*   *   *   *   *

I will say just this of *Aïda* at the 'Old Vic.' It was the most heroic show I have seen in London. A small stage, a small, but admirable, orchestra, beautiful lighting, inoffensive scenery, and this great spectacular opera, which ought to be performed in the Stadium, 'got over.'

I live in hope that some day a producer will buy a book on Egyptology and dress the opera correctly, for nothing could be more effective, no matter how small your stage. Someone deserves praise for putting on Pharaoh's head the Red and White crown of Egypt; surely the first time this has happened in the history of the opera!

*   *   *   *   *

The curtain fell on Act I, and the gallery went mad. Fancy an English gallery whistling, stamping, and yelling with joy at an Italian opera! 'Oh, this is nothing,' said the man with a cigar. 'When we like a thing, we let them know about it!'

He then told me that, when the bombs were dropping round Waterloo Station during the War, the 'Old Vic' audiences sat listening to Shakespeare, night after night. Macbeth had to raise his voice to carry it to them above the fire of the anti-aircraft batteries!

*   *   *   *   *

I explored the dress circle.

It was packed with people from every suburb in London. So were the stalls and the pit. In the interval, I went downstairs and joined a crush round a coffee urn. Here I met Chelsea in art silk, and Balham in a serge costume, also the masculine counterpart of each.

'Isn't it great?'

A young man, who was eating a substantial cake, asked me had I ever heard *Aïda* before? In any other theatre I might have said 'Yes,' and have left it at that, but here I told him what it is like to hear the opera in Egypt in the opera house for which Verdi wrote it, and, afterwards, to go home through moonlit streets with the palms rasping in the Ezbekeyih Gardens.

As I listened to the crowds talking, I gathered that the 'Old Vic' is a kind of compromise between a theatre and a club. They knew each other. They knew the actors and actresses. They had ideas about finance and production. A girl sold me a copy of the theatre journal, as people at a church bazaar sell you the parish magazine. On the front page, I read that: 'Early in Birthday Week [Shakespeare's] some kind member of the audience brought great bunches of rosemary from the country and filled the various offices with it because it was a *Hamlet* flower. . . .'

Does anyone feel such affection for any other theatre in London? Has any other theatre the life and enthusiasm this playhouse has? I began to revise my ideas on the National Theatre.

*   *   *   *   *

In the gloom of Waterloo Road, I passed my friend of the cigar. He was whistling most of the last act with tenacious enthusiasm, and I am certain that he will go on whistling it as he mends burst boilers, or looks after the bathroom taps, or carves out cabinets.

The 'Old Vic' is London's only theatrical inspiration.

LONDON may mean anything to a man.

To you, at home in a club chair, with Mrs. Browne sitting opposite, and the children asleep in the nursery, it means one thing and . . .

The squat timber ship, heavy with a small pine wood from the Baltic, comes rolling round North Europe with the salt caked to her smoke-stack and the cook's cabin flooded. Now and then it seems that she vanishes in the sweep of the sea, as if sucked down, her bridge heels over into the angry greyness but, bit by bit, with desperate persistence, she makes headway, and, in time, discovers the mouth of the Thames. She steams into Limehouse Reach, and slowly, for she is very tired, berths in the Surrey Commercial. There is a rattle of chains, and—one more cargo has been brought to London Town.

A hefty Scandinavian sailor looks at the twinkling chain, that is Rotherhithe Street, and feels glad that he is in London once again. His tow-coloured head cropped up early in English history, and those bleak blue eyes looked first at England over the poop of a viking galley. He is the same man who gave Alfred the Great much trouble; and, as he looks at the lights of Rotherhithe, his eyes are much the same as they were when he contemplated a raid on East Anglia but perhaps we are imaginative!

One fact is certain; the London night calls him! He wants to be ashore jingling money. He receives an advance of pay, and, with a gay whistle, is soon slouching his six feet two of blond manhood through the grim darkness of the docks, where stark cranes stand in rows outlined against the smoky gold of a London sky.

* * * * *

He is in London!

He likes London. He tells people at home about London, the greatness of it, the warmth of it, the excellence of it when you have been rolling in from the Baltic with salt on the funnel and the berths awash. A great place, London.

He whistles through Rotherhithe Tunnel and enters that

region of the Swede and the Dane—Shadwell. He goes on through dark streets, which smell of fried fish and fried sausage, he passes entries, where pale little girls whisper to him, but, being a northerner and not a southerner, he walks straight on, thinking of beer.

He enters a Danish café where men smoke long pipes, and he planks his money down, demanding drink. There is no one there to-night; no one he knows. He has another drink and goes on. (It is good to be back in dear old London!)

Out into Love Lane, across Cable Street, along Devonport Street into Commercial Road East. Here he meets the surge of London: the mellow lights that are, to him, London; the black-bearded men who are, to him, London; the sloe-eyed undulant maids who are, to him, London; the beckoning public-houses that are, to him, London! It does not seem strange to him that London should be an Oriental city. If you asked him for a symbol of London, he would probably draw a picture of an ample young Jewess with Corinthian legs.

Instinctively he calls at the corner 'pub' and puts down a pint of ale. He feels himself in the heart of London. He meets a friend who has just come in on a grain ship. He, too, is in the bosom of the metropolis. They stand each other drinks and talk shop, as all sailors do. It certainly has been an awful time at sea these last few weeks, but—it's good to be back in dear old London!

They go out into Commercial Road and think that it might be a brilliant, and rather daring, idea to walk towards White-chapel. The lights beckon, the passing omnibuses give that thrill of life so remarkable after solitude; and the crowds of small, pert odalisques charm without, perhaps, arousing any deeper feeling as they move past, always two by two, an astonishing contrast to the wildness of the northern sea.

*   *   *   *   *

They decide to eat. They are in London! They are sick of the food given by cooks in flooded kitchens. They go into a restaurant where a faded patriarch in an apron offers them the menu. They eat Hungarian goulash followed by kugel, and they drink (becoming reckless and liking each other tremendously by this time) a bottle of Alicante. Ah, how good to be in England, in London. . . .

They emerge and go on, following the omnibuses and the crowd, admiring the smouldering darkness of the girls, till they come to Aldgate, where various lines of traffic merge, where crowds merge, giving to Aldgate—or rather the northern side of it—an almost frantic excitement. It is the west end of the east! And here they pause. Few sailors—except those of America—ever travel beyond Aldgate Pump. Many have heard of the Nelson Column, and of Piccadilly and Leicester Square, and of Charing Cross; and many have identified these places beyond question at Aldgate!

This is the limit of London to the men who traffic on the seas. They do not know what lies beyond; and they do not want to know. Their bleak blue eyes are wide with the wonder of London: it certainly is a great city! What about another drink?

Like a couple of explorers on the edge of the unknown; they enter that well-known bar where the dust is heavy; and here they command beer.

'Cheerio!' they say in Scandinavian.

'Time, please!' says the chucker-out.

They put down their tankards and, drawing deep breaths, go into the night. London is going home! The black-eyed beauties of London, who parade at Aldgate, are all walking the same way towards Whitechapel, the London restaurants, with their Hebrew signboards, are closing down, the London streets, with their narrow alleyways, are lying deserted in the light of pale lamps. . . .

The dock police scrutinize their tickets; and they pass into the guarded darkness.

Good to be in London—the greatest city in the world!

A Suburban Dance

TAKE an omnibus or a tramcar in any direction, and you will arrive in time at a suburban Piccadilly. Lights are shining. A queue waits outside a cinema, the public-houses are busy, the cheap restaurants are full, the streets are packed with aimless crowds, there is a whist drive in a hall, and a dance in another. There is a zest in the air which is absent from more expensive places. This night life ceases promptly at eleven-forty-five, for its votaries have to be at work sharp at nine a.m. in the morning. It is the same at Brixton, Golders Green, Streatham, Cricklewood . . . little west ends of the suburbs, complete with their own society, their own 'men about town,' their own reigning beauties, their own heroes, villains, and enigmas.

You give eighteenpence to a young woman, who is imprisoned behind a brass grille; and you enter the dance hall.

The floor is covered with young men and girls fox-trotting to the music of an excellent band. The hall is large. Yellow lanterns hang from the roof. Your first impression is that the girls are extraordinarily pretty and the men surprisingly ordinary. The girls have dressed for the dance; the men do not possess evening clothes. Here and there a star dancer has changed into a special kind of trousers, grey or black Oxford trousers as a rule, which billow over pointed brown shoes. With these trousers he wears the coat and waistcoat of his lounge suit. Young men who do not dance linger in vague, drifting groups on the outskirts of the floor, smoking cigarettes and making comment. Pretty little wallflowers sit out by the dozen. Now and again two girls rise and dance together.

The music ends, the lights go up. Then a surprising thing occurs. In an instant men and girls have parted. The girls go over to one end of the room to sit on chairs ranged against the wall; the men group themselves in bands and coteries round the floor and light up the cigarettes, which they had left parked on the radiator.

* * * * *

You look with interest at the girls. Most of them work in the big shops in the district. Each one wears a knee-short, tasteful evening frock and light stockings. You look along the rows of chairs and realize that here are seen the prettiest, neatest legs in London. In the Ritz, the Savoy, Claridge's, the pretty woman is easily picked out from the crowd; in this eighteenpenny suburban dance 'hop' a new beauty dawns on the sight each minute; the girls are all between the ages of sixteen and twenty-five. Perhaps that is the secret; they have abundant vitality and youth. They have also abundant lip-stick and powder, and one or two have Eton-cropped their heads.

It strikes you over and again that they are too vital and brilliant for the dull youths who lean against the wall and smoke cigarettes and whisper.

*   *   *   *   *

'Will you dance with me?' you ask.

She hesitates coyly, and looks as though she intends to cut you ice-cold.

'I don't mind if I do,' she replies, leaving a large leather handbag over the arm of her chair, and rising.

She glides in your arms like a spirit. She knows all about dancing.

'Didn't those men look rather angry when I asked you to dance?' you say, as you go round.

She shakes her hair in your face, looks up, and laughs.

'I should shay sho!'

'But why?'

'Well, you see, you don't know me, and you're a stranger.'

'Oh, I see. Then I've made a mistake?'

'I should shay sho,' she says brightly, and begins to hum in tune with the music.

The music ends.

'You dance beautifully. Will you dance with me again?'

'I must go to my friend. If I nod my head—yes; I'd like to.'

Off she goes quickly. All the other girls have dropped their men with equal speed. No man offers his partner a cup of coffee from the meagre buffet. Now and again girls, two by two, will grope in their leather handbags, discover sixpence, and pay for their own refreshment.

*   *   *   *   *

In all the smart hotels and dance places in London you will find that, generally speaking, the men are older than the women. In the suburban dance halls the men and the girls are contemporary. In the smart dance places of London the dance is the least important thing: in the dance hall it is the only thing that matters. Once it is over, the girl has no use for her partner. She does not want to talk to him. She just shelves him and joins the pretty coloured bunch of *crêpe de Chine* against the wall. They sit whispering and smiling in a row, like a collection of bright little humming birds on one long perch.

Is it imagination, or is there suspicion between the male and the female?

There is no friendliness, no companionship, no dancers have apparently brought partners, each dance is the signal for the men to raid the humming birds, and the end of each dance is the signal for them to abandon them. You think that bishops, who fulminate against the immorality of the dance hall, should put on ordinary clothes and go to one or two of them.

* * * * *

You go out, where the omnibuses mass and the tramcars gather, realizing that they will all be at work again in the morning. You think that you have blundered by chance into a club whose members were too well bred to object when you violated rules. You marvel at the high standard of beauty. You wonder from how many dull homes Youth flies every night in a dance frock for a few hours of music, of rhythm. . . .

As in the fairy tale, midnight ends the ball; and the Cinderellas of the suburbs put on velour coats and go home through dark streets.

'Pub Crawlers' ᴏ ᴏ ᴏ ᴏ ᴏ ᴏ

WHEN the public-houses open in the evening, the pale old woman, with the tray of collar studs and boot-laces, begins her long and weary round. So does the man with one eye and many matches; so does the thin, consumptive-looking girl with a basket of flowers. They appeal to human nature in its most expansive moments.

When a normally hard-hearted man is emptying his fourth whisky down his red gullet, he sees beneath his glass a pale alabaster hand, not too clean perhaps, grasping a box of matches or a string of boot-laces and, turning, he looks into eyes full of dumb misery. Something surprisingly soft inside him makes him hand out a few pennies with a gruff refusal to profit by the transaction:

'You can keep the studs,' he says.

Now and again the varied commercial travellers meet by chance under a lamp.

'Fourpence at the "Crown" and nothink at all at the "Nag"!'

'Go on! Ain't there anythink doing at the "Bunch o' Gripes"?'

'No; they said, "'Ullo, missus, you're the blinkin' fifth that's been in during the last five minutes!"'.

It is a curious thing—but I have it on the authority of the people who live on saloon-bar generosity—that public-house philanthropy changes from night to night. On Monday the 'Nag's Head' may be full of kindness, and on Tuesday full of snubs; on Monday the 'White Horse' may rain pennies (and even sixpences), and on Tuesday you can put on your most wilted expression, and you won't get a blessed bean. So, you see, you have to keep on going round and round, night after night, taking the current of kindness as it comes.

You *have* to keep on, because there are children at home and a rent to be paid. . . .

Most remarkable of all the bar visitors is the Young Man with the Paper Shapes. Robert Louis Stevenson would have enjoyed him. He slips into a bar silently, and he stands by the door. Somehow the people become aware of him. Mrs. Jones, with her veil on her nose, pauses in mild alarm, with her second glass of stout poised above her ample bosom, as she says, *sotto voce*:

'Oo-er; look at 'im! What's he after?'

They see a pale young man gazing round the bar from beneath the brim of an old felt hat. He is fumbling with wads of folded newspaper contents bills, with which his clothes are padded. Quickly, he makes little tearing movements, he pinches ovals and oblongs and stripes from the folded bill, he teases it and pulls it, and then opens it, displaying four perfectly modelled filigreed figures cut in the paper.

A delighted murmur rises from the bar. Isn't it clever? How does he do it? He ought to be on the halls!

* * * * *

Without a change of expression, the young man brings out more folded bills, tears them, and exhibits this quick-change artistry to the bar. His *tour de force* is really remarkable (and it used to cost fourpence to perform before he bought old contents bills!) Taking a thick wad of bills from his pocket, he makes a series of incisions with his fingers, he does something else difficult to follow, and then he opens out a paper ladder until it touches the ceiling. The higher the ceiling of the bar, the more paper he uses; so that he does not perform this trick until he feels more or less sure of his audience. Then he sends round his hat, and you notice his well-shaped head. When he says, 'Thanks,' you realize that he is not an unlettered man.

* * * * *

'I have been doing this, with the exception of the War, for about fifteen years,' he will tell you. 'You see, it's the only thing I can do. I learned how to do it from a man who, I believe, invented a turn like this on the halls. There is, I am told, another fellow doing this in London, but I have never seen him. . . . Like it? One can't choose one's life! Sometimes I do quite well. I collected eight shillings in one place the other night. They vary. One interested man in a bar, and the whole bar forks out pennies and sixpences. . . .'

'Forgive my saying so, but you seem an unusual type to be living like this.'

'Unusual? Perhaps I am. The streets of London are full of unusual things. Did you know that a son of Sir —— plays a guitar in public-houses near here? I could show him to you to-night. When you have had to live on the streets in London, nothing ever surprises you!'

'Are you married?'

'Oh, yes! I have two children, but my son is all right: he is at —— '

He mentions a public school. You feel sure that this young man is some relation to Stevenson's Young Man with the Cream Tarts. Who would imagine that a man taking pennies in bars could have a son at an expensive school which has raised several Prime Ministers and many of the greatest soldiers this country has known.

'Well, you see, my wife's people look after him!'

'And you look after—yourself?'

'I try to! Good night! I must be moving on. The most favourable moment at the "George" is just now, for the night engineering staff at X's take a half-hour's break. Good night.'

He turns up his coat collar, turns down his hat brim over his pale, refined face, and, with a shy nod to the goggle-eyed bar, dives out into the darkness.

A Night Club

HE is just back on six months' leave after years of policing the Libyan desert from the top of a camel. The girl he is going to marry is a dear; and she dances well. After we had seen her home, and he stood in the night with a brand new silk hat in his hand, listening to that terribly final click of a front door closing behind the beloved, he said to me:

'I don't feel like turning in. Shan't sleep a wink to-night. Surely London hasn't closed down?'

I looked at his ingenuous brick-red face and knew that he was about to ask me to take him to a night club. Like all visitors and colonials who visit this city, he wanted to look upon life in the rough, he wanted to sit thrilled and horrified on the apex of his superiority and observe men and women—particularly women—dance along the primrose path to the everlasting bonfire. A kind of mental liqueur after a good evening.

I looked at his blue eyes and that healthy schoolboy enthusiasm in them, marvelling that a man, who is a terror to the thieving nomad when he swoops up out of the sand at the head of his patrol, should need any thrill in life. It occurred to me that I might as well cure him.

'The Hell Fire Club?' he said. 'Jove, we're going it a bit, aren't we?'

The taxicab turned and went back towards Piccadilly.

*   *   *   *   *

When we entered, three tired waiters were leaning against an aggressive yellow wall as if they were presiding over the funeral bakemeats. One yawned, and the others caught it. An anaemic young man, who is apparently never awake when the barbers are, played a piano with an expression he will wear later in Hades; a trap drummer crouched over his instruments with half-shut eyes; but no one danced.

We sat in an alcove and ordered ham and eggs. All round the tiny room, sitting in similar alcoves, were men and women drenched in gloom. The women looked frayed, the men looked bored. They seemed as though they were attending a wake in evening dress. You wondered where the body was.

'Is this a blind, or are they really like this?' asked the Man from the Desert.

'No; this is their usual state of mind. It's the same every night.'

'Then why don't they go home?'

'They can't; it's one of the mysteries of London.'

As we ate our ham and eggs, we looked round sympathetically. The only virtue of the place was its complete honesty: no one was pretending to enjoy it. You know, after a dinner-party, how you sit round discussing people, forgetting the clock, and then comes a time when discussion peters out and you still sit on under a spell thinking that there is something else to say: and there is not. You drift on in a tired stupor which it is difficult to break. It requires real effort to say: 'Well, what about bed?'

'Of course, it's attractive in a way,' said the Man from the Desert. 'As an American would say, it "keeps you guessing."'

'Yes, but there's nothing to guess. . . .'

'I feel that all these people are waiting for something dreadful to happen.'

'Well, you're wrong. It happened when they joined the club.'

*   *   *   *   *

Some excitement was caused, but not shown, when a man and a girl danced. Everybody watched for two minutes, perhaps; and the trap drummer opened his eyes.

A man at the next table called over the waiter, and, with a heavy air of decision, as if he were about to order a revolver and end his misery, said, 'Two black coffees.'

'Did you hear?' whispered the Man from the Desert. 'He's ordered two black coffins!'

The waiter moved off, as if he were thoroughly competent to find them!

*   *   *   *   *

'Jove!' cried the desert patrol suddenly, 'what a stunning girl! And she's alone. I wonder who she is? . . .'

'That would be difficult to say. I can tell you what she is: she is a dance instructress, one of the new professions. She has a good eye for clothes. Like a blonde barmaid, she attracts custom. If you would like to dance with her you can. Afterwards you will carelessly leave a pound note on the table. You understand?'

'But she's a lady!' whispered the desert patrol.

'We'll see,' I replied, calling the head waiter.

*   *   *   *   *

The girl smiled and moved across to us.

'Good evening,' she said.

'Do have a drink,' said the desert patrol.

'I'd adore some champagne,' replied the girl.

She was beautifully dressed. Her clothes were good and she wore them as only a woman can who has always worn good clothes. The desert patrol was right: she was a lady. The conversation skimmed a foolish surface. I caught the desert patrol looking at her in a way that told me that his mind was full of the problem: why had she 'come down' to this; what explanation lay behind her appearance in a fuggy, unhealthy little night club.

'Well, fancy you knowing the Vyners,' cried the desert patrol. 'Old Dick was killed in Egypt. I knew him well. I say, forgive me, do you come from that part of the world?'

The girl sipped her champagne and looked at the inoffensive face over the glass, seeming to hesitate.

'As a matter of fact,' she replied, 'I do, or rather I did. Let's dance. . . .'

They danced; and I admired them. She was a beautiful girl. She might have been his sister. When the dance was over they settled at her table and began talking. They danced again. The desert patrol looked worried. They settled again. A swarthy young man with incipient side-whiskers cut into their conversation, and the desert patrol, rising, excused himself and came back to me, looking rather pink about the ears:

'Let's go!' he said. 'I've had enough of this place. London's a pretty foul spot, old boy. . . . Oh, nothing: I'll tell you when we get outside. . . .'

We found our hats and walked into the cool night air. A taxicab cruised along the kerb as we walked towards Piccadilly. A policeman with a lamp on his belt tried shop doors; a vague

27*

figure moved out of the lamplight as we approached and half said something . . . chill, desolate Piccadilly. . . .

'What's the trouble?' I asked him.

'Who the devil do you think that girl is? She's the daughter of old Colonel X, a pal of my guv'nor's. I've heard about her. I believe my sister knows her. They have a big old place down in ——. She was a quiet, inoffensive kid until about a year ago, when she suddenly went crazy and left home. My sister wrote to me about it at the time, but I'd forgotten till I heard her name. And this is what she's doing, touting round these filthy night clubs. . . .'

'Did you attempt to reform her?'

'Well, I . . . anyhow she told me politely to keep my mouth shut and mind my own business. She isn't a bit repentant. Just fancy a girl brought up in the country with plenty of money and all that . . . and she seems happy. That's perhaps the queerest thing. I could understand it if she were too proud to go home; but she's too contented with this vile dancing life of hers to go home. How do you explain it?'

'The most unexpected people "go bad." It's a tragic thing. That's where you find them, now and again, in night clubs. There is something about the mad atmosphere that seems to act on them like a drug.'

'Can nothing be done about it?'

'Nothing. The first stage is that, and the next is drugs. For the final stage you watch the evening papers.'

'But it's criminal to let a girl like that slide away into the bad.'

'What can you do? She's over age. She's her own mistress. She can be cured only by herself.'

I told the desert patrol some of the queer people who have sunk themselves in the squalor of the London night.

'Well,' he said, 'you can keep London.'

STRANGE things happen now and then if you just take the first omnibus and sit there long enough.

It may have been a 2b or a 116 or an 11 or a 3—I don't know—but I sat there in the back corner seat with fourpennyworth of possibility stuck in the strap of my wristwatch, and was carried swiftly on the level of first floor windows through the varied scent of a warm London evening. (Some people eat fried fish all the year round.)

There were long grim streets, horrible as streets but thrilling as collections of little homes, each one in its way unique; and there were long holds-up at congested junctions, where tramcars and omnibuses tied themselves into knots and bunched together like a silly flock of sheep until a policeman walked to one side; and then they untied again.

*   *   *   *   *

When you are tired, or when you consciously turn off your brain as a tap is turned off, you can float along in a delicious haze, hardly existing, feeling that it is rather funny that you should be you, faintly amused, or placidly interested, in the life round you, much as a sleepy man in a cinema follows the pictures, grasping nothing of their significance or continuity: just conscious that things are flickering and fluttering in front of his eyes. I was conscious that the man and the girl in front of me were holding hands, and I thought how lucky for them that they had managed to coincide in time. A little matter of twenty years between them—a nothing to time—and where would they be now? Life is full of these hairbreadth escapes.

*   *   *   *   *

It was that time when London, its day's work over, does not quite know what to do with itself until bedtime. Men leant from windows in shirt sleeves reading the evening papers, women talked and shopped; young girls, who had hurriedly changed their work clothes, were two by two tripping along in their best clothes, setting out on that nightly parade which,

for lack of social occasions, is the only way they have of
meeting young men of their own age. All exceedingly proper
and conventional.

'Oh, he looks such a nice boy! Shall we turn round, Maudie?'

They turn, as two sheepish lads approach and raise their
hats.

'Didn't we meet you at the pictures last week?' say the boys
foolishly, putting up a barrage of pretence, knowing that they
did not, and knowing that the girls know they know it.

'No, you didn't,' say the girls, with swift feminine intuition,
if they feel the boys are 'wrong uns,' or 'P'raps you did';
and giggle.

This means that one of the boys may say: 'What about a
walk?' and, after pretending that mother would be annoyed,
and saying: 'Oh, I don't know. What do you think, Maudie?',
they giggle and remark: 'Well, we don't mind if we do.'

Not an elegant way of meeting your fellow creatures; but
what can they do? I suppose thousands of happy marriages
started like this.

*   *   *   *   *

Suddenly, I was startled out of this triviality by something
that looked remarkable. While I was still in a coma, and
regarding it freshly as if I had never seen it before, it appealed
to me as one of those hallucinations which bothered Don
Quixote from time to time. I left the omnibus quickly.

Here was an enormous green space stretching into the
evening mists. Everything that can happen on a green space
was happening simultaneously on this one. Bare-legged
children were paddling in a pond on the edge of the green.
Men and boys were playing cricket. There was tennis.
Hundreds of people lay on the grass. Placid old women sat
up stiffly knitting under trees. A young man lay luxuriously
with his head in a girl's lap. There were dogs barking, and,
somewhere, a band.

It looked as horrible as Utopia, a place where humanity
had suddenly decided to do as it liked and blow the conse-
quences. I plunged into it. A cricket ball whizzed over my
head. I passed through segments of varied enthusiasm, now
mixed up with tennis players, now in the middle of a political
meeting, now daringly walking across a juvenile Lord's, now

watching a serious grown-up game of cricket, now stepping over an occasional unconscious body stretched on the grass in an attitude of death.

But the most remarkable sight was an enclosure, containing a hearty band in which, over bumpy turf, girls were dancing with one another, while young men looked on, sniggering, and longing to have enough courage to join in. Occasionally one did; and the others laughed at him. This was a kind of cheap edition of Merrie England with the joy gone; the impetus, that led people to dance for the sheer love of life, absent.

Slowly the moon rose and gained strength. The enthusiasts left Utopia. Lovers drifted slowly under the moon. A boy asked me for a cigarette card. There was no sound but the clang of a tramcar bell. I felt, in the cool emptiness of this towny grass, that people had been happy; and I determined some day to go back and find out why.

'Where am I?' I asked a policeman.

He looked at me suspiciously, and replied:

'Peckham Rye.'

Our Last Inn   ◇   ◇   ◇   ◇   ◇   ◇

Written at the George Inn, Southwark,
September, 1926

WITHIN a hundred yards of London Bridge I am going to
bed by candle-light. The last office of the chambermaid was
to carry into this queer old room a big enamelled hip-bath
with the question: 'Hot or cold in the morning, sir?' A
canopied four-poster bed occupies a large portion of the room.
It is a high state couch of great splendour. It looks as though
it should be mounted on wheels so that it could be drawn
through the streets with a sultana lying inside on silk cushions.
Or it looks, with the white sheets turned back, as if ready for
the lying-in-state of a French President. That is possibly
far-fetched: most of all it looks as though against its generous
pillows should recline an eighteenth-century belle with a lace
cap on her Greuze-like head. She would, of course, be sipping
chocolate.

Placed against the side, from which, I suppose, I am to
enter this imposing bed, is a mounting-block of three steps
covered in carpet. How often in hotels all over the world have
I speculated idly on the past occupants of my room, a reflection
frequently assisted by a subtle perfume left behind in a wardrobe or a forlorn hairpin in a drawer; but here, in this forgotten
old inn, the last inn in Southwark, a man can actually see the
steps by which men and women long gathered to a sounder
sleep have mounted to their dreams. The candle-light casts
shadows: it flings a caricature of the four posts slantwise
against the farther wall, and, although it is a warm September
night, I feel chilled by the thought that, if I looked up suddenly
from this paper, I *might* see, shining on the bed-steps, the
ghost of a small naked foot.

Some rooms watch a man as a suspicious animal, unable to
make up its mind about him. This room is like that. I write
without fear of contradiction that it is the most remarkable
bedroom in London. There is something about it—a something common to many ancient rooms—that makes me anxious
to placate it and to find favour with its shadows. . . . The
fitful traffic of the Borough High Street goes by outside at
the end of the 'yard,' just shaking the window-frame slightly.
Downstairs, in the dark inn, a clock strikes eleven.

I have for years promised myself that I would some day
find time to spend a night here; and I have been postponing
the pleasure, as one does, now and then, postpone pleasure.
The George Inn, the last of the famous coaching inns of
Southwark, suffered in all the Borough fires, and, although
the site is that of the St. George Inn mentioned in 1554 as
situated on the north side of the Tabard, the present building
dates from the eighteenth century. Praise to those men who,
two hundred years ago, rebuilt the 'George' on the medieval
plan: it is the only galleried inn in London. If I opened the
bedroom door and crossed the adjacent sitting-room, I would
find myself on an oak gallery like the deck of a galleon. Here
it was, in the old days, that men leaned, watching the coach
swing in under the archway, commenting on the new arrivals
and the condition of the horses. Miss Murray, who has kept
the George Inn for the last fifty years, remembers when the
gallery was complete. Some time ago when Guy's Hospital,
who owned the land, sold it to the Great Northern Railway
Company, two sides of the old building with their galleries
were demolished to make way for a goods depot. The side
mercifully preserved is one of the unique treasures of London.

It seems to me that the shadows are like fingers pointing;
that this old room is trying to say to me: 'The time may come
when you, and those who love London, may have to fight for
all that is left of me,' and the knowledge that I would indeed
fight hard places me in sympathy with the shadows; which
no longer appear to watch doubtfully.

I have made friends with this queer old room.

*   *   *   *   *

I must go to bed; but I am not tired and I wish to postpone
the climb. . . .

I shall never forget my arrival here this evening. I hate
arriving at a modern hotel to be shot up in a lift to a stereo-
typed room in which to the servants I become 'Number 209.'
I have inherited, from who knows how many coaching ancestors, some perception of the technique of arriving at an inn.
It is something that this age has lost. Even a millionaire,
taking possession of the best suite in Claridge's, cannot achieve
the faintest ghost of the pleasure of arriving unexpectedly
and importantly at an inn which, recognizing you as 'the

quality,' flings itself into quick activity to give you the best it has. In my own life this has happened only twice— once in Somerset and once at Lillebonne, in France. There is a subtle flattery in the sudden bustle that follows your arrival; a delicious deference in the voice of the landlord, as he flings open the door and hopes 'it will do'; the smell and sizzle of a roasting chicken; the bent back of the chambermaid kindling a fire; the steps of the landlord ascending with a bottle of his best wine, all give you the feeling, impossible in the Ritz, that people are, not only serving you well, but that they are also glad to do so.

Something of the kindness of the old inn welcome lingers at the 'George.' People rarely stay here now. Few people realize that it is possible to sleep in London's last coaching inn.

Miss Murray was sitting reading in the little bar parlour, which is typical of all Old English inn parlours of the eighteenth century. Above the bottles and the decanters hung two horse-pistols discovered years ago in an oak chest. They were used by the coach guards. With them was found a pouch full of shot as big as marbles.

'Can I stay here?' I asked.

'Certainly,' smiled Miss Murray.

I learned afterwards how sincerely she loves this old inn of hers, so that I am now able to translate her smile into words. It meant:

'For five hundred years travellers have been staying at the "George" and the "George" is not dead yet. Of course you can stay.'

Then she showed me this room, with its great four-poster and I knew that here, at least, Time has not been able to pick the door lock. As I unpacked, I heard orders given about dinner; for the coffee-room was shrouded.

I am the only guest in the 'George.'

* * * * *

After dinner, served in the 'coffee-room' where the tables are placed between high-backed settles, I went into the bar parlour to drink port.

'Once,' said Miss Murray, 'we were busy with the hop merchants from the Hop Exchange near here. They used to come up from Kent and spend the night. But now they come up by motor and return the same evening. We do not have many visitors now. We do a luncheon trade; but no dinners.'

Years ago Miss Murray knew a man who said that he had met and chatted to Charles Dickens many a time in the coffee-room of the 'George':

'He brings it into *Little Dorrit*,' said Miss Murray, 'as the room where Tip Dorrit went to write a letter.'

The writing-table is still in the coffee-room, with pen, ink, and paper.

I do not know a spot in London which is more truly Dickens London than the bar and the coffee-room of this inn. The 'Cheshire Cheese' in Fleet Street has survived change, but in the process it has become self-conscious: the old 'George' is supremely unself-conscious. It caters, not for the American sightseer, but for the traveller and for the merchants of Southwark, for whom it has always catered. They have eaten its mutton for centuries. This inn has not been preserved: it is a genuine survival. There is life in the old 'George' still!

I sat drinking port in the room which Mr. E. V. Lucas so aptly describes in his *London Revisited* as 'a paradise of bottles,' wondering how long ago it is since the last coach clattered into the yard.

'I have no idea of the date,' said Miss Murray, 'but once, many years ago, an old gentleman came here and asked for a room. When I told him that I could put him up for the night he said, "And it isn't the first time either. The last time I stayed here I came on the coach!" So, of course, I gave him the best bedroom. He was over eighty years old. Ah, times have changed . . . all London has changed. . . .'

'Except the old "George."'

'Well, I've tried to keep it as I always remember it.'

At the side of the bar parlour is a glass window, which opens on to a passage. I became aware of a dark, spectral man standing outside, tapping on the window with his finger nail. The window was opened, and the light shone on him.

'Half a pint, miss!' he said.

He looked like Mr. Jingle. . . .

The candle has burned to the last two inches, and it is nearly midnight. I cannot say that the mighty bed invites me: it could never be so familiar. It looms before me like a state coach. Now the traffic is stilled. I would like to go out to the balcony and look down at the ghosts of the inn

yard, but the floors creak; and I might awaken the 'George.'
The strangest thing about to-night is that I am in London
in 1926!

Continued in the morning.

I am at the best of times an indifferent sleeper. I mounted the three steps and climbed into the great bed: and felt
marvellously awake. I heard a clock strike twelve.

I began to think of the Tabard, which stood nearby, and
of Chaucer. I enjoyed the feeling that I was lying so near
to London Bridge. I wondered if Shakespeare had ever
stayed at the 'George.' He must have known of it; possibly
he dined here on occasions . . . the silence of London. In the
West End the wheels go round to the small hours, but in
Southwark there is silence at midnight. The 'George' creaks
now and then. Strange, furtive creaks. . . . It is a curious
sensation to slip out of your period into another age. This
bed was a genuine escape from modern London; this room was
insulated from the London we know: it seemed to me, in that
hazy condition between sleep and wakefulness, that I might
at any moment hear the voice of the night watchman and
see the light of his lantern move across the ceiling.

'Twelve o'clock on a fine night. All's well!'

He would say something like that. . . . Surely the ghost of
the Dover Coach glides into the yard below on dark nights.
If ghosts were a little more convincing, how much more interesting life would be. I suppose many a fair refugee lay in
this bed during the French Revolution, dreaming of the sound
of tumbrils on the cobblestones of the Rue St. Honoré.
Many a fair refugee . . . many a fair refugee . . . and how many
times have runaway couples sought refuge here on their way
to London?

'The "George" is no place for ladies,' said Miss Murray to
me after dinner, 'if they want a lot of fussing. It's all right
if you take us as you find us and don't ask for the bathroom,
because we haven't got one and don't miss it, and manage to
have baths just the same!'

I suppose runaway ladies didn't want a lot of fussing. . . .
It must have been exciting to elope with a girl in a coach, to
hold her hand and say brave things as you swayed over rough
roads, hoping against hope that a horse would not cast a
shoe, looking out of the windows at the pale light left over

from the sunset, seeing the rain in the wheel ruts of the road. It must have been exciting. Then, you would come, at length, to some galleried inn at night with a yellow lamp shining among Virginia. creeper in the gallery; and the horses would be blowing and stamping on the cobbles as you hammered at the door asking for the best room and lights, dinner and a bottle of wine. For her ladyship and yourself . . . her ladyship . . .

And, as the coachman let down the little hanging steps, you would hand her out delicately. Hand in hand you would go up to the room and light every candle in every sconce; and hold her hands and look at her. Just as you were about to kiss her, a sleepy varlet with a bit of straw in his hair would blunder in with an apron full of wood logs for the fire. You would go over to the window in an offhand way and pull the curtain aside, watching them take the coach through to the stables.

'My soul . . .' you would begin, as the innkeeper entered with a cold shoulder of mutton.

Your man would tell you, when he brought up the luggage, that the Dover Coach was next yours in the stable. That would alarm you; and her ladyship's eyes would grow wide as the most beautiful saucers.

'My good fellow,' you would say to the innkeeper, 'did any gentlemen come over from France on the packet to-night?'

'Only one, me lord—in the next room, me lord.'

'And his name?'

'Sir Timothy Dagger, me lord.'

Merciful heavens, her husband. . . . Yes; it must have been exciting and complicated and—confound this bed!—probably not worth it in the long run when you met on wet grass in a mushroom mist, wondering which of you would be the man to finish his breakfast properly. . . .

At this point, I suppose, I fell asleep.

*　　　*　　　*　　　*　　　*

There came a knock on the door. The chambermaid entered and began to fill the hip-bath:

'A fine morning, sir,' she said.

Four huge jugs full of water went into the hip-bath and left enough water to splash in. I could not resist the temptation, before I shaved, of wandering out on the inn balcony and looking down towards the railway goods depot. What a revenge the railway has taken! I leaned on the gallery and looked at the ugly blank wall opposite and wished, with all my heart, that I could rebuild the lost portions of the 'George' and give London a coaching inn to be a joy and an escape.

Before breakfast I took a walk across London Bridge and watched the tangle of carts jammed round Billingsgate. I realized, as I took this short walk, that I had really spent a night in London.

(Another remarkable discovery is that the chambermaid, through sheer womanly kindness of heart, has darned two pairs of my socks!)

Dawn over London   ✑   ✑   ✑   ✑   ✑

THE vitality of Piccadilly ebbs after midnight hour by hour until three a.m., at which time a human figure becomes enigmatic in the emptiness of the Circus. At no time is the absence of the light-footed deity of Victorian London so noticeable: the hoardings in the centre of the roadway are like a scar.

Piccadilly at three a.m. has the dead appearance of an empty stage in an empty theatre. The mind, associating it with moving life and the excitement of great crowds, finds it uncanny: an abnormal sight, so cold and bare under the watchful yellow lights, so ready, it seems, for the bizarre. This is the time when policemen do not even smile as a man wearing a false nose slows up his motor-car in the Circus to inquire the nearest way to an obscure crescent in Maida Vale. At three a.m. Piccadilly would be an ideal stage for a performance of the Russian Ballet. All the comic and grotesque in life should come up like a toadstool at this time, in this place. . . .

    *   *   *   *   *

'You wouldn't hardly think Piccadilly could be so quiet, would you?' said the policeman.

'I suppose things happen now and then?'

'Not often. A drunk. A suspicious character loitering with intent. You have to keep your eyes open.'

He laughed.

'See that bin over there where they keep the grit for the road? One night I saw the lid move! I thought I'd "got 'em," but I looked again and, sure enough, it moved! It was just about the time when we were on the watch for a crook suspected of a big West End jewel robbery. "Now that's funny!" I thought, so I went over quietly and waited. The lid came up and banged down again, then it opened wide, and up sat a young fellow, just like a jack-in-the-box. "What are you doing in there?" I said. "I don't know where I am," he replied. "Do you know this bin is the property of the Westminster Council," I said, "and I could arrest you for trespassing?" I could see he was all right and I was only pulling his leg. . . .

'He was in a blinkin' awful mess! He was a young gent right enough—in evening dress—and he had grit in his hair and in his collar and his waistcoat pockets. "Help me out of this!" he said. "Not till you give an account of yourself," I said. "Who are you?" He scratched some more grit out of his head and said, "I'm the best man!" "Well," I said, "you're the worst-looking man I've seen in the Circus for many a long time, and that's a fact." ... To cut a long story short, it appeared that he'd been to a bachelor party, and his pals had put him in the bin for a lark. He must have been awful drunk, for he fell asleep. The job we had with his hat! He'd been sleeping on it! Anyhow, we punched it out. . . . Good night, sir!'

*   *   *   *   *

Leicester Square was empty save for a stray figure loitering like a ghost.

'Open all night.'

Here is the sequel to the desolation of Piccadilly. In the all-night cafés—in an atmosphere of stale smoke and hot coffee—is drawn all the life of the streets. The place is crowded with men and women sitting on little gold wicker chairs at close-packed tables. The room is full all night long. The air is loud all night long with the talk of these night birds. There is a curious refugee atmosphere. Most of the men wear their overcoats. The primitive magnet of warmth, light, and food has drawn them in from the cold and the dark. Meeting this unsuspected vitality in the night is rather like boarding a liner in the desolation of mid-ocean and finding yourself in a great restaurant. Just, as in a liner, you are conscious that the ocean is beyond the windows, so, in these places, the darkness of Piccadilly seems close, in spite of the bright light, the chatter, the waiters with their steaming trays. . . .

*   *   *   *   *

Who are these people? The eye that delights in crowds moves over them with interest, for this is the most varied crowd in London's twenty-four hours. There are young girls who have given up walking about outside. They sit together at tables, intent in conversation. There is a freemasonry between them and a uniform type of young man—pugilistic young men, or pale, tight-waisted young men with sallow faces, the type that tries to sell postcards under the Arc de Triomphe.

Mixed with them in the craziest fashion are smart people who have been having a night out . . . boys whose white shirt fronts shine obtrusively; young girls in evening cloaks, who lean bare arms on the table and smoke cigarettes reflectively, as they regard the obvious characters present with a cool interest which their grandmothers would have considered revolting. Silk hats appear. Ham and eggs quick! A bunch of tough-looking fellows comes in, their coat-collars turned up, their eyes searching beneath caps and the brims of hats. They discover their associates, and move over to them, settle down and whisper. It looks suspicious! You watch them, half expecting to see Lady Flash's diamonds pass from hand to hand.

Are they the London apache? Are they a third-class dance band off duty?

There are more dramatic possibilities here than in the entire East End of London, that libelled district which (mostly) goes to bed at ten.

*   *   *   *   *

A young man enters. A girl sits up and her eyes take fire:
'There he is, the dirty cad!'
Her three friends hold her down.
'Let me tell him what I think of him!'
'Hush! Don't be a fool, Maudie! Shut up!'
Somehow the flash of fire dies. A queer atmosphere! The girls from Knightsbridge and Kensington gaze through their cigarette smoke, mildly thrilled. Something ugly might, at any moment, bubble up in this varied, haphazard crowd which is sheltering from the darkness. That is the feeling. . . .

*   *   *   *   *

Outside, a derelict, an old shuffling man who has not given up begging, stands beneath a lamp and carefully opens a dirty newspaper in which is some horrid fragment picked from a restaurant refuse bin.

At the corner, where there is a pillar-box, a pretty girl, who has been running hard, posts a letter. Another girl, also running, cries:

'Oh, you little fool—now you've done it! And you deserve what's coming to you!'

Yet Piccadilly seems so dead under the watchful lamps. Over the rest of London is the peace of sleep. . . .

The London night is ending. . . .

It is not yet dawn and it is not night: it is that short between-time when the fates seem gathered in prayer over London. Already work has begun. Over the bridges pass the tramcars; from Covent Garden rises a rumble of effort; but it is still dark. The streets are empty; Big Ben's four gold faces shine to the four points of the compass; the Thames runs on in darkness under the lit bridges. It is cold.

I have seen dawn in many places; in Jerusalem I have seen light come fretfully like a thin sword above the mountains; a streak that widens and cuts a way out of the darkness for the shell-pink galleons to sail up from the east as they flush the minarets; I have seen the sun go up above the Sahara like a gong that calls the world to life; and I have seen the Egyptian sun leap in one second, round and hot, above the red Arabian hills. But dawn comes to London slowly.

A little wind slips out of the east and blows through the lamplit streets. Gradually, the lamplight loses its brilliance, and a kind of greyness, in which stars fade one by one, comes over all things. The black shadows, which have wrapped London during the night, pale moment by moment.

The Thames becomes a grey river, like a streak of blown smoke, and, slowly, the light touches, first, the dome of St. Paul's, then the high steeples of Wren's white churches. You stand, thinking that London, at this moment, looks like a harbour full of ships whose white masts lie against the sky. You become aware of a shrillness in the air. The London sparrows! Second by second the grey light strengthens. You see a great flight of small birds go north: the starlings that nest in London and fly with the dawn to the fields.

*　　　*　　　*　　　*　　　*

It is marvellous to stand alone, leaning over the parapet of the bridge, watching the curve of the Embankment grow clear like the image on a photographic plate in a dark room; and you are lost in the wonder of dawn and in the drama of dawn over a great city.

For now London's millions are coming out of dreams into reality. In thousands of homes the shrill clamour of the alarm clock is calling to duty, and, through the curtains, men and women see a thin streak of grey. And you know that this dawn means for some happiness, for some sorrow; you know that, among that dark mystery of roofs and chimneys, are some who welcome the light and some who fear it; some who awaken with a smile; some who awaken with a brain drugged by sleep for one merciful second before the weight of a misery reasserts it.

Every city on earth appears to have washed out its sins in the night. Dawn comes to them with eternal beauty and freshness. They seem to be making a fresh start every day. Through their streets, empty of men and women, is something which says:

'Here is a new day! See how clean and clear it is over your stones, as fresh and pure as the light that comes over hills and fields.'

London in the dawn is a clean, unwritten page.

You lean over the bridge and know that, in a few hours, the streets will be full of noise and people; the sensations of the evening papers are yet unborn. There may be a murder, a suicide . . . and you feel that, in some way, all the things which people will be discussing in the next dusk are now locked up in this calm greyness. It should seem an ominous greyness; but it does not. It is a pure, beautiful thing, like snow before men tread it into mud.

* * * * *

It is now light.

In the east there comes a pink flush low in the sky. The sun has risen. It is a smouldering, short-lived pinkness, as if the sun were fighting hard to show himself, uncertain, troubled. The colour changes, the pink clouds fade into the grey. The cross above St. Paul's is gold. The street lights go out. The feeling of other-worldliness has vanished with the dawn light, which went suddenly, as if London had flung off a wrap. Now all is clear to the eyes. Over the bridges sounds the rumble of wheels. London, the most masculine city in the world, seems standing clean and stripped, like a boxer entering a ring, for another twenty-four rounds with Fate.

Jarrold & Sons, Limited, The Empire Press, Norwich